AI & Big Data

FOR BUSINESSES

DEEP ATHENA

All information, procedures, and representations included in this book have been compiled and tested with the greatest knowledge and care pos-sible. However, the possibility of errors cannot be completely ruled out. For this reason, the information contained in this book is not associat-ed with any obligation or warranty of any kind. The author assumes no legal responsibility or liability arising from the use of this information, either in whole or in part.

Furthermore, the author does not guarantee that the procedures described are free from third-party rights. The mention of trade names, product names, etc., in this book also does not imply the acceptance that these names are exempt from intellectual property and trademark laws and that they may be used by anyone.

For reasons of better readability, the simultaneous use of masculine, feminine, and diverse (m/f/d) language forms, or man, woman, and diverse (m/w/d), is omitted. All designations of people apply equally to all gen-ders.

Published by DEEP ATHENA
(an Imprint of SMART &PRO AI Juan García)

https://deepathena.com
https://smartandpro.de
ES Version Proofreader: Juan García
DE Version Proofreader: Juan García / Lisa García
EN Version Proofreader: Juan García / Lisa García
Cover Design: Juan García
Cover Graphic: © GarryKillian, 1952, www.freepik.com
Sources consulted:
- General Data Protection Regulation (GDPR) European Union.
- California Consumer Privacy Act (CCPA) United States.
- AI-Manager: the AI Manager Handbook

Softcover ISBN: 9783912099072

DEEP ATHENA

the Artificial Intelligence Publishing House

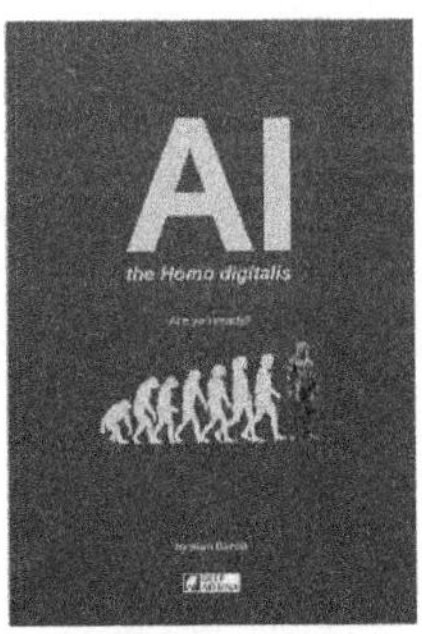

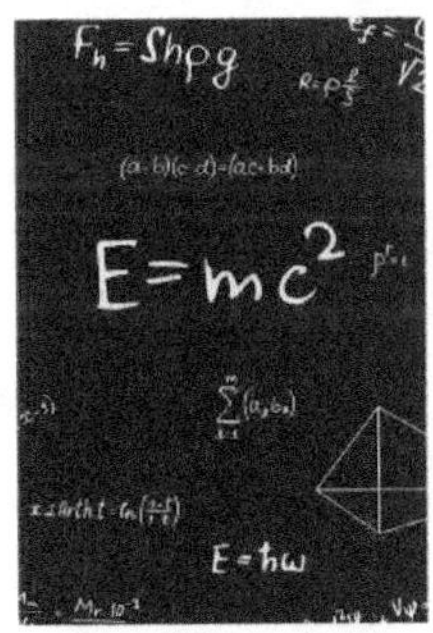

www.deepathena.com

All our books are translated into English, German, and Spanish.
You can find all the information on our website.

Index

Prologue

We are at the peak of an unprecedented revolution, an era in which Artificial Intelligence (AI) and Big Data have become transformative forces that are redefining every aspect of our society. From the way we make decisions to how we interact with the world around us, these technologies are radically changing the structure of business, scientific research, healthcare, entertainment, and practically everything. This process not only alters the way we understand the world and interact with it, but also invites us to rethink our role in it. We are witnessing a transformation that does not distinguish geographic borders, economic sectors, skin color, or educational levels.

This book, AI & Big Data, is not just a technical compendium but also a deep exploration of the impact these two disciplines have when working together. Although this book tries not to be a technical book, something difficult to avoid in this field, it does show you all the potential and provides you with all the knowledge to master these technologies. Artificial Intelligence, with its ability to learn, reason, and make decisions, needs data to feed its models and algorithms. Big Data, with its vast sea of information generated at breakneck speed, needs advanced tools like AI to process, analyze, and convert that data into practical knowledge. Together, these technologies create an ecosystem of innovation and discovery that is unparalleled in human history. We are not talking simply about isolated advances but about a new engine of change that drives the global economy, defines government strategies, and shapes the future of our daily interactions.

The purpose of this prologue is not to overwhelm you with technical terms or complex descriptions but to invite you to reflect on how these tools have ceased to be futuristic concepts and ignored by society to become tangible realities. They are realities that are already solving complex problems, optimizing processes, and in some cases, redefining the very nature of our existence. Imagine, for example, how Artificial Intelligence and Big Data are being used to predict disease outbreaks before they happen, improve the efficiency of global supply chains, or even personalize the education of millions of students around the world. The impact of these technologies goes beyond the merely technical; it touches fundamental aspects of our lives, from health and safety to leisure and culture.

AI & Big Data is an invitation to explore not only the technical and theoretical foundations of these disciplines but also their practical application and the ethical challenges they pose. This book aims to be a guide both for those who seek to understand these technologies from scratch and for professionals who want to deepen their integration and strategic use. In these pages, you will find a complete journey through the essential concepts but also a critical look at the social, cultural, and ethical implications of their adoption. Because, although these tools offer extraordinary opportunities, they also raise fundamental questions about privacy, security, and fairness that we must address as a society, since Big Data is not only a corporate issue; the way we store and manage data affects us all.

Artificial Intelligence and Big Data are not mere technological advances; they are a paradigm shift. They represent a new way of understanding the world, one in which data and algorithms become universal languages capable of crossing linguistic and cultural barriers. As you progress through the pages of this book, you will discover how companies are using these tools to predict trends, improve customer experience, and generally revolutionize entire sectors. This is a book full of ideas and use cases, but you will also find discussions about the limits of these technologies, the risks of their misuse, and the shared responsibility we have to ensure that their impact is positive for humanity. This is not a journey without risks, but it is one full of possibilities.

This prologue marks the beginning of a journey toward understanding how two concepts that were once science fiction are reshaping our reality. So, whether you are a curious professional, a passionate student, or simply someone interested in the impact of technology, I invite you to dive into this fascinating world. Because in this new chapter of history, we are all protagonists. It does not matter what your field or level of knowledge is, Artificial Intelligence and Big Data are shaping a future that involves us all. And you, as a reader, have the power to understand, question, and participate in this transformation.

Introduction

Over the past few decades, we have witnessed a transformation that has redefined the boundaries of innovation and human knowledge. Artificial Intelligence and Big Data are not merely technological tools; they represent a paradigm shift that is reshaping our society, our industries, and our way of understanding the world. These advances have ceased to be futuristic concepts and have become fundamental pillars of our everyday reality. However, their impact and potential are only beginning to be glimpsed in their full magnitude, even though they are arriving at a dizzying speed.

The digital era in which we live has generated an unprecedented amount of data. Every interaction, every transaction, and every click in the virtual world generates valuable information that, in the right hands, can reveal patterns, trends, and solutions to complex problems. But to extract value from this data, the intervention of Artificial Intelligence is necessary, a discipline that, supported by sophisticated algorithms and unimaginable computational power, has been revolutionizing the way we process, analyze, and use this information for several decades now.

The purpose of this book is to offer a deep and accessible exploration of these concepts, highlighting their impact in various areas and their relevance for the present and the future. In these pages, we will unravel how AI and Big Data complement and enhance each other, analyzing practical cases, concrete examples, and the opportunities and challenges they pose for professionals, companies, and society in general.

It is crucial to understand that this is not a book exclusively for technicians or specialists, as it does not aim to be technical but informative. However, as the prologue rightly points out, it is difficult to avoid being technical in these areas. I have been working on this book since 2023 with the aim of complementing my book "AI-Manager: The AI Project Manager's Handbook" in the field of Big Data. Unfortunately, due to other projects, I have not been able to finish it earlier, and I have also re-edited it 3 times due to all the events that have occurred in the field of Artificial Intelligence between 2023 and 2024. I finally decided to focus the book on Big Data because I made the decision to develop my books in a way that they complement each other. While we will delve into some technical aspects necessary to understand how these technologies work, AI and Big Data, we will also focus on the practical impact and the ethical, economic, and social implications of their implementation. With this broad approach, I seek to inspire and empower business leaders as well as students, entrepreneurs, and anyone interested in understanding the driving forces of change that will define the future. It is very important to understand that this book is designed and intended as a complement to my book "AI-Manager," which is a technical book designed to teach everything about Artificial Intelligence completely from scratch and in an easy way, both for newcomers to the field and for professionals in these areas. Therefore, it is important that you understand that each topic and each page of AI & Big Data are written and designed to complement the knowledge of AI-Manager. Additionally, as a further complement in a more ethical and perhaps philosophical part, you also have at your disposal "AI the *Homo Digitalis*," a book that not only explains what Artificial Intelligence is and the differences between AI, AGI, and ASI but also guides you on a reflective path showing you all the advantages and risks that this technology brings, including many examples of its use cases as well as hundreds of real situations that have taken place due to the implementation of AI in companies and in society in general. This means that if you miss some topics here or think they should have been covered in more depth, it is because you will find everything you need in my other books, as they have been designed to complement each other. This book aims to provide a deeper insight into the field of data and Big Data, as these are the fuel of all Artificial Intelligence, and therefore I seek here to delve more into this field, providing knowledge that complements the knowledge of the other books. Together, these books are the perfect combination, both to master AI professionally and to understand it and learn to use and apply it in the best way; and they offer you all the knowledge necessary to become a great Artificial Intelligence professional as well as a good user of Artificial Intelligence.

The methodology of this book, as well as any of my other books, is designed and thought out to support the learning curve and thus also the understanding of the other topics. Do not despair with the examples and use cases because, although we often use the same ones, for example, marketing, medicine, finance, autonomous vehicles, etc., this is due to their impact on our society and our lives in general. Furthermore, we will always use them in different contexts and will therefore break down their different aspects each time, both technical and ethical and privacy-related. As you will notice, these areas will be repeated quite a bit throughout the book. In any case, I always try to offer diverse examples by introducing areas that may be little discussed but are well known by everyone. The goal is to understand all their aspects, possibilities, and risks.

Artificial Intelligence and Big Data have the capacity to transform sectors as diverse as medicine, education, transportation, the environment, entertainment, biochemistry, and physics, among many others. However, they also present significant challenges, from data storage and management to its use, privacy, and security issues, leading to endless ethical debates about the responsible use of these technologies. In this context, understanding their fundamentals, applications, and limitations becomes an urgent necessity.

As we progress, we will explore not only the "what" and the "how" of AI and Big Data but also the "why." This book does not aim to provide definitive answers but to serve as a guide that provokes reflection, fosters learning and understanding, and encourages its readers to explore beyond conventional boundaries. This book aims to make the knowledge of these technologies accessible to everyone in a clear and simple way, although it is inevitable to enter into technicalities, so that everyone can learn to use these technologies as best as possible and implement them as ethically as possible. In a world where data and Artificial Intelligence have definitively become the new language of power and influence, knowledge and understanding of these tools become essential.

We will tackle the topics little by little and delve deeper as we progress throughout the book. We will see concepts and technologies several times and each time in different contexts or for different reasons, depending on the context being addressed or their importance in a particular area, as well as depending on the relationship being discussed. This means, for example, that if we address a topic and in this topic it is necessary to mention some technologies or aspects, these will be mentioned and addressed as necessary; later these technologies will be dealt with in depth. Everything in due course. This should also support your learning curve so that you become familiar with the terms, technologies, and concepts, and their relationships.

I invite you to embark on this journey with me. As you explore the ideas, discoveries, and narratives contained in these pages, my hope is that you will find not only information but also inspiration to imagine and build a future where technology and humanity work hand in hand to reach new horizons.

PART I

Fundamentals of AI

Part I: Fundamentals of AI

1. Introduction to Artificial Intelligence

Artificial Intelligence has ceased to be an exclusive concept of science fiction to become one of the most disruptive technologies of our era. From its beginnings as a theoretical field of study to its application in everyday life, AI has radically transformed the way we interact with technology and process information. Its impact spans numerous sectors and I would dare to say practically any sector one can imagine, from medicine to manufacturing, through transportation, customer service, security, music and cinema among many others.

In general terms, AI refers to the ability of machines to mimic human intelligence in problem-solving, learning, and decision-making. Over the years, this field has evolved from systems of explicit rules to complex models based on machine learning and deep learning, which have enabled the development of systems capable of recognizing patterns, processing natural language, and making autonomous decisions. Additionally, the combination of AI with other technologies, such as the Internet of Things (IoT), Big Data, augmented reality (AR), and virtual reality (VR), has further enhanced its capabilities, generating innovative applications in multiple fields.

The rise of AI has been driven by the exponential growth of data and the advancement of computing power. Thanks to these factors, Artificial Intelligence has ceased to be an experiment in academic laboratories to integrate into the daily lives of people and companies. Currently, and for years now, virtual assistants like Siri, Alexa, and Google Assistant, recommendation systems used on platforms like Netflix and Amazon, customer service chatbots, and autonomous vehicles are just some of the best-known examples of how AI is shaping the future now.

One of the greatest milestones in the history of Artificial Intelligence has been the development of deep learning models, which mimic the structure of the human brain through artificial neural networks, Deep Learning. These networks have enabled significant advances in areas such as image recognition, natural language processing, and automated decision-making. A prominent example of these advances is AlphaGo, the Artificial Intelligence system from DeepMind that managed to defeat world champions in the game of Go, a milestone that demonstrated the capability of AI to surpass humans in highly complex tasks. I remember that when AlphaGo faced the South Korean professional Go player Lee Sedol, if I recall correctly in March 2016, there were moments when he seemed cornered and at many times was unable to make a decision. AlphaGo defeated Lee Sedol with a result of 4 games won by AI against only 1 victory by Lee. This confrontation marked a milestone in the history of Artificial Intelligence because Go is a considerably more complex game than chess due to its immense number of possible combinations, which made it considered an almost insurmountable challenge for machines until that moment.

Lee Sedol, a South Korean Go legend, who was also a world Go champion at the time, is recognized for being the only human player to have won a game against this advanced AI; although he later decided to retire from professional play in 2019, citing the invincibility of Artificial Intelligence as one of the reasons for his retirement. To give you an example that you might understand, imagine that Magnus Carlsen retires from chess because he cannot beat Stockfish.

However, AI not only represents a technological revolution but also a challenge in terms of ethics, regulation, and privacy. As these technologies advance, fundamental and very important questions arise about their impact on society, employment, and automated decision-making. One of the main debates revolves around the use of AI in critical decision-making, such as medical diagnosis, the selection of job candidates, or the granting of credits. Although automating these processes can improve efficiency and reduce human bias, it also raises concerns about transparency, fairness, and accountability. Not to forget the very important quality of the data used to train the models that will later have to make these decisions, and something very important to remember is that AI is created by humans to imitate humans. We could talk about this at length, and if you have not yet realized the potential of these technologies, their advantages and risks, I assure you that it will not take long for you to notice.

Another key aspect to consider is security in the development and implementation of Artificial Intelligence. AI can be used for malicious purposes, such as the creation of deepfakes, the automation of cyberattacks, and the manipulation of public opinion through algorithms designed to spread disinformation. For this reason, it is crucial to establish regulatory frameworks and ethical principles that guide the responsible development and use of these technologies.

As we move forward in the 21st century, Artificial Intelligence will continue to evolve and play a fundamental role in the digital transformation of our society. AI research continues to expand, exploring areas such as Artificial General Intelligence (AGI), Artificial Super Intelligence (ASI), quantum computing, and the fusion of AI with biotechnology. These innovations will not only redefine the way we live and work but also generate new challenges and opportunities for the future. Each generation will have to face these advances, and previous generations will have no relevance in the future;

however, they do have relevance in the present, and a lot. Let me at this point recommend my book "AI the *Homo digitalis*," since here I talk in detail about these topics; it is a reading that is well worth it.

Understanding the fundamentals of AI is crucial not only for those who work in the development of these technologies but also for those seeking to understand their implications and opportunities in the modern world. Most people only see AI as a tool or a toy, and you can't blame them, because that's how it's being sold to them, but AI is really much more than that and it is something that humanity must take much more seriously. This is where true AI professionals come into play. Well-trained people who have delved deeply into both the technical and ethical aspects of these technologies; and I'm not referring to the self-proclaimed "experts" or the AI consultants that are suddenly everywhere today, I mean well-educated professionals with studies and experience in the field, and above all, with a deep understanding of what these technologies imply for our society. In the following sections, we will explore the nature of Artificial Intelligence, its historical evolution, and the key concepts that connect it with Big Data, providing a clear and structured view of this fascinating field.

1.1. What is AI?

Artificial Intelligence is a field of computer science that seeks to develop systems capable of performing tasks that normally require human intelligence. These tasks include learning, reasoning, problem-solving, perception, language understanding, and decision-making. In simple terms, AI is the ability of a machine to mimic human cognitive processes and execute complex functions autonomously or assisted.

The concept of Artificial Intelligence is not new; its foundations date back to the mid-20th century when the first scientists and mathematicians began to theorize about the possibility of creating machines that could learn and adapt. Over the decades, AI has evolved from systems based on simple rules to sophisticated machine learning and deep learning models that can analyze large volumes of data and improve their performance over time.

AI can be classified into different types according to its capability and application. In general terms, a distinction is made between weak AI and strong AI. Weak AI, also known as narrow AI, is designed to perform specific tasks such as voice recognition, automatic translation, or fraud detection in financial transactions. These systems do not possess consciousness or real understanding; they operate within a predefined set of parameters. On the other hand, Strong AI, which is not the same as AGI, is a philosophical idea that was first proposed by John Searle during the 1980s. This concept does not refer to the level of operational or cognitive capacity that an Artificial Intelligence might achieve, but rather to the idea that an AI truly possesses consciousness, mind, intentions, and genuine understanding, instead of merely imitating or simulating these processes. According to the Strong AI thesis, it is possible for a computational system to experience real mental states, comparable to those of a human being.

I constantly hear professionals in the AI field, "new experts," as I call them, and YouTubers among others, talking about "Strong AI" as if it were AGI, which is completely and utterly wrong. Strong AI is one thing, and AGI is another. If you want to properly understand these concepts, I recommend that you read my book "AI the *Homo digitalis*," as this book is dedicated, among other topics, to clarifying these concepts and also provides you with numerous examples and real-world cases for better understanding.

Advances in deep learning and neural networks have enabled the creation of AI models capable of diagnosing diseases, optimizing industrial processes, improving safety in autonomous driving, and developing increasingly sophisticated virtual assistants, among thousands of different applications.

Despite its benefits, AI also raises ethical challenges and concerns. Task automation, bias in algorithms, data privacy, and the impact on employment are just some of the issues that must be addressed as technology advances. It is essential that AI development is carried out responsibly and transparently, ensuring its use for the benefit of society; and as I always say, education starts at home and with oneself.

Artificial Intelligence is a constantly evolving discipline that seeks to equip machines with capabilities that were once exclusive to humans. Its impact is already evident in multiple areas and will continue to transform the way we live and work in the coming years and also in the short term. Understanding what AI is and how it works is essential to harness its advantages and mitigate its potential risks, and this involves professionals, users, and politicians alike, regardless of age, ethnicity, economic power, or nationality.

1.2. Evolution of AI and its Impact on Society

Artificial Intelligence has come a long way from its early conceptualizations to its modern implementation in various sectors of society. Its evolution has been marked by significant milestones that have redefined the way we interact with technology and use it to solve complex problems. Since I have talked about this in other books, and as I explained at the beginning of the book, this book is designed to complement those other books, I briefly present here, as a summary, the most important points in the journey of Artificial Intelligence.

As we already know, the foundations of Artificial Intelligence date back to the mid-20th century, when mathematicians and logicians began exploring the possibility of creating machines capable of imitating human thought. Alan Turing, with his famous "Turing test", was one of the pioneers in proposing that a machine could be considered intelligent if its behavior could not be distinguished from that of a human in a conversation. In the 1950s, John McCarthy coined the term "Artificial Intelligence" and laid the groundwork for research in the field, organizing the Dartmouth Conference in 1956, considered the formal starting point of AI.

During the 1960s and 1970s, researchers developed the first rule-based systems, such as expert systems, which simulated human knowledge in specific domains. However, the lack of computational capacity and excessive expectations led to a decline in funding and interest in AI, a period known as the "AI winter".

In the 1980s and 1990s, advances in Machine Learning (ML) revitalized AI research. New algorithms and especially artificial neural networks began to demonstrate their ability to learn from data, and this is where Big Data came into play, allowing many of the limitations of rule-based systems to be overcome. However, the lack of computing power remained an obstacle.

The real boom of AI came with the development of Deep Learning in the 2010s, driven by the increase in processor power (especially GPUs and TPUs), the availability of large volumes of data, and improvements in algorithms. Deep neural networks have enabled spectacular advances in image recognition, natural language processing, and automated decision-making, leading technology companies to implement Artificial Intelligence in commercial products, from virtual assistants to recommendation systems; for example, from your smartphone's Query keyboard to Apple's Siri.

The impact of AI on society has been profound and extends to various areas, such as:

- **Economy and employment:** Automation has optimized industrial processes, increased efficiency in various sectors, and at the same time has raised concerns about job loss in repetitive tasks.
- **Health:** AI has revolutionized medical diagnosis, drug discovery, and personalized care, significantly improving treatments and patient care.
- **Transport:** With the development of autonomous vehicles and traffic optimization systems, AI is redefining urban mobility.

- **Education:** Adaptive learning systems have allowed personalized teaching and improved the student experience.
- **Security and surveillance:** AI is used in facial recognition, cybersecurity, and crime prevention, although it also raises very important challenges regarding privacy and ethics.
- **Music:** AI has transformed musical composition, audio mixing and mastering, and even the generation of new artistic pieces, facilitating production and exploring new genres and sounds.
- **Cinema:** AI has optimized video editing, the generation of realistic visual effects, and content personalization, in addition to improving recommendations on streaming platforms.
- **Programming:** AI systems have completely revolutionized software development through autocomplete tools, automatic debugging, and code generation, accelerating development cycles.
- **Rescue:** AI is used in search and rescue systems, autonomous drones to locate people in emergency situations, and algorithms for predicting natural disasters, speeding up responses and improving success rates.
- **Industrial production:** AI-driven automation has optimized supply chains, predictive maintenance of machinery, and quality management, increasing productivity and reducing costs.
- **Marketing:** AI algorithms have enabled precise audience segmentation, personalization of advertising campaigns, and analysis of large volumes of data to predict trends and consumer behavior.
- **Customer service:** AI-based chatbots and virtual assistants have improved the availability and efficiency of customer service, providing quick and personalized responses, as well as automating repetitive tasks. AI always puts on a good face and responds kindly.

Despite the advances, AI faces challenges such as model interpretability, algorithmic bias, and the ethical implications of its use. Regulation and the development of responsible AI are key aspects to ensure that this technology benefits humanity without compromising privacy and individual rights. As you will see, these aspects will accompany us throughout the book, because in addition to being very important in the field of Artificial Intelligence, they are especially so when it comes to data; so if you feel that they are repeated often, it is because you really need to take them seriously and not ignore them.

The evolution of Artificial Intelligence is a reflection of the human potential to innovate and transform the world. Its impact on society will continue to expand, and its development raises fundamental questions about the future of work, education, and the relationship between humans and machines, and even the relationship between humans themselves.

1.3. Key AI Factors relevant to Big Data

Artificial Intelligence and Big Data are closely interrelated, as the success of AI systems depends largely on the quality, volume, and diversity of the data used for their training and operation. Below, I present the main Artificial Intelligence concepts that are fundamental in the context of Big Data. Since we will see them throughout the book, I will present them as briefly as possible, so as not to get into technicalities too early, just as an introduction.

Machine Learning algorithms

Machine Learning is a subset of AI that allows systems to learn patterns from data without the need for explicit programming. There are three main types of Machine Learning that are applied in the field of Big Data:

- **Supervised learning:** Uses labeled data to train models that can make predictions or classifications.
- **Unsupervised learning:** Analyzes unlabeled data to identify hidden patterns and underlying structures.
- **Reinforcement learning:** Based on interaction with an environment and obtaining rewards to optimize the behavior of an agent.

Artificial neural networks and Deep Learning

Artificial neural networks are models inspired by the human brain that process data hierarchically. In the context of Big Data, Deep Learning has become an essential technique due to its ability to handle large volumes of data and automatically extract features.

- **Convolutional Neural Networks (CNNs):** Mainly used in computer vision.
- **Recurrent Neural Networks (RNNs):** Applied in natural language processing and time series analysis.
- **Transformers:** Advanced models such as BERT and GPT, which have transformed and revolutionized data processing in text and natural language.

Generative models

Generative models, such as diffusion models and GANs (Generative Adversarial Networks), have gained great importance in the field of Big Data, as they can generate synthetic data to improve the quality and diversity of existing datasets.

Natural Language Processing (NLP)

NLP allows AI systems to understand, process, and generate human language. Within Big Data, NLP is used to analyze large volumes of text, extract relevant information, and improve decision-making.

- **Sentiment analysis:** Evaluation of opinions on social networks, surveys, and comments.
- **Topic modeling:** Identification of topics in large text corpora.
- **Machine translation:** AI-powered translation tools like Google Translate and DeepL, among many others.

Computer vision

Computer vision enables the analysis and interpretation of images and videos in large volumes of visual data. It is integrated and therefore used with various Big Data techniques and applications, such as:

- **Facial recognition:** Identification of people in images and videos.
- **Object detection:** Localization of elements in visual scenes.
- **Medical image analysis:** AI-assisted diagnosis in X-rays and magnetic resonance imaging.

Optimization and dimensionality reduction

In the context of Big Data, it is essential to reduce the amount of data without losing relevant information. Some key techniques include:

- **Principal Component Analysis (PCA):** Dimensionality reduction to improve data processing efficiency.
- **T-SNE and UMAP:** Methods used to visualize high-dimensional data.
- **Feature Selection:** Identification of the most relevant features for AI models.

Bias and Explainability in AI

As AI systems increasingly rely on large volumes of data, it is crucial to address issues of bias and explainability:

- **Bias mitigation:** Identification and correction of biases in datasets and AI models.
- **Explainable AI (XAI):** Methods to make models interpretable and understandable by humans.

As you can imagine, these concepts are key in the context of Big Data and are essential for building robust, efficient, and ethical Machine Learning models. Machine learning, deep learning, natural language processing, and computer vision are fundamental pillars in exploiting large volumes of data. Make no mistake that as technologies advance, the interaction between AI and Big Data will continue to evolve, providing new opportunities and challenges for data science and applied Artificial Intelligence.

2. Key Concepts of AI

The key concepts of Artificial Intelligence represent the fundamental basis upon which all applications, models, and technologies derived from this discipline are built. Without a solid understanding of these concepts, it is difficult to grasp how AI systems work, their scope, and their limitations. Before diving into specific details, it is important to establish an overview of the essential principles that define Artificial Intelligence in the modern context.

Let's make it clear that AI is not a single technology but a set of methodologies, algorithms, and approaches that enable machines to perform tasks that would normally require human intelligence. These capabilities include pattern recognition, decision-making, learning from data, understanding natural language, and visual perception, among others; and as we have seen, the combination of these elements has enabled the development of systems capable of improving processes across a wide variety of sectors, which we will delve deeper into as we progress through the book.

A key aspect to keep in mind is the relationship between Artificial Intelligence, Machine Learning, and Deep Learning. While AI is the general field that encompasses any attempt to endow machines with intelligence, Machine Learning represents a subset of AI that relies on using data to train models without the need for explicit programming. In turn, Deep Learning is an approach within Machine Learning that employs deep neural networks to extract features and patterns from complex data.

AI models depend heavily on data for their training and evolution. The quality and quantity of the data used can determine the effectiveness and accuracy of a model. For this reason, data management is an essential pillar in developing Artificial Intelligence solutions. Without adequate data, models lack the necessary information to learn and improve their performance. If you have already read any of my books, then you already know that I always emphasize the importance of data, and if you haven't read them, then you should read them before continuing with this book; at least AI-Manager and AI the *Homo digitalis*.

Another central concept is the tuning and optimization of AI models. Through techniques such as hyperparameter tuning, data normalization, and the selection of relevant features, models can improve their accuracy and reduce the margin of error in their predictions. This process requires not only technical knowledge but also a deep understanding of the problem to be solved and the limitations of the model used.

In addition, it is essential to consider the importance of interpretability and ethics in Artificial Intelligence. The explainability of AI models is a determining factor in their adoption in critical sectors such as healthcare and justice. A model that offers accurate predictions but whose internal logic is opaque can generate distrust and hinder its implementation in sensitive contexts. For this reason, increasing efforts are focused on developing techniques that allow explaining how and why a model has reached a particular conclusion. Here I must add that even the most renowned experts in the AI field say that "*no one really knows how the models make their decisions.*"

2.1. Machine Learning vs. Deep Learning

It is very important to understand and know how to differentiate these two areas, as it very often leads to confusion, something very serious when we talk about Artificial Intelligence projects. Well, in the context of Artificial Intelligence and Big Data, Machine Learning and Deep Learning are two essential approaches for data processing and automated decision-making. I have already mentioned these before, but while both belong to the general field of machine learning, they present key differences in their structure and capabilities.

Machine Learning is the overarching field and is based on algorithms that can learn patterns from data without being explicitly programmed for each task. These algorithms include models such as decision trees, support vector machines (SVM), and shallow artificial neural networks. The performance of ML depends heavily on the quality and quantity of the data provided, as well as the selection of relevant features for analysis. We will explore this in depth later.

Deep Learning, on the other hand, is a subcategory of Machine Learning that uses deep neural networks with multiple layers to analyze data in a more complex and abstract way. Thanks to its ability to process large volumes of information autonomously, DL has proven to be highly efficient in tasks such as image recognition, natural language processing, and pattern prediction in large datasets.

In relation to Big Data, both ML and DL benefit from the large availability of data to improve their models and generate more accurate predictions. While ML usually requires preprocessing and manual feature selection, DL is capable of extracting complex representations directly from raw data, making it particularly useful in environments with large volumes of unstructured information. You can find all the necessary information about data structure in my book "AI-Manager", so here we will only complement that knowledge by delving into Big Data technology.

Both ML and DL are fundamental in the Big Data ecosystem. The choice between one or the other depends not only on the project's objective but also on the amount of data available, the complexity of the problem, and the computational resources needed for its implementation.

2.2. AI Models and Their Dependence on Data

As I have already mentioned and we have seen, Artificial Intelligence in its modern form relies heavily on data. Without data, AI models lack the essential raw material for their training, validation, and continuous improvement. To give you an example, it is the same as humans without books. Let's briefly explore how AI models depend on data and why this relationship is key in the context of Big Data. Remember that the goal of this book is to explore Big Data and its relationship with AI, not AI itself.

What is an AI model?

An AI model is a mathematical representation of a cognitive process or a specific task that Artificial Intelligence tries to solve. It can be a supervised, unsupervised, or reinforcement learning algorithm, depending on the type of problem to be addressed. These models can take various forms, such as neural networks, decision trees, support vector machines, or probabilistic models.

Regardless of the type of model, they all share the need for data to learn patterns, make predictions, and improve their performance over time.

It is important to highlight that a model is not the same as an AI system. While an AI model is a mathematical representation of a cognitive process or a specific task, an AI system is based on data, AI models, and hardware, the latter being computational power and infrastructure, including the user interface. A model is just one part of the complete system, which requires other components to function effectively. You must be very clear about this from now on.

The Importance of Data in Machine Learning

Machine learning, as I have been explaining, is based on extracting patterns and relationships from large volumes of data. Without quality data, machine learning models simply cannot function properly. The relationship between AI models and data can be understood at several levels:

- **Model training:** AI models require labeled or unlabeled data to learn to make decisions. A facial recognition model, for example, needs thousands or millions of images to accurately identify human faces.
- **Generalization:** For a model to make accurate predictions on previously unseen data, it is essential that the training data be diverse and representative of real use cases.
- **Hyperparameter tuning:** Many AI models depend on the optimization of their internal parameters, and this tuning is only effective if adequate data is available. Additionally, of course, a proper understanding of the hyperparameters is needed.
- **Evaluation and continuous improvement:** AI models need test and validation data to measure their accuracy and correct possible biases or systematic errors. This means that data is needed for training, for testing, and for validation, and all must be different. You cannot use the same data you used in training to perform the test once training is complete. That data is already known to the model.

Data and Big Data: An Essential Symbiosis

The term Big Data refers to large volumes of data generated at high speed and with great variety. This data can come from multiple sources, such as IoT sensors, social networks, banking transactions, and medical records. The relationship between AI and Big Data is crucial because modern AI models require large volumes of data to achieve optimal performance. Some of the main reasons why Big Data is essential for AI are:

- **Greater accuracy:** The more data a model has, the better it can learn complex patterns and make more accurate predictions.
- **Bias reduction:** A large and well-balanced database helps reduce algorithmic biases and improves model fairness.
- **Automated decision-making:** Thanks to Big Data, AI models can adapt and improve in real time without constant human intervention.
- **Efficient processing capacity:** Big Data tools, such as Hadoop and Spark, make it possible to handle massive volumes of data to feed AI models in a scalable way.

Challenges in Data Management for AI

Although the availability of massive data has driven AI development, it also presents significant challenges, as I hope is already clear to you:

- **Data quality:** Incorrect, incomplete, or biased data can lead to inefficient models and wrong decisions.
- **Privacy and security:** The collection and processing of large volumes of data raise ethical and regulatory concerns.
- **Storage and processing:** Handling large volumes of data requires robust infrastructures and specialized technologies.
- **Updating and maintenance:** AI models need updated data to remain relevant and effective in changing environments.

The dependence of AI models on data is undeniable. Without data, AI cannot learn, improve, or offer useful predictions. The synergy between AI and Big Data has enabled significant advances in multiple industries; however, data management remains a key challenge to ensure the quality, security, and efficiency of AI models and systems. Therefore, understanding the relationship between AI models and data is fundamental for anyone interested in the development and application of Artificial Intelligence, and not just at the business level. Don't worry, because we will delve into each topic as we progress through the book, and many topics will "repeat" several times, but as you will see, always in different contexts; all very important to help you learn Big Data and understand its relationship with AI. We will look at everything little by little to ensure the assimilation and understanding of these topics.

2.3. Importance of Data in Model Training

So to speak, data is the essential fuel for the development and training of Artificial Intelligence models. As we have already mentioned, without quality data, even the most advanced algorithms will fail to provide accurate and reliable results. AI's dependence on data is absolute, since the effectiveness of machine learning and deep learning models depends on the quantity, variety, and quality of the data used during their training.

We have seen that Artificial Intelligence models learn patterns and trends from datasets, but now we observe that if these data contain erroneous, biased, or insufficient information, the model will learn incorrect or incomplete patterns, which will negatively affect its performance during the inference phase. For example, a facial recognition model trained with a dataset that lacks ethnic diversity will have difficulty accurately identifying faces from certain demographic groups. If you ask a generative model to generate images of a person of African ethnicity, a model that has only been trained with images of European people, then the model will generate images of people of European ethnicity, because it will basically understand that a "person" is "white," since that is how it was trained. On the other hand, if we overtrain the model or do it incorrectly, it could generate images only of people of African ethnicity because it prioritizes this ethnicity due to bias issues, basically trying to avoid racism when generating the image. As you can see, it is the same as educating a child. If you are racist, your child will be racist; if the child never sees a person of color, then when you say "describe a person" he will describe a person with white skin. However, if you place too much emphasis on avoiding racism, it can lead to biases and generate images only of people of color or other ethnicities. This has indeed happened with many models.

The relationship between data and AI models can be explained through the following factors:

1. Amount of data: In general terms, the more data a model has for training, the better its generalization capacity will be. However, in some cases, a large amount of noisy or irrelevant data can negatively affect performance. This is why the next point is very important.
2. Data quality: A well-structured dataset, free of errors and biases, will allow for more effective training. Quality is measured in terms of the accuracy, completeness, consistency, and representativeness of the data.
3. Data variety: Diversity in the data is key for a model to handle multiple real-world scenarios. The data must include different contexts, conditions, and variations within the problem domain.
4. Data labeling and annotation: In supervised learning, the data must be properly labeled so that the model can learn accurately. Poorly labeled data can lead to systematic errors in prediction. What does this mean? It means you cannot label an image of a dog as a cat, just as you cannot label a white person as a person of color. For example, an X-ray for disease analysis must be correctly labeled: "disease" or "no disease," "viral" or "bacterial," "pneumonia" or "cancer." Imagine here that you have an accounting teacher who does not understand the rule of three; it is the same thing. And by the way, I had a teacher in industrial business accounting who didn't understand it, so they do exist. And what does this mean? It means that he, my industrial business accounting teacher, saw it (the rule of three), memorized it, and just repeats it. This is what an AI model does if it is not properly trained. This can lead to overfitting or underfitting of the model.
5. Class balance: In classification problems, a dataset with an unbalanced class distribution can cause the model to favor the majority class, reducing its generalization capacity.

Common problems in data and their impact on AI

- **Data bias:** A biased dataset can generate models with unfair or erroneous results. This is especially critical in sensitive applications such as hiring or credit granting.
- **Insufficient data:** When the data volume is too small, the model fails to learn meaningful patterns and may fall into overfitting, where it memorizes the data instead of generalizing.
- **Noisy or erroneous data:** The presence of incorrect, duplicated, or inconsistent data can affect the model's performance.
- **Lack of representativeness:** If the training data do not reflect the reality of the problem to be solved, the model will be of little use in real-world scenarios.

Strategies to improve data quality

Since data is the foundation of a model's success, it is essential to apply strategies to improve its quality and ensure its adequacy for training. Some recommended practices include:

1. **Data preprocessing:** Apply cleaning, normalization, and transformation techniques to improve data quality.
2. **Data augmentation:** Generate new samples from existing data to improve representativeness and reduce overfitting.
3. **Filtering and noise removal:** Identify and remove outliers or inconsistencies within the dataset.
4. **Bias correction:** Balance classes and ensure the inclusion of representative data for all possible situations.
5. **Use of imputation techniques:** To handle missing values in the data without introducing significant errors.

A well-structured data strategy is essential to obtain accurate, reliable, and fair models. The implementation of good practices in data collection, cleaning, and processing is an indispensable requirement to ensure the optimal performance of any AI-based solution. Data preparation is a task that no one likes to do, but nevertheless, it is the most important aspect when it comes to Artificial Intelligence. Large companies leave this task in the hands of "specialized" companies, something I do not recommend at all, since it always leads to biases in the data. On the other hand, if you work in a medium or small company, God help you. This is why you must be very familiar with the field of data and Big Data and especially data analysis, because it is essential to know how to read the data to understand not only the information it offers but also to know how to find and mitigate all the errors it may contain.

2.4. AI without Data, is it possible?

Artificial Intelligence, as we know it today, is intrinsically, as you can see, linked to data. Most AI models, whether supervised, unsupervised, or even reinforcement learning algorithms, depend on large amounts of data for their training and operation. Without data, AI simply could not learn, reason, or make informed decisions.

AI models learn patterns and structures from data. In the case of Machine Learning, training data are fundamental for the model to generalize and make predictions about new data. In Deep Learning, data feed deep neural networks that adjust their weights and biases to improve their performance. Even in generative models, such as Generative Adversarial Networks (GANs) or language models like GPT, the quality and quantity of the training data determine the accuracy and relevance of their responses.

Data are also essential in the validation and evaluation of models. Without a dataset to assess their performance, there would be no way to determine the effectiveness of a model in practice.

In theory, an Artificial Intelligence system could be conceived that does not rely on pre-existing data but instead operates exclusively through manually programmed rules. This approach, known as expert systems, was very popular in the early days of AI and was based on logical rules defined by human experts. However, these systems have considerable limitations, as they cannot learn or adapt to new situations without human intervention.

Another alternative would be the use of evolutionary algorithms or systems that generate knowledge from simulations. However, these approaches, although they may reduce dependence on external data, still require initial information or simulated environments that act as a data source. So basically, it is the same thing: it is about the availability of information, in any of its formats, to learn.

Currently, all significant advances in AI are driven by the access to and processing of large volumes of data. From voice recognition and computer vision to content generation and automated decision-making, AI requires information to operate effectively. Even in attempts to reduce the amount of data needed through techniques such as reinforcement learning or few-shot learning, it is still essential to have base data.

Although one could imagine a concept of AI that works with predefined rules or generates its own knowledge through simulations, in practice, AI without data is not viable with current technology. The learning, adaptation, and continuous improvement of models depend on data. Without them,

Artificial Intelligence could not evolve or provide precise and useful solutions in the real world. This is where Big Data comes into play.

PART II

Big Data Fundamentals

Part II: Big Data Fundamentals

3. Introduction to Big Data

The term "Big Data" refers to data sets that are so large, fast, or complex that it is difficult or impossible to handle them with traditional data processing tools such as Access, Excel, and PowerBI, to name a few. The latter, Power BI, can handle larger volumes of data, especially when connected to optimized external data sources, such as cloud databases or Big Data technologies (like Hadoop or Spark). However, its capacity also has limits compared to specific Big Data solutions. The phenomenon of Big Data has transformed the way organizations manage, analyze, and use data, enabling them to gain valuable insights and make informed decisions.

The era of Big Data began with the explosion of the volume of data generated by the proliferation of digital devices, social networks, IoT sensors, and many other sources. It is estimated that 90% of the world's data was created in the last two years (approximately between 2022 and 2024), and this trend continues to accelerate. The key characteristics that define Big Data are commonly described through the "3 Vs": Volume, Velocity, and Variety. Sometimes, two other dimensions are added: Veracity and Value (becoming the 5 Vs), and this can be expanded in some cases.

Despite its enormous benefits, Big Data also presents significant challenges. Storing and managing large volumes of data require advanced infrastructures. Processing and analyzing this data demand new tools and technologies, such as Hadoop and Spark. In addition, data privacy and security are critical concerns, and ensuring the quality and veracity of the data is essential to obtain reliable results.

The technologies that support Big Data include Hadoop, a distributed processing framework; Spark, which facilitates in-memory data processing; and NoSQL databases, such as MongoDB and Cassandra, which efficiently handle unstructured data. Visualization tools like Tableau and Power BI also play a crucial role by making data understandable and useful for decision-making; furthermore, data can be analyzed with Python using libraries like Pandas for medium-sized datasets, or Dask and PySpark for Big Data scale datasets.

The future of Big Data is marked by integration with emerging technologies such as Artificial Intelligence and the Internet of Things, as well as by the growing use of cloud computing and Data Lakes, which enable flexible storage and access to large volumes of data in their original format.

Next, I will develop the 5 Vs one by one. Although they all go hand in hand, it is important to do it this way to understand each one, its importance, and its potential in terms of Big Data, as well as its relevance and connection to the development of Machine Learning models and therefore its relationship and relevance with AI.

3.1. Definition and characteristics of Big Data (the 5Vs)

3.1.1. Volume

Volume is one of the fundamental characteristics that define the concept of Big Data. It refers to the massive amount of data that is generated and stored daily on a global scale. This enormous quantity of data comes from diverse sources and accumulates at an unprecedented rate, challenging traditional data storage, processing, and analysis capabilities. Now let's explore the most relevant aspects of volume in the context of Big Data, including its origin, impact, challenges, and the technologies used to manage it.

Origin and growth of data volume

The volume of data has grown exponentially due to various technological and social trends. Among the most significant sources of data are:

1. Social networks: Platforms like Facebook, Twitter, Instagram, and LinkedIn generate massive amounts of data daily. Every interaction, such as a "like", a comment, or a post, contributes to the total data volume.

2. Mobile devices: Smartphones and other mobile devices are responsible for generating a huge amount of data, including text messages, emails, GPS locations, photos, and videos.

3. Internet of Things (IoT): Connected devices, such as sensors in smart homes, vehicles, factories, and cities, constantly generate data. These devices collect information about temperature, humidity, energy consumption, movement, and many other parameters.

4. Financial transactions: The financial sector produces a high volume of data through banking transactions, credit card purchases, stock market operations, and other economic activities.

5. Digital media: Streaming videos, music, and other digital content through platforms like YouTube, Netflix, and Spotify also contributes significantly to the data volume.

6. Health and medicine: The digitization of medical records, diagnostic images, clinical trial data, and patient monitoring through wearable devices generate enormous amounts of data.

The growth of data volume has been driven by the reduction of storage costs and the increase in the capacity of storage devices. It is estimated that the volume of global data doubles approximately every two years, posing enormous challenges and opportunities for organizations.

Impact of volume on organizations

The large volume of data has a significant impact on organizations, both in terms of opportunities and challenges. Organizations that can effectively manage and analyze large volumes of data can gain competitive advantages, such as:

Improved decision-making: Analyzing large volumes of data allows organizations to make more informed decisions based on concrete evidence rather than assumptions.

Personalization: With large volumes of data, companies can offer more personalized products and services, tailored to individual customer needs and preferences.

Innovation: Data can be a source of innovation, enabling organizations to develop new products, services, and business models based on insights obtained from data analysis.

Operational efficiency: Analyzing large volumes of data can help optimize operational processes, reduce costs, and improve overall organizational efficiency.

However, managing large volumes of data also presents several challenges:

Storage: Massive volumes of data require scalable and cost-effective storage solutions. Traditional storage infrastructures are often not suitable for handling the size and complexity of current data.

Processing: Efficiently processing large volumes of data requires powerful computing resources and advanced data processing techniques. Parallel processing and distributed architectures are essential to manage data volume.

Data quality: With large volumes of data, ensuring the quality and accuracy of the data is an ongoing challenge. Data can be incomplete, duplicated, or inconsistent, affecting the reliability of analyses.

Security and privacy: Managing large volumes of data raises important security and privacy issues. Organizations must implement robust measures to protect data and comply with privacy regulations.

Technologies to manage data volume

To address the challenges associated with data volume, various technologies and approaches have been developed. Some of the most important technologies include:

(*I will discuss the following points in much greater detail later.*)

- **Hadoop:** Hadoop is an open-source framework that enables distributed processing of large datasets across clusters of computers. It uses the Hadoop Distributed File System (HDFS) to store data in a distributed manner and the MapReduce programming model to process data in parallel.

- **Spark:** Apache Spark is a data processing engine that allows fast in-memory processing of large data volumes. Spark is known for its speed and ability to perform advanced analytics, such as Machine Learning and graph processing.

- **NoSQL:** NoSQL databases, such as MongoDB, Cassandra, and HBase, are designed to handle large volumes of unstructured and semi-structured data. They offer high scalability and flexibility in data management.

- **Data Lakes:** Data Lakes are storage repositories that allow storing large volumes of data in their native format, whether structured, semi-structured, or unstructured. They provide a flexible and scalable way to manage large volumes of data.

- **Data Warehouse:** Data Warehouses are storage systems optimized for structured data, specifically designed for analysis and reporting. Through ETL (Extract, Transform, Load) processes, data is cleaned, transformed, and stored in a structured format, allowing complex queries and obtaining strategic insights. They offer high performance in querying large volumes of data and are ideal for business intelligence and decision-making applications.

- **Data Lakehouse:** Data Lakehouses combine the capabilities of Data Lakes and Data Warehouses into a single platform. They allow storing data in its raw format, like a Data Lake, but with structures optimized for analysis, similar to a Data Warehouse. This hybrid architecture facilitates advanced analysis of structured and unstructured data, reducing costs and simplifying management by eliminating the need to maintain separate systems for storage and analysis.

- **Google File System (GFS):** Distributed File Systems (DFS), such as Google File System (GFS), allow storing and managing large volumes of data by distributing them across multiple nodes. These systems offer scalability, fault tolerance, and high performance when processing massive data. They are fundamental in Big Data environments and are used alongside frameworks like Hadoop and Spark to perform distributed data processing.

- **Object Storage:** Object storage is a scalable and flexible solution designed to store unstructured data. Instead of following a hierarchical file structure, data is stored as independent objects with metadata and a unique identifier. This approach facilitates the access and management of large volumes of files such as images, videos, backups, and log files. Popular examples include Amazon S3, Google Cloud Storage, and Azure Blob Storage.

- **In-Memory:** In-Memory storage uses RAM to store and process data, offering ultra-fast access and significantly reducing latency. This type of storage is ideal for applications that require real-time analysis, such as financial systems, online games, or e-commerce platforms. Tools like Redis, Memcached, or Apache Ignite are examples of In-Memory solutions used to speed up queries and improve overall performance.

- **Cloud Computing:** Cloud computing is a broad concept that encompasses the delivery of different services over the Internet, including storage, processing, databases, networks, and software. It provides scalability, flexibility, and cost-effectiveness by allowing organizations to use resources on demand without the need to maintain local infrastructures. There are different cloud service models:

▪ **IaaS (Infrastructure as a Service):** Virtualized infrastructure (servers, networks, storage) such as Amazon EC2 or Google Compute Engine.
▪ **PaaS (Platform as a Service**): Complete platforms to develop and run applications, such as Google App Engine or Heroku.
▪ **SaaS (Software as a Service):** Ready-to-use web applications, such as Google Drive or Microsoft 365.

Services like Amazon S3, Google Cloud Storage, and Azure Blob Storage allow organizations to store and process data without the need for expensive infrastructures.

Case studies and applications

The volume of data has led to innovative applications across various sectors. Some prominent case studies include:

- **Netflix:** Netflix uses large volumes of viewing data to personalize content recommendations for its users, enhance the user experience, and optimize the production of new content.

- **Tesla:** Tesla collects data from its vehicles in real time to improve the safety, performance, and efficiency of its cars. The data is also used to develop and refine autonomous driving technology.

- **Amazon:** Amazon uses large volumes of transaction data, user behavior, and customer feedback to optimize its supply chain, personalize product recommendations, and enhance the customer experience.

Future of data volume

The volume of data will continue to grow as more devices connect to the Internet and more real-time data is generated. According to UN data, approximately 134 million births were recorded worldwide in 2022. This equals a crude birth rate of around 17 births per 1,000 people, considering a global population of approximately 8 billion that year. It is important to note that these figures are estimates, as not all births are officially registered; the World Health Organization estimates that 36 million babies are born each year whose births are not registered. Although this can be explored and nuanced further, let's leave it here and now turn this into data.

According to recent data, approximately 1.220 billion smartphones were sold worldwide in 2024, representing a 7 percent growth compared to the previous year. In terms of market share, Apple and Samsung continue to lead global sales. According to data from forbesargentina.com, in 2024, Apple managed to position itself as the top smartphone seller, with 234.6 million units shipped and a market share of 20.1 percent. Samsung recorded sales of 226.6 million units, representing 19.4 percent of the market.

Now convert all this information into data. Into transactions, photos, videos, likes, comments, prices, dates, quantities, locations, groups.

Now imagine what this means, in the context of data, for these companies. Do you see where I am going with this?

Data is gold, and you are giving it away! But that's another story.

The development of new technologies and approaches will be crucial to manage and extract value from these massive volumes of data. The integration of Big Data with emerging technologies such as Artificial Intelligence, Machine Learning, and the Internet of Things will open new opportunities and challenges, further transforming the way organizations operate and make decisions.

Volume is a critical dimension of Big Data that presents both opportunities and challenges. Effectively managing large volumes of data requires advanced technologies, scalable infrastructures, and a deep understanding of data. As data volume continues to grow, organizations that can adapt and leverage this data will be better positioned to gain competitive advantages and lead in their respective sectors. For all these reasons, I am trying to make you understand that knowledge and control of data will open many doors for you professionally and will undoubtedly mark a before and after in your career.

3.1.2. Velocity

A crucial dimension of Big Data is Velocity, which refers to the speed at which data is generated, processed, and analyzed. In the context of Big Data, not only is the large amount of data important, but also the speed at which this data becomes available and can be used to make decisions. The velocity of data presents unique challenges and requires specific technological solutions to handle the continuous flow of information. Let's dive into the most relevant aspects of velocity in Big Data, including its origin, impact, challenges, and the technologies used to manage it. As you will see, everything is closely related and interconnected.

Origin and growth of data velocity

The speed at which data is generated and collected has increased dramatically in recent decades due to several technological and social factors:

1. Internet of Things (IoT): Connected devices, such as sensors, cameras, and other IoT devices, generate real-time data. These devices are present in homes, factories, vehicles, and smart cities, producing a constant stream of data that needs to be processed quickly.

2. Social media: Platforms such as X (Twitter), Meta (Facebook), and Instagram generate data at an impressive speed, with millions of posts, comments, and likes every minute. The rapid pace at which this data is generated requires solutions capable of processing it almost in real time.

3. Financial transactions: Real-time transactions in banks, stock markets, and e-commerce platforms contribute significantly to data velocity. Each transaction needs to be recorded and analyzed instantly to detect fraud and make business decisions.

4. Digital media: The streaming of multimedia content, such as videos on YouTube, streaming on Netflix, and music on Spotify also generates large volumes of data continuously. This data must be processed quickly to ensure a smooth user experience.

5. Real-time monitoring systems: Systems that monitor critical infrastructure, such as power grids, industrial plants, and transportation systems, generate high-speed data that must be analyzed in real time to ensure their safe and efficient operation.

Impact of velocity on organizations

The ability to process and analyze data quickly has a significant impact on organizations, allowing them to respond more agilely and effectively to changes and opportunities. Some of the most important benefits include:

Real-time decision-making: The ability to analyze data in real time allows organizations to make instant decisions based on up-to-date information. This is crucial in sectors such as finance, where quick decisions can mean the difference between gains and losses.

Improved customer experience: In e-commerce and digital services, the speed of data processing enables real-time personalization of the user experience, recommending relevant products or content and improving customer satisfaction.

Optimization of operational processes: In manufacturing and logistics, real-time analysis of operational data can help identify and resolve problems quickly, optimize production, and improve overall efficiency. This includes departments such as purchasing and sales, also influencing others like marketing and of course management.

Fraud detection and prevention: In the financial and insurance sectors, the speed of data analysis is crucial to detect fraudulent activities almost instantly, minimizing losses and improving security.

Challenges of data velocity

The speed of data presents several challenges that must be addressed to fully harness its benefits:

Real-time processing: Processing large volumes of data at high speed requires advanced infrastructures and technologies. Systems must be capable of handling the continuous data flow without significant delays.

Storage and management: Real-time data management also involves storing data quickly and ensuring it is available for immediate analysis. This requires scalable, efficient, and above all, reliable storage solutions.

Data integrity and quality: As data is generated and processed quickly, it is very important to ensure its quality and accuracy. Errors and inconsistencies in data can negatively affect analyses and the decisions based on them.

Security and privacy: Real-time data management increases the complexity of ensuring data security and privacy. Organizations must implement robust measures to protect sensitive data as it is collected and processed, also preventing malicious attacks. Here I recall that in 2024 Amazon experienced a notable increase in daily cyberattack attempts, rising from 100 million to 750 million over a period of six to seven months. This increase is partly attributed to the use of Artificial Intelligence by attackers, who employ generative AI tools to create more convincing phishing emails and develop advanced malware. To counter these threats, Amazon has implemented AI-based defenses, such as graph databases to monitor interactions and detect malicious behaviors, as well as honeypots that lure attackers to study their methods. Additionally, the company has collaborated with the US Department of Justice to dismantle platforms used by cybercriminal groups such as Anonymous Sudan. Furthermore, in November 2024, Amazon confirmed the theft of more than 2.8 million employee data records due to a vulnerability in MOVEit Transfer, a third-party provider. Although the compromised information included corporate email addresses and phone extensions, no confidential or personal data was accessed. This incident highlights the increasing sophistication of cyberattacks and the need for robust security measures.

Technologies to manage data velocity

To address the challenges of data velocity, several technologies and approaches have been developed that enable fast and efficient processing of large volumes of data:

- **Stream processing:** Stream processing platforms, such as Apache Kafka, Apache Flink, and Apache Storm, allow processing and analyzing data in real time. These platforms handle continuous data streams and perform operations such as filtering, aggregation, and analysis as data is generated.

- **Real-time databases:** Databases designed for real-time processing, such as Redis and Amazon DynamoDB, provide fast and efficient access to data, supporting applications that require low latency.

- **Edge computing:** Edge computing brings data processing closer to the source of generation, such as IoT devices. This reduces latency and enables fast decision-making without the need to send all data to a centralized data center.

- **In-memory storage technologies:** In-memory storage technologies, such as Apache Ignite and Memcached, allow extremely fast data access and processing, as the data is stored in RAM instead of on disks.

Case studies and applications

The speed of data has enabled innovative applications across various sectors. Some notable examples are:

- **Uber:** Uber uses stream processing technologies to analyze real-time data from its drivers and passengers, optimizing vehicle allocation, calculating dynamic fares, and improving the user experience.

- **Alibaba:** Alibaba uses real-time processing to manage millions of transactions during massive sales events such as Singles' Day, ensuring that its platform can handle the enormous volume of traffic and transactions without interruptions.

- **Walmart:** Walmart employs stream processing technologies to monitor and analyze real-time sales data, allowing dynamic inventory and pricing adjustments to maximize sales and minimize losses.

Future of data speed

The future of data speed is shaped by the integration of emerging technologies and the development of new processing architectures. Some emerging trends we can observe are:

5G and high-speed connectivity: The implementation of 5G networks will enable even faster data transmission, unlocking new real-time applications in areas such as autonomous vehicles, smart cities, and augmented reality.

Real-time Machine Learning: The combination of Big Data with real-time Machine Learning enables the development of autonomous systems that can learn and adapt instantly to new data and situations.

Process automation: The speed of data processing allows greater automation of business processes, optimizing operations and improving efficiency in real-time.

3.1.3. Variety

Variety is one of the fundamental characteristics of Big Data and refers to the different types of data that are generated and collected. In the Big Data era, it is not only important to handle large volumes of data or process them quickly but also to be able to manage and analyze data that come from various sources and have different formats and structures. Data variety presents both unique opportunities and challenges for organizations, both in its value and in the infrastructure required for its storage and management. Working with data variety makes the project much more complex and therefore much more delicate to achieve the best results.

Origin and types of data

The variety of data is due to the multitude of data sources that exist in today's environment. These data can be classified into three main categories: structured data, unstructured data, and semi-structured data. This point is perfectly explained in full detail and with plenty of examples in my book AI-Manager. Let's look at them briefly.

1. **Structured data:** These are data organized in a defined format, such as relational databases, spreadsheets, and tables. These data are easy to store, process, and analyze using traditional tools. Common examples include transaction records, financial data, and sensor data recorded in tabular formats.

2. **Unstructured data:** These are data that have no predefined structure and are more difficult to process and analyze. They include free text, images, videos, audio files, emails, and social media posts. These data require advanced techniques to be processed and to extract meaningful information from them.

3. **Semi-structured data:** These are data that are not fully structured but have some type of internal organization, such as XML, JSON, and HTML documents. These data contain tags and other markers that allow the identification of different elements within the data, making them easier to process compared to unstructured data.

Impact of variety on organizations

The ability to handle and analyze a variety of data offers multiple benefits to organizations, allowing them to obtain more complete and detailed insights. Some of the most significant impacts are:

Holistic business view: By integrating and analyzing different types of data, companies and organizations can obtain a more complete and accurate view of their operations, customers, and markets. This enables more informed and strategic decision-making.

Enhanced customer experience: The variety of data allows organizations to better understand their customers' needs and preferences, personalizing products and services to improve customer satisfaction and loyalty.

Innovation and product development: By analyzing varied data, organizations can identify new market opportunities and emerging trends, driving innovation and the development of new products and services.

Process optimization: Integrating data from different sources allows for the optimization of operational processes, improving efficiency and reducing costs. For example, the analysis of real-time sensor data can optimize predictive maintenance in manufacturing.

Challenges of data variety

Although data variety offers great opportunities, it also presents significant challenges that must be addressed to fully leverage its benefits:

Data integration: Integrating data from diverse sources and formats is a complex challenge. It requires advanced tools and techniques to consolidate and harmonize structured, unstructured, and semi-structured data into a single repository.

Data quality: Ensuring the quality and consistency of varied data is crucial for obtaining accurate insights. Data from different sources may be inconsistent, incomplete, duplicated, or of very dubious origin, which requires robust data cleaning and validation processes.

Storage and management: Storing and managing large volumes of varied data requires flexible and scalable storage solutions that can efficiently handle different types of data.

Analysis and processing: Unstructured and semi-structured data require advanced analysis and processing techniques, such as natural language processing, image recognition, and video analysis. This involves the use of specialized tools and technologies that can handle the complexity of these data.

Technologies to manage data variety

To address the challenges of data variety, various technologies and approaches have been developed to manage and analyze data of different types and formats:

(*Regarding the following points I will talk to you much more extensively later. Remember that we are introducing ourselves step by step*).

- **NoSQL databases:** NoSQL databases, such as MongoDB, Cassandra, and Couchbase, are designed to handle unstructured and semi-structured data. They offer flexibility and scalability, allowing efficient storage and querying of large volumes of data.

- **Data Lakes:** Data Lakes, as we have already seen earlier, are storage repositories that allow the storage of large volumes of data in their native format. In this context, they also provide a flexible way to manage structured, unstructured, and semi-structured data, facilitating access to and analysis of these data.

- **ETL tools:** Extract, Transform, and Load (ETL) tools, such as Apache Nifi, Talend, and Informatica, facilitate the integration and transformation of data from various sources. These tools allow cleaning, consolidating, and preparing data for analysis.

- **Data processing platforms:** Platforms such as Apache Hadoop and Apache Spark also enable distributed processing of large volumes of varied data. These platforms support the analysis of structured, unstructured, and semi-structured data using advanced parallel processing techniques.

- **Advanced analytics technologies:** Technologies such as natural language processing, machine learning, and image and video analysis allow extracting valuable insights from unstructured and semi-structured data. These technologies integrate with data processing platforms to perform complex analyses.

Case studies and applications

The variety of data has enabled innovative applications across various sectors. As examples, we can highlight:

- **Amazon:** Amazon uses varied data, including purchase transactions, product reviews, and web browsing data, to personalize product recommendations and improve the customer experience.

- **Netflix:** Netflix analyzes structured subscriber data along with unstructured data such as viewing history and content preferences to personalize recommendations and optimize the production of new content.

- **Ford:** Ford integrates vehicle sensor data, driver behavior data, and social media data to improve vehicle design, personalize services, and optimize safety and performance.

Future of data variety

The future of data variety is shaped by the integration of emerging technologies and the development of new management and analysis architectures. Some emerging trends include:

Artificial Intelligence and Machine Learning: The combination of Big Data with Artificial Intelligence and likewise Machine Learning allows us to develop advanced analysis systems that can autonomously handle and extract insights from varied data.

Internet of Things (IoT): The proliferation of IoT devices will generate a greater variety of real-time data, driving the need for advanced solutions to manage and analyze these data.

Cloud Computing: Cloud computing provides flexible and scalable storage and processing solutions to manage large volumes of varied data, facilitating access and analysis from anywhere.

Data fabric: The concept of data fabric, which integrates data and applications into a unified architecture, allows for more efficient and consistent management and analysis of varied data.

Variety is a critical dimension of Big Data, as it enables organizations to obtain more complete and detailed insights by integrating and analyzing different types of data.

3.1.4. Veracity

Veracity is also a critical dimension, and a very important one, of Big Data, which refers to the quality and reliability of the data. In an environment where data is generated and accumulated at an unprecedented speed and volume, veracity becomes a central challenge for organizations. Low-quality data can lead to erroneous conclusions and wrong decisions, which underscores the importance of ensuring the integrity and accuracy of the data used in analyses.

Origin and nature of data veracity

The veracity of data is influenced by multiple factors, including the data source, the way it is collected, and the cleaning and validation processes applied. Data can be inconsistent, incomplete, inaccurate, or duplicated for various reasons.

1. Data source: Data can come from multiple sources, each with different levels of reliability. Social networks, for example, can generate large volumes of data that are not always accurate or verifiable.

2. Collection methods: Data can be collected through sensors, IoT devices, surveys, transactional records, and other methodologies, each susceptible to errors and biases. Errors in device configuration or in the design of surveys can introduce inaccuracies.

3. Data quality: The quality of data is affected by factors such as duplication, lack of data, typographical errors, and obsolescence. Outdated data may not reflect the current reality and therefore can be misleading.

4. Data integration: When combining data from different sources, consistency and coherence issues may arise. The lack of standardization in formats and nomenclature can make precise data integration difficult.

Impact of veracity on organizations

The veracity of data has a significant impact on organizations, influencing the quality of decisions and the effectiveness of data-driven strategies. Some of the most important impacts include.

Decision making: Decisions based on inaccurate or unreliable data can lead to adverse outcomes. Data veracity is crucial to ensure that decisions are informed and precise.

Customer trust: Low-quality data can affect customer trust in an organization. For example, errors in billing data or in the personalization of services can decrease customer satisfaction and loyalty.

Regulatory compliance: In regulated sectors, such as healthcare and finance, data accuracy is essential to comply with regulations and avoid penalties. Incorrect data can lead to legal and regulatory non-compliance.

Operational efficiency: Managing incorrect data can lead to operational inefficiencies, as additional time and resources are needed to correct errors and validate information.

Challenges of data veracity

Ensuring the veracity of data in the context of Big Data presents several challenges that must be addressed to ensure that data is accurate and reliable. Using examples I will talk about this later, for now we will just familiarize ourselves with these points.

Data validation and cleaning: Validation and cleaning processes are essential to identify and correct errors in the data. This can include removing duplicates, correcting typographical errors, and verifying data consistency.

Data integrity: Maintaining data integrity throughout its entire lifecycle, from collection to analysis, is a critical challenge. This includes ensuring that data is not altered or corrupted during storage and processing.

Data standards and governance: Implementing data governance standards and policies is fundamental to ensure data quality and consistency. This includes defining quality standards, audit procedures, and clear roles and responsibilities for data management.

Data source: The reliability of the data source is a key factor to ensure veracity. Organizations must carefully evaluate and select data sources, preferring those recognized for their accuracy and reliability.

Technologies and approaches to manage data veracity

To face the challenges of data veracity, various technologies and approaches have been developed that improve the quality and reliability of data.

- **Data cleaning tools:** Tools such as Talend, Informatica, and OpenRefine enable data cleaning tasks, including duplicate removal, error correction, and format standardization.

- **Data quality platforms:** Platforms such as IBM InfoSphere QualityStage and Microsoft Azure Data Catalog provide comprehensive solutions for managing data quality, including validation, monitoring, and continuous quality improvement.

- **Blockchain technologies:** Blockchain technology offers a novel approach to ensure data integrity and traceability. Records on a blockchain are immutable and verifiable, helping to guarantee the accuracy and authenticity of data.

- **Machine Learning approaches:** Machine Learning algorithms can be used to detect anomalies and patterns in data that indicate errors or inconsistencies. These algorithms can help identify and correct data quality issues proactively.

- **Data governance:** Implementing robust data governance is crucial to ensure data quality. This includes defining policies and procedures, creating clear roles and responsibilities, and implementing quality and audit standards.

Case studies and applications

Data veracity has enabled innovative applications across various sectors. Some examples are.

- **Healthcare:** In the healthcare sector, data accuracy is fundamental for diagnosing and treating diseases. Health information systems (HIS) and electronic medical records (EMR) use advanced data cleaning and validation tools to ensure the quality of patient data.

- **Banking and finance:** Financial institutions use data quality platforms to ensure the accuracy of transactional and regulatory data. This is crucial for fraud detection, risk management, and regulatory compliance.

- **Retail:** In the retail sector, the quality of inventory and sales data is essential for efficient supply chain management and price optimization. Retailers use data quality tools to ensure that product and sales information is accurate and up to date.

Future of data veracity

The future of data veracity is marked by the integration of new technologies and innovative approaches to improve data quality and reliability. Some emerging trends include.

Artificial Intelligence and Machine Learning: The integration of AI and Machine Learning into data quality processes will allow faster and more accurate error detection and correction. Advanced algorithms will be able to identify patterns and anomalies in the data that indicate quality issues.

Blockchain and data traceability: The adoption of blockchain technologies will allow greater traceability and transparency in data, ensuring that records are immutable and verifiable. This will be especially important in sectors where data authenticity and integrity are critical.

Automation of data quality: Automating data cleaning and validation processes will reduce manual workload and improve efficiency. Advanced tools will enable continuous and proactive data quality management.

Improved data governance: Organizations will adopt more robust and structured approaches to data governance, ensuring that data is managed according to strict quality standards and complies with regulations.

Veracity in Big Data directly influences the quality of decisions and confidence in the data. Ensuring data veracity requires a multidimensional approach that includes advanced technological tools, robust quality standards, and effective data governance. It is essential to know the field of data very well, know how to read it, and understand it perfectly.

3.1.5. Value

Value is perhaps the most crucial dimension of Big Data, as it refers to the potential of data to generate significant benefits for organizations. While other dimensions such as volume, velocity, variety, and veracity are important for the management and processing of data, value focuses on the ultimate goal: turning data into useful information that can improve decision-making, optimize operations, generate new business opportunities, and ultimately increase profitability.

Definition and nature of value in Big Data

The value of Big Data does not lie in the data itself but in the insights and knowledge that can be extracted from it. For data to have value, it must be analyzed and transformed into actionable information. This information must be relevant, accurate, and timely, and it must directly support the strategic objectives of the organization.

The value of Big Data can manifest in various ways:

1. Improved decision-making: Data can provide a solid foundation for informed decision-making, reducing uncertainty and enabling business leaders to act with greater confidence and precision.

2. Operational efficiency: Data analysis can identify inefficiencies in processes, suggest improvements, and optimize resources, which can result in significant cost savings and increased productivity.

3. Personalization and enhancement of customer experience: By analyzing customer data, companies can personalize products, services, and marketing campaigns to better meet individual needs and preferences, improving customer satisfaction and loyalty.

4. Innovation and new product development: Data can reveal new market opportunities and emerging trends, driving innovation and the development of products and services that meet the changing demands of consumers.

5. Risk management and compliance: Data analysis can help identify and mitigate risks, ensure regulatory compliance, and protect the organization from fraud, cyberattacks, and other threats.

Impact of the value of Big Data on organizations

The value of Big Data has a profound impact on how organizations operate and compete in their respective markets. Companies that can extract value from their data are better positioned to lead in their industries, while those that fail to do so may fall behind. Here are some examples:

Competitive advantage: Organizations that use Big Data to improve decision-making and optimize operations can gain a significant competitive advantage. This is due to their ability to react more quickly to market changes and to seize new opportunities before their competitors.

Continuous innovation: The value of Big Data enables companies to maintain a culture of continuous innovation, using data to identify areas for improvement and product development. This is particularly important in highly dynamic industries where the ability to innovate quickly is key to success.

Improvement in customer satisfaction: By leveraging data to better understand customers and personalize the user experience, organizations can increase customer satisfaction and loyalty. This translates into higher customer retention rates and an increase in customer lifetime value.

Cost optimization: By analyzing large volumes of operational data, organizations can identify areas where costs can be reduced without compromising quality. This may include optimizing the supply chain, improving energy efficiency, and reducing waste.

Challenges to maximizing the value of Big Data

Although the potential value of Big Data is enormous, its effective realization is not without challenges. Some of the most common challenges organizations face when trying to extract value from their data are:

Information overload: With the vast amount of data available, one of the biggest challenges is to avoid information overload and focus on the data that really matters. Filtering relevant data from irrelevant data is crucial to avoid getting lost in a sea of information.

Lack of analytical skills: Extracting value from Big Data requires advanced analytical skills, including knowledge of statistical techniques, Machine Learning, and predictive analytics. The lack of talent in these areas can limit an organization's ability to leverage its data.

Data integration: Data often comes from multiple sources and in different formats, which can make integration and analysis difficult. The ability to consolidate and harmonize data from various sources is essential to obtain a complete and accurate view.

Security and privacy: As organizations collect and analyze large volumes of data, they must ensure that this data is protected against unauthorized access and complies with privacy regulations. Security breaches can not only jeopardize confidential information but also damage the organization's reputation.

Cost and complexity: Implementing and maintaining a Big Data infrastructure can be costly and complex. This includes the cost of technologies, data storage, and hiring skilled personnel.

Strategies to maximize the value of Big Data

To maximize the value of Big Data, organizations should adopt a series of strategies and approaches:

- **Focus on data quality:** Ensuring that data is accurate, complete, and up to date is essential to extract value from it. This includes implementing data cleaning and validation processes, as well as data governance to maintain consistent quality standards.

- **Investment in technology and talent:** Organizations should invest in advanced analytics technologies and in training and hiring personnel with skills in data science, data analysis, and Machine Learning. These investments are essential to develop the internal capability to extract value from Big Data.

- **Data-driven culture:** Promoting a culture in which decisions are based on data rather than assumptions is key to maximizing the value of Big Data. This involves educating all levels of the organization about the importance of using data and providing the necessary tools to do so.

- **Predictive and prescriptive analytics:** In addition to descriptive analytics, organizations should leverage predictive and prescriptive analytics to anticipate future trends and make proactive decisions. This includes using Machine Learning algorithms to predict customer behavior, identify risks, and optimize operations.

- **Partnerships and collaborations:** In some cases, collaborating with other organizations or technology providers can be an effective way to maximize the value of Big Data. This may include sharing data, technologies, and knowledge to achieve common goals.

Case studies and applications of the value of Big Data

The value of Big Data has been demonstrated in a variety of industries and applications.

- **Walmart:** Walmart uses Big Data to optimize its supply chain, personalize the shopping experience for its customers, and improve operational efficiency. By analyzing sales data and customer behavior in real time, Walmart can dynamically adjust its inventory and pricing to maximize sales and minimize costs.

- **UPS:** The logistics company UPS has implemented an advanced data analytics system called ORION (On-Road Integrated Optimization and Navigation) that optimizes delivery routes in real time. This has enabled UPS to save millions of liters of fuel and significantly reduce its operating costs.

- **Netflix:** Netflix uses Big Data to personalize content recommendations for each of its users, improve subscriber retention, and optimize the production of new content. By analyzing viewing data and user preferences, Netflix can predict which shows will be successful and make informed decisions about creating original content.

Future of the value of Big Data

The future of the value of Big Data is marked by the continuous integration of emerging technologies and the development of new applications.

Artificial Intelligence and Machine Learning: As Artificial Intelligence and Machine Learning become more deeply integrated into Big Data, organizations will be able to automate data analysis and discover patterns and insights that were previously impossible to detect.

IoT and real-time analytics: The proliferation of connected devices will generate a constant flow of real-time data, enabling organizations to make faster and more accurate decisions based on up-to-date information.

Data economy: As data becomes an increasingly valuable asset, organizations will explore new ways to monetize their data, whether through data sales, the creation of new data-based products, or participation in collaborative data economies.

Value is the dimension of Big Data that justifies investment in data and analytics technologies. Extracting value from data requires a combination of well-defined strategies, investments in technology and talent, and an organizational culture that values and uses data at all levels.

As you have seen regarding the "5Vs," they are very closely related, as well as with the techniques and technologies used for their management. Keep in mind that although everything may sound the same for this reason, they have different contexts, and this is a very important reason why you must master them perfectly to ensure the success of each project.

3.2. History of Data Storage and Processing

The history of data storage and processing is a chronicle of the technological evolution that has enabled humanity to handle information increasingly efficiently and effectively. From the earliest methods of recording information to today's advanced technologies of mass storage and distributed processing, this historical journey reflects continuous progress in our ability to manage data.

The earliest methods of data storage can be traced back to ancient civilizations that used rudimentary forms of record-keeping, such as clay tablets, papyrus, and parchment. These media were limited in capacity and durability but marked the beginning of documentation and preservation of critical information such as commercial records, laws, and treaties. The invention of paper by the Chinese in the 2nd century BC and its subsequent spread to other cultures represented a significant advancement in data storage, as it provided a more accessible and durable method for recording information.

The true change in data storage began with the invention of the printing press by Johannes Gutenberg in the 15th century. The printing press not only revolutionized the production and distribution of information but also allowed the preservation of large amounts of data in the form of books and documents. Blessed be the printing press. This advancement laid the foundation for the mass storage of information, a concept that would develop much further with the advent of the digital era.

The 19th century witnessed the first developments in mechanical data storage and processing. One of the most important milestones of this era was the invention of punched cards by Herman Hollerith in 1889. These cards, initially used to tabulate the United States census, allowed data to be stored mechanically and processes to be automated. Punched card technology became a standard for many decades, being used in early computers and data processing systems in large organizations.

The advent of electronic computers in the mid-20th century marked the beginning of a new era in data storage and processing. This was a turning point. The first generation of computers, such as the ENIAC and the UNIVAC, used vacuum tubes and magnetic tapes to store data and perform calculations. Magnetic tapes allowed sequential storage of large amounts of data, but their access speed was relatively slow compared to today's standards.

The development of hard drives in the 1950s was a crucial advancement in the history of data storage. The IBM 305 RAMAC, introduced in 1956, was the first commercial computer to use a hard drive for data storage. This device could store approximately 5 megabytes of data, a significant achievement for its time. Hard drives allowed random access to data, which considerably improved reading and writing speeds compared to magnetic tapes.

The 1960s saw the introduction of the first relational databases, a concept developed by Edgar F. Codd at IBM. Relational databases allowed data to be organized into interrelated tables, facilitating information retrieval through the use of structured queries in a standard language such as SQL. This structure became the backbone of database management systems (DBMS) still in use today.

During the 1970s and 1980s, data storage experienced significant advances with the introduction of higher-capacity disks, such as floppy disks, and the emergence of solid-state drives (SSD), which offered greater speed and reliability compared to traditional hard drives. At the same time, data processing became more sophisticated with the development of more powerful microprocessors and the introduction of more advanced operating systems that allowed multitasking and efficient resource management.

When I talk about data storage, I cannot help but remember my childhood, when my mother bought us a Sinclair ZX Spectrum +2, which had just 128K of memory. On that computer, we wrote code that was stored on cassette tapes, accompanied by the characteristic sounds that marked the loading process. It was a time when storage was limited at the user level, but imagination had no boundaries.

The 1990s marked the beginning of the network computing era and the explosion of online storage. The development of the World Wide Web and the expansion of the Internet drove the demand for large-scale data storage and processing. Organizations began using dedicated servers and data centers to handle large volumes of data generated by web applications and online transactions. This era also saw the popularization of distributed databases, which allowed organizations to store and access data across multiple geographic locations, improving redundancy and accessibility.

As the amount of data continued to grow exponentially, the first decade of the 21st century brought the need for new storage and processing architectures. Technologies such as cloud storage and distributed file systems like the Hadoop Distributed File System enabled organizations to store petabytes of data in a scalable and cost-effective way. At the same time, data processing benefited from the introduction of programming paradigms like MapReduce, which allowed parallel processing of large data sets distributed across multiple computing nodes.

The development of cloud storage technologies, such as Amazon S3, Google Cloud Storage, and Microsoft Azure, radically transformed the way organizations store and access their data. These platforms offer near-unlimited scalability, allowing organizations to store large volumes of data without the need to invest in physical infrastructures. Moreover, cloud computing facilitated real-time data processing, enabling organizations to make faster decisions based on up-to-date information.

The most recent advancement in the history of data storage and processing is the introduction of technologies such as in-memory storage and NoSQL databases. These technologies are designed to handle the specific needs of Big Data, such as high-speed data access and the ability to manage unstructured and semi-structured data. In-memory storage, used in systems like SAP HANA, allows organizations to access data at extremely high speeds by storing the entire database in RAM instead of on traditional disks.

NoSQL databases, such as MongoDB, Cassandra, and Couchbase, which we have already mentioned earlier, have gained popularity due to their ability to handle large volumes of distributed data and their flexibility to store different types of data. These databases do not rely on a fixed schema, making them ideal for modern applications that require high flexibility and scalability.

Today, the trend toward Artificial Intelligence and Machine Learning is further driving the evolution of data storage and processing. Machine learning systems require enormous amounts of data to train models, and this data must be processed quickly to generate useful insights. This need has led to the development of specialized architectures such as Data Lakes, which allow data to be stored in its native form and enable advanced analysis without the need for prior transformations.

The history of data storage and processing is a narrative of constant technological evolution, driven by the need to handle ever-larger amounts of information more efficiently and effectively. From the earliest manual recording methods to today's advanced cloud storage and distributed processing technologies, each stage has contributed to the development of human capacity to store, process, and leverage data in ways that drive innovation, improve operational efficiency, and enable informed decision-making. As technology continues to advance, we will undoubtedly see new revolutions in how data is stored and processed, which will continue to transform the global economy and society at large.

3.3. Evolution of Big Data Technologies

The evolution of Big Data technologies reflects how the growing need to manage, process, and analyze large volumes of data has driven the development of new tools, architectures, and approaches. As the amount of data generated by humanity has increased exponentially, Big Data technologies have evolved to meet the demands of real-time storage, processing, and analysis. This evolution has enabled organizations to transform data into valuable information, improving decision-making, optimizing operations, and discovering new business opportunities.

The concept of Big Data began to gain attention in the 1990s when organizations started facing unprecedented challenges related to the volume, velocity, and variety of data. At that time, traditional relational database management systems (RDBMS) could no longer effectively handle the growing amounts of unstructured and semi-structured data. This led to the development of new architectures and technologies specifically designed to address the unique challenges of Big Data.

One of the first key technologies in the evolution of Big Data was the distributed processing system. Instead of relying on a single centralized server to store and process data, distributed systems allow data to be split into smaller parts and distributed across multiple computing nodes. This approach not only improves scalability but also enables more efficient parallel processing. An important milestone in this area was the development of MapReduce, a programming model introduced by Google in 2004.

MapReduce was designed to process large amounts of data distributed across clusters of computers. The model consists of two main phases: the "Map" phase, where data is divided into smaller chunks and processed in parallel, and the "Reduce" phase, where the partial results are combined to produce the final output. MapReduce allowed organizations to efficiently process large datasets at scale, driving the development of data processing platforms like Apache Hadoop.

Hadoop, which was developed by Doug Cutting and Mike Cafarella in 2006, quickly became one of the most influential Big Data technologies. Hadoop is an open-source framework that uses the MapReduce programming model and the Hadoop Distributed File System to store and process large volumes of data. HDFS allows data to be stored across multiple computing nodes, providing high availability and redundancy. Hadoop was adopted by numerous organizations due to its ability to handle large amounts of unstructured data at low cost and with high scalability.

As Hadoop gained popularity, new technologies and tools emerged that integrated with its ecosystem to enhance data processing capabilities. Among these technologies are Pig and Hive, which provide high-level programming languages for data manipulation in Hadoop, and HBase, a NoSQL database that enables efficient storage and access to large volumes of data. Additionally, Sqoop and Flume were developed to facilitate data transfer between Hadoop and other data sources, such as relational databases and cloud storage systems.

However, as the volume and complexity of data continued to grow, the limitations of MapReduce became apparent. The batch processing model of MapReduce was not suitable for applications requiring real-time analytics or streaming data processing. This led to the development of new data processing technologies capable of handling real-time data streams.

One of the most influential technologies in this area is Apache Spark, which was developed in 2009 at the University of California, Berkeley. Spark was designed as a faster and more flexible alternative to Hadoop, capable of performing in-memory data analytics and handling real-time data streams. Unlike Hadoop, which writes and reads data to disk between each MapReduce operation, Spark keeps data in memory, enabling much faster iterative operations. Spark also supports a wide range of workloads, including batch processing, stream processing, Machine Learning, and graph analytics, making it a versatile tool for Big Data analysis.

Another important evolution in Big Data technologies was the introduction of NoSQL databases. Unlike traditional relational databases, which require a fixed schema and rely on the SQL language for queries, NoSQL databases are designed to handle large volumes of unstructured and semi-structured data with greater flexibility and scalability. There are several types of NoSQL databases, including key-value stores like Redis and DynamoDB, document databases like MongoDB, columnar databases like Cassandra, and graph databases like Neo4j. These databases have been widely adopted by organizations that need to manage large amounts of data in real time and at scale.

The development of cloud computing has also had a significant impact on the evolution of Big Data technologies. With cloud computing, organizations can store and process large volumes of data without the need to invest in physical infrastructure. Cloud service providers such as Amazon Web Services (AWS), Google Cloud Platform (GCP), and Microsoft Azure offer a wide range of scalable, flexible, and cost-effective data storage and processing services. These services include cloud storage like Amazon S3, cloud processing services like Amazon EMR and Google BigQuery, and data analytics services like AWS Redshift and Azure Data Lake.

The combination of Big Data with emerging technologies such as Artificial Intelligence and Machine Learning has led to the creation of new data analytics architectures and platforms. Machine Learning platforms like TensorFlow, PyTorch, and Scikit-learn enable organizations to develop predictive and classification models based on large volumes of data. These platforms integrate with Big Data technologies to perform advanced and real-time analytics, allowing organizations to make data-driven decisions and improve their operations.

In addition, the evolution of Big Data has led to the development of modern architectures like Data Lakes. A Data Lake is a storage repository that allows organizations to store large volumes of data in their native format without the need to transform or structure them beforehand. This contrasts with traditional data warehouses, which require data to be structured and transformed before storage. Data Lakes allow exploratory and experimental analysis of raw data, which is especially useful in Machine Learning and advanced analytics applications.

As the volume and variety of data continue to grow, Big Data technologies have continued to evolve to address new challenges and seize new opportunities. In recent years, there has been increasing interest in edge computing, an architecture in which data processing is performed close to the data source rather than in a centralized data center. This is particularly relevant in IoT applications, where devices generate large volumes of real-time data that need to be processed quickly to make immediate decisions.

Another emerging trend in the evolution of Big Data technologies is the use of Artificial Intelligence and Machine Learning to automate data management and processing. Data analytics platforms are beginning to incorporate AI and Machine Learning capabilities to automate tasks such as data cleaning, anomaly detection, and model optimization. This not only improves the efficiency of data processing but also enables organizations to gain insights more quickly and accurately.

The evolution of Big Data technologies has been driven by the need to handle increasingly large amounts of data with greater speed, flexibility, and efficiency. From early distributed systems and the development of Hadoop to the introduction of Spark, NoSQL databases, and cloud computing, each stage of this evolution has contributed to the creation of a modern data infrastructure that enables organizations to extract value from their data.

3.4. Importance of Big Data in Decision-Making

The importance of Big Data in decision-making has grown exponentially in recent years, transforming the way organizations, governments, and individuals approach problem-solving and strategic planning. Basically, today no decision is made without Big Data. Big Data provides a solid foundation for informed decision-making by offering detailed and in-depth analysis of large volumes of data that were previously difficult to process and analyze.

Let's review and look at some new aspects to understand the importance of Big Data in decision-making.

As we already know, in this digital era we live in, organizations generate and collect data at an unprecedented pace, coming from various sources, including business transactions, social networks, IoT sensors, mobile devices, and more. This data ranges from structured information in databases to unstructured data, such as text, images, and videos. However, the true value of this data does not lie in its mere accumulation but in the ability to analyze it and extract meaningful insights that can guide decision-making. And this is where Big Data truly plays a crucial role.

Data-driven decision-making is an approach that has become increasingly predominant in organizations of all kinds. This approach involves using data and analytics to guide strategic, operational, and tactical decisions, rather than relying solely on intuition or previous experience. Big Data facilitates this approach by providing a more complete and accurate view of the current situation, enabling leaders to make better-informed decisions and reduce uncertainty.

One of the ways Big Data has transformed decision-making is through predictive analytics. Predictive analytics uses statistical techniques and Machine Learning algorithms to identify patterns in historical data and make predictions about future events. For example, in the retail sector, companies can use Big Data to predict product demand based on past purchasing patterns, market trends, and external factors such as weather or social events. This allows companies to optimize their inventories, reduce waste, and maximize sales.

In addition to predictive analytics, Big Data is also fundamental for prescriptive analytics, which not only predicts what might happen but also suggests specific actions to achieve a desired outcome. In logistics, for example, companies can use Big Data to optimize delivery routes, taking into account variables such as traffic, weather conditions, and load restrictions. This not only improves operational efficiency but also reduces costs and enhances customer satisfaction.

Another area where Big Data has proven to be crucial in decision-making is in the personalization and improvement of customer experience. Organizations can analyze large volumes of customer behavior data, such as purchase history, online interactions, and social media feedback, to create detailed customer profiles. These profiles allow companies to personalize offers, products, and services to better meet individual customer needs and preferences. This not only improves customer loyalty but also increases conversion rates and revenue.

The financial sector is another example where Big Data has revolutionized decision-making. Financial institutions use Big Data to manage risks, detect fraud, and comply with regulations. For example, Big Data analysis algorithms can identify unusual patterns in transactions that may indicate fraudulent activities, enabling banks to take preventive measures before significant losses occur. Additionally, Big Data helps financial institutions assess customers' creditworthiness by providing a more accurate and complete view of their financial history.

In the governmental sphere, Big Data also plays an essential role in decision-making related to public policy, resource management, and emergency response. Governments can use Big Data to monitor population well-being, predict and mitigate natural disasters, and optimize resource allocation in areas such as health, education, and security. For example, during the

COVID-19 pandemic, governments used Big Data analytics to track the spread of the virus, predict hotspots, and make informed decisions about quarantines, vaccination, and other mitigation efforts.

Despite the numerous advantages Big Data offers in decision-making, there are also important challenges that must be considered. One of the most significant challenges is data quality. For decisions based on Big Data to be effective, the data must be accurate, complete, and up-to-date. Low-quality data can lead to incorrect conclusions and poor decisions, highlighting the importance of implementing robust data cleansing, validation, and governance processes.

Another challenge is the complexity of Big Data analysis. Large and varied data sets can be difficult to analyze, requiring advanced skills in data science, statistics, and Machine Learning. Additionally, organizations must have the appropriate technological infrastructure to efficiently process and analyze this data. This may involve significant investment in Big Data technologies, such as distributed processing platforms, NoSQL databases, and data visualization tools.

Data security and privacy are also key concerns in data-driven decision-making. As organizations collect and analyze large volumes of data, they must ensure that this data is protected against unauthorized access and complies with privacy regulations. Security breaches can not only put sensitive information at risk but also damage the organization's reputation and result in legal penalties.

It is important to highlight the need for an organizational culture that values data-driven decision-making. Although Big Data offers powerful tools to improve decision-making, its effectiveness largely depends on the willingness of leaders and employees to adopt a data-driven approach. This may require changes in organizational culture, including training in the use of data analysis tools, promoting collaboration between data teams and leadership, and fostering a mindset of continuous learning and improvement.

The importance of Big Data in decision-making cannot be underestimated. By providing a solid foundation for predictive, prescriptive, and descriptive analytics, Big Data enables organizations to make better-informed decisions, reduce uncertainty, and seize new opportunities. However, to maximize the value of Big Data, it is essential to work on challenges related to data quality, analysis complexity, security and privacy, and organizational culture.

3.5. Impact on Different Industries

The impact of Big Data on different industries has been profound, transforming the way companies operate, make decisions, and create value. Each industry has adopted Big Data in a unique way, leveraging its capabilities to address specific challenges and uncover new opportunities. Let's look at how Big Data has influenced various industries, including healthcare, retail, manufacturing, finance, agriculture, and media and entertainment.

In the healthcare industry, Big Data has revolutionized patient care and medical research. Hospitals and clinics now collect and analyze large volumes of patient data, including electronic medical records (EMR), diagnostic images, lab test results, and data from real-time monitoring devices. This data is used to personalize treatments, improve diagnoses, and predict disease outbreaks. Machine Learning algorithms applied to Big Data have enabled doctors to identify patterns that would otherwise be invisible, improving diagnostic accuracy and treatment effectiveness. Additionally, Big Data has facilitated research into complex diseases such as cancer by analyzing large genomic and clinical data sets, accelerating the discovery of new therapies.

In retail, Big Data has transformed the customer experience and supply chain management. Retail companies use Big Data analytics to better understand consumer purchasing behavior, enabling mass personalization of offers and promotions. Sales data, combined with social media data and online transactions, allows businesses to predict consumption trends and adjust their marketing strategies in real time. Big Data has optimized inventory management and logistics, enabling retailers to maintain optimal stock levels, reduce waste, and improve operational efficiency. Predictive analytics also help retailers anticipate seasonal demand and plan accordingly, reducing costs and improving customer satisfaction.

The manufacturing industry has adopted Big Data to improve operational efficiency, reduce downtime, and enhance product quality. Smart factories equipped with IoT sensors and real-time monitoring systems generate large volumes of data about machine status, process performance, and product quality. This data is analyzed to identify failure patterns and predict necessary maintenance before breakdowns occur, significantly reducing downtime and repair costs. Big Data analytics allow manufacturers to optimize production processes, identify bottlenecks, and improve product quality through early defect detection.

In the financial industry, Big Data has been key for risk management, fraud detection, and the personalization of financial services. Banks and other financial institutions analyze large volumes of transaction data, customer behavior, and financial markets to manage credit risk, detect fraudulent activities, and comply with regulations. Big Data algorithms can identify behavior patterns that may indicate fraud, such as unusual transactions or phishing attempts, and trigger alerts for immediate intervention. Financial institutions use Big Data to personalize product offers, such as loans and insurance, based on customer risk profiles and individual needs.

In agriculture, Big Data has given rise to precision farming, a practice that optimizes agricultural production by using data to make more informed decisions about planting, irrigation, fertilization, and harvesting. Farmers now use data from satellites, drones, soil sensors, and weather stations to monitor crop growth, predict yields, and improve the efficiency of resource use such as water and fertilizers. Big Data analytics allow farmers to identify best practices for different soil types and climate conditions, increasing productivity and reducing environmental impact. Big Data is used to monitor and predict pests and diseases, enabling early intervention and minimizing losses.

In media and entertainment, Big Data has transformed content creation, distribution, and consumption. Streaming platforms like Netflix and Spotify use Big Data to analyze user behavior and personalize content recommendations, improving subscriber retention and increasing viewing or listening time. Data analytics also enable media companies to optimize programming and content distribution based on audience preferences and real-time consumption trends. Here, Big Data is used to measure the impact of advertising campaigns, allowing brands to adjust their marketing strategies to maximize return on investment.

In education, Big Data has enabled the development of adaptive learning systems that personalize the educational experience for each student. Online learning platforms collect data on student performance, interactions, and behavior, and use this data to adjust content, difficulty, and lesson pace. This allows educators to identify areas where students need more support and provide personalized resources to improve learning outcomes. Big Data is used to analyze dropout rates, identify factors that contribute to academic success, and develop more effective educational policies.

Logistics and supply chain management have also greatly benefited from Big Data. Logistics companies use Big Data to optimize transportation routes, manage inventories, and improve demand forecasting. Real-time data on traffic, weather conditions, and delivery times allow companies to adjust vehicle routes to reduce transportation costs and improve delivery punctuality. Here, Big Data is implemented to improve supply chain visibility, enabling companies to track products from production to final delivery, which enhances efficiency and transparency across the supply chain.

In the energy sector, Big Data has facilitated the transition to renewable energy sources and the optimization of energy use. Energy companies use Big Data to analyze real-time energy consumption, predict demand, and adjust production to balance supply and demand. Data from smart sensors and energy meters allow companies to optimize grid operations and reduce energy waste. Big Data is used to improve the efficiency of renewable energies such as solar and wind by predicting energy generation and optimizing battery storage.

The transportation industry has also experienced significant changes thanks to Big Data. Public transport companies use real-time data on vehicle locations, traffic patterns, and passenger demand to optimize routes and improve service efficiency. Additionally, Big Data has been fundamental for the development of autonomous vehicles, which rely on the collection and analysis of large volumes of data to navigate safely in complex environments. Big Data analytics also enable transportation companies to better manage their fleets, reduce maintenance costs, and improve road safety.

In the field of security, Big Data has enhanced organizations' ability to detect and respond to cyber threats. Big Data-based cybersecurity systems analyze large volumes of data in real time to identify abnormal behaviors that could indicate an attack. These systems use Machine Learning to continuously improve threat detection accuracy, allowing organizations to respond more quickly and effectively to security incidents. Big Data is also used to prevent crime by analyzing data from previous incidents to identify patterns and predict possible future crimes, enabling law enforcement agencies to take proactive measures to protect communities.

The impact of Big Data on different industries is broad and deep, transforming the way organizations operate, make decisions, and create value. Big Data applications in healthcare, retail, manufacturing, finance, agriculture, media, education, logistics, energy, transportation, and security are driving innovations that improve efficiency, reduce costs, and provide more personalized and safer experiences for customers and citizens.

3.6. Success Stories with Big Data

Success stories with Big Data are abundant and span various industries, demonstrating how organizations have used massive data to transform their operations, improve customer experience, innovate in products and services, and make more informed decisions. These cases illustrate the power of Big Data to generate tangible value and offer a significant competitive advantage.

In the e-commerce sector, Amazon is one of the most prominent examples of success with Big Data. The company has developed a sophisticated recommendation system based on the analysis of large volumes of data about user behavior. This system suggests products to customers based on their purchase history, previous searches, and browsing patterns, which has significantly increased conversion rates and the average order value. Additionally, Amazon uses Big Data to optimize its supply chain and logistics, ensuring that products are available in the right place at the right time. The company also applies predictive analytics to anticipate product demand and adjust its inventory in real time, minimizing costs and improving operational efficiency.

Another success case in the entertainment industry is Netflix. The streaming platform has used Big Data to revolutionize the way content is created, distributed, and consumed. Netflix collects and analyzes data on its users' viewing preferences, including the type of content they watch, what time they watch it, whether they complete a series or movie, and how much time they spend searching for content. This information allows Netflix to personalize content recommendations for each user, which has significantly improved subscriber retention. Additionally, Netflix uses this data to make informed decisions about producing original content. A notable example is the series "House of Cards," which was largely developed based on data analysis indicating that users preferred political dramas starring Kevin Spacey. The series was a huge success, validating Netflix's data-driven approach to content production.

In the healthcare industry, the case of IBM Watson is a prominent example of how Big Data can be used to improve medical care. IBM Watson is an Artificial Intelligence platform that analyzes large volumes of medical data, including scientific research, electronic medical records, and genomic data, to help doctors make informed decisions about patient treatment. For example, Watson has been used in oncology to analyze data from cancer patients and suggest personalized treatment options based on tumor genetics and the latest medical literature. This approach has allowed doctors to offer more effective and personalized treatments, improving outcomes for patients. Watson has also been used to accelerate medical research, helping researchers identify new connections between genes and diseases that can lead to the development of new therapies.

In the financial sector, JP Morgan Chase has implemented Big Data to improve fraud detection and risk management. The company uses advanced data analysis algorithms to monitor millions of transactions in real time and detect behavior patterns that could indicate fraudulent activities. These algorithms can quickly identify suspicious transactions, such as unauthorized access attempts or unusual money transfers, and trigger automatic alerts for security team intervention. Additionally, JP Morgan Chase uses Big Data to assess the credit risk of clients, analyzing historical data and financial behavior patterns to predict the likelihood of default. This has allowed the company to reduce losses from fraud and improve the accuracy of risk assessment, which in turn has strengthened its position in the financial market.

In the field of agriculture, the case of John Deere is an outstanding example of how Big Data can transform traditional farming into precision agriculture. John Deere has developed a Big Data platform called FarmSight, which collects real-time data from agricultural equipment, field sensors, and weather data. This data is analyzed to provide farmers with detailed information about soil conditions, crop growth, and irrigation and fertilization needs. With this information, farmers can make more informed decisions about crop management, resulting in increased productivity and reduced use of resources such as water and fertilizers. FarmSight also allows farmers to monitor their equipment performance in real time and plan predictive maintenance, which reduces downtime and operating costs.

In the energy sector, General Electric (GE) has used Big Data to optimize the performance of its wind turbines. GE has developed an analytics platform called Predix, which collects real-time data from sensors installed on wind turbines. This data includes information about wind speed, blade vibration, temperature, and energy production. Predix analyzes this data to optimize the performance of each turbine, automatically adjusting blade orientation and rotation speed to maximize energy generation. Additionally, the platform predicts when turbine components are likely to fail, allowing maintenance to be carried out before a breakdown occurs, thus reducing maintenance costs and increasing operational efficiency. The use of Big Data has enabled GE to improve the efficiency and profitability of its wind farms, positioning the company as a leader in the renewable energy industry.

Walmart, the retail giant, is another example of success with Big Data. The company uses Big Data to comprehensively optimize its operations, from the supply chain to customer experience. Walmart analyzes large volumes of sales data, inventories, and customer behavior to predict product demand and adjust its inventories in real time. This has allowed Walmart to reduce storage costs and minimize stockouts, ensuring that products are available for customers when they need them. Additionally, Walmart uses Big Data to personalize online promotions and offers based on each customer's preferences and purchasing behavior. This approach has significantly improved customer loyalty and increased sales both online and in physical stores.

In the transportation sector, UPS has achieved remarkable success with Big Data through its ORION system (On-Road Integrated Optimization and Navigation). ORION is a route optimization platform that uses Big Data to analyze millions of data points, such as delivery addresses, traffic conditions, and time constraints, to design the most efficient delivery routes for UPS drivers. The system updates in real time, allowing drivers to adjust their routes on the go in response to traffic changes or new delivery requests. Since the implementation of ORION, UPS has significantly reduced fuel consumption, operating costs, and carbon emissions while improving delivery punctuality and customer satisfaction.

In the telecommunications field, Verizon has used Big Data to improve network quality and customer experience. The company collects and analyzes large volumes of data on network performance, device usage, and customer behavior to proactively identify and resolve issues. For example, Verizon can detect areas where network coverage is poor and take steps to improve it, such as installing new cell towers or optimizing existing antennas. Additionally, Verizon uses Big Data to personalize service offers and pricing plans based on each customer's usage and preferences, which has improved customer retention and increased revenue per user.

Toyota, in the automotive industry, has adopted Big Data to develop connected vehicles that offer a better driving experience and improve road safety. Toyota's connected vehicles collect real-time data on driver behavior, road conditions, and vehicle performance. This data is analyzed to offer recommendations to the driver, such as maintenance alerts or alternative route suggestions in case of traffic. Toyota also uses Big Data to improve vehicle design and production, identifying usage and performance patterns that can be used to optimize future models. Big Data analysis also allows Toyota to develop more advanced autonomous driving technologies, increasing safety and driving efficiency.

These examples show how Big Data has been successfully implemented across a variety of industries, improving operational efficiency, personalizing customer experience, optimizing products and services, and providing a competitive advantage. Companies that have adopted Big Data have been able to transform their operations and discover new growth opportunities, standing out in an increasingly competitive and data-driven market.

3.7. Future of Big Data

The future of Big Data is shaping up as fertile ground for innovation and transformation, with technological and methodological developments that promise to redefine how organizations collect, store, process, and use data. As we see the amount of data generated continue to grow at an exponential rate, the future focus of Big Data will center on the ability to manage this explosion of information more efficiently, securely, and effectively, while maximizing the value derived from the data. There are several emerging trends that are shaping what we can expect in the Big Data landscape in the coming years.

The rise of quantum computing also promises to have a profound impact on the future of Big Data. Although still in its early stages of development, quantum computing offers the possibility of performing calculations and data analysis at speeds that would be impossible to achieve with classical computers. This would allow solving extremely complex problems, such as simulating molecules for drug discovery or optimizing global supply chains, in a significantly reduced time. As quantum computing technology matures, we are likely to see its integration into Big Data systems to tackle challenges that are currently beyond our computational capabilities.

Data privacy and security will remain a critical topic in the future of Big Data. As organizations collect and store increasing amounts of data, protecting this information from unauthorized access and security breaches will be a priority. Emerging technologies such as homomorphic encryption and privacy-preserving techniques like differential privacy will allow organizations to analyze sensitive data without compromising individual privacy. These techniques are being developed to enable the processing and analysis of encrypted data, ensuring that personal information remains secure even while being used to generate valuable insights.

The rise of cloud-based Big Data platforms is another trend that will continue to shape the future. The flexibility, scalability, and reduced costs of cloud solutions have led more and more organizations to migrate their data operations to cloud platforms. Cloud service providers are continuously enhancing their Big Data offerings, including advanced analytics capabilities, integration of AI and Machine Learning, and mass storage services.

Another key topic we will discuss frequently due to its importance is the concept of Data Lakes, which has already gained traction and will continue to evolve and adapt to the changing needs of Big Data analytics. Data Lakes allow the storage of large volumes of data in its original and unstructured format, facilitating more flexible and accessible analysis.

In parallel, data governance will become a central concern as organizations navigate an increasingly complex regulatory environment. The need to comply with data protection regulations such as the General Data Protection Regulation (GDPR) in Europe and the California Consumer Privacy Act (CCPA) in the United States will drive the adoption of stricter data governance policies. Organizations will need to implement robust data governance frameworks that not only ensure regulatory compliance but also optimize data quality, integrity, and availability across the organization.

Another emerging trend is data monetization. As organizations accumulate large volumes of data, they are realizing that the data itself is a valuable asset that can be commercialized. Data monetization can take many forms, from the direct sale of data to third parties to the creation of new products and services based on data analysis. Data exchange platforms are emerging as a new market where companies can buy, sell, or trade data securely and in a controlled manner, generating new revenue streams.

Additionally, cross-industry collaboration around the use of Big Data is a trend likely to gain strength. Industries are beginning to recognize the value of sharing data with each other to gain more complete and accurate insights. This collaboration can lead to innovations that benefit multiple sectors. For example, mobility data generated by the automotive industry can be valuable for the transportation, urban planning, and environmental sectors, helping to develop smarter and more sustainable cities.

Advanced automation driven by Big Data is a direction in which many organizations are investing. Automation is not only limited to manufacturing or IT operations but extends to decision-making in areas such as marketing, finance, and talent management, basically human resources. This trend toward advanced automation is creating a more agile and dynamic business environment where decisions can be made quickly based on accurate and up-to-date data.

4. Big Data Technologies and Tools

Since the beginning of the book, I have been talking about techniques, tools, and technologies related to Big Data, but now we are going to look at them in more depth. As I said at the beginning, we are going to look at each thing little by little so that you can get used to them. Big Data technologies and tools have been fundamental in enabling companies and organizations to manage, analyze, and extract value from the vast amount of data generated in the digital age. As I hope you can already see, these technologies cover a wide spectrum, from data storage and processing to analysis and visualization, each with specific characteristics that make them suitable for different types of applications. This section serves as a window into the key components of the Big Data technology ecosystem.

In recent years, the exponential growth of data has driven the need for technological solutions capable of handling massive volumes of information. As companies and organizations of all kinds seek to leverage their data for competitive advantage, the demand for technologies that can store, process, and analyze this data efficiently has increased dramatically. The competition here is very broad.

One of the pillars of Big Data technologies is storage infrastructure. As data volumes have grown, storage technologies have had to adapt to offer scalable, durable, and accessible solutions. Initially, data was stored on physical servers located on the premises of organizations, but over time, distributed architectures such as distributed file systems and cloud storage solutions have become predominant. These technologies allow organizations to store large amounts of data in multiple geographic locations, ensuring redundancy and availability while optimizing costs and the ability to scale based on needs.

Data processing is another component within the Big Data ecosystem. The speed at which data must be processed is a critical factor, especially when working with real-time data streams. Traditional database and data processing technologies could not scale adequately to meet these new demands, which led to the development of new processing paradigms. Distributed processing, powered by technologies such as Apache Hadoop and Apache Spark, has enabled large datasets to be processed in parallel across clusters of computers. These tools have become the backbone of Big Data processing, offering the ability to handle large-scale processing tasks more quickly and efficiently.

In addition to storage and processing, data analysis tools play a crucial role in the Big Data ecosystem. These tools are designed to uncover patterns, trends, and hidden insights within large volumes of data. The analysis can range from descriptive analytics, which provides an overview of historical data, to predictive and prescriptive analytics, which help forecast future events and recommend actions. Big Data analytics tools such as Tableau, QlikView, and Power BI enable users to intuitively visualize data, facilitating the interpretation of complex results and data-driven decision-making.

Another important category within Big Data technologies is NoSQL databases. Unlike traditional relational databases, which are structured in tables and rely on the SQL language for queries, NoSQL databases are designed to handle unstructured and semi-structured data, such as text, images, and documents. These databases are highly scalable and flexible, making them ideal for modern applications that require the management of large volumes of diverse data. Some examples of NoSQL databases include MongoDB, Cassandra, and Couchbase, each optimized for different types of workloads and data storage needs.

Data integration is another critical area within the Big Data ecosystem. With data coming from multiple sources, formats, and systems, the ability to efficiently integrate this data is essential for obtaining a unified and coherent view. Data integration tools such as Apache Kafka and Apache NiFi enable organizations to move and transform data between systems smoothly, ensuring that data is available for analysis at the right time. These tools are fundamental for building data pipelines that support real-time analysis and informed decision-making.

As organizations collect and store increasing volumes of data, protecting this data against unauthorized access, loss, or corruption becomes critical. Data security technologies such as encryption, tokenization, and access control are implemented to ensure that data is protected at all stages of its lifecycle. Data governance ensures that data is accurate, consistent, and accessible to those who need it while complying with regulations and internal policies.

The evolution of Big Data technologies has also led to the emergence of integrated platforms that combine multiple capabilities into a unified solution. These platforms, such as AWS Big Data, Google Cloud Big Data, and Azure Synapse Analytics, offer a complete set of tools for data storage, processing, analysis, and management. By centralizing these capabilities on one platform, organizations can simplify their data operations, reduce complexity, and accelerate the time to value from their data.

This general overview of Big Data technologies and tools lays the groundwork for exploring in greater depth the specific categories that make up this ecosystem. In the following subsections, we will examine in detail storage solutions, data processing tools, analytics platforms, NoSQL databases, data integration technologies, and security and governance considerations, among other critical aspects that enable organizations to harness the full potential of their data in the digital age.

4.1. Hadoop and its Ecosystem

4.1.1. Hadoop Architecture

The architecture of Hadoop is one of the cornerstones of the Big Data ecosystem, designed to handle large volumes of data distributed across multiple servers. Hadoop was created to overcome the limitations of traditional data processing systems, which could not scale efficiently to manage the size and complexity of data generated in the digital age. The architecture of Hadoop is composed of several key components that work together to provide a scalable, flexible, and resilient platform for data storage and processing.

At its core, Hadoop is based on a distributed architecture that allows data to be stored and processed across a cluster of servers known as nodes. This architecture is designed to handle common hardware failures in large-scale computing environments, ensuring that the system continues operating even if some nodes fail. This is achieved through data replication and the distribution of task processing, enabling Hadoop to maintain data availability and integrity at all times.

The first fundamental component of the Hadoop architecture is the Hadoop Distributed File System (HDFS). HDFS is the distributed file system that allows large volumes of data to be redundantly stored across several nodes in the cluster. HDFS splits large files into smaller blocks and distributes them across the nodes, with each block replicated on multiple nodes to ensure data reliability and availability. By default, HDFS creates three copies of each block, storing them on different nodes to minimize the risk of data loss due to hardware failures.

HDFS is composed of two main types of nodes: the NameNode and the DataNodes. The NameNode is the master node that manages the file system structure, keeping a record of where the blocks of each file are stored on the DataNodes. It acts as a centralized directory that allows users and applications to locate and access data within the cluster. Since the NameNode is a single point of failure, Hadoop implements a secondary NameNode that periodically backs up the state of the file system to minimize the impact of a failure of the primary NameNode.

The DataNodes, on the other hand, are the worker nodes that physically store the data blocks and perform read and write operations on them. Each DataNode periodically communicates with the NameNode, reporting on the status of the blocks it stores and receiving instructions about the operations it should perform. The DataNodes are also responsible for replicating data blocks when a node fails, ensuring that there are always enough copies available in the cluster.

The second key component of the Hadoop architecture is the MapReduce processing engine. MapReduce is the programming model that allows large distributed data sets to be processed in parallel across a cluster of nodes. The model is based on two main phases: the Map phase and the Reduce phase. In the Map phase, the input data is divided into smaller chunks that are processed in parallel on the nodes of the cluster. Each node applies a mapping function to its chunks of data, generating key-value pairs as intermediate results. In the Reduce phase, the generated key-value pairs are grouped and processed to produce the final output, which is written back into HDFS.

The MapReduce processing engine is managed by two main types of nodes: the JobTracker and the TaskTrackers. The JobTracker is the master node that coordinates the execution of MapReduce tasks across the entire cluster. It receives job requests from users, splits the work into smaller tasks, and assigns them to the TaskTrackers, which are the worker nodes that execute the mapping and reducing tasks on the data. The JobTracker also monitors the progress of each task and reassigns tasks in case a TaskTracker fails or becomes unreachable.

The TaskTrackers, like the DataNodes in HDFS, are responsible for executing the assigned tasks and reporting their progress to the JobTracker. Each TaskTracker manages a set of tasks in parallel, using the resources of the node on which it runs to efficiently process the data. At the end of the mapping phase, the TaskTrackers temporarily store the intermediate results on their local disks before sending them to the nodes that execute the reduce tasks. This distributed and parallel approach allows Hadoop to process large volumes of data quickly and efficiently, even in clusters of thousands of nodes.

In addition to HDFS and MapReduce, the Hadoop architecture includes several other components that extend its capabilities and allow for more flexible and advanced data processing. Among these components are Apache Pig and Apache Hive, which provide high-level languages for data manipulation and querying in Hadoop. Pig uses a language called Pig Latin, which allows users to define complex data processing flows declaratively without needing to write detailed MapReduce code. Hive, on the other hand, offers an abstraction layer over Hadoop that allows users to perform SQL queries on data stored in HDFS, making data access easier for those familiar with the SQL language.

Another important component is Apache HBase, a distributed NoSQL database that runs on top of HDFS and is designed to handle large volumes of structured and semi-structured data. HBase enables fast, real-time access to large data sets, making it ideal for applications that require frequent reads and writes on large data tables. HBase complements the Hadoop architecture by providing a highly scalable and efficient data storage solution for data that does not fit well into the file-based model of HDFS.

It is also worth mentioning YARN (Yet Another Resource Negotiator), which is a key component of Hadoop responsible for resource management and task scheduling within the cluster. YARN allows Hadoop to support multiple processing engines, such as MapReduce and Spark, on the same cluster, improving flexibility and resource utilization. YARN manages the allocation of resources such as CPU and memory to the different applications running in the cluster, ensuring that tasks are completed efficiently and without interference.

The Hadoop architecture is designed to be highly extensible, which has allowed the integration of a wide range of tools and technologies into its ecosystem. This extensibility has made Hadoop a central platform in the world of Big Data, capable of supporting a wide variety of use cases and applications across different industries. Hadoop's ability to scale horizontally, handle failures, and process large volumes of data efficiently has made it an indispensable tool for organizations looking to leverage the power of Big Data to improve their operations and make more informed decisions.

The combination of HDFS for distributed storage, MapReduce for parallel processing, and a set of additional tools for data manipulation and querying makes the Hadoop architecture a powerful and versatile solution to tackle the challenges of Big Data.

4.1.2. HDFS (Hadoop Distributed File System)

Now we are going to look at HDFS in depth. It is specifically designed to manage large volumes of data in a distributed environment. HDFS is inspired by the Google File System and has become one of the most important technologies for data storage and management in the Big Data era. Its design focuses on providing high availability, scalability, and fault tolerance, which are crucial aspects when it comes to handling large-scale data in computer clusters.

The design of HDFS is based on the idea that data should be stored in blocks distributed across multiple nodes in a cluster. This distribution allows data to be accessed efficiently and enables the system to withstand common hardware failures without losing data or interrupting operations. The ability of HDFS to handle failures is one of its most distinctive features, and it is made possible by replicating data blocks on different nodes within the cluster.

In HDFS, large files are split into blocks of a predetermined size, which by default is 128 megabytes, although this size can be configured according to the specific needs of the application. These blocks are distributed across different nodes in the cluster, known as DataNodes. Each block is replicated across several DataNodes (usually three), ensuring that data remains available even if one or more nodes fail. This replication is crucial for the resilience of the system as it ensures that data is not lost in the event of hardware failures.

The HDFS system is organized in a master-slave architecture, where the master node, known as the NameNode, manages the metadata of the file system, while the DataNodes are responsible for the physical storage of the data. The NameNode keeps a record of the location of each data block within the system, as well as crucial information about the structure of files and directories stored in HDFS. This record is stored in the memory of the NameNode, allowing quick access to information when a read or write operation is performed in HDFS.

The NameNode is a critical component in the HDFS architecture because without it the system could not function. However, this design presents a challenge: the NameNode is a single point of failure. To mitigate this risk, Hadoop, as we have already seen, allows the implementation of a Secondary NameNode, which periodically backs up the metadata of the primary NameNode. Although the Secondary NameNode cannot directly replace the NameNode in case of failure, its function is crucial for system recovery, as it allows the metadata to be restored in case of a system reboot.

The DataNodes, for their part, store the data blocks and are responsible for read and write operations. Each DataNode regularly communicates with the NameNode, reporting on the blocks it stores and their health status. If the NameNode detects that a DataNode has failed, it instructs other DataNodes to replicate the blocks stored on the failed node, thereby ensuring that the number of replicas remains at the desired level.

A key feature of HDFS is its ability to manage read and write operations efficiently in a distributed environment. When a client wants to read a file from HDFS, it first communicates with the NameNode to obtain the location of the file's blocks. Once the client has this information, it connects directly to the corresponding DataNodes to read the data blocks. This approach allows data reading to be performed in parallel, which significantly improves the speed and efficiency of read operations.

As for write operations, when a client wants to write a file to HDFS, the file is split into blocks and sent to the DataNodes for storage. The client first requests from the NameNode a list of DataNodes where each block will be stored. Then, the client sends the data block to the first DataNode in the list, which stores it and sends it to the next DataNode, and so on, until all replicas are completed. This chain operation ensures that data is distributed efficiently and that the consistency of the replicas is maintained.

HDFS also includes a mechanism for automatic failure recovery known as heartbeats. DataNodes periodically send heartbeat signals to the NameNode to indicate that they are functioning correctly. If a DataNode does not send a heartbeat within a specified time, the NameNode marks it as failed and triggers the replication of the blocks stored on that node to other available DataNodes. This automatic failure recovery process is fundamental to maintaining data availability and integrity in a Hadoop cluster.

Another important feature of HDFS is its ability to handle large data sets and files efficiently. Since HDFS is designed to store large files, it is particularly suitable for applications that generate or consume large volumes of data, such as Big Data analytics, data mining, and machine learning. In addition, HDFS is optimized for sequential read and write operations, making it ideal for workloads where data is processed in large blocks, such as server log processing or data aggregation.

The scalability of HDFS is another of its strong points. As data storage and processing needs increase, more nodes can be added to the cluster to increase storage capacity and system performance. This horizontal scaling is essential for handling the exponential growth of data in modern organizations. Moreover, HDFS is designed to run on common, non-specialized hardware, allowing organizations to deploy scalable and cost-effective storage solutions without the need to invest in expensive hardware infrastructure.

HDFS also integrates well with other tools and technologies in the Hadoop ecosystem, such as MapReduce for distributed data processing, YARN for resource management and job scheduling, and Apache HBase for real-time data storage. This integration enables organizations to build complete and efficient data pipelines that span from data ingestion to processing and analysis.

Despite its numerous advantages, HDFS also has some limitations. For example, it is not designed to handle a large number of small files, as this can overload the NameNode, which must keep track of every file in the system. Additionally, due to its write-once, read-many design, HDFS is not ideal for applications that require frequent writes or updates to existing files. However, these limitations are generally outweighed by the unique capabilities of HDFS to handle large volumes of distributed data efficiently and reliably.

4.1.3. MapReduce

Let's now look at what exactly MapReduce is. MapReduce is a programming model and a distributed data processing engine that enables organizations to handle and analyze large volumes of data in parallel across a cluster of servers. This model was developed by Google and presented in a research paper in 2004, and since then it has been widely adopted in the Hadoop ecosystem, becoming one of the fundamental components for large-scale data processing. MapReduce is designed to be highly scalable, fault-tolerant, and resource-efficient, making it ideal for processing large datasets in distributed environments.

The MapReduce programming model is based on two main functions: Map and Reduce. These functions are used to break down a complex processing task into simpler operations that can be executed in parallel on different nodes of a cluster. The distributed approach of MapReduce allows large datasets to be processed simultaneously by multiple nodes, resulting in a significant reduction in processing time compared to traditional sequential processing methods.

The Map function is the first phase in the MapReduce model. Its main objective is to take an input dataset, split it into smaller fragments (usually in the form of key-value pairs), and apply a mapping function to each fragment. This mapping function generates an intermediate set of key-value pairs that are then grouped and passed to the reduction phase. The mapping process is executed in parallel on all available nodes of the cluster, allowing large volumes of data to be handled efficiently.

The mapping phase begins when the MapReduce system takes the input dataset and divides it into manageable-sized blocks. These blocks are distributed to processing nodes (also called Map Task Trackers) within the cluster. Each processing node applies the mapping function to its assigned data block, producing key-value pairs as output. For example, in a word count process, the mapping function would take a block of text as input and produce key-value pairs where the key is the word and the value is the number one (indicating an occurrence of the word).

Once all data blocks have been processed by the mapping nodes, the generated key-value pairs are grouped by key in a phase known as shuffle and sort. During this phase, the system organizes the key-value pairs so that all instances of the same key are grouped together. This process is crucial for the efficiency of the next phase, as it ensures that values associated with the same key are presented together to be processed by the reduction function.

The Reduce function is the second phase of the MapReduce model and is responsible for processing the grouped key-value pairs generated in the mapping phase. The purpose of the reduction function is to take all the values associated with a specific key and combine them to produce a final result. This result can be a summary, an aggregation, or any other operation that meaningfully combines the values. The reduction phase is also executed in parallel across multiple nodes of the cluster, allowing large volumes of data to be processed efficiently.

In practice, the reduction phase takes the grouped key-value pairs and assigns them to processing nodes (also known as Reduce Task Trackers). Each reduction node applies the reduction function to its assigned group of data. Continuing with the word count example, the reduction function would take all the values associated with a specific word (for example, all instances of the key "wordX") and sum them to determine the total number of times that word appears in the dataset. The final result would be a key-value pair where the key is the word and the value is its total frequency in the dataset.

One of the key features of MapReduce is its fault tolerance. Since the data is processed in parallel across multiple nodes, it is possible that one or more nodes may experience failures during the execution of a task. MapReduce handles these failures by rescheduling the failed tasks on other available nodes in the cluster. This recovery capability allows the system to continue operating without significant interruptions, which is essential in production environments where reliability is critical.

Another important advantage of MapReduce is its scalability. As data volumes increase, more nodes can be added to the cluster to distribute the workload and maintain reasonable processing times. This horizontal scalability is fundamental in Big Data applications, where datasets can grow exponentially and processing needs can vary considerably.

MapReduce is also highly flexible and can be applied to a wide variety of data processing problems. Although it was originally designed for tasks such as text processing, its generalized mapping and reduction model can be adapted to handle a variety of operations such as data filtering, sorting, aggregation, graph analysis, and more. This makes it a versatile tool within the Big Data ecosystem, suitable for a wide range of applications.

Despite its many advantages, MapReduce also has some limitations. One of the most common criticisms is its inefficiency for tasks that require multiple stages of processing. Since each mapping and reduction phase in MapReduce is independent, tasks that require multiple processing steps can become inefficient due to the need to read and write intermediate data to HDFS between each stage. This can result in significant I/O overhead and increased processing time.

To address these limitations, other processing engines have been developed that can complement or even replace MapReduce in certain contexts. For example, Apache Spark is a newer technology that offers an in-memory processing model, allowing multiple stages of data processing to be handled more efficiently than MapReduce. However, MapReduce remains a valuable tool in many applications, especially those involving large-scale data processing that can be easily divided into independent mapping and reduction tasks.

In terms of implementation, MapReduce is easy to integrate into the Hadoop ecosystem, making it a natural choice for organizations already using Hadoop for data storage and processing. The combination of HDFS for data storage and MapReduce for processing allows organizations to build robust and scalable data pipelines that can handle large volumes of data efficiently and reliably.

MapReduce has been fundamental in the evolution of Big Data and remains a key technology in many data processing environments. Although technologies continue to evolve and new tools emerge, the impact of MapReduce on how we process large volumes of data is undeniable. Its simple yet powerful programming model has enabled organizations worldwide to harness the power of distributed data and scale their operations to meet the challenges of Big Data.

4.2. Apache Spark

4.2.1. Introduction to Apache Spark

Apache Spark is a distributed data processing platform that has revolutionized the way large volumes of data are handled in the era of Big Data. Developed at the University of California, Berkeley, and first released in 2014, Spark was designed to overcome the limitations of its predecessor, Hadoop MapReduce, offering significantly faster performance thanks to its ability to process data in memory. This improvement in speed and efficiency has led Spark to be widely adopted across various industries, becoming an essential tool for massive data processing.

One of the most outstanding features of Apache Spark is its ability to perform in-memory data processing operations. Unlike Hadoop MapReduce, which writes intermediate data to disk between each processing stage, Spark allows data to remain in memory throughout the process, which drastically reduces disk read and write times and significantly improves execution speed. This capability is especially beneficial for applications that require multiple processing stages, such as iterative algorithms and real-time analytics.

The core of Apache Spark is built on a distributed programming model called Resilient Distributed Dataset (RDD). RDDs are collections of objects that can be distributed across a cluster and processed in parallel. RDDs are immutable, meaning they cannot be changed once created, and any transformation applied to them generates a new RDD. This immutability provides several advantages, such as fault tolerance, since RDDs can be reconstructed from their original data if a node fails during processing.

Another key feature of Apache Spark is its parallel processing model. RDDs can be automatically partitioned across multiple nodes in the cluster, allowing operations to be performed in parallel on multiple machines. This not only improves processing efficiency but also facilitates horizontal scaling, meaning more nodes can be added to the cluster to handle increasing data volumes without sacrificing performance.

Spark is also highly flexible and supports multiple programming languages, including Scala, Java, Python, and R. This compatibility with various languages makes it accessible to a wide range of developers and data scientists, enabling them to harness the power of Spark without needing to learn a new language. The Spark API is designed to be intuitive and easy to use, making it simpler to implement complex data processing applications.

In addition to its in-memory processing capability and support for multiple languages, Apache Spark includes several built-in components that extend its functionality beyond basic data processing. One of these components is Spark SQL, which allows users to perform structured queries on distributed data using a SQL-like language. Spark SQL is especially useful for integrating structured and unstructured data and allows Spark applications to easily integrate with existing databases and business intelligence tools.

Another important component of Apache Spark is Spark Streaming, which provides capabilities for processing real-time data streams. Spark Streaming allows streaming data to be processed and analyzed as it arrives, which is crucial for applications that require real-time response, such as fraud detection, network monitoring, and real-time recommendations. Spark Streaming is built on the same core as Spark, allowing streaming applications to leverage the same infrastructure and API as batch processing applications, making it easier to implement hybrid solutions that combine real-time and batch processing.

Spark also includes MLlib, a Machine Learning library that provides a set of algorithms and tools for building Machine Learning models on large datasets. MLlib is designed to be scalable and efficient, allowing Machine Learning algorithms to be applied to distributed data across a cluster without needing to move the data to a central machine. This significantly reduces training time and allows models to be applied to much larger datasets than would be possible with traditional Machine Learning libraries.

GraphX is another component of Apache Spark designed for distributed graph processing and analysis. GraphX allows data to be represented and manipulated in the form of graphs, which is useful for a wide range of applications, from social network analysis to route optimization and the analysis of complex relationships. Like other Spark components, GraphX is fully integrated with the Spark core and can work alongside RDDs and other Spark data structures.

One of the reasons Apache Spark has been so widely adopted is its ability to integrate with other technologies in the Big Data ecosystem. Spark can run on Hadoop YARN, allowing organizations to leverage their existing Hadoop infrastructure to manage resources and run Spark applications alongside Hadoop applications. Additionally, Spark is compatible with HDFS, meaning it can read and write data directly from Hadoop's distributed file system, facilitating the migration and coexistence of Hadoop and Spark applications on the same infrastructure.

Another key integration of Apache Spark is with Apache Mesos, a cluster management system that allows multiple applications to efficiently share a cluster. By running on Mesos, Spark can share resources with other distributed applications, improving cluster utilization and making it easier to implement multitenant solutions in production environments.

Spark can also integrate with modern database and data storage systems such as Apache Cassandra, HBase, and Amazon S3. This ability to connect to different data sources and storage systems allows Spark to be used in a wide range of applications, from Big Data analytics in the cloud to real-time processing in distributed databases.

Despite its many advantages, Apache Spark also has some considerations that need to be kept in mind. For example, although Spark's in-memory processing offers significant speed advantages, it also requires a large amount of RAM in the cluster. This can be a limiting factor in environments where hardware resources are scarce or expensive. Additionally, Spark is best suited for applications that can benefit from in-memory parallelization; for simpler jobs or where distributed processing is not necessary, lighter solutions may be more efficient.

The continuous evolution of Apache Spark has also led to the development of an active community and an ecosystem of tools and libraries that extend Spark. This includes tools for job management, application debugging, and performance monitoring, as well as additional libraries for specific tasks such as geospatial data processing or text analysis.

As you can conclude yourself, Apache Spark is an extremely powerful data processing platform that has changed the way large volumes of data are handled and analyzed. Its ability to process data in memory, along with its flexibility, scalability, and support for multiple languages and applications, has made it an essential tool in the arsenal of any Big Data professional. As data processing demands continue to grow, Apache Spark is well positioned to remain a leading technology in the field of distributed data processing.

4.2.2. Main Components of Spark

Apache Spark is a data processing platform that has stood out for its modular architecture, which is composed of several main components that work together to provide a comprehensive solution for processing large volumes of data. Each of these components has a specific role within the Spark ecosystem, offering functionalities that range from basic data manipulation to advanced real-time analysis and machine learning. Below is a detailed description of each of these main components.

The core of Apache Spark is known as Spark Core. This is the underlying processing engine that manages Spark's fundamental tasks, such as task scheduling, memory management, fault recovery, task distribution across the cluster, and basic data input and output operations. Spark Core provides the foundation on which all other Spark components are built and supports the distributed programming model based on Resilient Distributed Datasets. RDDs are the central data abstraction in Spark, enabling immutable and distributed processing of collections of objects across the cluster. RDDs can be created from data stored in distributed storage systems such as HDFS, S3, or by transforming other existing RDDs.

One of the main benefits of Spark Core is its ability to perform in-memory processing, which allows data to be kept in RAM during processing, avoiding the need to write data to disk between operations. This feature is key to Spark's performance, allowing many applications to be considerably faster than if disk-based approaches were used. In addition, Spark Core supports transformation and action operations on RDDs, such as map, filter, reduce, and aggregate, which enable a wide range of data processing operations.

Another fundamental component of Spark is Spark SQL. Spark SQL is the Spark module that provides capabilities for working with structured data, that is, data that has a well-defined schema like tables in a relational database. Spark SQL introduces a new data abstraction called DataFrame, which is similar to a table in a database and can be manipulated using a SQL-like query language. DataFrames are an evolution of RDDs, optimized for processing structured and semi-structured data. Spark SQL allows running SQL queries on DataFrames, which facilitates the integration of Spark with traditional database systems and business intelligence tools. Additionally, Spark SQL includes a query optimizer called Catalyst, which automatically optimizes queries to improve performance.

Spark Streaming is another key component of Apache Spark, designed for real-time data stream processing. Spark Streaming allows users to process and analyze data arriving in real-time from various sources, such as Kafka, Flume, TCP sockets, files, and more. Spark Streaming divides the data stream into small time units called batches and processes them using the same programming model as Spark Core, making it easier to build streaming applications that seamlessly integrate with other Spark operations. This allows Spark Streaming applications to take advantage of Spark's in-memory processing capabilities and high-level APIs, providing a powerful and scalable solution for real-time analysis. The results of streaming processing can be stored in file systems, databases, or displayed in real time.

MLlib is Spark's machine learning library, designed to scale the processing of machine learning algorithms on large volumes of distributed data. MLlib includes a wide range of machine learning algorithms, ranging from linear and logistic regression to clustering, classification, and collaborative filtering. The library is optimized to work in parallel on a Spark cluster, allowing machine learning models to be trained and applied to large-scale datasets efficiently. MLlib also provides tools for model validation, such as cross-validation and metric evaluation, which facilitate the development of accurate and robust models. In addition, MLlib supports integrations with other machine learning tools and libraries, allowing users to leverage a wide range of analytical capabilities within the Spark ecosystem.

GraphX is another important component of Apache Spark, oriented toward the processing and analysis of distributed graphs. GraphX provides an API for building and manipulating graphs (data structures that represent relationships between entities, such as social networks, road maps, or dependency graphs). This module enables performing graph analysis operations, such as shortest path search, community detection, and node ranking, in a distributed environment. GraphX combines the flexibility of RDD data processing with the efficiency of graph modeling, allowing graph applications to easily integrate with other Spark operations. This is especially useful in use cases where data has an inherently graphical nature, such as in social network analysis, transportation route analysis, or modeling complex relationships between entities.

Spark ML is an extension of MLlib and is designed to simplify the construction of machine learning pipelines. A machine learning pipeline is a workflow that encapsulates all stages of a machine learning process, from data preparation to model evaluation. Spark ML provides a unified API that allows building and chaining various pipeline stages, such as feature selection, data normalization, model training, and prediction. This API facilitates experimentation and optimization of models, as it allows quickly changing and adjusting different pipeline components. Additionally, Spark ML supports model persistence, which makes it easier to deploy trained models in production applications.

An important underlying component in Spark is YARN, which is a resource management platform used in Hadoop that Spark can leverage to manage resources in a cluster. Although YARN is not exclusively part of Spark, its integration is crucial for deploying Spark applications on Hadoop clusters, allowing Spark to share resources with other applications and ensuring efficient cluster utilization. YARN facilitates resource allocation, task scheduling, and distributed application management, which is essential for running Spark in large-scale production environments.

Each of these Apache Spark components contributes to making Spark a robust and versatile platform for distributed data processing. By combining in-memory processing, support for structured and unstructured data, real-time streaming capabilities, advanced machine learning tools, and graph analysis, Spark provides a complete solution for tackling a wide range of challenges in the world of Big Data. This modular architecture allows users to leverage only the components they need for their specific applications, while the integration of all these elements within a single framework facilitates the development of complex applications that require multiple types of data processing.

4.2.3. Comparison with Hadoop

Apache Spark and Hadoop are two of the most prominent technologies in the Big Data ecosystem, used for processing and analyzing large volumes of data. Although both platforms are employed to address similar challenges in terms of scalability, handling distributed data, and parallel processing, they differ significantly in their architecture, approach, and performance. Throughout this comparison, we will analyze in depth and detail the main differences between Spark and Hadoop, highlighting the key aspects that distinguish them and the scenarios in which each is more suitable.

One of the most fundamental differences between Apache Spark and Hadoop lies in their approach to data processing. Hadoop is based on a batch processing paradigm, MapReduce, where data is processed in multiple stages, and between each of these stages, the intermediate results are written to disk before being read again for the next stage. This approach is effective for handling large volumes of data, but it also introduces significant I/O overhead due to the continuous writing and reading to disk. This can make Hadoop less efficient, especially in applications that require multiple processing stages or handle real-time data.

In contrast, Apache Spark was designed to overcome these limitations through in-memory processing. Spark allows data to be kept in RAM throughout the processing lifecycle, which drastically reduces the need to write to disk between stages. This approach not only improves performance by minimizing disk I/O but also allows Spark to execute data processing jobs up to 100 times faster than Hadoop in certain applications. This in-memory processing capability makes Spark the preferred option for applications that require real-time analysis or involve multiple iterations, such as in machine learning.

Another key difference between Spark and Hadoop is the flexibility and breadth of their ecosystems. Hadoop is essentially a framework for data storage and processing, composed mainly of HDFS and MapReduce. While there are other tools in the Hadoop ecosystem, such as Hive, Pig, and HBase, these are usually more focused on specific use cases and rely on the underlying infrastructure of HDFS and MapReduce to function.

On the other hand, Spark offers a more integrated ecosystem with multiple native components that enable more diverse data processing. In addition to in-memory processing through Spark Core, Spark includes Spark SQL for working with structured data, Spark Streaming for real-time stream processing, MLlib for machine learning, and GraphX for graph analytics. These components are designed to work cohesively, using the same Spark core, making it easier to implement complex solutions that require several types of data processing within a single framework.

Scalability is another area where Spark and Hadoop are compared, although both are designed to be highly scalable, allowing the processing of petabytes of data in a cluster of thousands of nodes. Hadoop has historically been known for its ability to scale horizontally, meaning that more nodes can be added to the cluster to handle increasing data volumes without affecting performance. Spark is also highly scalable, but due to its reliance on in-memory processing, scaling may require a significant investment in hardware with large RAM capacity to maintain performance.

Resource management in both systems also shows notable differences. Hadoop uses YARN as its resource manager, which is responsible for allocating cluster resources, such as CPU and memory, to the different applications running in the cluster. YARN allows Hadoop to run multiple applications simultaneously, efficiently managing the available resources to avoid conflicts and maximize cluster utilization.

Apache Spark, although it can also run on YARN, has its own cluster manager called Spark Standalone, which is simpler and less dependent on Hadoop's configuration. However, Spark benefits from integration with YARN when running in a Hadoop environment, allowing Spark to share a cluster with Hadoop applications and take advantage of Hadoop's infrastructure for resource management.

In terms of compatibility and integration, Spark has the advantage of being able to work directly with the Hadoop ecosystem, especially with HDFS. This allows organizations that already have an existing Hadoop infrastructure to integrate Spark without needing to replace their current environment. Additionally, Spark can read and write data from HDFS, making it easy to migrate or cohabitate Hadoop and Spark applications in the same cluster. Spark is also compatible with a wide range of other data sources, including NoSQL databases like Cassandra and HBase, giving it additional flexibility compared to Hadoop.

Regarding ease of use, Spark stands out for its more user-friendly API and its support for multiple programming languages, including Scala, Java, Python, and R. This contrasts with Hadoop, where developing MapReduce applications can be more complex and is generally done in Java. The simplicity and flexibility of Spark's API have contributed significantly to its popularity, as they allow developers to build and test data processing applications more quickly and efficiently.

Although Spark offers many advantages in terms of performance and flexibility, Hadoop remains a viable option in certain scenarios, especially when it comes to large-scale batch data processing where hardware cost is an important consideration. Hadoop, with its disk-based approach, can be more economical in terms of hardware resources, as it does not require large amounts of RAM to function effectively. This makes it a suitable solution for organizations looking for a more cost-effective option for massive data processing where latency is not a critical concern.

The comparison between Apache Spark and Hadoop reveals that each platform has strengths and limitations that make it more suitable for different types of applications. Spark is ideal for applications that require fast, in-memory processing and that involve multiple processing stages or real-time analysis. On the other hand, Hadoop is more suitable for large-scale batch processing tasks where disk I/O efficiency and the ability to scale horizontally at low cost are more important. Organizations should consider these factors when deciding which platform to use for their Big Data processing needs, taking into account both their specific requirements and existing infrastructure.

4.3. NoSQL Databases

4.3.1. Concept and Types of NoSQL Databases

NoSQL databases have emerged as a key solution in the era of Big Data and modern applications, where scalability, flexibility, and performance requirements often exceed the capabilities of traditional relational databases. NoSQL, which stands for "Not Only SQL" or "No SQL," refers to a class of database management systems that differ from relational databases in several fundamental aspects. These databases are designed to handle large volumes of distributed data, be highly scalable, and offer a flexibility in the data model that conventional relational databases cannot match.

The concept of NoSQL databases arose as a response to the limitations of traditional relational databases in modern application environments, especially in terms of horizontal scalability, the ability to handle unstructured or semi-structured data, and the need to provide high and consistent performance in applications that generate large volumes of real-time data. Relational databases rely on a predefined schema, which means that the data must fit into a rigid tabular structure. This can be a significant limitation when dealing with data with variable structures or when the application requirements evolve over time.

On the other hand, NoSQL databases are schematically flexible, meaning they can handle data that does not follow a rigid schema, allowing data to be stored and retrieved without the need for a fixed predefined schema. This flexibility is particularly useful in agile development environments, where data requirements can change quickly, and in applications that handle large volumes of unstructured data, such as user activity logs, documents, multimedia, and more.

There are several types of NoSQL databases, each designed for specific use cases and particular data types. These can be mainly categorized into four types: key-value databases, column databases, document databases, and graph databases.

The first type of NoSQL database is the key-value model. In this type of database, data is stored as key-value pairs, where a unique key is used to identify and access an associated value. This model is extremely simple and efficient, making it suitable for applications that require fast data access, such as distributed caches and user session storage. The values can be any type of data, from simple text strings to complex data structures. Since data access is performed through a unique key, key-value databases are very efficient in terms of performance and horizontal scalability, as data distribution between nodes can be easily managed by hashing the keys. Popular examples of key-value databases include Redis, Amazon's DynamoDB, and Riak.

The second type of NoSQL database is the column model or column-oriented databases. Unlike relational databases, which store data in rows within tables, column-oriented databases store data in columns. This means that each column is stored separately and can be queried and manipulated independently. This model is particularly efficient for processing analytical queries on large volumes of data, as it allows reading and processing only the necessary columns instead of entire rows, reducing the amount of data that must be read from disk. Column-oriented databases are ideal for data analysis applications, where it is necessary to perform aggregations and operations on large datasets. Notable examples of column databases include Apache Cassandra and HBase.

The third type is the document model. Document databases store data in documents, which are usually in JSON, BSON, XML, or other similar formats. Each document is a self-contained set of data that can contain different fields and structures, providing great flexibility for handling semi-structured and unstructured data. This model is very suitable for applications that manage complex and hierarchical data, such as user data or multimedia content. The self-descriptive nature of documents allows different types of data to coexist in the same database without the need for a fixed schema. This is particularly useful in applications where the data may change dynamically or where different types of data are handled in the same system. MongoDB and Couchbase are widely used examples of document databases.

The fourth type is the graph model, which focuses on representing and manipulating data as graphs, where entities are represented as nodes and the relationships between these entities as edges. Graph databases are designed to handle highly connected data and are ideal for applications that require the exploration and analysis of complex relationships between data, such as social networks, recommendation systems, fraud analysis, and more. In a graph, it is easy to model direct relationships between nodes, allowing queries involving multiple hops in the network of relationships to be performed more efficiently than in relational databases. Neo4j is one of the best-known examples of graph databases and has been widely used in applications that require in-depth analysis of connections and relationships between entities.

In addition to these four main types, there are also other specialized types of NoSQL databases, such as time series databases, which are optimized to handle large volumes of time-series data, and multi-value databases, which allow storing multiple values in a single field, providing greater flexibility for certain types of applications.

The use of NoSQL databases presents several benefits, such as horizontal scalability, which allows data and workload to be distributed across multiple servers, which is essential for applications that handle large volumes of data and traffic. Another benefit is high availability and fault tolerance, achieved through data replication across multiple nodes in the cluster, ensuring that data remains accessible even in the event of failures in some nodes. Additionally, the flexibility in the schema allows developers to work with data without the need to define rigid structures in advance, making it easier to adapt to changes in application requirements.

However, the use of NoSQL databases can also present challenges. For example, the lack of support for ACID transactions (Atomicity, Consistency, Isolation, and Durability) in many NoSQL databases can be a drawback for applications that require a high level of data consistency. Although some NoSQL databases, such as MongoDB, have begun to offer support for ACID transactions, this is an aspect that organizations should consider when choosing between relational and NoSQL databases. Additionally, the diversity of data models in NoSQL may require greater expertise from developers and architects to choose the right solution and design the database optimally.

In terms of applications, NoSQL databases are used in a wide range of industries and use cases, including e-commerce, social networks, Big Data analytics, Internet of Things, and mobile applications, among others. Their ability to handle data at scale, offer consistent performance, and provide flexibility in data modeling makes them an attractive option for modern applications that require a highly scalable and adaptable data architecture.

4.3.2. MongoDB

MongoDB is one of the most popular and widely used NoSQL databases in the world, known for its flexibility, scalability, and ability to handle large volumes of unstructured and semi-structured data. It was originally developed by the company 10gen, which later changed its name to MongoDB Inc., and was released to the public in 2009. MongoDB was designed to provide a more flexible and scalable alternative to traditional relational databases, adapting to the needs of modern applications that handle constantly changing data and require fast and efficient response.

One of the fundamental aspects of MongoDB is its document-based data model. Instead of using a fixed tabular schema, as in relational databases, MongoDB stores data in BSON (Binary JSON) documents, a binary format that is an extension of the JSON format. These documents can contain different types of data, including nested structures and lists, which provides great flexibility to represent complex data. Each document in MongoDB is associated with a unique key, which is used to identify and access the document. This document structure is ideal for handling semi-structured and unstructured data, where data requirements can change rapidly.

The use of BSON in MongoDB offers several advantages. First, it allows storing data in a format that is easy to read and manipulate for both developers and applications. Second, BSON is a binary format, which means it is more compact and efficient than JSON in terms of storage and data transmission, especially when working with large volumes of data. Additionally, BSON supports various data types, including integers, strings, booleans, dates, and arrays, as well as more complex structures such as nested documents. This provides MongoDB with the ability to handle a wide variety of data efficiently and flexibly.

In terms of architecture, MongoDB is designed to be highly scalable. It supports horizontal scalability through a process known as sharding, which allows splitting and distributing data across multiple servers or nodes. Each node stores a part of the total dataset, enabling MongoDB to handle large volumes of data and distribute the workload efficiently. Sharding in MongoDB is implemented using a shard key, which determines how data is distributed among the different nodes. This allows applications using MongoDB to scale linearly as their data storage and processing needs grow.

Another key aspect of MongoDB's architecture is its focus on high availability and fault tolerance. MongoDB implements a mechanism called replication, where data is replicated across multiple nodes within a server cluster. This is achieved through a replica set, which is a group of nodes containing the same copies of the data. Within this set, one node acts as the primary and the others as secondaries. All write operations are performed on the primary node and then replicated to the secondary nodes to ensure data consistency. If the primary node fails, one of the secondary nodes automatically becomes the new primary, ensuring that the system remains operational without significant interruptions.

In addition to its scalability and availability, MongoDB is known for its flexibility in data modeling. Since MongoDB does not require a fixed schema, developers can modify the structure of documents at any time, making it easier to adapt to changes in application requirements. This contrasts with relational databases, where any change in the database structure usually requires complex and potentially disruptive modifications to the schema. This flexibility is especially useful in agile development environments, where data requirements can change quickly during the development lifecycle.

MongoDB also includes a rich and expressive query language, allowing users to perform complex operations of searching, filtering, aggregation, and data manipulation. Although MongoDB does not use SQL like traditional relational databases, its query language is easy to learn for developers familiar with JSON, as it follows a similar structure. MongoDB allows performing advanced operations such as data aggregation through its aggregation framework, which enables users to perform operations like filtering, grouping, and transforming data in a single step using a series of stages in a pipeline. This aggregation framework is extremely powerful and can be used to perform complex analysis directly in the database, eliminating the need to move data to an external analysis tool.

In terms of performance, MongoDB is optimized to offer fast read and write operations. Through the use of indexes, MongoDB allows queries to be executed efficiently, which is crucial in applications where performance and responsiveness are essential. MongoDB also supports compound, geospatial, and text indexes, providing greater flexibility in optimizing queries for different types of applications. Additionally, MongoDB allows parallel execution of operations, which further improves performance in high-traffic environments.

Another important aspect of MongoDB is its ability to integrate with various technologies and platforms. MongoDB offers drivers for a wide range of programming languages, including Java, Python, Ruby, C#, PHP, and JavaScript (through Node.js), making it easy to adopt in a variety of development environments. Additionally, MongoDB integrates well with other tools and platforms in the Big Data ecosystem, such as Hadoop and Apache Spark, allowing organizations to use MongoDB as part of their broader data processing pipelines.

MongoDB has also been widely adopted across various industries and types of applications. Its flexibility, scalability, and performance have made it a popular choice for web applications, e-commerce, content management systems, data analytics, Internet of Things, and more. Its ability to handle unstructured and semi-structured data makes it especially suitable for applications that need to store and process large volumes of user-generated data, such as activity logs, sensor data, and multimedia content.

Despite its many advantages, MongoDB also has some limitations that should be considered. For example, although MongoDB supports ACID transactions, this support is relatively recent and may not be as robust as in traditional relational databases. This can be an important consideration for applications that require a high level of data consistency. Additionally, MongoDB's flexibility in terms of schema can also be a double-edged sword, as the lack of a rigid schema can lead to data inconsistency if not managed properly.

In terms of administration, MongoDB requires a solid understanding of its architecture and features to optimize performance and ensure data integrity. This includes index management, replication and sharding configuration, and performance and resource usage monitoring. However, MongoDB Inc. offers a range of tools and services, such as MongoDB Atlas, a fully managed cloud platform that simplifies the deployment, management, and scalability of MongoDB, reducing the administrative burden for organizations.

Overall, MongoDB has established itself as one of the most versatile and powerful NoSQL databases in today's technology landscape. Its ability to handle data in a flexible and scalable format, along with its optimized performance and rich feature set, make it a solid choice for a wide range of modern applications that require a database that can grow and adapt with the application's needs. Its continued adoption across various industries and its ongoing evolution indicate that MongoDB will remain an important tool in the technological infrastructure of many organizations in the years to come.

4.3.3. Cassandra

Apache Cassandra is a distributed NoSQL database designed to handle large volumes of data across multiple servers, offering high availability, horizontal scalability, and fault tolerance. It was initially developed at Facebook in 2008 to handle the growing demand for data storage and processing, especially in messaging and social networking applications. Later, Cassandra became an open-source project under the Apache Software Foundation, which has enabled its adoption and continuous development across a wide range of industries.

Cassandra is based on a column-oriented data model, which is different from the traditional relational data model based on rows and tables. In Cassandra, data is organized into columns within rows, and the rows are grouped into column families. Each row in Cassandra can have a different number of columns, providing great flexibility to store data that may vary in structure. Column families in Cassandra are conceptually similar to tables in relational databases, but without the rigidity of a predefined schema, allowing Cassandra to handle semi-structured data more efficiently.

One of the most distinctive aspects of Cassandra is its distributed architecture without a single point of failure. Unlike traditional databases that rely on a master server to manage write and read operations, Cassandra employs a peer-to-peer design in which all nodes in the cluster are equal and can receive and process read and write requests. This decentralized architecture allows Cassandra to be highly available and fault tolerant, as there is no single node whose failure can cause a service outage. If a node in the cluster fails, the other nodes can continue handling operations without significant interruptions.

Scalability is another fundamental feature of Cassandra. The system is designed to scale horizontally, which means that more nodes can be added to the cluster to handle higher volumes of data and traffic without affecting performance. This is made possible by the use of sharding and replication. Cassandra splits the data among the nodes in the cluster using a hash algorithm that assigns each row to a specific range of keys. This technique, known as partitioning or sharding, allows the data to be distributed evenly across the nodes, optimizing resource usage and ensuring consistent performance even as the cluster grows.

Cassandra also implements data replication to ensure durability and availability of information. Data is replicated across multiple nodes in the cluster according to a configurable replication factor. This means that each piece of data is stored on several nodes, allowing read and write operations to continue even if one or more nodes fail. Additionally, the consistency level of operations in Cassandra can be adjusted according to the needs of the application. Cassandra supports various consistency levels, ranging from eventual consistency, where writes propagate asynchronously to the replicated nodes, to strong consistency, where write and read operations ensure that all replicated nodes are synchronized before an operation is confirmed.

The consistency model of Cassandra is flexible and allows developers to choose the appropriate consistency level for each operation based on the needs of their application. For example, an application that prioritizes availability over immediate consistency may opt for eventual consistency, while an application that requires guarantees that all write operations are immediately reflected in all replicas may opt for strong consistency. This flexibility is one of the reasons why Cassandra is popular in critical applications where availability and responsiveness are essential.

Cassandra uses its own query language called CQL (Cassandra Query Language), which is designed to be similar to SQL but adapted to Cassandra's data model. CQL provides a familiar way for developers who are used to SQL to interact with data in Cassandra while also leveraging the unique features of Cassandra's column data model. CQL supports a wide range of operations, including creating and managing tables (column families), inserting and updating data, and executing queries to retrieve data. Although CQL is similar to SQL, it is optimized to work with the distributed architecture and scalability features of Cassandra.

In terms of performance, Cassandra is optimized to handle large volumes of data and high traffic levels with low latency. Its ability to perform write and read operations in parallel across multiple nodes in the cluster allows Cassandra to handle millions of operations per second with consistent performance. This makes it ideal for mission-critical applications that require predictable performance and scalability, such as transaction management systems, real-time data analytics, and applications that generate large volumes of data, such as IoT.

Cassandra's high availability is also reinforced by its ability to operate in geographically distributed environments. Cassandra allows data replication across data centers in different geographic locations, which is crucial for applications that require high global availability. This also allows organizations to meet data localization requirements and data protection regulations by replicating data in data centers located in different regions.

However, as with any technology, Cassandra also has some considerations and challenges. For example, although Cassandra is highly scalable and available, managing and administering a Cassandra cluster can be complex, especially as the cluster grows. Configuring and maintaining the cluster, monitoring performance, managing nodes, and optimizing queries require a deep understanding of Cassandra's architecture and inner workings. Additionally, Cassandra's data model, while flexible, may require a rethinking of how data is modeled compared to relational databases, which can involve a learning curve for developers and database administrators.

Another challenge is eventual consistency, which, although it provides high availability and scalability, may not be suitable for all applications. In scenarios where immediate data consistency is critical, such as in financial systems or inventory control systems, eventual consistency can introduce complications that require careful handling to ensure data integrity.

Cassandra has been widely adopted across various sectors, including telecommunications, banking, e-commerce, and cloud services. Companies like Netflix, Apple, eBay, and Reddit use Cassandra to handle their large-scale data storage and processing needs, highlighting Cassandra's ability to support data-intensive workloads and deliver robust and scalable performance in high-demand production environments.

5. Data Storage and Processing

Data storage and processing is a central aspect of managing Big Data and implementing Artificial Intelligence solutions. As we have seen at the beginning of the book, as the volume of data grows exponentially, organizations face increasing challenges in storing, managing, and efficiently processing this data to extract valuable information and make informed decisions. In this chapter, I want to focus on exploring the technologies, strategies, and tools used to store and process data in the context of Big Data, as well as understanding how these techniques integrate into the overall architecture of modern data systems.

Data storage refers to how data is saved and organized for later access and use. In a Big Data environment, data comes from a variety of sources and is in different formats, requiring storage solutions that are flexible, scalable, and capable of handling structured, semi-structured, and unstructured data. Additionally, storage must be cost-efficient and performant, providing fast and reliable access to data when needed. To address these needs, various storage technologies and approaches have been developed, such as relational databases, NoSQL databases, distributed file systems, and cloud storage.

Data processing, on the other hand, involves the operations and transformations performed on data to convert it into useful information. This can include simple operations such as data cleaning and filtering, to complex analyses such as machine learning and data mining. In the context of Big Data, data processing must be capable of handling large volumes of data in parallel, requiring distributed processing architectures that can scale horizontally. Technologies like Hadoop, Spark, and real-time analytics tools have been developed to meet these demands, allowing organizations to process and analyze their data at scale and with high efficiency.

The concept of data storage and processing encompasses a wide range of technologies and approaches, which can be grouped into three main categories: data storage, batch data processing, and real-time data processing. Each of these categories addresses different aspects of data management, and it is important to understand how they interrelate and complement each other.

In the data storage category, the different options available for effectively storing large volumes of data are explored. This includes everything from traditional relational database systems to more modern technologies such as distributed file systems and NoSQL databases. These solutions are designed to handle the great diversity of data that characterizes Big Data, including text, images, videos, sensor logs, and other types of data. Additionally, storage strategies that allow organizations to optimize the use of their storage resources are examined, such as data compression, deduplication, and replication.

Batch data processing is a technique used to efficiently process large volumes of data. In this approach, data is collected over a period of time and then processed in blocks or "batches". This method is suitable for tasks that do not require an immediate response and where parallel processing can be leveraged to speed up the execution of data-intensive jobs. Technologies like Hadoop MapReduce have been fundamental in the development of batch processing solutions, allowing organizations to analyze petabytes of data in a distributed and efficient manner.

Real-time data processing, on the other hand, focuses on the need to process and analyze data as it is generated, providing information and results almost instantly. This approach is crucial in applications where rapid decision-making is essential, such as in fraud detection, network monitoring, and real-time personalization of online services. Technologies like Apache Kafka and Apache Storm have been designed to handle continuous data streams and provide real-time processing capabilities, allowing organizations to quickly react to events and changes in their data environment.

Data storage and processing are essential components in Big Data infrastructure, and their proper implementation is critical to the success of any data analysis initiative. By understanding the different technologies and approaches available, as well as how they integrate into the overall architecture of a data system, organizations can optimize their data management and maximize the value they derive from their data assets.

5.1. Distributed Storage Systems

5.1.1. Amazon S3

Amazon S3, or Amazon Simple Storage Service, is one of the most widely used and recognized cloud storage solutions worldwide. Launched by Amazon Web Services (AWS) in March 2006, Amazon S3 has revolutionized the way organizations store, manage, and access large volumes of data. Its highly scalable, durable, and accessible design has allowed businesses of all sizes to adopt the cloud as a viable solution for their storage needs, eliminating the need to manage physical storage infrastructures and enabling a pay-as-you-go model that adapts to fluctuating data storage demands.

Amazon S3 is an object storage service, meaning it stores data as objects within "buckets" rather than files in a traditional file system or records in a database. Each object in S3 consists of the actual data, descriptive metadata, and a unique key that identifies the object within the bucket. This object storage model is ideal for handling large volumes of unstructured data, such as media files, documents, backups, sensor data, and log files, where the structure of the content is less important than the ability to efficiently store and retrieve large amounts of information.

One of the fundamental features of Amazon S3 is its durability and availability. Amazon guarantees 99.999999999 percent (11 nines) durability for objects stored in S3, meaning data is almost entirely protected against loss. This durability is achieved by automatically replicating data across multiple devices and locations within an AWS region, ensuring that data remains safe even in the event of hardware failures or natural disasters in a data center. Additionally, Amazon S3 offers 99.99 percent availability, ensuring that data is accessible when needed without significant interruptions.

Scalability is another key aspect of Amazon S3. The service is designed to handle any amount of data, from a few gigabytes to petabytes and beyond, without users having to worry about storage capacity or performance. S3's automatic scalability allows organizations to quickly adapt to increases or decreases in their storage needs without managing or provisioning additional infrastructure. This is especially useful in scenarios where data volume can change unpredictably, such as web applications, cloud services, or Big Data analytics.

In terms of data management, Amazon S3 provides a range of advanced tools and features to help organizations organize, protect, and optimize the use of their data. These include object versioning, which allows maintaining multiple versions of an object to guard against accidental deletion or data corruption; cross-region replication, which automatically copies objects between different AWS regions to improve redundancy and facilitate disaster recovery; and granular access control, allowing administrators to define detailed access policies to control who can access which data and under what circumstances.

In addition to these features, Amazon S3 supports integration with other AWS services, making it an integral part of the AWS ecosystem. For example, data stored in S3 can be analyzed directly using tools such as Amazon Athena, an interactive query service that allows analyzing data in S3 using standard SQL. It can also be integrated with Amazon Glacier, a long-term storage service for infrequently accessed data, enabling organizations to automatically move data from S3 to Glacier to reduce storage costs.

Another important feature of Amazon S3 is its ability to efficiently handle large volumes of traffic and data requests. S3 is designed to provide high performance, meaning it can handle thousands of simultaneous read and write requests, which is crucial for high-demand applications that require fast and consistent access to data. Additionally, S3 supports data transfer through multiple methods, including HTTP, HTTPS, and the native S3 protocol, providing flexibility in how data can be accessed and managed.

In terms of security, Amazon S3 offers multiple layers of protection for stored data. Data can be encrypted both in transit and at rest using a variety of encryption options, including server-side encryption (SSE) with keys managed by AWS, and client-side encryption, where the client manages the encryption keys. Additionally, S3 integrates with AWS Identity and Access Management (IAM) to provide detailed role-based access control and also supports the use of bucket policies to define specific rules about how data can be accessed and manipulated. This is essential to meet security and compliance requirements in sectors such as banking, healthcare, and government.

Amazon S3 also offers tools for cost optimization, allowing users to choose between different storage classes according to their data access needs. For example, Amazon S3 Standard is ideal for frequently accessed data, while Amazon S3 Standard-IA (Infrequent Access) and Amazon S3 One Zone-IA are designed for data that is accessed less frequently but still requires fast access when needed. For data that is accessed very rarely and can tolerate longer retrieval times, Amazon Glacier and Glacier Deep Archive offer low-cost storage options. These options allow organizations to balance their performance and cost needs, optimizing their storage spending.

Amazon S3 is designed to be highly available and accessible from anywhere in the world. Data stored in S3 can be accessed from any location with an internet connection, making it ideal for global applications that require fast and reliable access to data in multiple regions. Additionally, S3's integration with Amazon CloudFront's Content Delivery Network (CDN) enables accelerated content distribution to end users worldwide, improving performance and user experience.

From my point of view, Amazon S3 is a robust, scalable, and flexible cloud storage solution that has transformed how organizations handle large volumes of data. Its durability, availability, and set of advanced features make it an essential tool for any organization looking for a reliable cloud storage solution. From its ability to scale seamlessly to its integration with other AWS tools and services, S3 provides companies with the tools they need to manage their data efficiently and securely in a Big Data environment.

5.1.2. Google Cloud Storage

Google Cloud Storage is a cloud storage solution provided by Google Cloud Platform, designed to store and manage large volumes of data with high availability, security, and scalability. It is an integral part of Google's infrastructure and is used by both large enterprises and small startups to store everything from unstructured data, such as media files, to structured and semi-structured data that requires fast and reliable access.

Google Cloud Storage offers an object storage model, meaning data is organized into "buckets," within which objects are stored. Each object in Google Cloud Storage consists of the actual data, optional metadata describing the object, and a unique identifier that allows access to the object. This approach is ideal for handling unstructured data, allowing large volumes of data to be stored without the limitations of traditional databases or file systems.

One of the most notable features of Google Cloud Storage is its native integration with other Google Cloud services, making it a preferred option for companies already using Google's infrastructure. This includes seamless integration with data analytics tools like BigQuery, Machine Learning services like AI Platform, and data processing systems like Dataflow and Dataproc. This integration allows Google Cloud Storage users to easily move data between different GCP services, facilitating the construction of complex and automated data pipelines.

Like Amazon S3, Google Cloud Storage is also designed to offer high durability and availability. Google guarantees 99.999999999 percent (11 nines) durability for stored data, achieved by replicating data across multiple locations within a region or even globally, depending on the selected storage class. This ensures that data remains safe and accessible even in the event of hardware failures or natural disasters in a data center. Data replication is transparent to the user, meaning no additional configuration is required to ensure data durability.

In terms of availability, Google Cloud Storage offers different storage classes that allow users to balance cost and performance according to their needs. These classes include:

1. Standard Storage, designed for frequently accessed data. It is ideal for data-intensive applications, such as websites, mobile apps, and Big Data analytics. Standard Storage ensures high availability and low access latency, making it suitable for workloads that require fast and constant data access.

2. Nearline Storage, optimized for data accessed less frequently but still needed almost immediately when required. Nearline Storage is ideal for backups, archived data accessed once a month or less, and other situations where cost is a key factor but access latency remains important.

3. Coldline Storage, suitable for rarely accessed data that needs to remain available at any time, such as disaster recovery backups. Coldline Storage offers a significantly lower cost compared to Standard and Nearline Storage but with a slightly higher retrieval cost.

4. Archive Storage, the most cost-effective option for data that is accessed very rarely, such as long-term archive files or compliance data that must be retained for many years. Archive Storage is ideal for situations where data can tolerate longer retrieval times but where storage cost is the main concern.

These storage classes allow users to optimize their storage costs by choosing the most suitable class for each type of data they handle, without compromising accessibility or durability.

Google Cloud Storage also stands out for its ability to handle data-intensive workloads at a global scale. Thanks to Google's infrastructure, data stored in Google Cloud Storage can be accessed from anywhere in the world with low latency, which is essential for global applications requiring a consistent user experience across all regions. Additionally, integration with Google Cloud CDN enables faster delivery of content stored in Google Cloud Storage to end users worldwide, improving the performance of web applications and streaming services.

Security is a priority in Google Cloud Storage, which offers a range of advanced features to protect data. Data can be encrypted both in transit and at rest using encryption keys managed by Google or, alternatively, keys managed by the customer for greater control over data security. Google Cloud Storage also integrates with Google Cloud Identity and Access Management to provide detailed role-based access control, allowing administrators to define specific access policies for different users and groups within the organization.

In terms of performance, Google Cloud Storage is optimized to provide fast access to large volumes of data. It can handle thousands of read and write operations per second, which is essential for high-demand applications that require fast and consistent access to stored data. Google Cloud Storage uses advanced caching and network optimization techniques to minimize latency and maximize performance, making it an ideal solution for applications that depend on fast and reliable access to large volumes of data.

In addition to its technical features, Google Cloud Storage offers a range of tools for efficient data management. This includes the ability to perform bulk operations, such as uploading and downloading large volumes of data, object versioning to guard against accidental deletion, and lifecycle policies that allow users to automate the movement of data between different storage classes based on predefined rules. These tools make it easier to manage large volumes of data and help organizations optimize their storage usage.

Google Cloud Storage also supports the creation of public and private buckets, allowing users to share data publicly or restrict access as needed. Public buckets are useful for hosting static files for websites, sharing data with the public, or collaborating on open projects. Private buckets provide full control over who can access the data, which is crucial for protecting sensitive information or complying with privacy and security regulations.

The compatibility of Google Cloud Storage with multiple programming languages and platforms makes it accessible to a wide variety of developers and application architectures. Google provides client libraries and SDKs for languages such as Python, Java, Ruby, Go, and JavaScript, making it easy to integrate Google Cloud Storage into new or existing applications. Additionally, Google Cloud Storage is compatible with the Amazon S3 API, allowing applications to migrate from Amazon S3 to Google Cloud Storage with minimal adjustments.

Google Cloud Storage is an integral part of Google's Big Data and Machine Learning strategy. As the central storage point for many data workflows in Google Cloud, it is common to see it used together with other Google solutions, such as BigQuery for large-scale data analysis, or AI Platform for training and deploying machine learning models. This makes Google Cloud Storage not just a place to store data but also a foundation for building advanced solutions that leverage the full power of Google's cloud.

5.2. Real-Time Processing vs. Batch Processing

5.2.1. Characteristics and Differences

Data processing is one of the most important parts and processes in managing large volumes of information, and there are two main approaches to carry out this processing: real-time processing and batch processing. Both methods have distinct characteristics and are used in different contexts depending on the specific needs of an organization or application. Understanding the fundamental differences between these two approaches is essential for choosing the right strategy for a Big Data project or for implementing data analysis systems.

Batch processing refers to executing data processing operations on a large set of accumulated data, usually at defined time intervals. This approach is traditionally used for tasks that do not require immediate results and where the amount of data to be processed is considerable. Batch processing tasks are usually executed in the background, often during periods of low system activity, such as at night or on weekends, to minimize the impact on overall system performance. One of the key characteristics of batch processing is its efficiency in handling large volumes of data. Because data is processed in blocks or batches, this approach allows for the optimization of system resources such as memory and computing capacity. Batch processing is ideal for tasks such as data aggregation, periodic report generation, billing, and data cleansing. These processes can be resource-intensive, but since they are performed on a complete data set rather than in real time, they can be executed in a more controlled and optimized manner.

Another characteristic of batch processing is that it tends to be less costly in terms of computing resources. By running at predefined times with more predictable resource usage, organizations can plan and optimize their infrastructure more efficiently. Additionally, batch processing is more fault-tolerant, as if an error occurs during the execution of a batch, the process can be restarted from the beginning of the batch or from a checkpoint without affecting the ongoing data or processes.

On the other hand, real-time processing, as the name implies, refers to processing data as it is generated or arrives in the system. This approach is critical in applications where the immediacy of information is vital, such as in financial trading systems, fraud detection, network monitoring, and online recommendation systems. In these cases, data must be processed almost instantly to enable rapid decision-making based on the most up-to-date information available.

One of the most notable characteristics of real-time processing is its ability to handle continuous data streams and provide applications with the ability to respond immediately to events or changes in the data. Unlike batch processing, which accumulates data over time before processing it, real-time processing acts on each event or piece of data as soon as it becomes available. This requires a highly efficient and low-latency processing system that can handle large volumes of data in real time without creating bottlenecks or significant delays.

Real-time processing also involves a more intensive and constant use of system resources, as the system must always be ready to process incoming data at any moment. This can make real-time processing more costly in terms of infrastructure, as it requires more powerful or scalable hardware, as well as a software architecture capable of supporting unpredictable and fluctuating workloads. Additionally, latency in processing is a critical consideration in real-time systems, as any delay can affect the accuracy and effectiveness of decisions made based on the processed data.

Consistency and fault tolerance in real-time processing systems also present unique challenges. Due to the need to process data continuously and without interruption, systems must be designed to handle failures without losing data or interrupting the processing flow. This often requires the implementation of distributed and redundant architectures that can continue functioning even if one or more components fail.

In terms of fundamental differences between batch processing and real-time processing, the former is more suitable for tasks where accuracy and thoroughness are more important than speed, while the latter is essential for applications where speed and responsiveness are critical. Batch processing is ideal for scenarios where large volumes of data need to be processed efficiently and at a relatively low cost, and where results can be delivered at defined intervals without affecting the usefulness of the data. For example, the generation of monthly financial reports or batch payment processing are typical tasks that are better handled with batch processing.

In contrast, real-time processing is indispensable in situations where every fraction of a second counts, and where the ability to make informed decisions in real time can have a significant impact on system performance or the success of the organization. Recommendation systems on e-commerce platforms, which need to analyze user actions and respond in real time with personalized suggestions, are a clear example of the need for real-time processing.

At a technical level, these differences are reflected in the underlying architectures and the technologies used to implement each type of processing. Batch processing architectures are usually optimized to handle large volumes of data in parallel and with high resource efficiency, while real-time processing architectures are designed to minimize latency and maximize availability and responsiveness. Tools like Apache Hadoop and Apache Spark are commonly used in batch processing, while technologies like Apache Kafka, Apache Flink, and Apache Storm are more suitable for real-time processing.

Despite their differences, it is important to note that in practice, many organizations combine both approaches to meet their data processing needs. For example, a company may use real-time processing to monitor financial transactions for fraud patterns in real time, while employing batch processing to conduct in-depth analysis of the same data over weeks or months. This combination allows organizations to leverage the advantages of both approaches, ensuring both immediacy and thoroughness in data analysis.

Put another way, batch processing and real-time processing are two fundamental approaches to handling large volumes of data, each with particular characteristics and advantages that make them suitable for different types of tasks and applications. Understanding the differences and applications of each approach is crucial for designing efficient and effective data systems that can meet processing demands both in the short and long term.

5.2.2. Tools for Real-Time Processing

Real-time processing has become an essential component in many modern applications that require the ability to analyze and respond to data immediately. To facilitate this type of processing, several tools have been developed that enable handling continuous data streams and performing complex analyses in real time. Two of the most prominent tools in this field are Apache Kafka and Apache Flink. These technologies not only enable real-time processing but also offer scalability, resilience, and flexibility, making them fundamental components of any modern data architecture.

Apache Kafka is a distributed event streaming platform primarily used to build real-time data pipelines and streaming applications. Originally developed by LinkedIn and later donated to the Apache Software Foundation, Kafka is designed to handle large volumes of data with high speed and low latency. Its architecture is based on the concept of distributed logs, where messages are stored in "topics" that act as channels to which data producers can send messages and from which consumers can read those messages. Kafka is characterized by its ability to handle millions of events per second, making it ideal for applications that require a constant and fast data flow, such as monitoring systems, social media analysis, and e-commerce platforms. One of Kafka's main features is its durability and persistence. Data in Kafka is stored on disks, ensuring that messages are not lost even if the system fails. This approach also allows data consumers to read messages at their own pace, facilitating the construction of decoupled and scalable systems. Kafka enables data replication across multiple nodes, ensuring high availability and fault tolerance, which are critical aspects in applications that cannot afford interruptions in the data flow.

Another advantage of Kafka is its flexibility in terms of data processing. Although Kafka is primarily used as a messaging platform, its ecosystem has expanded to include components such as Kafka Streams and Kafka Connect. Kafka Streams is a stream processing library that allows developers to build real-time data processing applications directly on top of Kafka.

This includes operations such as filtering, aggregation, and joining data streams, all in real time. Kafka Connect, on the other hand, facilitates the integration of Kafka with other systems, enabling the ingestion and export of data between Kafka and databases, storage systems, and other real-time applications.

Apache Flink is another powerful tool in the realm of real-time processing. Unlike Kafka, which focuses on data transmission, Flink is specifically designed for real-time data stream processing with advanced analysis capabilities. Flink is a distributed processing engine that enables the execution of analytical tasks both in real time and in batch, although its true strength lies in real-time processing. Initially developed by the Technical University of Berlin and later adopted by the Apache Software Foundation, Flink is known for its ability to handle stateful data streams and perform complex calculations in real time with low latency and high accuracy.

One of the distinguishing features of Apache Flink is its stream-based processing model. Unlike other systems that treat data streams as a set of mini-batches, Flink processes each event as it arrives, enabling continuous real-time processing. This is particularly useful for applications that require immediate and continuous data analysis, such as fraud detection, network monitoring, or real-time sensor data analysis. Flink also offers advanced state handling, meaning it can maintain information about past events and use it to influence the processing of future events. This capability is crucial for tasks like pattern detection, where it is necessary to remember the context of previous events. Flink also stands out for its ability to handle complex operations such as time windows, stream joins, and stateful event-based processing, all in real time. Time windows allow data streams to be grouped and analyzed based on time intervals, which is useful for operations like calculating moving averages or aggregating data within a specific period. Flink supports different types of windows, including tumbling, sliding, and session windows, providing flexibility in how real-time data can be processed.

Another important feature of Flink is its focus on consistency and fault management. Flink ensures that real-time calculations are consistent through its exactly-once processing model, which guarantees that each event is processed exactly once without duplication or loss. This is achieved through a mechanism called checkpoints, which saves the application's state at regular control points. In the event of a failure, Flink can restart processing from the last checkpoint without losing data or compromising processing consistency.

Both Apache Kafka and Apache Flink are complementary tools in many real-time processing scenarios. Kafka is often used for ingesting and transmitting large volumes of data, acting as a backbone for real-time data pipelines. The data flowing through Kafka can be processed in real time using Flink, which handles the more complex analysis and processing tasks. This combined approach allows for the construction of robust and scalable data systems that can handle everything from simple data transmission to advanced real-time analysis.

In addition, Kafka and Flink are designed to integrate well with other technologies and platforms. For example, it is common to see architectures where Kafka acts as the messaging system feeding data to Flink, while the results processed by Flink are sent to other databases, storage systems, or machine learning applications for further analysis. This flexibility and interoperability make Kafka and Flink indispensable tools in any real-time data processing ecosystem.

Both technologies are open source, which has contributed to widespread adoption and a vibrant ecosystem of developers and users who continue to improve and expand their capabilities. This also means they are supported by a wealth of resources and documentation, making them easier to learn and implement in real-time data projects. While Apache Kafka is ideal for transmitting and managing large real-time data streams, Apache Flink excels at processing and analyzing that data. These tools, when used together, offer a complete and powerful solution for handling and processing real-time data, enabling organizations to make informed decisions almost instantly and respond quickly to events and changes in their data environment.

5.3. Data Processing Models (MapReduce, DAGs)

Since I have talked about MapReduce in a previous section, I will now focus on DAGs and finally make a comparison so that the differences are clearer for you.

5.3.1. Directed Acyclic Graphs (DAGs)

Directed Acyclic Graphs, commonly known as DAGs, are a mathematical structure widely used in data processing, distributed file systems, and in scheduling and optimization algorithms. A DAG is a type of graph composed of a set of nodes connected by directed edges, where each edge has a direction going from one node to another, and, crucially, the graph contains no cycles. That is, there is no path that starts at a node and, following the directions of the edges, returns to that same node.

The concept of acyclicity is fundamental in a DAG because it ensures that the graph has an inherent hierarchical order. This order is manifested in that it is possible to arrange the nodes in such a way that all edges point in the same direction without forming loops. This property makes DAGs extremely useful in situations where it is necessary to represent dependencies or workflows, such as in distributed data processing systems, program compilation, task scheduling, and workflow modeling.

In the context of data processing, DAGs are used to model and manage complex workflows that involve multiple stages or tasks that must be executed in a specific order due to their dependencies. For example, in a Big Data environment, processing a large amount of data often involves a series of operations that must be executed in a particular sequence: reading data from multiple sources, cleaning it, transforming it, analyzing it, and then storing the results. Each of these operations may depend on the results of the previous operation, and these dependencies can be represented clearly and structurally through a DAG.

A DAG in this context would be a graph in which each node represents a task or an operation, and the directed edges between nodes represent the dependencies between these tasks. For example, if task B depends on the results of task A, in the DAG there would be a directed edge from node A to node B. Due to the acyclic nature of the DAG, it is guaranteed that there are no circular dependencies that could cause a deadlock or an infinite loop in the workflow. This allows tasks to be scheduled and executed efficiently, respecting the order of dependencies.

The use of DAGs is particularly prominent in data processing engines like Apache Spark and Apache Tez, which use DAGs to plan and execute distributed data processing jobs. In these systems, the DAG is used to represent the entire process of a job, from reading the data to writing the final results. The nodes of the DAG correspond to the different processing stages, and the edges represent the data dependencies between these stages.

Apache Spark, for example, transforms a program written in its API into a DAG that represents the different transformations and actions that will be applied to the data. Each transformation in Spark, such as a map or a reduce, becomes a node in the DAG, and the relationships between these nodes are established based on how the data flows through the program. Spark uses this DAG to optimize the order in which operations are executed, minimizing data movement between nodes in the cluster and leveraging in-memory computation when possible. Once the DAG has been built, Spark uses it to schedule the parallel execution of tasks across the cluster, ensuring that all dependencies are respected and that the job is completed as efficiently as possible.

Apache Tez is another processing engine that uses DAGs as a core part of its architecture. Tez was designed to improve the performance of MapReduce jobs on Hadoop, allowing more complex and flexible workflows to be represented and executed using DAGs. In Tez, a DAG can represent workflows that include multiple MapReduce jobs, which traditionally would have had to be executed sequentially. By representing the entire workflow as a DAG, Tez can optimize the execution of these tasks more globally, reducing latency and improving overall system performance.

The importance of DAGs is not limited to the scheduling and execution of tasks in data processing engines. They also play a crucial role in other domains such as compiler programming, where they are used to represent and optimize the flow of instructions in a program; in database management, where DAGs can represent query plans that specify the order in which database operations should be executed; and in social network analysis, where DAGs can model hierarchical or dependency relationships between users or events.

In addition to their applicability in distributed systems and scheduling algorithms, DAGs have significant applications in representing data structures and modeling systems in computer science. For example, DAGs are used in the representation of decision trees, control flow graphs in programming, and in the internal structure of distributed version control systems like Git, where they are used to model the relationships between different versions of a code repository.

Another crucial feature of DAGs is that they allow efficient parallelization in distributed environments. Because a DAG defines a partial order of operations, it is possible to identify subsets of nodes that are independent of each other and can therefore be executed in parallel. This is especially valuable in large-scale data processing systems, where the ability to execute tasks in parallel can drastically reduce the total processing time. Execution engines like Spark and Tez leverage this property to maximize parallelism and minimize bottlenecks in data processing.

An additional aspect to consider in the use of DAGs is their optimization. In practice, building an efficient DAG for a data processing job involves not only correctly representing the dependencies between tasks but also optimizing the DAG structure to minimize the number of steps and the execution time. This may include reordering nodes, merging tasks that can be executed together, and minimizing data transfer between nodes in the cluster. DAG optimizations can have a significant impact on the overall system performance, making tasks complete more quickly and with lower resource usage.

It is important to highlight that while DAGs are a powerful tool for modeling and executing complex workflows, they also require careful handling. Building and managing DAGs in distributed systems involves understanding not only the dependencies between tasks but also how resources are managed and how failures are handled. In systems where consistency and fault tolerance are critical, such as in distributed databases or real-time data analysis systems, the correct implementation and management of DAGs is essential to ensure that systems operate reliably and efficiently.

The concept of directed acyclic graphs is fundamental in data processing and task scheduling in distributed environments. Their ability to represent dependencies and order tasks in a way that maximizes efficiency and minimizes errors has made DAGs a cornerstone in the design of modern data processing systems, from execution engines like Spark and Tez to scheduling and optimization algorithms in a variety of computational domains.

5.3.2. Comparison between DAGs and MapReduce

The comparison between data processing models based on MapReduce and directed acyclic graphs is fundamental to understanding how and when to use each of these paradigms in practice. Both approaches are widely used in processing large volumes of data but have significant differences in terms of architecture, flexibility, and use cases.

MapReduce is a more traditional model that became popular with the rise of Apache Hadoop. It is based on two main operations: Map and Reduce. This model is highly effective for processing tasks that can be broken down into a series of independent operations that can then be aggregated. A key aspect of MapReduce is its simplicity and robustness in handling large volumes of data, especially in scenarios where the data does not require iterative or real-time processing. MapReduce excels in use cases such as log analysis, data aggregation, and large-scale data processing in distributed clusters.

On the other hand, DAGs, used in systems like Apache Spark, Apache Tez, and other modern execution engines, offer greater flexibility by allowing data operations to be structured in a directed graph, where each node represents an operation and the edges represent the dependencies between these operations. Unlike MapReduce, where the data flow is limited to a fixed sequence of steps, DAGs allow greater optimization by reordering and grouping operations, minimizing intermediate reads and writes, and making the most of memory and parallelism. This approach is especially beneficial in applications that require iterative processing, such as Machine Learning, graph analysis, and real-time processing, where the ability to perform in-memory computations significantly reduces latency.

In terms of use cases, MapReduce is ideal for scenarios where the main task is to efficiently process large-scale data without the need for in-memory optimization or real-time processing. For example, web index generation, log processing for retrospective analysis, and ETL (Extract, Transform, Load) tasks are cases where MapReduce shines. In these cases, MapReduce's ability to handle large volumes of data in distributed clusters, its robustness, and its focus on fault tolerance make it a reliable and scalable solution.

Conversely, DAGs are used in more dynamic and complex applications where flexibility in execution and optimization capability are crucial. In the context of Apache Spark, for example, a DAG allows operations such as joins, filters, and aggregations to be executed in a single pass through the data, efficiently using memory to avoid costly I/O operations. This is fundamental in Machine Learning applications, where multiple iterations over the data are required to adjust models, and in real-time data stream processing, where decisions must be made quickly on the fly.

Another notable difference is how these models handle node failures in a cluster. MapReduce is designed to be highly fault-tolerant, replicating data across multiple nodes and ensuring that failed tasks are automatically reassigned to other available nodes. This feature is essential in critical applications where data integrity and task completeness are paramount. DAGs can also handle failures, but the strategy depends more on the underlying engine. In Spark, for example, resilience is ensured through RDDs, which allow lost data to be recomputed automatically using the DAG, providing a balance between performance and fault tolerance.

Additionally, the complexity of implementation and use is different between the two models. MapReduce, with its more linear approach, can be easier to understand and apply for simple or well-defined processing tasks. However, its rigidity can become a drawback in applications that require more advanced optimizations. In contrast, DAGs offer much greater flexibility and efficiency but at the cost of increased complexity in their implementation and optimization. Developers must understand how to structure the operation graph to make the most of the execution engine's capabilities, which may require deeper knowledge of distributed processing and resource management.

In terms of performance, DAGs typically outperform MapReduce in applications where minimizing I/O operations is critical and where intensive in-memory processing can be performed. The ability of DAGs to reduce intermediate operations and keep data in memory throughout the process provides superior performance in applications involving complex or iterative operations. MapReduce, on the other hand, is more suitable for applications that do not benefit significantly from in-memory optimization or that have simpler and more linear requirements.

The choice between MapReduce and DAGs largely depends on the type of application and the specific requirements of data processing. MapReduce remains a great tool and suitable for many batch data processing applications, while DAGs offer a more modern and optimized solution for applications that require greater flexibility, parallelism, and efficiency in handling complex or iterative tasks. Understanding the strengths and limitations of each approach is important to select the right tool and maximize performance and efficiency in Big Data environments.

PART III

Integration of AI and Big Data

Part III: Integration of AI and Big Data

6. Relationship between AI and Big Data

We have talked about AI, and we have talked about Big Data; now we are going to talk about both in their relationship. This chapter, which deals with the relationship between Artificial Intelligence and Big Data, although at this point I hope you already understand, is fundamental to grasp how these two technologies have deeply intertwined in recent years, driving significant advances across various industries and applications. The convergence of AI and Big Data is not accidental; rather, it is the result of a technological evolution in which each of these disciplines has enhanced the capabilities of the other, generating a virtuous cycle of innovation and development.

As I said before, we are looking at things step by step and discussing them as needed, to delve deeper when the time comes. It is very important to first get familiar and understand the relationships. This is why if you feel that some things are being repeated, it is normal. I also remind you that we always look at everything in different contexts to better assimilate the information, which ensures you an optimal learning curve. Therefore, it means that if you are already understanding it, it is working.

Artificial Intelligence, which is based on complex algorithms and mathematical models, as you are seeing yourself, requires large volumes of data to train, validate, and optimize these models. The ability to collect, store, and process data on a massive scale is essential for AI algorithms to learn and improve their accuracy. Without proper access to quality data, AI models lack the "fuel," "food," "raw material," "input," call it what you want, necessary to function efficiently. This need has led to the expansion of Big Data infrastructures that not only store large amounts of data but also facilitate their analysis and real-time use, a critical factor for AI applications that require quick responses, such as autonomous driving or LLMs (Large Language Models) like ChatGPT, Claude, and Gemini.

On the other hand, we have also seen that Big Data benefits enormously from AI techniques. The amount of data generated today is so immense that traditional analysis methods are inadequate for extracting value from it effectively. Here, AI offers advanced solutions, such as machine learning, to identify hidden patterns, make accurate predictions, and make decisions based on data and not on assumptions or theories. This not only optimizes the use of data but also opens new possibilities for innovation in fields such as medicine, finance, and marketing, where the ability to process large volumes of information intelligently is key to gaining the most competitive advantages.

The value generated by the combination of AI and Big Data is another central point in this relationship. Organizations that have adopted these technologies report significant improvements in efficiency, accuracy, and responsiveness. In many cases, the value of these technologies does not lie only in the individual capabilities of AI or Big Data, but in how they complement each other to offer solutions that would be impossible to achieve with only one of them. For example, in the personalization of offers in marketing, it has taken a new turn since AI algorithms can analyze behavioral patterns in large datasets to create detailed customer profiles and adapt offers in real time, increasing the effectiveness of campaigns and improving the customer experience.

In terms of challenges, the integration of AI and Big Data is not without difficulties. Managing large volumes of data, the need for robust and scalable infrastructures, and the complexity of AI algorithms are just some of the obstacles that organizations must overcome to fully leverage the synergies between these two areas. However, these challenges simultaneously also present opportunities for innovation and the development of new technologies that facilitate integration and maximize the value derived from data.

As we move forward in this digital era, without a doubt, the relationship between AI and Big Data will continue to evolve with new technologies and approaches that expand the boundaries of what is possible. The ability to handle large-scale data and use advanced AI techniques to analyze them will be a key differentiator for companies seeking to remain competitive in an increasingly complex and demanding global market. A deep understanding of how these technologies interrelate and enhance each other is therefore essential for any professional who wants to lead in this field. You cannot achieve good results if you do not know AI in depth or understand the data you are working with. I constantly repeat this to my clients, my Partners, and my students, and I repeat it to you as well because it is very important. Get it into your head.

6.1. How Big Data Drives AI

6.1.1. Access to Large Volumes of Data

Access to large volumes of data is a crucial factor that has driven the development and effectiveness of Artificial Intelligence in the past decade. As organizations, both in the public and private sectors, have increasingly adopted digital technologies, the amount of data generated has grown exponentially. Do you remember the example with the birth rate and the sale of smartphones? Well, this is where I wanted to get. This increase has not only opened new possibilities for Artificial Intelligence but has also redefined what is possible in terms of data analysis, decision-making, and process automation.

The concept of Big Data, which refers to datasets so large and complex that they require advanced technologies for processing and analysis, has allowed Artificial Intelligence to access unprecedented volumes of data. This data availability is fundamental for training AI models, as the performance of these models is usually directly related to the quantity and quality of the available data. In the context of supervised learning, for example, AI models require large amounts of labeled data to learn how to perform specific tasks, such as image classification, speech recognition, or market behavior prediction.

Large volumes of data not only improve the accuracy of AI models but also enable the development of more complex and sophisticated algorithms. With access to massive data, deep learning models can be trained to recognize patterns and make predictions with a level of accuracy that would be impossible with smaller datasets like the ones you probably work with at your company. A notable example is the development of natural language models, such as those used in virtual assistants like those from Apple or Google or automatic translators like DeepL, which are trained with billions of words to improve their ability to understand and generate human language text. If you have been a DeepL user and didn't know where the name came from, I hope by now it is clearer to you.

Access to large volumes of data has also facilitated the development of Artificial Intelligence systems that can operate in real time. In sectors such as digital advertising, banking, and healthcare, the ability to process data in real time and make immediate decisions is essential, and this is where the technologies we have seen earlier come into play. So I hope you understand the importance of all this. For example, the recommendation systems used by e-commerce platforms rely on the ability to quickly analyze large amounts of data about user behavior to suggest relevant products. Similarly, in fraud detection, banks use AI systems that analyze thousands of transactions in real time to identify suspicious patterns and prevent fraud before it happens.

Access to large volumes of data has enabled Artificial Intelligence to tackle problems that were previously unapproachable due to the lack of sufficient data. In medical research, for example, the availability of large health record databases has allowed the development of predictive models that can identify the risk of diseases more accurately than ever before. These models are based on the analysis of clinical data from millions of patients, allowing researchers to discover patterns and risk factors that would not be evident in studies with fewer data.

The storage and processing of these large volumes of data have been facilitated by the evolution of Big Data infrastructures, such as distributed storage systems and parallel processing platforms. Tools like Hadoop, Amazon S3, and Google Cloud Storage have been fundamental in providing the necessary storage capacity to handle large amounts of data, while processing technologies like MapReduce and Apache Spark have enabled efficient and effective analysis of this data.

It is important to remember, to highlight again, that inaccurate or incomplete data can lead to biased or incorrect AI models, which can have negative consequences in their application. Additionally, data privacy is a growing concern, especially in contexts where sensitive personal data is handled, such as in health or finance.

Access to large volumes of data has been a key enabler for advances in Artificial Intelligence. It has allowed the development of more precise and complex models, the ability to operate in real time, and the possibility of tackling problems that were previously unapproachable. However, it has also introduced new challenges in terms of management, quality, security, and data privacy, which must be carefully managed to maximize the benefits of Artificial Intelligence while minimizing the associated risks. Before the "boom," there were no laws regulating this, but with the massive arrival of AI systems in our lives, this has started to change and will change even more.

6.1.2. Improvement in Model Accuracy

As we have seen earlier, improving the accuracy of Artificial Intelligence models is one of the central goals in AI research and application, especially in contexts where accuracy and reliability are critical. The accuracy of a model refers to its ability to make correct predictions, whether in classification tasks, regression, or any other type of predictive analysis. As the volumes of accessible data have increased, so has the ability of AI models to improve their accuracy, since the quality and quantity of available data are determining factors in the performance of these models.

Access to large volumes of data allows AI models to be trained with a greater diversity of examples, which in turn improves their ability to generalize, that is, to make accurate predictions on unseen data. When a model is trained with a small or limited dataset, it runs the risk of being overly specific or of "memorizing" the training data, the phenomenon known as "overfitting."

However, with a large and diverse dataset, it is more likely that the model will capture underlying general patterns in the data, which translates into better accuracy when faced with new data.

The use of advanced techniques such as model ensembling has also proven effective in improving accuracy. Ensembling involves combining multiple models to make predictions, with the idea that the combination of different approaches can compensate for the weaknesses of any individual model. This can lead to significant improvements in accuracy, as the strengths of each model are leveraged.

6.2. Challenges and Opportunities

As we have already seen with some applications and use cases I have mentioned, the integration of Artificial Intelligence and Big Data has revolutionized multiple sectors, providing advanced analytical capabilities and large-scale automation. However, this integration is not without challenges and problems, some of which are technical, while others are related to data management, security, ethics, and infrastructure. These challenges can complicate the development, implementation, and maintenance of effective solutions that combine AI and Big Data, and it is crucial to understand them in order to address them properly.

One of the most significant challenges is data quality and preparation. Artificial Intelligence relies heavily on data to train its models and make decisions. However, data coming from various sources are often heterogeneous, noisy, and unstructured. This means that before they can be used by AI algorithms, the data must be cleaned, transformed, and organized. This data preprocessing process is complex and time-consuming, and errors at this stage can lead, as we already know, to inaccurate or biased models. Moreover, in Big Data environments, where massive volumes of data are handled in real time, ensuring data consistency and integrity is even more difficult.

Another major technical challenge is scalability. AI applications require a large amount of computational resources, especially when processing large volumes of data. This includes not only storage and processing capacity but also the infrastructure to handle real-time data streams and continuous analytics. As data volumes grow, AI solutions must be able to scale without compromising performance. Achieving this scalability requires careful planning of the infrastructure, including the selection of appropriate technologies such as cloud computing, distributed storage, and parallel processing techniques. However, scalability also introduces additional complexities in terms of resource coordination, latency, and operational efficiency.

The integration of AI and Big Data also poses significant challenges in terms of security and privacy. As you have seen from the beginning, the data used in these systems often include sensitive and personal information, making the protection of user privacy a priority. However, the secure handling of large volumes of data is inherently complicated. As data are collected from multiple sources and integrated into AI systems, the risks of exposure to security breaches, cyberattacks, and data leaks increase. Additionally, data privacy regulations, such as the General Data Protection Regulation (GDPR) in Europe, impose strict requirements on how data must be handled, stored, and shared. Complying with these regulations while maximizing the value of the data for AI is a difficult balance to achieve.

Biases in AI algorithms represent another critical challenge. Since AI models learn from the data they are trained on, any bias present in the data can be amplified by the model, leading to unfair or incorrect decisions. This problem is particularly acute in the context of Big Data, where data may come from various sources with different levels of quality and representation. Addressing biases requires a conscious and proactive approach, including diversifying datasets, implementing regularization techniques, and continuously evaluating model performance from a fairness perspective. However, even with these measures, completely eliminating biases can be extremely difficult, especially in complex AI and Big Data systems.

In addition, the integration of AI and Big Data faces organizational and management challenges. Implementing advanced technologies requires a shift in organizational culture as well as the formation of multidisciplinary teams with skills in data science, data engineering, and AI development. Organizations often find it difficult to attract and retain qualified talent, which can limit their ability to develop and implement effective solutions. Collaboration between different departments is also essential, but not always easy to achieve, especially in large organizations where data silos and lack of communication can hinder the effective integration of AI and Big Data.

Decision-making based on AI and Big Data also faces challenges in terms of interpretability and transparency. If it is already difficult today, imagine as AI models become more complex, it may be hard for users and decision-makers to understand how and why a model arrived at a particular conclusion. This lack of transparency can lead to a lack of trust in AI solutions, especially in sectors where interpretability is crucial, such as healthcare, finance, and the legal field. Challenges in interpretability can also make it difficult to identify errors or biases in models, which in turn can lead to suboptimal or even harmful decisions.

The technological infrastructure and system integration also present a considerable challenge. Big Data solutions are often based on distributed architectures and heterogeneous systems, which can complicate integration with AI tools, which often have their own specific hardware and software requirements. Aligning these different technologies and ensuring they work in harmony requires detailed technical planning and a deep understanding of the capabilities and limitations of each component. The lack of standardization in the platforms and tools used both in Big Data and AI can further aggravate this challenge, making interoperability and effective integration difficult.

One of the biggest challenges in the integration of AI and Big Data is cost. Developing, implementing, and maintaining these technologies requires a significant investment in hardware, software, cloud infrastructure, and specialized talent. For many organizations, especially small and medium-sized enterprises, these costs can be prohibitive. Additionally, the implementation of these technologies is often accompanied by a steep learning curve, which can delay the realization of benefits and increase operational costs in the early stages. This forces organizations to conduct a detailed cost-benefit analysis and carefully consider whether investing in AI and Big Data aligns with their long-term strategic objectives.

7. Integrated Platforms and Tools

The development of Artificial Intelligence and advanced data analytics requires not only theoretical knowledge but also practical tools that enable the effective and scalable implementation of solutions. Machine Learning libraries and frameworks have revolutionized the way predictive models and intelligent systems are created, making technologies that were previously reserved only for large corporations accessible to both researchers and companies. Added to this are integrated platforms, which combine computing power, storage, and specialized services in accessible and collaborative environments, optimizing processes from data collection to model deployment. Understanding and mastering these tools is key to transforming data into real and competitive value, allowing current challenges to be met effectively in any sector.

At this point, we are going to look at the most important and widely used tools and the most recommended platforms in this regard.

7.1. Machine Learning tools

7.1.1. Introduction to TensorFlow

TensorFlow is an open-source platform developed by Google for the creation and deployment of Machine Learning and Deep Learning models. Since its initial release in 2015, it has become one of the most popular and widely used tools for the development of Artificial Intelligence applications, ranging from academic research to industrial production applications.

TensorFlow was originally designed to facilitate the implementation of deep neural networks, also known as Deep Learning, which require handling large volumes of data and complex mathematical operations. The core of TensorFlow is built on a system of computational graphs that allows mathematical operations to be represented and executed efficiently and scalably, leveraging both CPUs and GPUs for parallel processing.

One of the key aspects of TensorFlow is its ability to build computation graphs. In TensorFlow, a graph is a structured representation of a set of mathematical operations and their relationships. Each node in the graph represents an operation, such as a multiplication or a convolution, while the edges represent the data flowing between those operations. This structure allows TensorFlow to optimize and execute calculations efficiently, distributing operations across multiple hardware devices when necessary.

TensorFlow not only allows model creation through its low-level mathematical operations but also offers high-level interfaces to facilitate development. Keras, which has been integrated into TensorFlow since version 2.0, is one of these high-level interfaces that simplifies the construction, training, and evaluation of Deep Learning models. With Keras, developers can define models more intuitively using a Python-based API, making rapid experimentation and the implementation of more complex models easier.

In addition to model construction, TensorFlow provides robust tools for training and optimizing Machine Learning models. These include optimization algorithms such as gradient descent and its variants, methods for regularization, and advanced techniques such as reinforcement learning and federated learning. This makes TensorFlow versatile and suitable for a wide range of applications, from image classification to natural language processing and recommendation systems.

TensorFlow's support for multiple platforms is another highlight. Models built in TensorFlow can be deployed in a variety of environments, including high-capacity servers, mobile devices, and embedded systems. TensorFlow Lite, a lightweight version of the library, is specifically designed to run models on mobile and embedded devices with limited resources, such as smartphones, tablets, and IoT devices. This has enabled TensorFlow to be used in applications that require real-time inference at the edge, such as voice recognition, image processing, and sensor analysis.

TensorFlow has also been designed with scalability and production in mind. TensorFlow Serving is a system designed to facilitate the deployment of Machine Learning models in production environments, allowing continuous model updates without service interruption. TensorFlow Extended (TFX) is another component that provides a complete platform for the production of Machine Learning models, covering everything from data management to monitoring models in production.

The community around TensorFlow is large and active, which has contributed significantly to its growth and evolution. Google, along with other contributors from the open-source community, continues to develop and improve TensorFlow, leading to the introduction of new features, performance improvements, and expanded support for various hardware architectures. Extensive documentation, tutorials, and examples provided by the community make TensorFlow accessible to both beginners and experts in Machine Learning.

TensorFlow also supports other programming languages besides Python, such as C++, JavaScript, and Java, which broadens its applicability in different contexts. TensorFlow\.js, for example, allows Machine Learning models to run directly in the browser, opening up new possibilities for interactive web applications that can perform client-side inference without needing to send data to a server.

Another important aspect is TensorFlow's ability to integrate with other tools and libraries in the Machine Learning ecosystem. TensorFlow can be used alongside frameworks such as Apache Spark for processing large volumes of data, or with visualization tools like TensorBoard, which allows monitoring and analyzing model performance during training. TensorFlow has established itself as the essential tool in the field of Machine Learning and Deep Learning due to its flexibility, scalability, and robustness. Its ability to support everything from research to production on a variety of platforms has made TensorFlow a preferred choice for developers and data scientists around the world. Continuous innovation and community support ensure that TensorFlow will remain a key tool in the evolution of Artificial Intelligence and Machine Learning.

7.1.2. Available Models in Scikit-learn

Scikit-learn is one of the most widely used libraries in the Python ecosystem for implementing Machine Learning algorithms. Its simple design and consistent interface allow developers and data scientists to quickly experiment with different models without the need for complex implementation. Over the years, Scikit-learn has gained popularity due to its accessibility and the breadth of available models, covering a wide range of supervised and unsupervised learning techniques, as well as preprocessing, validation, and model selection tools.

One of the main attractions of Scikit-learn is the diversity of regression algorithms it offers. Among them, the most basic is linear regression, which models the relationship between a dependent variable and one or more independent variables through a straight line. Although simple, linear regression is extremely useful and is used as a starting point for many analyses. For problems where the relationship between variables is more complex, Scikit-learn offers variants such as polynomial regression and Ridge and Lasso regression, which include regularization to prevent overfitting.

Another fundamental group of models available in Scikit-learn are classification algorithms. Here, one of the best-known algorithms is logistic regression, which despite its name, is used for binary classification. It models the probability of a positive class versus a negative one, being an essential tool in problems such as fraud detection or disease prediction. Other classification models provided by Scikit-learn include decision tree-based classifiers, which divide the feature space into regions defined by simple rules, and k-Nearest Neighbors (k-NN) classifiers, which classify points based on the classes of the nearest data points in the feature space.

For more complex and nonlinear tasks, Scikit-learn includes Support Vector Machines (SVM), which are very effective in high-dimensional spaces. SVM seeks to maximize the margin between classes, making it robust to outliers and capable of handling cases where classes are not linearly separable by transforming the feature space. Additionally, the Support Vector Machine model allows the use of kernels to transform the data into a higher-dimensional space, where a linear separation can be more easily found.

Scikit-learn also offers a variety of clustering algorithms, one of the main methods of unsupervised learning. Among these are the k-means algorithm, which groups data into k clusters based on the minimum Euclidean distance from a centroid, and hierarchical clustering, which creates a hierarchy of clusters in a dendrogram tree, allowing the observation of how data clusters at different levels of similarity. Another important algorithm is DBSCAN (Density-Based Spatial Clustering of Applications with Noise), which finds arbitrarily shaped clusters based on point density, being useful in identifying outliers and irregularly shaped clusters.

In addition to regression, classification, and clustering models, Scikit-learn offers advanced tools such as Random Forests and Gradient Boosting. Random Forests are an ensemble of decision trees trained on different subsets of the dataset, then combined to improve accuracy and reduce overfitting. Boosting models, such as Gradient Boosting Machines (GBM), build a strong model by combining multiple weak models in a learning sequence, where each new model tries to correct the errors made by the previous ones.

Scikit-learn also offers models for dimensionality reduction tasks, such as Principal Component Analysis (PCA) and Linear Discriminant Analysis (LDA). PCA is a statistical technique that transforms the original data into a new set of uncorrelated variables called principal components, while LDA seeks to maximize the separation between classes while maintaining the variability within each class. Both methods are essential in data preprocessing to reduce complexity and computation time.

The library is not limited to learning algorithms only. Scikit-learn also includes tools for data preparation, such as normalization, standardization, and handling of missing data, which are crucial before feeding the data into any Machine Learning model. The pipeline function of Scikit-learn is particularly useful for chaining multiple processing and modeling stages, ensuring that operations are applied in a sequential flow, which is important in cross-validation and hyperparameter tuning.

Additionally, Scikit-learn offers model validation tools such as cross-validation and hyperparameter tuning through grid search or random search, allowing users to find the best configuration for a given model without the risk of overfitting to the training set. These capabilities make Scikit-learn a comprehensive library that enables not only building and training models but also evaluating their performance and optimally tuning their parameters.

Scikit-learn has gained popularity not only for its robustness and flexibility but also for its accessibility. Its detailed documentation, practical examples, and active community have made Scikit-learn an indispensable tool for those looking to implement Machine Learning techniques efficiently and effectively. By offering such a wide range of models and tools, Scikit-learn allows tackling almost any Machine Learning problem, from the simplest to the most complex, facilitating experimentation and the application of these techniques in production environments.

7.1.3. Framework Comparison

Choosing the right framework for developing Machine Learning models is a critical decision that can significantly influence the implementation process and the results obtained. In today's ecosystem, there are several popular frameworks, each with its own strengths, weaknesses, and specific use cases. The most prominent include TensorFlow, PyTorch, Scikit-learn, and Keras. Each of these frameworks has been designed with different priorities in mind, making them more suitable for certain tasks and less for others.

TensorFlow, developed by Google, is one of the most widely used frameworks in the field of Deep Learning. Its main strength lies in its ability to handle large-scale complex mathematical operations, making it the preferred choice for training Deep Learning models on large datasets. TensorFlow is highly scalable and supports both distributed training and inference across multiple platforms, from high-performance servers to mobile devices. Its flexibility is another significant advantage, as it allows developers to define custom neural network architectures. However, this same flexibility can make TensorFlow more complicated to learn and use for beginners. Its learning curve can be steep, and its API, while powerful, has been criticized for being less intuitive compared to other options.

PyTorch, developed by Facebook, has gained widespread adoption in the academic and research community due to its simplicity and ease of use. Unlike TensorFlow, PyTorch allows the construction of neural networks using a more intuitive and dynamic approach, making experimentation and rapid development easier. One of the most notable features of PyTorch is its ability to perform computations in dynamic computational graphs, allowing greater control over data flow and easier debugging. Additionally, PyTorch integrates well with other Python tools, making it a preferred choice for researchers who want to quickly prototype and experiment with new ideas. However, PyTorch has not traditionally been as robust in production as TensorFlow, although this is changing over time thanks to improvements in its ecosystem and the introduction of tools such as TorchServe.

Scikit-learn, although not a Deep Learning framework in the traditional sense, is a fundamental tool in the Machine Learning toolkit, especially for supervised and unsupervised learning tasks on small to medium-scale problems. Its simplicity, consistency, and wide range of algorithms make it the ideal choice for those looking to implement Machine Learning models quickly without the need for a steep learning curve. Scikit-learn is especially useful for problems that do not require the computational capacity of Deep Learning models, such as regression, basic classification, and clustering. However, its focus on more traditional algorithms makes it less suitable for tasks involving large volumes of data or the need for complex neural architectures, where frameworks like TensorFlow or PyTorch are more appropriate.

Keras, originally a high-level API built on top of TensorFlow, was designed with simplicity and rapid prototyping in mind. Keras allows developers to build and train Deep Learning models easily and quickly, with a focus on ease of use. Its API is intuitive, making it an excellent choice for beginners and for those looking to develop and test ideas quickly. Although Keras provides an abstraction that simplifies many of the complex aspects of Deep Learning, this simplification sometimes comes at the cost of flexibility and control. As TensorFlow has integrated Keras as its official high-level API, users can now benefit from the combination of Keras's simplicity with TensorFlow's power.

The choice between these frameworks largely depends on the type of project being developed and the specific needs of the team or developer. For example, for applications requiring the construction and training of Deep Learning models on large volumes of data, TensorFlow is a natural choice due to its scalability and support for distributed training. On the other hand, PyTorch is more suitable for research and rapid development environments where flexibility and debugging capability are more important. Scikit-learn remains the preferred choice for those working with structured data who need to implement traditional Machine Learning models quickly and efficiently. Keras, with its focus on ease of use, is ideal for those seeking a simplified development experience without losing access to TensorFlow's underlying capabilities.

Each framework has its place within the Machine Learning ecosystem, and often, the decision on which to use will depend on factors such as the team's familiarity with the framework, the nature of the problem to be solved, and the requirements for scalability and production. These frameworks are not mutually exclusive and, in many cases, can complement each other within the same project, providing the development team with the necessary tools to tackle Machine Learning problems efficiently and effectively.

7.2. Integrated platforms (Databricks, Google Cloud AI)

7.2.1. Features of Databricks

Databricks is a comprehensive platform designed to facilitate data engineering, analytics, machine learning, and real-time processing, all within a unified cloud-based environment. Originally created by the founders of Apache Spark, Databricks has been developed to fully leverage this distributed processing engine, integrating its capabilities with a range of additional tools that enable businesses to efficiently manage the entire data lifecycle.

One of the main features of Databricks is its ability to handle large volumes of data through a scalable and distributed environment. The platform allows users to perform massive data processing tasks using cloud-managed clusters, eliminating the need to manually manage the underlying infrastructure. Users can dynamically adjust the size of the processing clusters according to the workload, optimizing both performance and cost. Databricks also stands out for its native support for multiple programming languages, including Python, Scala, R, and SQL, making it easier for data scientists, data engineers, and analysts to collaborate. This flexibility in language use allows teams to work in a common environment without having to change their usual tools or workflows. Additionally, Databricks offers collaborative cloud-based notebooks that enable teams to work together in real time, share analyses and results, and comment directly on the code, improving communication and productivity.

Another key aspect of Databricks is its deep integration with Apache Spark, allowing it to execute large-scale data processing tasks extremely efficiently. In addition to Spark, Databricks easily integrates machine learning libraries such as MLlib and TensorFlow, facilitating the building, training, and deployment of machine learning models within the same platform. This ability to integrate data and machine learning models in a single workflow is one of the aspects that distinguishes Databricks in the data platform landscape.

In terms of security and compliance, Databricks offers a complete set of features to protect data and meet regulations. The platform includes data encryption in transit and at rest, role-based access controls, and support for integrations with external authentication tools such as Active Directory and OAuth. Additionally, Databricks provides detailed audits and activity logs, allowing organizations to comply with regulations like GDPR and CCPA while ensuring data integrity and confidentiality.

Another important feature of Databricks is its integration capability with multiple cloud services, including Amazon Web Services, Microsoft Azure, and Google Cloud Platform. This multicloud compatibility allows businesses to leverage their existing investments in cloud infrastructure and create hybrid or fully cloud-based workflows. The platform also supports integration with various storage tools and databases, such as Amazon S3, Azure Blob Storage, and Google Cloud Storage, making it easier to access and manipulate large volumes of data.

Databricks also focuses on performance optimization, offering technologies such as Delta Lake, which improves the reliability and performance of data workflows. Delta Lake allows handling of structured and unstructured data in a format that ensures data consistency and availability, eliminating common issues such as corrupt or inconsistent data. This technology is crucial for applications that require high availability and accuracy in data processing, such as real-time analytics and machine learning.

Databricks' focus on automation and ease of use is evident in its task management features. The platform allows job scheduling, dependency tracking, and management of complex workflows through an intuitive interface. Users can automate the execution of scripts and models, perform A/B tests, and manage data pipelines, all within the same platform, greatly simplifying the development and deployment process of big data and machine learning solutions.

Databricks also fosters an active community and a partner ecosystem that provide additional resources, integrations, and support. The platform offers extensive documentation, tutorials, and discussion forums that help users make the most of the platform's capabilities. Additionally, Databricks organizes events and workshops that allow professionals to stay up to date with the latest trends and technologies in big data and machine learning.

Databricks brings together multiple tools and capabilities in a unified environment, enabling businesses to efficiently manage the entire data lifecycle, from ingestion to analytics and machine learning. Its integration with Apache Spark, multicloud flexibility, focus on security and scalability, along with its commitment to automation and ease of use, make Databricks a standout option for organizations looking to maximize the value of their data in the digital age.

7.2.2. Google Cloud AI services

Google Cloud AI is a comprehensive suite of services and tools designed to facilitate the implementation and development of artificial intelligence applications in the cloud. These services enable businesses and developers to access advanced AI capabilities without the need to build complex infrastructures from scratch, accelerating innovation and time to market.

One of the most prominent services of Google Cloud AI is AI Platform, a platform that provides tools for the entire lifecycle of machine learning model development, from data preparation to production deployment. AI Platform allows users to train models in managed environments using scalable and optimized infrastructures and supports popular frameworks such as

TensorFlow, PyTorch, and Scikit-learn. The platform also offers AutoML services, which automate the process of creating high-quality custom models without requiring deep ML expertise, democratizing access to advanced AI technologies.

AutoML is another key service in the Google Cloud AI portfolio, designed for those who want to develop custom AI models but lack the technical expertise to do so manually. AutoML provides a simple interface that allows users to upload their data, choose a target, and let the platform handle the heavy lifting, from data preprocessing to model optimization. This service is particularly useful in applications such as computer vision, natural language processing, and tabular data analysis, where model quality and accuracy are critical.

In the field of computer vision, Google Cloud offers Vision AI, a service that enables the analysis of images and videos to identify objects, faces, text, and more. This service is based on pre-trained models that have been fine-tuned with vast amounts of data, allowing users to implement robust solutions with high accuracy without the need to train their own models from scratch. Vision AI is widely used in industries such as security, retail, and healthcare, where image detection and analysis play a crucial role.

In the area of natural language processing, Google Cloud AI provides Natural Language API, a service that allows applications to understand and analyze written text in various languages. This API can identify entities, perform sentiment analysis, classify content, and understand text structure, which is extremely useful in applications such as opinion analysis, chatbots, and search engines. Additionally, Google Cloud offers Dialogflow, a platform for building conversational interfaces such as chatbots and virtual assistants, which integrates with multiple communication channels, including websites, mobile apps, and virtual assistant devices.

Speech-to-Text and Text-to-Speech are other significant services in the Google Cloud AI ecosystem, enabling accurate conversion between voice and text. Speech-to-Text transcribes audio in real time or from prerecorded files, supporting a wide range of languages and dialect variants. Text-to-Speech, on the other hand, generates human-like voice from text, with multiple customization options regarding tone, speed, and style, allowing AI applications to interact more naturally with users.

Google Cloud also offers Recommendations AI, a service that helps businesses provide personalized recommendations to their customers based on the analysis of large volumes of behavioral data. This tool is essential for e-commerce applications, where personalization can significantly increase conversion rates and customer satisfaction.

Another area of focus is AI Infrastructure, which includes a range of services and tools designed to support large-scale ML model training and deployment. This includes compute instances optimized for ML, such as Tensor Processing Units (TPUs), which are specialized chips designed by Google to accelerate deep learning model processing. TPUs are a powerful option for training complex models quickly, reducing costs and development time.

Google Cloud AI also facilitates the integration of trained models in the cloud with data applications through BigQuery ML, a service that allows analysts and data scientists to create and run ML models directly within BigQuery, Google Cloud's data warehouse. This greatly simplifies the model-building process, as it does not require transferring data between different environments or using external infrastructures.

Google Cloud AI's focus on security and privacy is another critical aspect, providing capabilities such as data encryption and compliance with regulations like GDPR. This ensures that AI applications built on Google Cloud can operate within strict regulatory frameworks, protecting user privacy and data integrity.

Google Cloud AI is a robust and truly versatile platform that provides a wide range of services designed to facilitate the implementation of artificial intelligence in business applications. From development and training tools to specific APIs for vision, language, and recommendations tasks, Google Cloud AI covers all the needs a company may have on its journey toward digital transformation through artificial intelligence.

7.2.3. Success Cases of using integrated Platforms

Integrated platforms have been fundamental for numerous companies in their journey toward digital transformation through the use of Artificial Intelligence and Big Data. These platforms, such as Google Cloud AI, Databricks, and others, have enabled organizations to tackle complex challenges, optimize their operations, and create new business opportunities.

A prominent example is Zillow, the real estate company that uses Databricks in combination with Apache Spark to enhance its predictive analytics and Machine Learning capabilities. Zillow processes large volumes of data to predict real estate values in real time, a complex task that requires handling heterogeneous data such as market trends, property characteristics, and demographic data. With Databricks, Zillow has been able to significantly reduce the processing time of its predictive models, allowing it to offer more accurate and up-to-date estimates to its users. The platform has facilitated collaboration between data scientists and engineers, optimizing the workflow of data modeling and analysis, resulting in greater efficiency and faster decision-making.

In the healthcare sector, Sanofi, one of the largest pharmaceutical companies in the world, has used Google Cloud AI to improve its drug research and development processes. Sanofi has implemented Machine Learning and Big Data tools to analyze vast amounts of genomic and clinical data, aiming to identify patterns that can accelerate the development of new treatments. Thanks to the integration of platforms such as Google Cloud AI, Sanofi has been able to reduce the time required for data analysis, improve the accuracy of its predictive models, and ultimately accelerate the arrival of new medications to the market. This integration has also enabled Sanofi to comply with data privacy and security regulations, which are crucial in the pharmaceutical sector.

Another success case is Toyota, which has leveraged Big Data and Machine Learning capabilities in its manufacturing process through the use of integrated platforms such as Google Cloud AI and Databricks. Toyota has implemented predictive maintenance models to optimize the performance of its production plants. Using data from sensors installed in machinery and vehicles, Toyota predicts failures before they occur, allowing the company to reduce unplanned downtime and maintenance costs. This approach has not only improved operational efficiency but also increased product quality by preventing defects before they become major issues. The integration of these platforms has enabled Toyota to manage large volumes of data in real time, optimizing its manufacturing processes and strengthening its position in the global automotive market.

In the e-commerce sector, Alibaba has used integrated platforms to significantly improve its product recommendation capabilities. Alibaba has implemented advanced Machine Learning systems in its e-commerce platform to analyze user behavior and offer personalized recommendations in real time. Using tools such as TensorFlow and the Google Cloud AI infrastructure, Alibaba processes large volumes of user data, from purchase histories to interactions on the platform, to create recommendation models that enhance the user experience and increase conversion rates. This approach has allowed Alibaba not only to boost its sales but also to improve customer loyalty by offering more relevant and personalized products and services.

In the financial sector, JPMorgan Chase has used Google Cloud AI to automate the analysis of legal contracts, a process that traditionally required a large amount of time and human resources. With the implementation of natural language processing models developed in Google Cloud, JPMorgan Chase has been able to analyze thousands of contracts in a fraction of the time it used to take, reducing human errors and improving operational efficiency. This automation has enabled the bank to better manage legal risks and comply with financial regulations more effectively.

These success cases highlight how integrated platforms have been essential for organizations to face complex challenges and explore new opportunities. From optimizing manufacturing processes to personalizing the customer experience and accelerating drug development, companies are leveraging the advanced capabilities of these platforms to transform their operations and remain competitive in an increasingly digital and data-driven business environment.

PART IV

Data Modelling and Analysis

Part IV: Data Modeling and Analysis

8. Data Preprocessing and Cleaning

Data preprocessing and cleaning are fundamental steps in any data analysis, machine learning, or artificial intelligence project. The quality of the data used has a direct impact on the accuracy, robustness, and reliability of subsequent models and analyses. This chapter focuses on essential techniques and practices for preparing raw data before it is used in predictive models, ensuring that this data is accurate, complete, and in a suitable format.

Data preprocessing covers a variety of tasks ranging from error correction to transforming data into a format more appropriate for analysis. Raw data is often plagued with problems such as missing values, duplicates, inconsistencies, and errors. Additionally, it may be distributed across different formats or structures, making it difficult to use directly in analytical models or machine learning algorithms. That is why data preprocessing and cleaning are not only necessary but are critical stages that require meticulous attention.

One of the most important aspects of preprocessing is ensuring data quality. As I hope is very clear to you by now, data quality is a determining factor in the performance of any predictive model or analysis. Low-quality data can lead to incorrect conclusions, which in turn can negatively affect decision-making based on those analyses. Therefore, identifying and correcting quality problems is a priority in data preprocessing. I say this sincerely and will repeat it as many times as necessary, it is very important that you become proficient in this field. This is a factor that, in addition to giving you better results, can also position you as a candidate with more potential and therefore worth considering.

8.1. Importance of Data Quality

8.1.1. Improvement in Model Performance

Improving model performance is a crucial goal in the development and application of machine learning and data analysis techniques. The quality of data preprocessing and cleaning plays a decisive role in obtaining efficient, accurate, and generalizable models. When addressing performance improvement, multiple aspects can be considered, ranging from feature selection to the proper preparation of input data.

One of the most influential factors in improving model performance is the quality of the data being used. Well-preprocessed, clean, and organized data allow learning algorithms to detect patterns more clearly and accurately. The removal of noise, duplicates, and irrelevant data reduces the likelihood that the model will learn incorrect or insignificant patterns, known as overfitting. For example, in a noisy dataset with outliers or errors, the model may overfit to these anomalous data, reducing its ability to generalize to new, unseen data. Careful cleaning and correction of such errors directly improve the model's ability to make more accurate predictions in the future.

Another key aspect is the normalization and standardization of features. Raw data often contains variables in different scales or units, which can unbalance the training of certain machine learning models, especially those that rely on distance measures, such as clustering or regression algorithms. Normalizing the data (that is, rescaling feature values to fall within a uniform range) or standardizing it (rescaling values to have a mean of zero and a standard deviation of one) can help algorithms converge more quickly and find more effective solutions. This results in improved model accuracy and speed.

Handling missing values is also fundamental for improving performance. Incomplete data can introduce uncertainty and bias into a model, especially if missing values are common or follow a pattern that is not completely random. There are various techniques to handle missing values, such as deleting affected rows or columns or imputing missing values using techniques like mean, median, or more advanced methods such as machine learning-based imputation. Choosing the right method for dealing with missing values can make a significant difference in the model's predictive capacity, as it helps preserve useful information without introducing significant bias.

Feature selection is another essential aspect of improving model performance. Not all features in a dataset are relevant to the problem being solved. Some features may be redundant or not provide significant additional information, while others may even be detrimental if they introduce noise. Using feature selection techniques, such as selection based on feature importance, eliminating highly correlated features, or using techniques like LASSO, which can enforce the selection of a more relevant subset of features, can reduce the dimensionality of the problem. This not only improves the model's performance in terms of accuracy but also reduces computational cost and model complexity.

Additionally, creating new features (feature engineering) can be crucial for improving model performance. Sometimes, the data in its original form does not contain all the information needed to make accurate predictions. By creating new features, such as aggregations, interactions between variables, or logarithmic and polynomial transformations, you can provide the model with a better representation of the problem, allowing it to detect more complex patterns and thus enhance its predictive capacity.

Managing imbalanced data is another factor that affects model performance, particularly in classification problems where some classes may be underrepresented in the data. This can lead the model to be biased toward majority classes, ignoring or mispredicting minority classes. Techniques such as oversampling the minority class, undersampling the majority class, or using advanced techniques like Synthetic Minority Over-sampling Technique (SMOTE) can help balance the dataset and improve the model's ability to correctly predict all classes.

Regularization is a powerful technique to improve model performance by preventing overfitting. Models such as linear or logistic regressions, neural networks, and other algorithms can overfit the training data, capturing noise instead of important underlying relationships. Regularization techniques, such as L1 (LASSO) and L2 (Ridge), introduce a penalty term that constrains the model's coefficients, forcing it to focus on the most important features and avoid unnecessary fitting to the training data. This not only improves the model's generalization to new data but also makes the model more interpretable and manageable.

Improving model performance largely depends on how data is managed and preprocessed before model training. The combination of data cleaning techniques, feature selection and creation, normalization, handling of imbalanced data, and regularization not only optimizes model accuracy but also ensures that these models are more robust, efficient, and applicable in real-world situations.

8.1.2. Tools to Ensure Data Quality

As you already know, ensuring data quality is fundamental in any data analysis or artificial intelligence project, as low-quality data can lead to incorrect results and ineffective models. To ensure that data is of high quality, there are various tools and techniques that address different aspects of the data preparation and cleaning process. Below are some of the most relevant tools in this field.

One of the most widely used tools is OpenRefine. OpenRefine is an open-source tool that allows users to clean data, transform it from one format to another, and explore large datasets with ease. OpenRefine is particularly useful for detecting and correcting inconsistencies in data, such as typos, variations in capitalization, or the presence of duplicate values. The intuitive user interface allows users to perform complex operations without advanced programming knowledge, making it an accessible option for a wide range of professionals.

Trifacta Wrangler is another powerful tool that facilitates data cleaning, transformation, and enrichment. Trifacta uses an artificial intelligence and machine learning-based approach to suggest data transformations, helping users identify and correct data quality issues efficiently. The tool allows real-time visualization of data transformations, providing immediate feedback on the impact of the operations performed and ensuring that the resulting data meets the required standards for subsequent analysis.

Talend Data Quality is a suite of tools that provides a comprehensive set of functions to ensure data quality, including validation, data profiling, cleaning, and deduplication. Talend Data Quality allows users to define custom rules to ensure data consistency and accuracy, as well as identify patterns and anomalies that may indicate underlying data issues. Integration with other Talend tools facilitates data flow throughout the organization, ensuring that data quality is maintained across the entire process.

Ataccama ONE is another comprehensive tool that combines data quality management with governance and data profiling. Ataccama ONE allows users to automate the data cleaning process and ensure that data complies with defined business rules. The tool also provides continuous monitoring capabilities, enabling organizations to identify and correct data quality issues in real time, minimizing the impact on analyses and decision-making.

Pandas is a Python library that, although not designed exclusively for data cleaning, is widely used for this purpose due to its flexibility and power. Pandas allows efficient manipulation and analysis of structured data, providing functions for detecting null values, removing duplicates, transforming columns, and creating new features. The ability to integrate Pandas with other Python libraries makes it a popular choice among data scientists and data engineers.

Great Expectations is a relatively new tool that has gained popularity for its focus on data validation. Great Expectations allows users to define expectations about their data, which are rules or constraints that the data must meet. These expectations can be as simple as ensuring that there are no null values in a column or as complex as validating complete statistical distributions. The tool generates automatic reports on the state of the data in relation to these expectations, making it easier to identify problems and correct them early before they affect analyses or models.

DataCleaner is another tool that specializes in data cleaning and profiling. DataCleaner provides a wide range of functions for detecting duplicate data, identifying outliers, and normalizing data. The tool also includes integration capabilities with databases and other data sources, facilitating the application of data quality rules in complex and distributed environments.

For enterprise environments that require a robust and scalable solution, Informatica Data Quality is one of the leading options. Informatica offers a comprehensive platform that includes advanced capabilities for data quality management, from cleaning and standardization to validation and enrichment. The platform integrates well with other enterprise data management systems, enabling a holistic view and centralized control over data quality across the organization.

In big data environments, where datasets can be extremely large and complex, tools like Apache Griffin provide quality control capabilities at scale. Apache Griffin allows the definition of custom data quality metrics and applies these metrics to large, distributed datasets. The tool offers a user interface for configuring and monitoring data quality, as well as the ability to generate alerts and reports when problems are detected.

DQ Analyzer, a data profiling tool from Uniserv, focuses on identifying data quality issues and suggesting improvements. The tool is especially useful for companies that handle large volumes of customer data, allowing them to improve data quality through duplicate detection, field validation, and data normalization.

These tools provide a comprehensive set of options to ensure that the data used in any analysis or artificial intelligence project is of high quality, minimizing errors and maximizing the accuracy of the resulting models and analyses. The choice of the right tool or set of tools depends on the specific environment, project requirements, and available technological infrastructure, but all these tools play a crucial role in the continuous maintenance and improvement of data quality.

8.2. Data Cleaning and Transformation Techniques

8.2.1. Duplicate Removal

Duplicate removal is a crucial step in data preprocessing that ensures datasets are clean, consistent, and free of redundancies that could distort analyses and the results of Artificial Intelligence models. Duplicates can arise from various sources, such as data entry errors, database merges, and multiple data import processes. If not handled properly, duplicates can lead to biased or inaccurate results, negatively affecting the quality of any analysis or model based on that data.

The first step in removing duplicates is identifying them within the dataset. This task can be simple or complex, depending on the nature of the data and how duplicates are defined. In simple cases, a duplicate might be an exact row that appears more than once. However, in more complicated situations, duplicates may not be identical across all columns, requiring a more detailed analysis to determine if the rows are indeed redundant. For example, two customer records may have similar names and addresses but with small spelling variations, making a duplicate not immediately obvious.

The tools and methods for identifying and removing duplicates vary depending on the work environment and the technology used. In the Python environment, Pandas is one of the most popular libraries for data handling. Pandas provides functions such as

```
drop_duplicates()
```

which allow identifying and removing duplicate rows from a DataFrame. This method can be configured to check for duplicates across all columns or within a specific subset, allowing flexibility in how a duplicate is defined.

For projects involving larger and more complex databases, tools like SQL can be used to manage duplicates. SQL queries can identify duplicates through commands such as

```
select distinct
```

or by using subqueries with

```
row_number()
```

to remove duplicates based on specific criteria. This approach is particularly useful in relational database environments where data is structured across multiple tables and it is necessary to consider the relationships between different datasets.

In scenarios where duplicates are not exactly identical, more advanced fuzzy matching techniques must be applied. Tools like OpenRefine allow matching based on string similarities, which is useful for identifying records that are duplicates but may have small differences in data entry, such as typographical errors. This type of analysis can use algorithms like Levenshtein, Jaro-Winkler, or clustering techniques to determine the similarity between records.

Another approach to duplicate removal is rule-based deduplication. Here, rules are established based on key dataset attributes, such as combinations of names, email addresses, and phone numbers. The definition of custom rules is particularly useful in systems where duplications may occur in non-trivial ways and where a more nuanced analysis is needed to determine if records are truly duplicates.

In Big Data environments, where datasets can be extremely large, deduplication can become a challenge due to performance limitations. Tools like Apache Spark can be used to handle deduplication in large volumes of data. Spark allows duplicate removal in a distributed environment, where data is processed in parallel across a computer cluster, ensuring that duplicates are efficiently removed without compromising the overall system performance.

Additionally, to ensure the integrity of the duplicate removal process, it is important to keep a record of the deleted data. This allows auditing and verifying that the deleted records were indeed duplicates and not unique data that was mistakenly removed. Maintaining a log or record of these operations also helps with traceability, especially in regulated environments where every data operation must be documented and justifiable.

Duplicate removal not only improves the accuracy and efficiency of machine learning models but also optimizes storage use and reduces processing time, as models do not need to handle redundant information. By eliminating duplicates, it is ensured that each record in the dataset is unique and meaningful, which in turn contributes to the overall quality of the analysis and the reliability of the results obtained from that data.

Duplicate removal is an essential component of the data cleaning process and crucial for any data analysis or modeling project. Proper identification and removal of duplicates using the right tools and methods ensure data integrity, thereby improving the quality and reliability of the results derived from its analysis.

8.2.2. Normalization and Standardization

Normalization and standardization are two fundamental techniques in data preprocessing, especially when working with Machine Learning algorithms. Both techniques are essential to ensure that numerical data falls within an appropriate range and is comparable to each other, which is crucial for the performance of machine learning models.

Normalization

Normalization is the process of scaling the values of a variable to a specific range, usually between 0 and 1. This is especially useful when you want to prevent variables with different units or magnitudes from dominating the model. Normalization is common in algorithms that depend on distance, such as k-means clustering or distance-based methods like k-NN.

The most common method to normalize a dataset is min-max scaling, where each value is scaled using the following formula:

```
X_normalized = (X - X_min) / (X_max - X_min)
```

In this formula:

- `X` is the original value of the feature.
- `X_min` is the minimum value in the dataset for that feature.
- `X_max` is the maximum value in the dataset for that feature.

Normalization is particularly useful when you have a dataset where the attributes have different scales. For example, in a dataset that includes both age (which might range between 0 and 100 years) and annual income (which might range between thousands and millions), normalization ensures that both variables have the same importance in the calculations performed by the model.

An implementation in Python using Pandas might look like this:

```
import pandas as pd
from sklearn.preprocessing import MinMaxScaler

# Example of a DataFrame
df = pd.DataFrame({
    'Age': [20, 30, 40, 50],
    'Income': [20000, 50000, 80000, 110000]
})

# Initialize the MinMaxScaler
scaler = MinMaxScaler()

# Apply normalization
df_normalized = pd.DataFrame(scaler.fit_transform(df),
columns=df.columns)

print(df_normalized)
```

In this example, normalization converts the original values into a range between 0 and 1, making both features comparable in terms of scale.

Standardization

Standardization, on the other hand, transforms the data to have a mean of 0 and a standard deviation of 1. This process is crucial in algorithms such as neural networks and regression methods, where it is assumed that the data is normally distributed.

The formula to standardize a value is:

```
X_standardized = (X - μ) / σ
```

Where:

- `X` is the original value.
- `μ` is the mean of the values in the dataset.
- `σ` is the standard deviation of the values in the dataset.

Standardization is particularly important when the data follows a normal or approximately normal distribution. By standardizing the data, models that assume normality in the data can function more efficiently and accurately.

An example of standardization in Python using Pandas and Scikit-learn is the following:

```
import pandas as pd
from sklearn.preprocessing import StandardScaler

# Example of a DataFrame
df = pd.DataFrame({
    'Age': [20, 30, 40, 50],
    'Income': [20000, 50000, 80000, 110000]
})

# Initialize the StandardScaler
scaler = StandardScaler()

# Apply standardization
df_standardized = pd.DataFrame(scaler.fit_transform(df),
columns=df.columns)

print(df_standardized)
```

In this case, the standardized values have a mean of 0 and a standard deviation of 1, which facilitates their use in models that are sensitive to data distributions.

Comparison and choice of techniques

The choice between normalization and standardization depends on the Machine Learning algorithm and the nature of the data. For example, normalization is preferred in techniques like clustering and distance-based methods, where the different scales of the variables can affect the distance calculations. In contrast, standardization is essential in methods like linear regression, SVM, or neural networks, where the distribution of the data influences the model's convergence and accuracy.

It is important to keep in mind that in some cases, you may need to apply both techniques at different stages of preprocessing, depending on the structure and behavior of the data. Additionally, some models, such as decision trees and boosting algorithms, are less sensitive to the scale of the data, and in those cases, normalization or standardization might not be necessary.

The correct application of normalization or standardization is crucial to improve the performance and accuracy of models, ensuring that all features contribute equitably and effectively to the modeling process. This decision must be based on a deep understanding of the algorithm you are going to use and the nature of the data you are working with.

8.2.3. Transformations and Handling of Categorical Variables

Handling categorical variables is a crucial part of data preprocessing, especially in the context of machine learning. Categorical variables are those that represent discrete categories or labels, instead of continuous numerical values. Common examples include gender, colors, product types, among others. Since many machine learning algorithms require numerical data, it is necessary to transform these categorical variables into a suitable format for processing.

Types of categorical variables

Before diving into transformation techniques, it is important to understand that categorical variables can be classified into two main types:

1. **Nominal:** These are categories without inherent order. For example, colors like "`red`", "`blue`", and "`green`" do not have a logical order.
2. **Ordinal:** These categories have an inherent order. For example, "`low`", "`medium`", and "`high`" have a natural order.

Categorical variable transformation methods

There are several techniques to transform categorical variables into a format that machine learning models can process. The most common ones are detailed below.

One-Hot Encoding

One-Hot Encoding is one of the most widely used techniques for transforming nominal categorical variables. It involves creating a new binary variable (0 or 1) for each category of the original variable. This method ensures that no artificial order is introduced into the categorical variables.

For example, if there is a variable "`color`" with categories "`red`", "`blue`", and "`green`", One-Hot Encoding would create three new variables:

- `color_red`
- `color_blue`
- `color_green`

If a data point has the value "red" for the variable "`color`," it would be represented as:

```
color_red = 1, color_blue = 0, color_green = 0
```

In Python, this can be implemented using the Pandas library:

```
import pandas as pd

# Example DataFrame
df = pd.DataFrame({
    'Color': ['red', 'blue', 'green', 'red', 'green']
})

# Apply One-Hot Encoding
df_one_hot = pd.get_dummies(df, columns=['Color'])

print(df_one_hot)
```

Ordinal Encoding

Ordinal Encoding is suitable for ordinal categorical variables. It assigns a numerical value to each category based on its order. This method preserves the inherent order relationship in the variable. For example, if there is a variable "`size`" with categories "`small`," "`medium`," and "`large`," values can be assigned as:

- small = 1
- medium = 2
- large = 3

In Python, ordinal encoding can be performed as follows:

```
import pandas as pd
from sklearn.preprocessing import OrdinalEncoder

# Example DataFrame
df = pd.DataFrame({
    'Size': ['small', 'medium', 'large', 'small', 'large']
})

# Initialize the OrdinalEncoder
ordinal_encoder = OrdinalEncoder(categories=[['small', 'medium',
'large']])

# Apply ordinal encoding
df['Size_ordinal'] = ordinal_encoder.fit_transform(df[['Size']])

print(df)
```

Frequency Encoding

Frequency Encoding assigns each category a numerical value based on how frequently it appears in the dataset. This method is useful when the frequency of categories is relevant to the model.

For example, if a category appears more frequently, it will be assigned a higher value. This type of encoding can be especially useful in models where the frequency of categories has a significant impact on the outcome.

Here is an example of how it can be implemented in Python:

```
import pandas as pd

# Example DataFrame
df = pd.DataFrame({
    'Color': ['red', 'blue', 'green', 'red', 'green', 'red']
})

# Calculate frequency
freq_encoding = df['Color'].value_counts(normalize=True)

# Map frequencies to categories
df['Color_freq'] = df['Color'].map(freq_encoding)

print(df)
```

Target Encoding

Target Encoding (also known as Mean Encoding) assigns each category the average of the `target` variable for the observations where that category appears. This method can be useful but must be used carefully due to the risk of overfitting.

For example, if there is a variable "`neighborhood`" and you want to predict house prices, you can encode "`neighborhood`" with the average price of houses in that neighborhood.

Here is a basic example of how it could be implemented:

```
import pandas as pd

# Example DataFrame
df = pd.DataFrame({
    'Neighborhood': ['A', 'B', 'A', 'C', 'B'],
    'Price': [200000, 250000, 220000, 180000, 260000]
})

# Calculate the mean price for each neighborhood
mean_encoding = df.groupby('Neighborhood')['Price'].mean()

# Map means to neighborhood categories
df['Neighborhood_encoded'] = df['Neighborhood'].map(mean_encoding)

print(df)
```

Considerations when choosing a technique

The choice of encoding technique depends on several factors, including the type of categorical variable (nominal or ordinal), the machine learning model being used, and the nature of the data. For example:

- For linear models and tree-based models, One-Hot Encoding is usually a safe and effective option.
- Ordinal Encoding is ideal for categorical variables that have a natural order, but it should not be used with nominal variables.
- Frequency Encoding and Target Encoding can be powerful but should be handled with caution to avoid overfitting, especially when working with small datasets.

Additionally, it is important to consider the impact on the dataset size. One-Hot Encoding can significantly increase the dimensionality of the dataset, which might slow down model training or increase storage requirements.

Proper handling of categorical variables is essential for building accurate and efficient machine learning models. By applying these transformations correctly, the model's predictive ability and its capacity to generalize to new data can be significantly improved.

8.3. Handling Missing and Anomalous Data

8.3.1. Identification and Treatment of Missing Data

The identification and treatment of missing data is a crucial step in data preprocessing, especially in Machine Learning projects. Missing data can introduce biases and reduce the accuracy of predictive models, so it is essential to address them systematically and effectively.

Identification of Missing Data

Before treating missing data, the first step is to identify it. Missing data can appear in various ways, depending on how the dataset was collected. Commonly, missing values are represented as `NaN` (Not a Number) in libraries like Pandas in Python, but they can also appear as blank spaces, zeros, or even as extremely high or low values that are not possible in the data context.

In Python, identifying missing values in a data frame can be done as follows:

```
import pandas as pd

# Example DataFrame with missing values
data = {
    'A': [1, 2, None, 4],
    'B': [5, None, None, 8],
    'C': [9, 10, 11, 12]
}

df = pd.DataFrame(data)

# Identify missing values
print(df.isnull())

# Count missing values by column
print(df.isnull().sum())
```

This code shows which values are missing (True indicates the value is missing) and counts how many values are missing in each column. This type of analysis is the first step to decide how to handle missing data.

Types of Missing Data

Missing data can be classified into three main categories:

1. MCAR (Missing Completely at Random): The data is missing completely at random and is not related to any other variable in the dataset. For example, if a sample is lost due to a technical error unrelated to the data characteristics.

2. MAR (Missing at Random): The data is missing randomly but is related to another observable variable. For example, if a person's income is missing depending on their education level, but not on another variable in the dataset.

3. MNAR (Missing Not at Random): The data is missing in a way that is not random and is related to the missing variable itself. For example, if people do not report their income due to the sensitivity of the data.

The treatment of missing data depends on the type of missing data and the potential impact on the analysis or model.

Eliminating Missing Data

One of the most direct approaches is to delete the rows or columns that contain missing data. This is suitable when the amount of missing data is minimal and the integrity of the analysis is not compromised by deleting that data.

In Python, this can be done with:

```
# Drop rows with any missing value
df_dropped_rows = df.dropna()

# Drop columns with any missing value
df_dropped_columns = df.dropna(axis=1)
```

Imputing Missing Data

When it is not possible to remove missing data, the missing values can be replaced with appropriate values (imputation). The most common imputation techniques are:

- Imputation with the mean
- Imputation with the median
- Imputation with the mode

- Imputation with a constant value
- Imputation based on a predictive model

To avoid repeating these points, I will explain and elaborate on them in the following sections.

Using Algorithms that Handle Missing Data

Some Machine Learning algorithms can effectively handle missing data without the need for prior imputation. For example, decision trees and some ensemble-based models like Random Forest can deal with missing data during the training process.

Considerations for Handling Missing Data

It is important to consider the impact of handling missing data on the analysis or predictive model. Imputation can introduce biases if not done properly, and deleting missing data can significantly reduce the dataset size, affecting the representativeness of the data.

Additionally, it is advisable to perform a sensitivity analysis to evaluate how different missing data treatment techniques affect the model results. This allows selecting the most appropriate approach for the specific context.

The identification and treatment of missing data is a step that requires a careful approach to ensure that no biases are introduced and that the analysis or predictive model is as accurate as possible.

8.3.2. Outlier Detection

Outlier detection is a critical step in data preprocessing, especially in data analysis and in building Machine Learning models. Outliers are observations that deviate significantly from the rest of the data. These may result from measurement errors, incorrect data entries, or real phenomena occurring in the data distribution, and they can disproportionately influence the results of the analysis and the performance of predictive models.

Importance of outlier detection

Outliers can have a significant impact on statistical and Machine Learning models. In linear models, such as regression, a single outlier can drastically alter the estimated coefficients, leading to incorrect inferences. In clustering or classification analysis, outliers can distort decision boundaries or the groupings formed by the data.

For these reasons, detecting and properly handling outliers is essential to ensure that models are accurate and generalizable.

Methods for outlier detection

There are several methods to detect outliers, each with its own advantages and disadvantages. The most common methods include univariate analysis, multivariate analysis, and specific Machine Learning techniques.

1. Univariate analysis

This method focuses on detecting outliers in a single variable at a time. Some of the most commonly used techniques are:

- **Visualization with boxplots:** A boxplot is a graphical tool that shows the distribution of a variable through its quartiles. Values that lie beyond the "whiskers" of the plot are considered outliers.

```
import matplotlib.pyplot as plt
import seaborn as sns

# Example of creating a boxplot
sns.boxplot(x=df['A'])
plt.show()
```

- **Identification based on Tukey's rule:** According to this rule, any observation that lies more than 1.5 times the interquartile range (IQR) above the third quartile or below the first quartile is considered an outlier.

```
Q1 = df['A'].quantile(0.25)
Q3 = df['A'].quantile(0.75)
IQR = Q3 - Q1

lower_bound = Q1 - 1.5 * IQR
upper_bound = Q3 + 1.5 * IQR

outliers = df[(df['A'] < lower_bound) | (df['A'] > upper_bound)]
```

2. Multivariate analysis

Multivariate analysis considers the relationship between multiple variables to identify outliers. Some of the most commonly used techniques are:

- **Mahalanobis distance:** This metric calculates the distance of each data point from the center of a multivariate distribution, taking into account correlations between variables. Points with large Mahalanobis distances are considered outliers.

```
import numpy as np
from scipy.spatial.distance import mahalanobis
from scipy.stats import chi2

mean = np.mean(df[['A', 'B', 'C']], axis=0)
cov = np.cov(df[['A', 'B', 'C']].values.T)
inv_covmat = np.linalg.inv(cov)

df['Mahalanobis'] = df.apply(lambda x: mahalanobis(x[['A', 'B',
'C']], mean, inv_covmat), axis=1)
df['p_value'] = df['Mahalanobis'].apply(lambda x: 1 - chi2.cdf(x,
df=2))

outliers = df[df['p_value'] < 0.01]
```

- **Principal Component Analysis (PCA):** PCA can reduce the dimensionality of the data and highlight observations that do not align with the principal components, which may indicate they are outliers. We will look at this later to avoid repeating too much here.

3. Machine Learning Techniques

Some Machine Learning algorithms are designed to detect outliers automatically, considering complex patterns in the data. Some examples include:

- **Isolation Forest:** This algorithm is based on building decision trees that isolate individual observations. Observations that require fewer splits to be isolated are considered outliers.

```
from sklearn.ensemble import IsolationForest

iso_forest = IsolationForest(contamination=0.05)
df['outlier'] = iso_forest.fit_predict(df[['A', 'B', 'C']])
```

- **Support Vector Machine (SVM) for outlier detection**: Using a modified version of SVM called One-Class SVM, it is possible to identify the contour that contains most of the data and detect values that fall outside this contour.

```
from sklearn.svm import OneClassSVM

svm = OneClassSVM(gamma='auto', nu=0.05)
df['outlier'] = svm.fit_predict(df[['A', 'B', 'C']])
```

Considerations for handling outliers

Once outliers are identified, decisions must be made on how to handle them. Some of the most common options are:

- **Removing outliers:** If outliers are errors or not representative of the general population, they can be removed from the dataset.

- **Imputation:** Instead of removing outliers, it is possible to impute values that are more consistent with the rest of the dataset.

- **Treating outliers as a special category:** In some contexts, it is useful to treat outliers as a separate category or transform them to reduce their impact.

- **Using robust algorithms:** Instead of removing or transforming outliers, models that are less sensitive to outliers can be used, such as using medians instead of means.

The choice of the appropriate technique depends on the specific context and the nature of the dataset. Ignoring outliers can lead to misleading results and underperforming models, while proper treatment can improve the accuracy and generalization of the predictive model.

8.3.3. Imputation Methods

Data imputation is a fundamental process in data preprocessing, especially when working with datasets that contain missing values. Missing values can arise for various reasons, such as measurement errors, data entry errors, or simply because the information was not available at the time of collection. Leaving these missing values untreated can lead to biased or incorrect results in analyses and predictive models. There are several imputation methods that can be used depending on the nature of the data and the context of the analysis.

Simple imputation

1. Mean, median, or mode imputation

This is one of the simplest and most common methods for imputing missing values. It involves replacing the missing values with the mean, median, or mode of the variable in question. The choice between mean, median, or mode depends on the nature of the data.

- **Mean:** It is appropriate for numerical variables that follow an approximately normal distribution. However, it is sensitive to the presence of outliers.

```
df['column'].fillna(df['column'].mean(), inplace=True)
```

- **Median**: It is more robust to outliers and is useful for skewed numerical variables.

```
df['column'].fillna(df['column'].median(), inplace=True)
```

- **Mode:** It is mainly used for categorical variables, replacing the missing values with the most frequent category.

```
df['column'].fillna(df['column'].mode()[0], inplace=True)
```

2. Imputation with a constant value

In some cases, it is useful to impute missing values with a constant value that makes sense within the context of the analysis. For example, in a dataset where income is recorded, missing values could be imputed with a value such as "0" if it is assumed that the lack of income indicates no earnings.

```
df['column'].fillna(0, inplace=True)
```

Advanced imputation

1. Model-based imputation

This method uses machine learning algorithms to predict the missing values based on other features of the dataset. The models most commonly used for this purpose include linear regression, decision trees, and random forests.

- **Linear regression:** A regression model is built where the variable with missing values is predicted based on other variables.

```
from sklearn.linear_model import LinearRegression

# Split the dataset into complete and incomplete observations
complete_data = df[df['column'].notnull()]
missing_data = df[df['column'].isnull()]

# Train a regression model on the complete data
reg = LinearRegression()
reg.fit(complete_data[['feature1', 'feature2']],
complete_data['column'])

# Predict the missing values
predicted_values = reg.predict(missing_data[['feature1',
'feature2']])

# Fill the missing values with the predictions
df.loc[df['column'].isnull(), 'column'] = predicted_values
```

- **Random Forests:** This method is particularly useful for complex datasets with nonlinear interactions between variables.

```
from sklearn.ensemble import RandomForestRegressor

rf = RandomForestRegressor()
rf.fit(complete_data[['feature1', 'feature2']],
complete_data['column'])

predicted_values = rf.predict(missing_data[['feature1',
'feature2']])

df.loc[df['column'].isnull(), 'column'] = predicted_values
```

2. Imputation with k-Nearest Neighbors (k-NN)

KNN is another machine learning approach that imputes missing values using the mean, median, or mode of the closest observations (neighbors) in the feature space. This method is flexible and can capture complex relationships between variables.

```
from sklearn.impute import KNNImputer

imputer = KNNImputer(n_neighbors=5)
df[['column1', 'column2']] = imputer.fit_transform(df[['column1',
'column2']])
```

Time series imputation

For data that have a temporal nature, it is important to consider methods that respect the temporal structure of the data.

- **Forward Fill:** Imputes missing values with the last known previous value.

```
df['column'].fillna(method='ffill', inplace=True)
```

- **Backward Fill:** Imputes missing values with the next known subsequent value.

```
df['column'].fillna(method='bfill', inplace=True)
```

- **Interpolation:** Calculates the missing values using linear or polynomial interpolation based on the previous and subsequent values.

```
df['column'].interpolate(method='linear', inplace=True)
```

Additional considerations

The choice of the imputation method should be made carefully, considering the impact it may have on subsequent analyses and models. For example, mean imputation may reduce variability in the data, while model-based imputation may introduce biases if the predictive model is not well calibrated.

In some cases, especially when the percentage of missing data is very high, it may be more appropriate to consider methods such as multiple imputation analysis, where multiple imputed datasets are generated and the results are combined to obtain a more robust estimate.

Imputation is a tool to improve data quality and ensure that analyses are representative and accurate. However, it is always advisable to assess the impact of imputation on the results and, when possible, perform sensitivity analyses to understand how imputation decisions affect the conclusions obtained.

9. Data Modeling

Data modeling is one of the most crucial and complex phases within the data analysis process and the development of machine learning models. In general terms, data modeling involves transforming raw data into a format that can be used to extract meaningful information, make predictions, and make data-driven decisions. This process covers everything from feature selection and transformation to the construction, training, and evaluation of predictive models. It is essential in any data science project, as it defines how the data is structured and how machine learning models are applied.

Data modeling begins with the identification and selection of relevant features, a process known as feature selection. This step is fundamental to reduce the dimensionality of the dataset and improve both the efficiency of the model and its ability to generalize to unseen data. The selected features or variables must have a strong correlation with the target variable and be free from noise or redundancy. There are several techniques for feature selection, ranging from simple statistical methods to more complex approaches based on the importance of features within machine learning models.

Another key aspect of data modeling is dimensionality reduction. This process is crucial when working with datasets containing a large number of variables, which can lead to problems such as overfitting or the curse of dimensionality. Dimensionality reduction seeks to project the data into a lower-dimensional space without losing relevant information. Methods such as principal component analysis and linear discriminant analysis are popular techniques that allow reducing the number of features while retaining as much variance or discrimination between classes as possible. We will delve deeper into these two methods as we move forward to analyze both.

Once the features have been selected and transformed, the next step in data modeling is model construction and training. Building a model involves choosing a suitable learning algorithm, which can vary depending on the type of problem (regression, classification, clustering, etc.) and the nature of the data. For example, in regression problems, models such as linear regression or polynomial regression can be used, while for classification, algorithms such as decision trees, support vector machines, or neural networks can be employed.

Model training consists of adjusting the model's parameters so that it can learn from the training data. During this phase, a loss or error function is minimized, which measures how well the model is making predictions. It is essential to keep in mind the problem of overfitting during training, which means the model learns the details and noise of the training data too well, losing its ability to generalize.

The data modeling process would not be complete without the evaluation and tuning of the models. After training the model, it is necessary to evaluate its performance using a separate dataset, commonly called a validation or test set. Performance metrics, such as accuracy, recall, F1-score, or mean squared error (in the case of regression problems), allow measuring the model's effectiveness and comparing it with other models or versions of the same model. Additionally, it may be necessary to adjust hyperparameters, which are parameters that are not learned during training but are set before the training process. These hyperparameters can include the number of layers in a neural network, the maximum depth of a decision tree, or the learning rate in an optimization algorithm.

Data modeling is an iterative process that often requires multiple cycles of tuning and reevaluation to achieve the optimal model. As the data environment changes, it may be necessary to reevaluate or retrain existing models, highlighting the importance of having a continuous lifecycle in model development.

This process is fundamental to ensure that machine learning models are accurate, efficient, and applicable to real-world problems.

Let’s look at it in more depth.

9.1. Feature Selection

Feature selection is a fundamental step in the data modeling process, as it involves identifying and choosing the most relevant variables from a dataset to build more accurate and efficient predictive models. Proper feature selection not only improves model accuracy but also reduces computational complexity, decreases the risk of overfitting, and facilitates model interpretation.

The need for feature selection arises mainly due to the abundance of data available today. In many machine learning applications, datasets may contain hundreds or thousands of variables (or features), many of which may be irrelevant or redundant for the specific prediction task. Using all available features is not always the most effective, as this can increase noise in the model and make it harder to extract meaningful patterns.

The feature selection process can be approached using different methods that are generally divided into three categories: filter methods, wrapper methods, and embedded methods.

Filter methods evaluate the relevance of each feature independently of the machine learning model to be used later. These methods rely on statistical metrics to select the most relevant features. For example, techniques such as the chi-square test for categorical variables or Pearson's correlation coefficient for numerical variables can be used to identify which features have the strongest relationship with the target variable. One of the main advantages of filter methods is their speed and simplicity, as they do not depend on the type of model being applied. However, their drawback is that they do not take into account interactions between features, which can lead to suboptimal selection.
Wrapper methods, on the other hand, consider the impact of the features on a specific learning model. In this approach, a subset of features is selected, and the model is trained with them, evaluating its performance. This process is repeated with different combinations of features to identify which set of variables produces the best model performance. Among the most common wrapper methods is forward sequential selection, where the process starts with an empty set of features, and features are added one by one, selecting at each step the feature that most improves the model's performance. There is also backward sequential selection, which starts with all features and removes them one by one. Although these methods can produce better results, they are computationally expensive, especially in datasets with a large number of variables.

Embedded methods combine the advantages of filter and wrapper methods. These methods perform feature selection during the model's training process. A common example is the use of regularization algorithms, such as Lasso (Least Absolute Shrinkage and Selection Operator), which adds a penalty to the model's loss function to reduce irrelevant feature coefficients to zero, effectively eliminating them from the model. Another example is the use of decision trees or random forests, where the importance of features can be directly evaluated based on how they are used in the model's decision process.

The feature selection process can also include techniques such as selection based on feature importance derived from trained models, where the most relevant features are analyzed according to an already trained model, and dimensionality reduction techniques, such as principal component analysis, although the latter focuses more on transforming features than selecting them.

In practice, feature selection is an iterative process that often requires combining several methods and continuously evaluating model performance. Depending on the nature of the problem and the dataset, different approaches may be more appropriate. In any case, proper feature selection is crucial to build robust models that not only offer high predictive performance but are also interpretable and scalable.

An example of how a feature selection process could be implemented in Python using Scikit-learn might look like this:

```
from sklearn.feature_selection import SelectKBest, f_classif
from sklearn.datasets import load_iris
from sklearn.model_selection import train_test_split
from sklearn.ensemble import RandomForestClassifier
from sklearn.metrics import accuracy_score

# Load the dataset
data = load_iris()
X, y = data.data, data.target

# Split the dataset into training and test sets
X_train, X_test, y_train, y_test = train_test_split(X, y,
test_size=0.3, random_state=42)

# Apply feature selection using ANOVA F-test
selector = SelectKBest(score_func=f_classif, k=2) # Selects the 2
best features
X_train_selected = selector.fit_transform(X_train, y_train)
X_test_selected = selector.transform(X_test)

# Train a model with the selected features
model = RandomForestClassifier(random_state=42)
model.fit(X_train_selected, y_train)
```

```
# Evaluate the model
y_pred = model.predict(X_test_selected)
accuracy = accuracy_score(y_test, y_pred)

print(f"Model accuracy with selected features: {accuracy:.4f}")
```

This code demonstrates how to select the two most relevant features using the ANOVA F-test method and train a random forest model with them. This feature selection process can be adjusted for different models and selection methods according to the specific requirements of the problem and the dataset.

Now let's break down the topic to analyze it more precisely and get a better understanding.

9.1.1. Feature Selection Techniques

Feature selection is a critical step in building machine learning models, and there are various techniques that can be used to identify the most relevant variables that improve the model's performance. These techniques, depending on their approach, can be classified into three main categories: filter methods, wrapper methods, and embedded methods. Each of these techniques has its own set of specific methods that can be used depending on the nature of the problem and the type of data.

1. Filter Methods

Filter methods are independent of the machine learning model and are based on statistical properties of the data. They evaluate the relevance of each feature before any model is applied and select the most important ones based on certain statistical metrics.

- **Chi-squared test:** It is a statistical test used to examine the independence between two categorical variables. In feature selection, it is used to assess the relationship between each feature and the target variable. Features with higher chi-squared values are considered more relevant.

```
from sklearn.feature_selection import SelectKBest, chi2
X_new = SelectKBest(chi2, k=10).fit_transform(X, y)
```

- **Mutual Information:** Measures the dependency between two variables, evaluating how much information about one variable can be obtained through the other. It is useful for both categorical and continuous variables.

```
from sklearn.feature_selection import mutual_info_classif
```

```
mutual_info = mutual_info_classif(X, y)
```

- **Pearson Correlation Coefficient:** Used to measure the linear correlation between two continuous variables. Features with a high correlation with the target variable (positive or negative) are generally more useful.

```
from scipy.stats import pearsonr
correlation, _ = pearsonr(X[:,0], y)
```

- **ANOVA (Analysis of Variance):** Evaluates whether there are significant differences between the means of different categorical groups. It is widely used when the target variable is categorical and the features are continuous.

```
from sklearn.feature_selection import SelectKBest, f_classif
X_new = SelectKBest(f_classif, k=10).fit_transform(X, y)
```

2. Wrapper Methods

Wrapper methods consider a specific learning model and use its performance as a criterion for feature selection. These methods are usually more computationally intensive as they involve evaluating the model multiple times.

- **Recursive Feature Elimination (RFE):** RFE is an iterative method that trains a model and removes the least important features based on the weights assigned by the model. This process is repeated until the desired number of features is reached.

```
from sklearn.feature_selection import RFE
from sklearn.ensemble import RandomForestClassifier
rfe = RFE(estimator=RandomForestClassifier(),
n_features_to_select=10)
X_new = rfe.fit_transform(X, y)
```

- Sequential Feature Selection: This method sequentially includes or excludes features and evaluates the model's performance at each iteration. There are two variants: Forward Selection, which starts with an empty set and adds features, and Backward Elimination, which starts with all features and removes the least relevant ones.

```
from sklearn.feature_selection import SequentialFeatureSelector
sfs = SequentialFeatureSelector(RandomForestClassifier(),
n_features_to_select=10)
X_new = sfs.fit_transform(X, y)
```

3. Embedded Methods

Embedded methods perform feature selection during the model training process. Unlike filter and wrapper methods, these methods are integrated into the model creation and do not require a separate feature selection step.

- **Lasso (Least Absolute Shrinkage and Selection Operator)**: Lasso is a form of linear regression that includes a penalty for the sum of the absolute values of the model coefficients. This penalty tends to shrink the coefficients of less important features to zero, effectively removing them from the model.

```
from sklearn.linear_model import Lasso
lasso = Lasso(alpha=0.1)
lasso.fit(X, y)
selected_features = X[:, lasso.coef_ != 0]
```

- **Elastic Net:** It is a generalization of Lasso that combines the Lasso penalty with Ridge Regression (which penalizes the sum of the squares of the coefficients). This allows handling datasets with highly correlated features.

```
from sklearn.linear_model import ElasticNet
enet = ElasticNet(alpha=1.0, l1_ratio=0.5)
enet.fit(X, y)
selected_features = X[:, enet.coef_ != 0]
```

- **Random Forest Importance:** Decision tree models and random forests provide a natural way to select features by computing the importance of each feature during training. Features that are more frequently used to split nodes are usually more important.

```
from sklearn.ensemble import RandomForestClassifier
model = RandomForestClassifier()
model.fit(X, y)
importances = model.feature_importances_
```

Practical Application

Suppose we are working with a dataset that contains a large number of variables, and we want to use a Random Forest model to predict the class of a sample. We can use RFE to select the most important features and then train the model using only these selected features.

```
from sklearn.datasets import load_iris
from sklearn.ensemble import RandomForestClassifier
from sklearn.feature_selection import RFE
from sklearn.model_selection import train_test_split
from sklearn.metrics import accuracy_score
```

```
# Load the dataset
data = load_iris()
X, y = data.data, data.target

# Split the dataset into training and testing sets
X_train, X_test, y_train, y_test = train_test_split(X, y,
test_size=0.3, random_state=42)

# Apply RFE to select the best features
rfe = RFE(estimator=RandomForestClassifier(),
n_features_to_select=2)
X_train_rfe = rfe.fit_transform(X_train, y_train)
X_test_rfe = rfe.transform(X_test)

# Train the model with the selected features
model = RandomForestClassifier(random_state=42)
model.fit(X_train_rfe, y_train)

# Evaluate the model
y_pred = model.predict(X_test_rfe)
accuracy = accuracy_score(y_test, y_pred)

print(f"Model accuracy with RFE: {accuracy:.4f}")
```

Feature selection is a fundamental process that, if done correctly, can significantly improve the performance and interpretability of machine learning models.

9.1.2. Feature Importance in Machine Learning Models

The importance of features in Machine Learning models is an essential concept that directly influences the predictive capability and interpretability of the models. Understanding and evaluating the importance of each feature allows data scientists and Machine Learning engineers to optimize their models, improve prediction accuracy, and in many cases, reduce computation time and model complexity. Feature importance also plays a crucial role in informed decision-making, especially in contexts where model interpretability is critical, such as in medicine or finance.

1. Concept of feature importance:

Feature importance, in the context of Machine Learning, refers to the extent to which a feature influences a model's prediction. This importance can vary depending on the type of model used and the relationship between the features and the target variable. Some features may have a direct and significant impact on the model's output, while others may have little or no effect. Correctly identifying these differences is vital for building efficient and effective models.

2. Feature importance in different types of models:

Different Machine Learning algorithms assess feature importance in various ways. Below are some common approaches used in different types of models:

- Decision Trees and Random Forests: In these models, the importance of a feature can be determined by evaluating how much it reduces impurity (measured by criteria such as Gini or entropy) at each tree split. Features that are frequently used to split nodes with high information gains are considered more important. In Random Forests, the importance of each feature is averaged across all trees in the model.

```
from sklearn.ensemble import RandomForestClassifier
model = RandomForestClassifier()
model.fit(X, y)
importances = model.feature_importances_
```

- Linear Models (such as Linear or Logistic Regression): In these models, the importance of a feature is directly related to the coefficient assigned to it. A higher absolute value of the coefficient indicates that the feature has a greater impact on the prediction. However, it is important to normalize the features before interpreting the coefficients, especially if the features have different scales.

```
from sklearn.linear_model import LogisticRegression
model = LogisticRegression()
model.fit(X, y)
coefficients = model.coef_
```

- Gradient Boosting Machines (GBMs): Similar to decision trees, in boosting models (such as XGBoost or LightGBM), feature importance is calculated based on how much they contribute to reducing the loss function over the iterations. Features that are selected more often and that contribute significantly to error reduction are considered more important.

```
import xgboost as xgb
model = xgb.XGBClassifier()
model.fit(X, y)
importances = model.feature_importances_
```

3. Methods for assessing feature importance:

There are several methods to assess feature importance in a Machine Learning model:

- **Permutation Feature Importance:** This method evaluates the importance of a feature by measuring the decrease in model accuracy when the feature's values are randomized. If permuting a feature significantly decreases accuracy, that feature is important to the model.

```
from sklearn.inspection import permutation_importance
result = permutation_importance(model, X, y, n_repeats=10,
random_state=42)
importances = result.importances_mean
```

- **SHAP (SHapley Additive exPlanations)**: SHAP is a game-theory-based method that provides a consistent way to assign importance to features. It calculates the contribution of each feature to the model's prediction, considering all possible combinations of features. This and other methods will be covered throughout the book.

```
import shap
explainer = shap.TreeExplainer(model)
shap_values = explainer.shap_values(X)
shap.summary_plot(shap_values, X)
```

- **LIME (Local Interpretable Model-agnostic Explanations):** LIME explains individual predictions of any Machine Learning model by fitting an interpretable model (such as a linear regression) to the local predictions of the complex model. The importance of a feature is measured by its coefficient in this local model. Lime, like SHAP, will be covered throughout the book, as both SHAP and LIME are closely tied to data features, and therefore appear at other relevant points in relation to data features. So do not worry. If you want to work with AI and Big Data it is very important to understand everything thoroughly, and it does not matter how often a term is repeated. Here we work with programming and data, and understanding both the code and the information the data provides is front and center.

```
import lime
from lime.lime_tabular import LimeTabularExplainer
explainer = LimeTabularExplainer(X_train,
feature_names=feature_names, class_names=class_names,
mode='classification')
exp = explainer.explain_instance(X[0], model.predict_proba)
exp.show_in_notebook()
```

4. Practical implications of feature importance:

Correctly assessing feature importance has several practical implications:

- **Dimensionality reduction:** By identifying less important features, they can be removed from the model, which reduces complexity and improves computational efficiency, without sacrificing (or even improving) the model's accuracy.

- **Model interpretability:** Knowing which features are most important allows stakeholders to better interpret the model and make informed decisions. This is especially relevant in sectors where decisions must be justified, such as in medicine or finance.

- **Improved model performance:** Focusing training on the most important features can lead to more accurate and generalizable models by avoiding noise and focusing on the strongest signals.

- **Detection of irrelevant or redundant features:** Evaluating feature importance helps identify features that do not provide relevant information or are highly correlated with other features. These can be removed to avoid issues such as overfitting.

5. Considerations when assessing feature importance:

It is crucial to keep in mind that feature importance can vary depending on the type of model used. A feature that is important in a linear model may not be important in a decision tree model, and vice versa. Additionally, some evaluation techniques, such as permutation or SHAP, can be computationally intensive, especially on large datasets.

It is also important to remember that interpreting feature importance should be done with caution, as the relationship between features and the target variable can be non-linear or interactive, which may not be adequately captured by all evaluation methods.

For example, suppose we are working on a classification model with a dataset where features are correlated. A Random Forest model may identify some features as more important than others, but this could be due to the nature of the model splitting nodes hierarchically, and not necessarily because those features are the most relevant in absolute terms.

In code, we could assess feature importance using a RandomForestClassifier model and the built-in feature importance method:

```
from sklearn.ensemble import RandomForestClassifier
from sklearn.datasets import load_iris
import pandas as pd

# Load the dataset
data = load_iris()
X, y = data.data, data.target
```

```
# Train the Random Forest model
model = RandomForestClassifier(n_estimators=100, random_state=42)
model.fit(X, y)

# Get the feature importances
importances = model.feature_importances_

# Create a DataFrame to visualize the importance
feature_names = data.feature_names
importance_df = pd.DataFrame({'Feature': feature_names,
'Importance': importances})
importance_df = importance_df.sort_values(by='Importance',
ascending=False)

print(importance\_df)
```

This example shows how to identify the most important features in a model, which in turn could guide decision-making on how to improve the model, reduce its complexity, or interpret it better.

Understanding feature importance is a very important step in the development and optimization of Machine Learning models, providing improvements in both accuracy and interpretability, key aspects for real-world applications and therefore vitally important for decision-making.

9.1.3. Tools for Feature Selection

The process of feature selection is a crucial step in building Machine Learning models, as it allows identifying and using only those features that contribute significantly to the model's prediction. There are various tools and libraries that facilitate the implementation of feature selection techniques, both automatic and manual.

1. Scikit-learn

Scikit-learn is one of the most widely used libraries in Python for Machine Learning. It offers several functions for feature selection, including filter-based, wrapper, and embedded methods. Some of the techniques available in Scikit-learn include:

- **SelectKBest:** This technique selects the best features based on a statistical scoring function. For example, the chi-square statistic (chi2) can be used for categorical features or ANOVA (`f_classif`) for continuous features. This method is a type of filter-based feature selection.

```
from sklearn.feature_selection import SelectKBest, f_classif
X_new = SelectKBest(f_classif, k=10).fit_transform(X, y)
```

- **RFE (Recursive Feature Elimination):** This is a wrapper method that selects features by recursively eliminating them and building the model with the remaining features. The goal is to select a subset of features that produce the best model.

```
from sklearn.feature_selection import RFE
from sklearn.linear_model import LogisticRegression
model = LogisticRegression()
rfe = RFE(model, n_features_to_select=10)
X_new = rfe.fit_transform(X, y)
```

- **SelectFromModel:** This technique selects features based on their importance according to a specific model, such as a decision tree model or a linear model with regularization. It is commonly used with models that have coefficients or feature importance attributes, such as random forests.

```
from sklearn.ensemble import RandomForestClassifier
from sklearn.feature_selection import SelectFromModel
model = RandomForestClassifier()
model.fit(X, y)
selector = SelectFromModel(model, prefit=True)
X_new = selector.transform(X)
```

2. XGBoost

XGBoost is an efficient and scalable implementation of gradient boosted decision trees. Besides being a powerful algorithm for classification and regression tasks, XGBoost also offers integrated capabilities for feature selection based on feature importance.

- **Feature importance:** XGBoost calculates the importance of each feature based on gain, coverage, or weight. These measures indicate how important each feature is for improving the model during different iterations of the boosting process.

```
import xgboost as xgb
model = xgb.XGBClassifier()
model.fit(X, y)
importances = model.feature_importances_
```

- **Plot_importance:** This function graphically visualizes feature importance, making it easier to interpret and select the most relevant features.

```
xgb.plot_importance(model)
```

3. LASSO (Least Absolute Shrinkage and Selection Operator)

LASSO is a regularization technique used both for feature selection and to prevent overfitting in linear models. By applying an L1 penalty, LASSO can shrink some feature coefficients to zero, effectively eliminating them from the model.

- LASSO in Scikit-learn: Scikit-learn offers an implementation of LASSO that can be used for feature selection in linear models.

```
from sklearn.linear_model import Lasso
model = Lasso(alpha=0.1)
model.fit(X, y)
coef = model.coef_
```

4. Boruta

Boruta is an algorithm designed to work with random forest models to identify all relevant features. It is an all-or-nothing approach that aims to ensure no important feature is missed in the selection process.

- Using Boruta in Python: The BorutaPy library in Python makes it easy to implement this algorithm.

```
from boruta import BorutaPy
from sklearn.ensemble import RandomForestClassifier
model = RandomForestClassifier()
boruta = BorutaPy(model, n_estimators='auto', verbose=2,
random_state=42)
boruta.fit(X, y)
```

5. FSelector (in R)

FSelector is a library in R that offers multiple feature selection methods, including Chi-square, information gain, and the Random Forest attribute importance method. It is widely used in the R environment due to its versatility.

- Using FSelector in R

```
library(FSelector)
weights <- information.gain(Species~., iris)
subset <- cutoff.k(weights, 2)

print(subset)
```

6. SHAP (SHapley Additive exPlanations)

As we have already seen in the previous section, SHAP is a technique based on game theory that provides interpretable explanations of model predictions. It is particularly useful for feature selection as it quantifies the contribution of each feature to the predictions.

Here is the Python code again

```
import shap
explainer = shap.TreeExplainer(model)
shap_values = explainer.shap_values(X)
shap.summary_plot(shap_values, X)
```

7. LIME (Local Interpretable Model-agnostic Explanations)

We have already started to see LIME in the previous section in its relation to data features. It also provides local explanations of model predictions. It can be used to identify the importance of features in individual predictions, which is useful for feature selection in models that require interpretability.

Here is the code again so you don't have to look it up in the previous section

```
import lime
from lime.lime_tabular import LimeTabularExplainer
explainer = LimeTabularExplainer(X_train,
feature_names=feature_names, class_names=class_names,
mode='classification')
exp = explainer.explain_instance(X[0], model.predict_proba)
exp.show_in_notebook()
```

8. Featuretools

Featuretools is a library in Python designed for automated feature engineering. Although its main focus is generating new features, it can also be used to select the most relevant features by creating new transformations and aggregations of the data.

- Using Featuretools in Python

```
import featuretools as ft
es = ft.EntitySet(id="customers")
es = es.entity_from_dataframe(entity_id="transactions",
dataframe=df, index="id")
feature_matrix, feature_defs = ft.dfs(entityset=es,
target_entity="transactions")
```

9.2. Dimensionality Reduction Techniques

Dimensionality reduction is an essential technique in data preprocessing and in building Machine Learning models, particularly when working with datasets that contain a large number of features or variables. The presence of too many features can not only lead to model overfitting but also increase computational cost and make the model harder to interpret. Additionally, many features may be redundant or irrelevant, which does not contribute to improving model performance. Therefore, dimensionality reduction seeks to simplify the data while preserving as much relevant information as possible. Below are some of the most important and widely used techniques for dimensionality reduction.

We are going to perform a general overview first and then we will dive deeper into PCA, as it is one of the most important parts for data analysis and work, and I can assure you it is one of the most useful. My recommendation is that you familiarize yourself as much as possible with PCA.

1. Principal Component Analysis (PCA): Principal component analysis is a statistical technique that transforms a set of possibly correlated variables into a set of linearly uncorrelated variable values called principal components. The first principal component captures the greatest possible variance in the data, the second component captures the greatest possible variance under the constraint of being orthogonal to the first, and so on. PCA is widely used because it is efficient and easily interpreted, although its main limitation is that the new variables (principal components) may be less interpretable in terms of the problem domain. We will analyze it in depth in the next chapter.

```
from sklearn.decomposition import PCA

# Applying PCA
pca = PCA(n_components=2)
X_reduced = pca.fit_transform(X)
```

2. Linear Discriminant Analysis (LDA): Linear discriminant analysis is another technique that, unlike PCA, is supervised, which means it uses output class information to maximize the separation between classes. LDA tries to find a linear combination of features that best separates two or more classes of data. It is especially useful in classification problems when the classes are well separated in the feature space. We will also analyze it in the next chapter.

```
from sklearn.discriminant_analysis import LinearDiscriminantAnalysis
as LDA
```

```
# Applying LDA
lda = LDA(n_components=2)
X_reduced = lda.fit_transform(X, y)
```

3. Autoencoders: Autoencoders are a type of neural network used to learn a compressed representation of the dataset. An autoencoder consists of two main parts: the encoder, which reduces the dimensionality of the data, and the decoder, which reconstructs the original data from the reduced representation. Autoencoders are especially useful when working with nonlinear and complex data where techniques like PCA may not be effective.

```
from keras.layers import Input, Dense
from keras.models import Model

# Creating a simple autoencoder
input_dim = X.shape[1]
encoding_dim = 2  # Reduction to 2 dimensions

input_layer = Input(shape=(input_dim,))
encoder = Dense(encoding_dim, activation='relu')(input_layer)
decoder = Dense(input_dim, activation='sigmoid')(encoder)

autoencoder = Model(inputs=input_layer, outputs=decoder)
autoencoder.compile(optimizer='adam', loss='mse')
autoencoder.fit(X, X, epochs=50, batch_size=256, shuffle=True)
```

4. t-Distributed Stochastic Neighbor Embedding (t-SNE): t-SNE is a nonlinear dimensionality reduction technique that is particularly useful for visualizing high-dimensional data. It works by minimizing the Kullback-Leibler divergence between the distribution of pairs of points in the high-dimensional space and the distribution in the low-dimensional space. t-SNE is excellent for visualizing the inherent structure of the data, but it is not recommended for large datasets due to its high computational demand.

```
from sklearn.manifold import TSNE

# Applying t-SNE
tsne = TSNE(n_components=2)
X_reduced = tsne.fit_transform(X)
```

5. Multiple Correspondence Analysis (MCA): Multiple correspondence analysis is a technique similar to PCA but designed to handle categorical variables. It is useful in situations where dimensionality reduction is needed for datasets containing multiple categorical variables. MCA transforms the categorical variables into a Euclidean space where the distances reflect the associations between the categories of the variables.

```
# Applying MCA in R
library(FactoMineR)
```

```
res.mca <- MCA(df, ncp=2)
```

6. Kernel PCA: Kernel PCA is an extension of PCA that uses kernel tricks to perform PCA transformation in a nonlinear feature space. This allows Kernel PCA to capture nonlinear relationships in the data, which is an advantage over linear PCA when working with data that is not well represented in a linear space.

```
from sklearn.decomposition import KernelPCA

# Applying Kernel PCA
kpca = KernelPCA(kernel='rbf', n_components=2)
X_reduced = kpca.fit_transform(X)
```

7. Non-Negative Matrix Factorization (NMF): NMF is a technique that factorizes a matrix into two smaller matrices, whose entries are all non-negative. It is mainly used in tasks such as feature extraction and dimensionality reduction in data like images and texts. The non-negativity constraint facilitates the interpretation of the factors in terms of additive combinations.

```
from sklearn.decomposition import NMF

# Applying NMF
nmf = NMF(n_components=2)
X_reduced = nmf.fit_transform(X)
```

8. Isomap: Isomap is a nonlinear dimensionality reduction technique that seeks to preserve the geodesic distances between all points in the dataset. It is particularly useful when the data lies on a low-dimensional manifold embedded in a high-dimensional space. Isomap is suitable for dimensionality reduction in data with manifold structure.

```
from sklearn.manifold import Isomap

# Applying Isomap
isomap = Isomap(n_components=2)
X_reduced = isomap.fit_transform(X)
```

9. Curse of Dimensionality: The curse of dimensionality refers to various phenomena that occur when working with data in high-dimensional spaces. As the number of dimensions increases, the data tends to spread out more, and the distances between data points become less meaningful. Dimensionality reduction techniques are essential to mitigate these effects and improve the efficiency of machine learning algorithms.

10. Feature Selection vs. Dimensionality Reduction

Although feature selection and dimensionality reduction may seem similar, they differ in their approaches. Feature selection involves removing irrelevant or redundant features, while dimensionality reduction transforms the features into a lower-dimensional space. Both methods can be used complementarily to improve model performance.

The choice of the appropriate dimensionality reduction technique does not depend on you but depends on the type of data, the nature of the relationship between the variables, and the goal of the analysis. Linear techniques such as PCA and LDA are efficient and easy to interpret, while nonlinear techniques such as t-SNE and autoencoders are more powerful at capturing complex relationships, although they can be more difficult to interpret and more computationally expensive.

10.1. Principal Component Analysis (PCA)

Now let's look at it in detail. Principal component analysis is one of the most popular and widely used techniques for dimensionality reduction. Its main goal is to transform a set of possibly correlated variables into a new set of uncorrelated variables called principal components. This transformation is carried out so that the first principal component captures the maximum possible variance in the data, the second principal component captures the maximum possible variance under the constraint of being orthogonal to the first, and so on. This unsupervised technique is based on the mathematics of singular value decomposition (SVD) and has extensive applications in areas such as data compression, visualization, and noise reduction.

The PCA process involves several fundamental steps, from centering the data to constructing the principal components. Below are the most relevant aspects of PCA:

1. Centering the data: Before applying PCA, it is crucial that the data are centered, meaning the mean of each feature is subtracted. This step ensures that the calculated principal components reflect variability relative to the mean of the data. Mathematically, this involves transforming the data set X into a new set X' where each column has a mean of zero.

```
import numpy as np

# Suppose X is our data matrix with n samples and m features
X_meaned = X - np.mean(X, axis=0)
```

2. Calculating the covariance matrix: The covariance matrix is fundamental in PCA because its decomposition allows identifying the directions in which the data vary most. The covariance matrix C is calculated as:

$$C = \frac{1}{\mathrm{n} - 1} X'^T X'$$

where X' is the centered data matrix. The covariance matrix is symmetric, and its eigenvalues and eigenvectors contain the information needed to construct the principal components.

```
cov_matrix = np.cov(X_meaned, rowvar=False)
```

3. Decomposing the covariance matrix: Next, the eigenvalue decomposition of the covariance matrix is performed. The eigenvalues (λ) indicate the variance explained by each principal component, while the eigenvectors (v) provide the directions in the original feature space.

```
eigen_values, eigen_vectors = np.linalg.eigh(cov_matrix)
```

4. Selecting principal components: The eigenvalues are sorted from largest to smallest, and the corresponding eigenvectors form the directions of the principal components. It is common to select only the first principal components that explain a significant percentage of the total variance. This allows reducing the dimensionality of the data set while preserving most of the original information.

```
# Sort eigenvalues and eigenvectors
sorted_index = np.argsort(eigen_values)[::-1]
sorted_eigenvalue = eigen_values[sorted_index]
sorted_eigenvectors = eigen_vectors[:, sorted_index]
```

5. Transforming the data: The original data are projected onto the new directions of the principal components to obtain a new reduced data set. This is done by multiplying the original centered matrix by the selected eigenvector matrix.

```
# Select the first n principal components
n_components = 2
eigenvector_subset = sorted_eigenvectors[:, 0:n_components]

# Transform the data
X_reduced = np.dot(X_meaned, eigenvector_subset)
```

6. Interpreting the principal components: Each principal component is a linear combination of the original variables, and the weight of each variable in this combination is given by the elements of the corresponding eigenvector. In practical terms, the first principal components are usually the most interpretable because they capture the main structure of the data. However, since PCA is a linear transformation, the new variables (principal components) may be less intuitive or interpretable compared to the original variables.

7. Explained variance and choosing the number of components: A key aspect of PCA is deciding how many principal components to keep. This is based on the analysis of the cumulative explained variance ratio, which shows how much information (variance) from the original data is retained as more principal components are added. The choice of the number of components is usually based on a predefined explained variance threshold (for example, 95 percent).

```
import matplotlib.pyplot as plt

# Calculate cumulative explained variance
explained_variance = np.cumsum(sorted_eigenvalue) /
np.sum(sorted_eigenvalue)

# Plot cumulative explained variance
plt.plot(range(1, len(explained_variance) + 1), explained_variance)
plt.xlabel('Number of Components')
plt.ylabel('Cumulative Explained Variance')
plt.show()
```

8. Applications and limitations of PCA: PCA is widely used in areas such as data compression, noise reduction, visualization of high-dimensional data, and as a preprocessing step in building machine learning models. However, PCA has some limitations. For example, it only captures linear relationships between variables, which may not be suitable in cases where the relationships are nonlinear. Additionally, PCA is sensitive to the scale of the variables, so it is recommended to normalize or standardize the data before applying the technique.

Principal component analysis is essential for simplifying complex data sets, making analysis and visualization easier without losing too much relevant information. Although it is a technique based on linearity, its simplicity and effectiveness make it a popular option for a wide variety of applications in machine learning and data analysis.

10.2. Linear Discriminant Analysis (LDA)

Linear discriminant analysis is a supervised dimensionality reduction and classification technique used primarily when you want to maximize the separation between different classes in a data set. Unlike PCA, which is an unsupervised technique that seeks to maximize the total variance of the data, LDA seeks to maximize the variance between classes while minimizing the variance within classes, making it a powerful tool for classification.

LDA not only reduces the dimensionality of the data but also preserves the discriminative information that is crucial for distinguishing between different classes. It is commonly used in problems where the classes are well defined and the goal is to project the data into a lower-dimensional space that maximizes class separability.

Let's look in detail at the key steps and concepts involved in LDA:

1. Assumptions and objectives of LDA: LDA is based on some fundamental assumptions. The first is that the classes should follow a Gaussian distribution with identical covariance for all classes, although with different means. The main objective of LDA is to find a linear projection of the data that maximizes the distance between the class means and minimizes the variance within each class. This is achieved by projecting the data into a new space where the signal-to-noise ratio (the ratio between the variance between classes and the variance within classes) is maximized.

2. Calculating means and covariance matrices: To begin, the means of each class and the overall mean of the data are calculated. The within class scatter matrices (or covariance) S_W and the between-class scatter matrices S_B are calculated. These matrices are crucial for constructing the linear discriminant because they reflect the variance within and between the classes. The within-class scatter matrix S_W is:

$$S_W = \sum_{i=1}^{C} \sum_{x_j \in X_i} (x_j - \mu_i)(x_j - \mu_i)^T$$

where C is the number of classes, X_i are the samples belonging to class i, and μ_i is the mean of class i.

The between-class scatter matrix S_B is:

$$S_B = \sum_{i=1}^{C} N_i \, (\mu_i - \mu)(\mu_i - \mu)^T$$

where N_i is the number of samples in class i, and μ is the overall mean of all samples.

```
import numpy as np

def compute_mean_vectors(X, y):
mean_vectors = []
for cl in np.unique(y):
mean_vectors.append(np.mean(X[y == cl], axis=0))
return mean_vectors

def scatter_matrices(X, y, mean_vectors):
n_features = X.shape[1]
S_W = np.zeros((n_features, n_features))
S_B = np.zeros((n_features, n_features))
overall_mean = np.mean(X, axis=0)
for cl, mv in zip(np.unique(y), mean_vectors):
class_sc_mat = np.zeros((n_features, n_features))
for row in X[y == cl]:
row, mv = row.reshape(n_features, 1), mv.reshape(n_features, 1)
class_sc_mat += (row - mv).dot((row - mv).T)
S_W += class_sc_mat
n = X[y == cl].shape[0]
mean_diff = (mv - overall_mean).reshape(n_features, 1)
S_B += n * mean_diff.dot(mean_diff.T)
return S_W, S_B
```

3. Determination of eigenvalues and eigenvectors: To find the directions of maximum discrimination, the characteristic equation of the matrix $S_W^{-1}S_B$ is solved, whose eigenvalues and eigenvectors provide the optimal projection direction. The eigenvalues reflect the magnitude of between class variance captured by the corresponding projection. The eigenvectors corresponding to the largest eigenvalues form the bases of the new dimensions onto which the data will be projected.

```
eig_vals, eig_vecs = np.linalg.eig(np.linalg.inv(S_W).dot(S_B))
```

4. Selection of discriminant components: The eigenvalues are sorted in descending order, and the eigenvectors corresponding to the largest eigenvalues are selected to form the projection matrix. This matrix transforms the original data into the lower dimensional space that maximizes class separation.

```
eig_pairs = [(np.abs(eig_vals[i]), eig_vecs[:, i]) for i in
range(len(eig_vals))]
eig_pairs = sorted(eig_pairs, key=lambda k: k[0], reverse=True)

W = np.hstack([eig_pairs[i][1].reshape(X.shape[1], 1) for i in
range(n_components)])
```

5. Data transformation and projection: Finally, the original data are projected onto the new space using the projection matrix W. This reduces the dimensionality of the data while preserving the relevant information for classification.

```
X_lda = X.dot(W)
```

6. Applications and common uses: LDA is commonly used in classification problems where it is desired to reduce the dimensionality of the data while maintaining clear separation between classes. It is especially useful in problems where classes overlap, and the model needs to find a projection that maximizes discrimination. Some examples include image classification, pattern recognition, and bioinformatics. LDA has also been used for dimensionality reduction before applying other machine learning algorithms, such as SVM or KNN, to improve their performance in terms of computation time and accuracy.

7. Comparison with PCA: Unlike PCA, which does not consider the class to which each sample belongs, LDA is supervised and uses class information to find the projections. This makes LDA more suitable when the goal is classification rather than simply reducing dimensionality without a specific task in mind.

8. Limitations of LDA: LDA assumes that the classes have Gaussian distributions with equal covariance across classes, which may not be the case in practice. Additionally, LDA can have issues when the classes are not well linearly separable or when the number of samples is small compared to the number of features.

10.3. Applications and Use Cases

Dimensionality reduction techniques such as principal component analysis and linear discriminant analysis have extensive and varied applications in the field of machine learning and data analysis. Their use is justified by the need to simplify models, improve computational efficiency, and effectively handle the problem of the "curse of dimensionality". Below are some of the most relevant applications and use cases of these techniques, covering different areas and types of problems.

Data preprocessing for predictive modeling: In many machine learning applications, datasets may contain a large number of variables that, if all used, can generate complex and overfitting-prone models. In such cases, reducing dimensionality before training the model is crucial. PCA is commonly used to transform the feature set into a new lower-dimensional space that retains most of the original variance. This step not only simplifies the model but also reduces training time and improves the model's generalization to new data. On the other hand, LDA is used in classification tasks to project the data into a space that maximizes class separation, which is particularly useful in multiclass classification problems.

Image recognition and computer vision: In computer vision applications such as facial recognition and image classification, high-resolution images have thousands of pixels, each representing a dimension in the feature space. PCA is commonly applied to reduce the number of pixels while preserving the most important information, facilitating analysis and classification. For example, in the Eigenfaces technique used for facial recognition, PCA is applied to identify the principal directions of variation in a set of facial images, reducing dimensions and enabling a more compact and manageable representation of faces. LDA is also used in combination with PCA in these cases to enhance discrimination between different image categories.

Bioinformatics and genomic data analysis: In bioinformatics, the analysis of genomic data such as gene expression profiles or DNA sequencing data often involves a large number of variables (genes) with a limited number of samples. This type of high-dimensional, low-sample data is particularly suitable for dimensionality reduction. PCA is used to identify patterns in genomic data and reduce the number of features to those that explain most of the variability in the data. LDA, on the other hand, is useful for classifying cancer types or diseases based on gene expression profiles by finding linear combinations of genes that best distinguish between different disease classes.

Financial analysis and risk reduction: In finance, portfolio management and risk analysis involve working with large amounts of market data, such as stock prices, interest rates, and other economic indicators. PCA is widely used to identify latent factors that explain variations in these data, helping fund managers simplify risk analysis and diversify their portfolios based on these factors. This technique allows reducing the number of variables to consider, which is especially useful in building risk models and identifying the main sources of variability in the markets.

Signal processing and time series analysis: In signal processing, such as in electroencephalography (EEG) or seismology, the recorded signals often contain noise and redundancies. PCA is used to extract the principal components that contain the most relevant information, removing noise and reducing the dimensionality of the signals. This allows more efficient analysis and the identification of significant patterns in the signals. LDA can also be applied when the goal is to classify these signals into different categories, such as identifying types of brain activity from EEG data.

Marketing and customer behavior analysis: In marketing, dimensionality reduction techniques are used to analyze large volumes of customer data, such as purchase transactions, online behavior, and responses to advertising campaigns. PCA can be used to segment customers based on their behavior patterns, allowing companies to customize their offers and marketing strategies. Additionally, LDA can be applied to categorize customers into predefined groups based on their characteristics and behaviors, facilitating decision-making in targeted marketing and campaign optimization.

Survey and questionnaire data analysis: Data obtained from surveys and questionnaires often have many questions (dimensions) that may be correlated with each other. PCA is used to identify the underlying latent dimensions that explain most of the variability in responses, helping researchers better understand patterns in the data and reduce the number of questions needed in later analyses. This is especially useful in social and behavioral studies, where the goal is to summarize respondents' attitudes and opinions into a smaller set of factors.

Applications in the field of economics: In economics, macroeconomic models and time series are often composed of a large number of variables, such as interest rates, inflation, GDP, and other economic measures. PCA is used to reduce the dimensionality of these models, allowing economists to identify the main factors driving changes in the economy. This facilitates modeling and predicting key economic variables as well as identifying relationships between different economic indicators.

These examples illustrate how dimensionality reduction techniques such as PCA and LDA are fundamental in a wide range of applications across different fields, from bioinformatics and computer vision to financial analysis and marketing. The ability to simplify and focus data without losing critical information is what makes these techniques so valuable in practice. These techniques not only improve computational efficiency but also help create more interpretable and robust models, which is crucial in many real-world applications as you can surely already imagine.

11. Construction and Training of Models

11.1. Dataset Preparation

The preparation of the dataset is a fundamental step in the construction and training of Machine Learning models. This process ensures that the data is in an optimal state to be used by learning algorithms, which directly influences the performance and accuracy of the model. The quality and structure of the dataset largely determine the model's ability to generalize to unseen data and, therefore, its usefulness in practical applications. Below are the main aspects and steps involved in preparing a dataset for training Machine Learning models.

1. Data collection

The first step in preparing the dataset is the collection of relevant and sufficient data for the specific Machine Learning task. The data can come from various sources such as databases, CSV files, APIs, sensors, surveys, or directly from the web. It is important to ensure that the collected data is representative of the problem being addressed. At this stage, it is also necessary to consider the amount of data required to train an effective model, bearing in mind that more data generally allows for more robust models but also increases the time and resources needed for processing and training.

2. Exploratory Data Analysis (EDA)

Before proceeding with cleaning and transforming the data, it is crucial to perform an Exploratory Data Analysis. EDA allows understanding the distribution of the data, identifying patterns, detecting anomalies, and observing relationships between variables. During this stage, graphs, descriptive statistics, and other analytical tools can be used to obtain an overview of the data. EDA helps discover if there are outliers, missing data, or if some variables are not useful for the model, which will guide the next preprocessing phases.

3. Data cleaning

Data cleaning is a critical process to ensure that the data is of high quality. This step includes removing duplicates, correcting typographical errors, and removing or imputing missing data, among others. It is important to ensure that the data is as clean as possible, as errors at this stage can propagate and negatively affect the model's performance. Cleaning also involves managing outliers, which can distort results if not handled properly.

4. Data transformation

Once the data is clean, data transformation should be considered to make it more suitable for the learning algorithm to be used. This process may include normalization or standardization of numerical variables, encoding of categorical variables, and the creation of new features derived from existing ones. Normalization and standardization are particularly important in algorithms that depend on the distance between data points, such as k-means or SVM, since differences in variable scales can influence the results. Regarding categorical variables, techniques such as one-hot encoding are used to convert categories into a numerical representation that models can process.

5. Dataset splitting
To properly evaluate the performance of a Machine Learning model, it is essential to split the dataset into training and test sets. Generally, it is recommended to reserve between 20% and 30% of the data for testing, although this proportion may vary depending on the size of the dataset and the nature of the problem. In addition to this basic split, cross-validation is commonly performed during training to ensure that the model does not overfit to a specific subset of the data. In cross-validation, the dataset is divided into k subsets, and the model is trained k times, each time using a different subset as the test set and the rest as the training set.

6. Handling class imbalance
In classification problems, it is common for classes to be unbalanced, meaning that some classes are overrepresented in the dataset. This imbalance can cause the model to be biased toward the majority class, ignoring or misclassifying the minority class. To handle this problem, techniques such as oversampling the minority class, undersampling the majority class, or using methods like SMOTE (Synthetic Minority Over-sampling Technique), which generates synthetic examples of the minority class, can be applied. Class weights in the learning algorithm can also be adjusted to compensate for the imbalance.

7. Feature engineering and feature selection
Feature engineering involves creating new variables from existing ones that can improve the model's performance. This may include creating interactions between variables, transforming existing variables, or creating temporal aggregates in the case of time series. Feature selection, on the other hand, involves identifying and retaining only the most relevant features for the model, eliminating those that are irrelevant or redundant. Feature selection techniques, such as importance-based selection or backward stepwise elimination, help reduce the dimensionality of the dataset, improving the model's efficiency and interpretability.

8. Handling temporal and sequential data
When working with temporal or sequential data, such as time series or sensor data, it is important to consider the temporal structure of the data. The order and temporal dependency between observations must be respected during data preparation. In these cases, additional variables can be created to capture trends, seasonality, or temporal lags. Additionally, care must be taken when splitting the data to ensure that there is no temporal data leakage between the training and test sets, which could lead to an inaccurate evaluation of the model's performance.

9. Documentation and reproducibility
It is essential to document the entire data preparation process, including the decisions made at each step and the scripts used to perform the transformations. This ensures the reproducibility of the work and allows other researchers or professionals to replicate and understand the process that led to the model's construction. Proper documentation also facilitates debugging and process adjustments in future iterations of the model.

Each of these steps must be carefully executed to ensure that the Machine Learning model can effectively learn from the data and generalize well to unseen data.

11.2. Model Training Techniques

Model training in Machine Learning is a critical stage where algorithms learn patterns from data to make future predictions or classifications. There are various model training techniques, each with its own characteristics, advantages, and disadvantages. These are some of the most commonly used techniques in model training.

One of the most common techniques is linear regression, which is used to model the relationship between a continuous dependent variable and one or more independent variables. During training, the model learns the coefficients that best fit the training data, minimizing the difference between the model's predictions and the actual values. This adjustment is done using a process known as "minimization of the sum of squared errors."

In contrast, logistic regression is used when the dependent variable is categorical, commonly binary. Instead of predicting a continuous value, the model estimates the probability that an observation belongs to a particular class. Training in logistic regression involves optimizing the likelihood function, which measures the agreement between the model's predictions and the actual classes in the training data.

Another training technique is the training of neural networks, which is based on adjusting the weights of the connections between neurons in a network. This process is carried out through the backpropagation algorithm, which iteratively adjusts the weights to minimize a cost function, generally using variants of the gradient descent method. Neural networks can be very powerful, especially in complex tasks such as image classification or natural language processing, but they also require large volumes of data and significant computing power.

Decision trees represent another popular technique for training classification and regression models. A decision tree is trained by repeatedly splitting the data into subsets based on the feature that provides the greatest reduction in impurity, measured by metrics such as entropy or variance. The goal is to create a branched structure where each leaf represents a class or a prediction value. To improve accuracy and reduce the risk of overfitting, techniques such as tree pruning or tree combinations, as in the case of random forests, can be used.

Training support vector machines (which we have already discussed earlier) is another technique used in classification and regression. The goal of SVM is to find the hyperplane that best separates the classes in the feature space. During training, SVM optimizes the margin between the classes closest to the hyperplane, known as support vectors. There are versions of SVM for nonlinear problems that use the kernel trick to project the data into a higher-dimensional space where they can be linearly separable.

A technique that has gained popularity is the training of ensemble models, which combine multiple base models to improve overall performance. There are several forms of ensemble methods, such as bagging and boosting. In the case of bagging, as in random forests, multiple models are trained on different subsets of the data and their predictions are combined to form a single final prediction. Boosting, on the other hand, trains models sequentially, so that each subsequent model tries to correct the errors made by the previous models.

Additionally, an advanced technique is the training of deep neural networks (Deep Learning). This type of training involves multiple layers of neurons (hence the term "deep"), where each layer extracts increasingly abstract features from the data. The training process in Deep Learning is similar to that of traditional neural networks but on a much larger scale, both in terms of the number of parameters to be adjusted and the computing capacity required.
Finally, model training must include a careful approach to avoid overfitting, where the model fits too closely to the training data and loses the ability to generalize to new data. This can be mitigated through techniques such as cross-validation, the use of regularization, and early stopping in the case of neural networks.

It is essential to choose the appropriate training technique according to the nature of the problem, the available data, and the model's objective. Each technique has its own considerations regarding result interpretation, scalability, and training time, so the selection must be aligned with the specific needs of the project, always keeping in mind the complexity, which undoubtedly affects the work.

11.3. Hyperparameter Tuning and Evaluation

Hyperparameter tuning and evaluation is a crucial stage in the machine learning model training process, as hyperparameters control the behavior of the model and its ability to learn from data. Unlike parameters learned during training, such as weights in a neural network, hyperparameters must be set before training and determine fundamental aspects of the learning process. Proper selection and tuning of these hyperparameters is essential to maximize the model's performance on unseen data.

There are several methods to tune hyperparameters, and one of the most common is grid search. This method involves defining a set of possible values for each hyperparameter and training the model for all possible combinations of these values. Although this approach ensures that all combinations are explored, it can be computationally expensive, especially when the number of hyperparameters and possible values is large. Grid search is exhaustive, but its main limitation is scalability, as the number of combinations grows exponentially with the number of hyperparameters.

Another more computationally efficient technique is random search. Instead of testing all possible combinations, this method randomly selects combinations of hyperparameter values within the defined ranges. This allows covering a wide area of the search space with fewer trials, which can be beneficial when time and resources are limited. Studies have shown that, in many cases, random search can find hyperparameter combinations that are just as good or even better than grid search in less time.

An advanced technique for hyperparameter optimization is Bayesian optimization. This approach uses probabilistic models to estimate the objective function and selects the hyperparameters that are likely to improve the model's performance. Unlike the previous methods, Bayesian optimization does not treat each hyperparameter trial independently but uses information from previous trials to make more informed choices in subsequent iterations. This can lead to faster and more efficient optimization, especially in problems where hyperparameter tuning is costly.

Hyperparameter tuning should also be accompanied by rigorous evaluation to avoid issues such as overfitting. A common practice is to use cross-validation to evaluate model performance on multiple partitions of the dataset. In k-fold cross-validation, for example, the data is divided into k subsets, and the model is trained on k-1 subsets and evaluated on the remaining subset. This process is repeated k times, changing the evaluation subset each time, and the results are averaged. This provides a more robust estimate of model performance and helps ensure that the selected hyperparameters work well in general, not just on a specific partition of the data.

It is also important to consider regularization techniques during hyperparameter tuning. Regularization is a strategy used to penalize model complexity and prevent overfitting. In regression models, regularization terms such as L1 regularization (Lasso) or L2 regularization (Ridge) add an additional term to the loss function that penalizes the model's coefficients. The penalty value is controlled by a hyperparameter that must be carefully tuned. In neural networks, regularization can include techniques such as dropout, where certain neurons are randomly ignored during training to prevent the model from becoming too reliant on any specific set of neurons.

Early stopping should be considered as part of the hyperparameter tuning process, especially in deep neural networks. Early stopping monitors the model's performance on a validation set during training and halts the process when performance starts to degrade, indicating that the model is beginning to overfit the training data. The stopping point becomes an additional hyperparameter that needs to be tuned to achieve an optimal balance between learning and generalization.

To illustrate how these concepts are implemented in code, here is a simple example using `scikit-learn` in Python:

```
from sklearn.datasets import load_iris
from sklearn.model_selection import GridSearchCV
from sklearn.ensemble import RandomForestClassifier
from sklearn.model_selection import cross_val_score

# Load the Iris dataset
data = load_iris()
X, y = data.data, data.target

# Define the model
model = RandomForestClassifier()
# Define the hyperparameters for grid search
param_grid = {
'n_estimators': [50, 100, 200],
'max_depth': [None, 10, 20, 30],
'min_samples_split': [2, 5, 10]
}

# Implement grid search with cross-validation
grid_search = GridSearchCV(estimator=model, param_grid=param_grid,
cv=5)
grid_search.fit(X, y)

# Best set of hyperparameters
best_params = grid_search.best_params_
print("Best hyperparameters found:", best_params)

# Evaluate the model with the best hyperparameters
best_model = grid_search.best_estimator_
```

```
scores = cross_val_score(best_model, X, y, cv=5)

print("Average accuracy with the best hyperparameters:",
scores.mean())
```

In this code, grid search is used to tune the hyperparameters of a Random Forest model, and evaluation is done using cross-validation. This combination of techniques ensures that the resulting model is well-tuned and generalizes well to new data.

Hyperparameter tuning and evaluation is a task that requires a deep understanding of the model, the data, and the problem at hand, and must be carried out carefully to maximize model effectiveness.

12. Predictive and Descriptive Analysis

Predictive and descriptive analysis plays a crucial role in the interpretation and utilization of data within Artificial Intelligence and Big Data systems. These approaches are used to extract value from data by identifying patterns, making predictions about future behavior, and providing a deep understanding of what is happening in the data.

Descriptive analysis focuses on summarizing and explaining what has already happened. This type of analysis is the starting point for data exploration, where characteristics and patterns in historical data are examined. By using descriptive statistics, charts, and other techniques, descriptive analysis allows analysts to understand distributions, trends, and relationships in the data. It is fundamental for the creation of reports, dashboards, and executive summaries that help organizations better understand their current situation and make decisions based on what the data reveals about past events. This approach is key in areas such as fraud detection, sales analysis, and customer segmentation, where understanding past patterns is essential for informed decision-making.

On the other hand, predictive analysis goes a step further by using mathematical models and algorithms to forecast future outcomes based on historical data. This type of analysis relies on Machine Learning techniques and advanced statistics to build models that can predict behaviors, trends, and future events with a certain degree of probability. In this context, predictive analysis not only relies on identifying past patterns but also extrapolates them to make predictions. It is widely used in a variety of applications, such as demand forecasting in the supply chain, failure prediction in predictive maintenance, credit risk assessment in the financial sector, and personalized marketing offers. The ability to anticipate future events allows organizations not only to react but also to be proactive in making strategic decisions.

The success of predictive analysis largely depends on the quality of the prediction models and the data used to train them. Regression and classification algorithms, for example, are fundamental in this type of analysis. Regression is used to predict continuous values, such as future sales, while classification models are applied to predict categories or classes, such as whether a customer will buy a product or not. Within predictive analysis, there are also more advanced techniques such as neural networks and time series models, which allow for capturing complex patterns and dependencies in the data.

Time series analysis is a specialized branch within predictive analysis that focuses on modeling and forecasting data that are sequential over time, such as the daily sales of a store, stock prices, or production levels in a factory. ARIMA (AutoRegressive Integrated Moving Average) models and recurrent neural networks (RNNs) are advanced techniques used in this field to capture both trends and seasonality in temporal data. These models allow for accurate predictions and help companies better plan their resources and strategies based on forecasts of future events.

Clustering and segmentation, although techniques that can fall within descriptive analysis, can also be used in a predictive context. By grouping data into segments or clusters, predictive models can be refined and personalized for each specific group, increasing the accuracy of predictions. For example, in marketing, customer segmentation allows predictive models to more accurately anticipate purchasing behavior within each specific segment.

It is important to note that the accuracy and usefulness of predictive and descriptive analysis are closely tied to the quality of the data and the model's ability to generalize well. This is where the process of data preprocessing and cleaning comes into play, because without quality data, even the best models will fail to provide useful predictions.

12.1. Regression and Classification Algorithms

12.1.1. Linear and Logistic Regression

Linear regression and logistic regression are two of the most fundamental algorithms in predictive analysis, mainly used to model the relationship between variables and make predictions based on available data. Although both methods share some similarities in terms of their basic structure, they are applied in different contexts and produce different types of results, making them indispensable tools in the field of Machine Learning and data analysis.

Linear regression is a statistical model that assumes a linear relationship between a dependent variable (the one to be predicted) and one or more independent variables (the features or inputs). This relationship is expressed through a linear equation, where the dependent variable is a linear combination of the independent variables plus an error or noise term. The general formula for simple linear regression with a single independent variable is:

$$y = \beta_0 + \beta_{1x} + \epsilon$$

Where:

- y is the dependent variable.
- x is the independent variable.
- β_0 is the intercept, the value of y when $x = 0$.
- β_1 is the slope of the line, indicating the change in y per unit change in x.
- ϵ is the error term, which captures the influence of other variables not included in the model.

In multiple linear regression, where there are several independent variables, the equation expands to:

$$y = \beta_0 + \beta_1 x_1 + \beta_2 x_2 + \cdots + \beta_n x_n + \epsilon$$

This model is mainly used in situations where the goal is to predict a continuous value, such as the price of a house based on its size and location, or the temperature depending on various weather conditions. The training of the model involves finding the optimal values of $\beta_0, \beta_1, \dots \beta_n$ that minimize the difference between the model's predictions and the actual observed values, which is typically achieved using the method of least squares.

On the other hand, logistic regression, although similar in structure to linear regression, is used to predict a categorical outcome, usually binary, such as yes/no, true/false, or the presence/absence of a characteristic. Instead of directly modeling the dependent variable, logistic regression models the probability of an event occurring, using the logistic or sigmoid function to ensure that predictions are in the range of 0 to 1:

$$P(y = 1|x) = \frac{1}{1 + e^{-(\beta_0 + \beta_1 x)}}$$

Where:

- $P(y = 1|x)$ is the probability that the dependent variable is 1 given the value of x.
- x is the base of the natural logarithm.
- β_0 and β_1 are the model coefficients, similar to those in linear regression.

In logistic regression, the model's objective is to find the values of β_0 and β_1 that maximize the likelihood of the observed data under the model. This is generally achieved through an optimization process known as maximum likelihood estimation, rather than the method of least squares used in linear regression.

An important feature of logistic regression is its ability to handle classification problems where the dependent variable has two or more categories. Although the basic logistic regression model applies to binary problems, there are extensions such as multinomial logistic regression for problems with more than two categories.

The use of linear regression is common in situations where the relationship between variables is linear and the goal is to predict a numerical value. For example, a linear regression model could be used to predict a company's revenue based on variables such as advertising spending and the number of employees.

In contrast, logistic regression is widely used in classification problems. A typical example would be predicting whether a customer will buy a product based on their demographic data and previous purchasing behavior. Here, the goal is to predict a probability of class membership, not a direct numerical value.

Regarding implementation in code, below is a basic example of how both types of regression could be implemented using Python and the `Scikit-learn` library:

```
from sklearn.model_selection import train_test_split
from sklearn.linear_model import LinearRegression, LogisticRegres-
sion
from sklearn.metrics import mean_squared_error, accuracy_score
from sklearn.preprocessing import StandardScaler

# Let's assume X is the feature set and y is the target variable.

# Split the data into training and testing sets
X_train, X_test, y_train, y_test = train_test_split(X, y,
test_size=0.2, random_state=42)
```

```
# Scale the data
scaler = StandardScaler()
X_train_scaled = scaler.fit_transform(X_train)
X_test_scaled = scaler.transform(X_test)

# Linear Regression
print("Linear Regression")

# Create the linear regression model
linear_model = LinearRegression()
linear_model.fit(X_train, y_train)

# Make predictions
y_pred_linear = linear_model.predict(X_test)

# Evaluate the model
mse = mean_squared_error(y_test, y_pred_linear)
print(f'Mean Squared Error: {mse}')

# Logistic Regression
print("\nLogistic Regression")

# Create the logistic regression model with more iterations
logistic_model = LogisticRegression(max_iter=1000)
logistic_model.fit(X_train_scaled, y_train)

# Make predictions
y_pred_logistic = logistic_model.predict(X_test_scaled)

# Evaluate the model
accuracy = accuracy_score(y_test, y_pred_logistic)
print(f'Accuracy: {accuracy}')
```

This code, it shows how to train and evaluate a linear regression model and a logistic regression model using `Scikit-learn`. Linear regression is evaluated using the mean squared error (MSE), while logistic regression is evaluated using accuracy, which measures the proportion of correct predictions.

As you can see, both linear and logistic regression are tools for predictive analysis, but each is suitable for different types of problems. Linear regression is ideal for predicting continuous values and modeling linear relationships, while logistic regression is crucial for classification problems, providing a robust way to model probabilities and make categorical predictions. Understanding when and how to apply each is fundamental to success in data analysis and the construction of effective predictive models.

12.1.2. Support Vector Machines (SVM)

Although we have already mentioned them, let's now talk more in depth about support vector machines. These, the SVM, are a supervised learning technique used for both classification and regression problems, although their most frequent use is in classification tasks. SVM is particularly effective in situations where the goal is to find a clear and robust decision boundary between different data classes, especially in datasets where the classes are not linearly separable.

The basic principle behind SVM is to identify an optimal hyperplane that separates the data classes in a multidimensional feature space. In binary classification problems, the hyperplane is a line in two dimensions, a plane in three dimensions, and so on in higher dimensions. This hyperplane is chosen in such a way that it maximizes the "margin" between the classes, where the margin is defined as the distance between the hyperplane and the closest data points from each class, known as support vectors.

The problem of finding the optimal hyperplane can be formulated as an optimization problem, whose objective is to maximize the margin between the classes. Mathematically, it can be expressed as follows:

Given a training set $(x_1, y_1), (x_2, y_2), \dots, (x_n, y_n)$, where x_i are the feature vectors and y_i are the corresponding labels (generally y_i is +1 or -1 for binary classification problems), the goal is to find a vector w and a bias b such that the hyperplane defined by $w \ \ x + b = 0$ separates the data classes. The optimal hyperplane is the one that maximizes the distance (margin) between the data points of the two classes closest to that hyperplane.

In mathematical terms, this can be formulated as the following optimization problem:

$$min = \frac{1}{2}||w||^2 \text{ subject to } y_i(w \cdot x_i + b) \geq 1 \text{ for all i}$$

The term $\frac{1}{2}||w||^2$ is a form of regularization that minimizes the norm of the vector w, which helps to find the hyperplane that maximizes the margin.

In many cases, data classes are not linearly separable in the original feature space. This is where SVM extends its power through the use of "kernel tricks" or "kernel trick". The basic idea of the kernel is to map the original data to a higher-dimensional feature space where the classes are linearly separable. The most common kernels include the linear kernel, polynomial kernel, and the radial basis function (RBF) kernel. The latter is especially popular in practical applications due to its ability to handle complex nonlinear relationships.

The RBF kernel is defined as:

$$K(x_i, x_j) = \exp\left(-\gamma \left\|x_i - x_j\right\|^2\right)$$

where γ is a parameter that controls the range of influence of a single training example.

In addition to classification problems, SVM can also be used for regression, known as "SVR" (Support Vector Regression). Instead of finding a hyperplane that separates the classes, SVR tries to find a hyperplane that is as close as possible to the data points, but within an acceptable error margin.

The practical implementation of SVM in Python can be easily done using the `Scikit-learn` library, which offers an accessible interface and allows experimenting with different kernels and configurations. Here is a basic example of how to train an SVM model for classification:

```
from sklearn import datasets
from sklearn.model_selection import train_test_split
from sklearn.svm import SVC
from sklearn.metrics import accuracy_score

# Load an example dataset
iris = datasets.load_iris()
X = iris.data
y = iris.target

# We only use two classes to simplify
X = X[y != 2]
y = y[y != 2]

# Split the dataset into training and testing
X_train, X_test, y_train, y_test = train_test_split(X, y,
test_size=0.2, random_state=42)

# Create the SVM model with a linear kernel
model = SVC(kernel='linear', C=1.0)

# Train the model
model.fit(X_train, y_train)

# Make predictions
y_pred = model.predict(X_test)

# Evaluate the model
accuracy = accuracy_score(y_test, y_pred)
```

```
print(f'Model accuracy: {accuracy}')
```

This code trains an SVM model on the Iris dataset, using a linear kernel. The model's accuracy is evaluated on the test set, providing a measure of how well the model has learned to classify new observations.

SVM are particularly useful in applications where classes are well separated and the goal is to maximize the separation margin. However, they can also be less efficient in problems with large datasets or when classes are not clearly separable in the original feature space. In these cases, additional techniques may be needed, such as selecting an appropriate kernel or implementing dimensionality reduction methods to improve model performance.

Support vector machines remain a fundamental tool in the arsenal of Machine Learning techniques, appreciated for their ability to provide robust and well-generalized models, especially in classification tasks.

12.1.3. Neural Networks

Neural networks are one of the most advanced and widely used techniques in the field of Machine Learning and Artificial Intelligence. In fact, I am sure that even if you are not an expert and are just starting out, you are already seeing them everywhere. Inspired by the structure and functioning of the human brain, neural networks are composed of layers of artificial neurons that process information similarly to biological neurons. These networks have proven to be extremely effective for a variety of complex tasks, such as voice recognition, image classification, natural language processing, and more.

Basic architecture of a neural network

A typical neural network is composed of several layers of neurons, organized in an architecture that includes:

- **Input Layer:** This layer receives the input data, which can be any type of numerical information, such as pixels of an image, feature values in a dataset, etc. Each neuron in this layer corresponds to a feature or variable in the dataset.

- **Hidden Layers:** Between the input layer and the output layer, there are one or more hidden layers. These layers do not interact directly with the outside world and are where most of the processing occurs. The neurons in the hidden layers perform calculations through activation functions, which determine whether a neuron should "fire" or not, that is, whether it should pass its value to the next layer.

- **Output Layer:** This layer provides the final output of the neural network. In a binary classification problem, for example, the output layer may have a single neuron indicating the probability of a specific class. In a multiclass classification problem, there may be several neurons, each representing a different class.

How a Neural Network works

The process of how a neural network works involves the following flow:

- **Forward propagation**: The input data passes through the different layers of the network. In each layer, the neurons receive the input values, apply an activation function, and pass the result to the next layer. This process continues until it reaches the output layer.

- **Activation function:** Activation functions introduce nonlinearities into the network, allowing it to learn complex patterns. Some common activation functions include the sigmoid function, the hyperbolic tangent (tanh), and the ReLU (Rectified Linear Unit) function, the latter being one of the most widely used due to its effectiveness in deep networks.

- **Error calculation:** Once the network output is obtained, it is compared with the target value (ground truth) using a loss function, which measures how far the network's prediction is from the expected result. In classification problems, the most common loss function is cross-entropy, while in regression the mean squared error is usually used.

- **Backpropagation:** To adjust the weights of the neural network and reduce the error, a process called backpropagation is used. This process calculates the gradient of the loss function with respect to each weight in the network and then updates the weights in the opposite direction of the gradient, usually using an optimization algorithm such as gradient descent.

- **Weight update:** With the information obtained in the previous step, the weights are adjusted so that the next time the data passes through the network, the error is reduced. This process is repeated over multiple iterations or epochs until the model converges to an acceptable error level.

Types of Neural Networks

There are different types of neural networks, each adapted to specific types of tasks:

Multilayer Perceptron (MLP): This is the most basic type of neural network, composed of fully connected layers of neurons. It is suitable for general classification and regression tasks but has limitations in tasks that require spatial or sequential processing.

Convolutional Neural Networks (CNN): Especially designed to process data with a grid-like structure, such as images. CNN use convolutional layers to extract spatial features and pooling layers to reduce dimensionality, making them very effective in image and video recognition.

Recurrent Neural Networks (RNN): These networks are designed to work with sequential data, such as time series or text. RNN use feedback (or loops) to remember information across input sequences, allowing them to handle temporal dependencies.

Long Short-Term Memory Networks (LSTM): A variant of RNN that includes special mechanisms to handle long-term memory, allowing the network to remember relevant information over long periods of time. They are widely used in tasks such as machine translation and natural language processing.

Implementation of a Neural Network in Python

With the following code I show you a basic example of how to implement a neural network with Python using the popular `TensorFlow` and `Keras` library:

```
import tensorflow as tf
from tensorflow.keras.models import Sequential
from tensorflow.keras.layers import Dense

# Define the sequential model
model = Sequential()

# Add an input layer (4 neurons) and a hidden layer (8 neurons) with
ReLU activation
model.add(Dense(8, input_dim=4, activation='relu'))

# Add a second hidden layer (8 neurons) with ReLU activation
model.add(Dense(8, activation='relu'))

# Add the output layer (1 neuron) with sigmoid activation for a bi-
nary classification problem
model.add(Dense(1, activation='sigmoid'))

# Compile the model with the Adam optimizer and binary cross-entropy
loss function
model.compile(loss='binary_crossentropy', optimizer='adam', met-
rics=['accuracy'])
```

```
# Show the summary of the model architecture
model.summary()

# Assuming X_train and y_train are the training data
# Train the model
# model.fit(X_train, y_train, epochs=100, batch_size=10)
```

This code implements a simple neural network model with two hidden layers and one output layer designed for a binary classification problem. The ReLU activation function is used in the hidden layers, while the sigmoid function is used in the output layer to predict probabilities. The Adam optimizer is used to update the weights during training, and the binary cross-entropy loss function is employed to measure the model's accuracy in binary classification problems.

Applications of Neural Networks

Neural networks have a wide range of applications due to their flexibility and ability to learn complex patterns. Some of the most notable applications include:

Image recognition: CNNs are widely used in image classification tasks, object detection, and image segmentation.

Natural language processing: RNNs and LSTMs are applied in tasks such as machine translation, text summarization, and sentiment analysis.

Games and simulations: Neural networks are employed in Artificial Intelligence for games, such as AlphaGo, where they are combined with reinforcement learning to create agents that can learn to play games autonomously.

Financial prediction: In the financial field, neural networks are used to predict stock prices, credit risks, and detect fraud.

Recommendation systems: Amazon, Netflix, and other platforms use neural networks to recommend products and personalized content to users based on their previous behaviors and preferences.

Neural networks have revolutionized Artificial Intelligence and Machine Learning, providing advanced solutions for problems that were previously unapproachable. With their ability to learn from large volumes of data and discover complex patterns, these networks continue to drive innovations in a variety of fields, from healthcare to finance and entertainment, including virtual reality, augmented reality, education, and hundreds of other fields.

12.2. Time Series Analysis

12.2.1. Time Series Decomposition

Time series decomposition is a fundamental technique in temporal data analysis that allows a time series to be broken down into several basic components. These components help to understand and model the patterns present in the data over time, which is crucial for forecasting and informed decision-making. The main components of a time series typically include trend, seasonality, and noise or residual component.

Components of a Time Series

- **Trend:** The trend is the component of the time series that represents the general direction of the data movement over time. It can be upward, downward, or constant, and reflects long-term changes in the data. For example, in a company's sales analysis, an upward trend may indicate sustained growth in sales over time.

- **Seasonality:** Seasonality is the recurring pattern that repeats at regular intervals over time, usually based on a specific period such as yearly, quarterly, monthly, or weekly. These patterns are common in data such as retail sales, where peaks can be observed during the holiday season.

- **Cyclical component:** Similar to seasonality, the cyclical component reflects repetitive patterns, but these do not occur at regular intervals like seasonality. Cycles are usually related to economic factors, such as recessions and expansions, and can last several years.

- **Noise or residual:** The noise component is the part of the time series that cannot be explained by the trend, seasonality, or cycles. It is unpredictable and represents random variability in the data.

Methods of Time Series Decomposition

There are several methods to decompose a time series into its basic components. The two most common approaches are additive decomposition and multiplicative decomposition.

1. Additive decomposition: In this approach, it is assumed that the components of the time series are added together. That is, the time series y_t is represented as:

$$y_t = T_t + S_t + R_t$$

where T_t is the trend, S_t is the seasonality, and R_t is the residual component. This method is used when the magnitude of the seasonal and trend fluctuations does not vary significantly with the level of the time series.

2. Multiplicative decomposition: In this approach, it is assumed that the components of the time series are multiplied together. The time series y_t is represented as:

$$y_t = T_t \times S_t \times R_t$$

this method is suitable when the seasonal and trend fluctuations change proportionally with the level of the time series.

Implementation of Time Series Decomposition in Python

Time series decomposition can be effectively implemented using Python libraries such as `statsmodels`. Below an example of how to decompose a time series using the additive method.

```
import pandas as pd
from statsmodels.tsa.seasonal import seasonal_decompose
import matplotlib.pyplot as plt

# Load the time series data

# Assuming the data is in a DataFrame with a 'date' column for dates
and 'value' for the values
data = pd.read_csv('path_to_your_data.csv', parse_dates=['date'],
index_col='date')

# Perform the additive decomposition
result = seasonal_decompose(data['value'], model='additive')

# Plot the components
result.plot()
plt.show()

# Access individual components
trend = result.trend
seasonal = result.seasonal
residual = result.resid
```

Let's see what we have done in this code:

1. Load the data: A time series is loaded from a CSV file and the date column is set as the index.

2. Decomposition: The `seasonal_decompose` function from the `statsmodels` library is used to decompose the time series into its components using the additive model.

3. Visualization: The decomposed components of the time series (trend, seasonality, and residual) are plotted.

Applications of Time Series Decomposition

- **Analysis and forecasting:** Decomposition allows analysts to clearly identify underlying trends and seasonal patterns, which is crucial for forecasting future values of the time series with greater accuracy.

- **Anomaly detection:** By separating trend and seasonality, analysts can detect anomalies or abrupt changes in the data that do not fit historical patterns, which could indicate unusual events or problems in the data collection system.

- **Time series modeling:** Knowing the components of a time series allows modelers to better select and adjust predictive models, such as ARIMA models, which can model trend and seasonality more effectively.

- **Seasonal adjustment:** In many cases, it is useful to remove the seasonal component from the data to analyze the "seasonally adjusted" series. This is common in economic analysis, where seasonal data can obscure the underlying trend.

Considerations when using Time Series Decomposition

1. Stationarity: Before applying certain time series models, it is important to assess whether the series is stationary. A time series is stationary if its statistical properties, such as the mean and variance, are constant over time. If a series is not stationary, it may be necessary to differentiate it or adjust its components to make it stationary.

2. Interaction between components: In some cases, the components of the time series may interact in complex ways. For example, seasonality may vary depending on the trend. This may require a more sophisticated approach, such as decomposition using more advanced methods or the incorporation of nonlinear models.

Time series decomposition is a powerful technique for understanding and modeling temporal data. It allows the separation of the different elements that contribute to the behavior of the series, which facilitates both analysis and forecasting. This technique is widely used in fields such as economics, meteorology, quality control, and many others where the analysis of temporal data is crucial.

12.2.2. ARIMA Models

ARIMA models (Autoregressive Integrated Moving Average) are a class of statistical models widely used for time series analysis and forecasting. These models are especially useful when dealing with data that show a trend or seasonality and are applied in various fields such as economics, meteorology, engineering, and more.

Fundamental Concepts of the ARIMA Model

The ARIMA model is a combination of three main components: autoregression (AR), moving average (MA), and differencing (*I*, for "Integrated"). These components are combined to create a model that can capture the dynamics of a complex time series. The ARIMA model is commonly represented as ARIMA(p, d, q), where:

- **Autoregression (AR) - *p*:** The autoregressive component implies that the current value of the time series depends linearly on its previous values, with a degree of dependence that decreases over time. The parameter p indicates the number of lags used in the model.

- **Differencing (I) - *d*:** The integrated part of the model implies taking differences between consecutive observations to make the time series stationary, that is, to remove the trend. The parameter d indicates the number of times the data have been differenced.

- **Moving Average (MA) - *q*:** The moving average component suggests that the current value of the time series is influenced by the error (residual) of previous observations. The parameter q determines the number of moving average terms to include in the model.

Decomposition of the ARIMA Model

An ARIMA model is built by combining these three elements and is mathematically expressed as:

$$Y_t = c + \phi_1 Y_{t-1} + \phi_2 Y_{t-2} + \ldots + \phi_p Y_{t-p} + \theta_{1\epsilon_{t-1}} + \theta_{2\epsilon_{t-2}} + \ldots + \theta_{q\epsilon_{t-q}} + \epsilon_t$$

Where:

- Y_t is the predicted value at time t.
- c is a constant.
- $\phi_1, \phi_2, \ldots \phi_p$ are the autoregressive coefficients.
- ϵ_t is the random error or noise term.
- $\theta_1, \theta_2, \ldots \theta_q$ are the moving average coefficients.

Steps to build an ARIMA Model

1. Identification of stationarity: Before applying an ARIMA model, it is crucial to check if the time series is stationary. A series is stationary if its statistical properties, such as the mean and variance, are constant over time. If not, differencing can be applied until the series stabilizes.

2. Determination of parameters (*p*, *d*, *q*): Selecting the values of *p*, *d*, and *q* is a key step. This can be done using the autocorrelation function (ACF) and the partial autocorrelation function (PACF) to determine the appropriate lags.

3. Model estimation: Once the parameters are selected, the model is estimated by fitting the ϕ and θ coefficients.

4. Model diagnostics: After fitting the model, diagnostics are performed to check its validity. This includes checking the model residuals, which should appear as white noise (that is, without correlation).

5. Forecasting: Finally, the model is used to make future predictions, which is the main application of ARIMA in time series analysis.

Implementation in Python

The following code shows how to implement an ARIMA model using the `statsmodels` library in Python. This example includes the steps of identification, fitting, and forecasting.

```
import pandas as pd
import numpy as np
from statsmodels.tsa.arima.model import ARIMA
import matplotlib.pyplot as plt
import warnings
warnings.filterwarnings("ignore")

# Load time series data
data = pd.read_csv('path_to_your_data.csv', parse_dates=['date'],
index_col='date')

# Check stationarity and apply differencing
differenced_data = data.diff().dropna()
```

```
# Determine parameters p, d, q using ACF and PACF (manual determina-
tion or testing)

# Fit the ARIMA model (example with p=1, d=1, q=1)
model = ARIMA(data, order=(1, 1, 1))
model_fit = model.fit()

# Model summary

print(model_fit.summary())

# Forecasting
forecast = model_fit.forecast(steps=10)

print(forecast)

# Plot the result
data.plot(label='Original')
forecast.plot(label='Forecast', color='red')
plt.legend()
plt.show()
```

Code Explanation

1. Data loading and differencing: The time series data is loaded and differencing is applied to ensure the series is stationary.

2. Model fitting: An ARIMA model is fitted using the selected parameters. In this case, an ARIMA(1, 1, 1) model is used as an example.

3. Forecasting: The trained model is used to make predictions of future values of the time series.

4. Visualization: The original data is plotted along with the forecasts to compare the results.

Applications of ARIMA Models

Sales forecasting: In retail and other industries, ARIMA is used to forecast future sales based on historical data, allowing for proper inventory planning.

Financial value prediction: ARIMA is widely used in finance to predict stock prices, indexes, interest rates, and more.

Quality control: In manufacturing processes, ARIMA helps predict the behavior of time series related to product quality, allowing the implementation of preventive measures.

Economic analysis: Economists use ARIMA to forecast key economic indicators such as GDP, inflation, and unemployment, supporting decision-making at the government and corporate levels.

Considerations and Limitations

Parameter selection: Correct identification of the values of p, d, and q is fundamental for the success of the model. If selected incorrectly, the model may fail to properly capture the dynamics of the time series.

Stationary data: ARIMA requires the data to be stationary. If the data is not stationary, the model may produce incorrect results, highlighting the importance of proper differencing.

Seasonal ARIMA models (SARIMA): For time series that exhibit strong seasonality, a simple ARIMA model may not be sufficient, so it can be extended to a SARIMA model that includes seasonal components.

ARIMA models are powerful tools in time series analysis, providing a solid framework for modeling and forecasting temporal data in a wide variety of contexts.

12.2.3. Recurrent Neural Networks (RNN)

In previous sections we have talked about neural networks and looked at some different ones. And these, of course, we have also mentioned. Now is the time, and due to their importance, to go deeper into them. Recurrent neural networks are a class of neural networks designed to process sequences of data, as I mentioned earlier, for example text, which makes them especially suitable for tasks where the order of the data is important. Unlike traditional neural networks, which assume that inputs are independent of each other, RNNs are capable of maintaining an internal memory that allows them to capture temporal or sequential dependencies in the data. Let's look at them in more detail.

Fundamental Concepts of Recurrent Neural Networks (RNN)

RNNs are characterized by having recurrent connections, which means that the output of a neural unit at a given moment is fed back as input to the same unit at the next time step. This mechanism allows them to store information across the sequence, which is crucial for tasks such as time series prediction, natural language processing, machine translation, and speech recognition.

Basic Structure of an RNN

The basic structure of an RNN can be described with the following equation:

$$h_t = \sigma(W_{hh}h_{t-1} + W_{xh}x_t + b_h)$$

$$y_t = W_{hy}h_t + b_y)$$

where:

- x_t is the input at time t.
- h_t is the hidden state at time t, which acts as the network's memory.
- W_{xh}, W_{hh}, and W_{hy} are weight matrices that determine the connections between the different layers.
- b_h and b_y are the corresponding biases.
- σ is a nonlinear activation function (for example, tanh or ReLU).

The hidden state h_t is updated at each time step, which allows the network to capture information from all previous inputs in the sequence.

Problems of classical RNNs

Despite their advantages, classical RNNs have certain limitations, mainly the problem of vanishing and exploding gradients during training. This occurs because, when many layers or long sequences are used, the gradients that propagate through the network can become extremely small or large, which makes effective learning difficult. This problem limits the ability of RNNs to learn long-term dependencies.

Variants of RNNs: LSTM and GRU

To address the mentioned problems, more advanced variants of RNNs have been developed, such as LSTM (Long Short-Term Memory) and GRU (Gated Recurrent Unit).

LSTM (Long Short-Term Memory)

LSTMs are designed to handle long-term dependencies by using a more complex structure that includes "gates" that regulate the flow of information through the network. LSTMs include:

1. Forget Gate f_h: Decides how much information from the previous state should be forgotten.

2. Input Gate i_t: Determines how much new information should be stored in memory.
3. Output Gate o_t: Decides which part of the current memory is used to calculate the output.

These gates allow LSTMs to maintain relevant information for longer than traditional RNNs.

GRU (Gated Recurrent Unit)

GRUs are a simplification of LSTMs that combine the input gate and the forget gate into a single "update gate." Although they are less complex than LSTMs, GRUs often offer comparable performance in many tasks and have the advantage of being faster to train.

Implementation of an RNN in Python

Let's look at an example of how to implement an RNN using the `TensorFlow` and `Keras` libraries to predict a time series.

```
import numpy as np
import matplotlib.pyplot as plt
from tensorflow.keras.models import Sequential
from tensorflow.keras.layers import SimpleRNN, LSTM, Dense

# 1. Generation of the sinusoidal time series
def generate_sequence(n_timesteps):
X = np.array([i / float(n_timesteps) for i in range(n_timesteps)])
y = np.sin(2.0 * np.pi * X)
return y

n_timesteps = 100
data = generate_sequence(n_timesteps)

# Plot the time series
plt.plot(data)
plt.title("Sinusoidal Time Series")
plt.show()

# 2. Preparing the data with a sliding window
def create_dataset(data, n_steps):
X, y = [], []
for i in range(len(data)):
end_ix = i + n_steps
if end_ix > len(data) - 1:
break
seq_x, seq_y = data[i:end_ix], data[end_ix]
X.append(seq_x)
y.append(seq_y)
return np.array(X), np.array(y)
```

```
n_steps = 10
X, y = create_dataset(data, n_steps)

# Reshape for RNN input: [samples, timesteps, features]
X = X.reshape((X.shape[0], X.shape[1], 1))

# Split the data into training and test sets
split = int(0.8 * len(X))
X_train, X_test = X[:split], X[split:]
y_train, y_test = y[:split], y[split:]

# 3. Define the RNN model with LSTM
model = Sequential([
LSTM(50, activation='tanh', input_shape=(n_steps, 1)),
Dense(1)
])

# Compile the model
model.compile(optimizer='adam', loss='mse')

# Model summary
model.summary()

# 4. Train the model
model.fit(X_train, y_train, epochs=200, verbose=1, valida-
tion_data=(X_test, y_test))

# 5. Prediction and Evaluation
yhat_train = model.predict(X_train, verbose=0)
yhat_test = model.predict(X_test, verbose=0)

# Plot results
plt.figure(figsize=(10,6))
plt.plot(range(len(y_train)), y_train, label='Train Actual')
plt.plot(range(len(y_train), len(y_train) + len(y_test)), y_test,
label='Test Actual')
plt.plot(range(len(y_train)), yhat_train, linestyle='--',
color='red', label='Train Predicted')
plt.plot(range(len(y_train), len(y_train) + len(y_test)), yhat_test,
linestyle='--', color='green', label='Test Predicted')
plt.legend()
plt.title("Time Series Prediction with RNN")
plt.show()
```

Code Explanation

1. Data sequence generation: Here a data sequence is generated based on the sine function to serve as an example dataset.

2. RNN model definition: A simple RNN is built with a `SimpleRNN` layer that has 50 units. The `tanh` activation function is used, common in RNNs due to its ability to handle sequential signals.

3. Compilation and training: The model is compiled using the `Adam` optimizer and the mean squared error (`mse`) loss function. Then, the model is trained on the generated data.

4. Prediction and visualization: The trained model is used to make predictions on the same input data, and the results are plotted to visualize the prediction versus the actual values.

Applications of RNNs and Their Variants

Natural language processing (NLP): RNNs are widely used in NLP tasks such as machine translation, language modeling, and text generation.

Time series prediction: RNNs, especially LSTM and GRU, are used in finance to predict stock prices, in meteorology to forecast the weather, and in other fields where data has a sequential nature.

Speech recognition: RNNs are fundamental in speech recognition systems, where they need to interpret audio sequences to convert them into text.

Music generation: RNNs are used in music generation, where they learn musical patterns from large volumes of audio data.

Considerations and Challenges

- **Computationally expensive training:** RNNs can be slower to train than other types of neural networks due to their sequential dependency, which also means they are not easy to parallelize.

- **Long-term memory:** Although LSTM and GRU improve the RNNs' ability to remember long-term information, they can still struggle with extremely long sequences.

- **Overfitting:** RNNs, due to their high capacity to model complex dependencies, can overfit the training data if appropriate precautions are not taken, such as using regularization.

RNNs and their LSTM and GRU variants are powerful tools in sequence analysis, offering advanced solutions for a wide range of problems where sequential data is key. Implementing these networks requires careful considerations about their architecture and parameters, but their ability to model temporal dependencies makes them a preferred choice for many advanced applications.

12.3. Clustering and Segmentation Models

We have already mentioned k-means and hierarchical clustering earlier, now let's break them down along with DBSCAN. Let me remind you at this point that this book is designed to complement my book AI-Manager, which offers you a broader and more complex view of both machine learning algorithms and methods as well as data analysis and visualization. So if you feel you are missing information, I advise you to buy the book, as they are written and designed to complement each other.

12.3.1. k-means Algorithm

The k-means algorithm is a widely used clustering technique in machine learning and data analysis to group a dataset into a specific number of groups or clusters, where each observation belongs to the cluster with the nearest centroid. It is an iterative algorithm that tries to minimize the internal variance of each cluster, which means reducing the squared distance between the observations and their respective centroids.

Basics of the k-means Algorithm

The k-means algorithm works through the following steps:

- **Initialization**: k random points are chosen in the data space as the initial centroids of the clusters. These points can be selected randomly or by using a method like k-means++ to improve the efficiency and accuracy of the algorithm.

- **Cluster assignment:** Each data point is assigned to the nearest centroid, determining the cluster to which it belongs. Proximity is generally measured using Euclidean distance, although other distance metrics can also be used.

- **Centroid update:** Once all points have been assigned to a cluster, the centroids of each cluster are recalculated as the average of all data points belonging to that cluster.

- **Repeat:** The assignment and update steps are repeated until the centroids no longer change significantly, meaning that the data points have converged into stable clusters. Alternatively, the process can be stopped after a fixed number of iterations or when the variation in centroids between iterations falls below a predefined threshold.

Choosing the Number of Clusters (k)

A critical aspect of the k-means algorithm is the choice of the number of clusters k. Determining the optimal value of k may not be trivial and is generally done using methods such as the Elbow Method, Silhouette Analysis, or more advanced techniques like the Gap Statistic.

- **Elbow Method:** This method involves calculating the sum of squared errors (SSE) for different values of k. k is plotted against SSE, and the value of k is selected where the reduction in SSE starts to slow down, forming an "elbow" in the graph.

- **Silhouette Analysis:** This technique measures how close points in a cluster are to points in other clusters. The optimal k is the one that maximizes the average silhouette value, which ranges between -1 and 1.

- **Gap Statistic:** This technique compares the within-cluster variation for different values of k with what is expected under a null (random) distribution. A "gap" value is calculated that measures the difference between both, and the optimal k is chosen where this gap is maximum, indicating the greatest separation between the actual data structure and random noise.

Limitations of the k-means Algorithm

Despite its popularity, k-means has some important limitations:

1. **Dependence on initial value:** The quality of the resulting clustering can depend significantly on the initial centroids. Different initializations can lead to different results, known as the sensitivity to initialization problem.

2. **Fixed number of clusters:** k-means requires the number of clusters k to be specified before execution, which can be challenging if prior knowledge of the appropriate number of clusters is lacking.

3. **Spherical clusters:** k-means assumes that clusters have a spherical shape and similar sizes, which may not be suitable for data with more complex cluster structures or non-spherical shapes.

4. **Sensitivity to outliers:** The k-means algorithm is sensitive to outliers and noise in the data, as centroids can be heavily influenced by outlier points.

Applying the k-means Algorithm in Python

Let's develop an example of how to implement the k-means algorithm using the `scikit-learn` library in Python.

```
import numpy as np
import matplotlib.pyplot as plt
from sklearn.cluster import KMeans
from sklearn.datasets import make_blobs

# Generate sample data
X, _ = make_blobs(n_samples=300, centers=4, cluster_std=0.60, ran-
dom_state=0)

# Apply k-means
kmeans = KMeans(n_clusters=4, random_state=0)
kmeans.fit(X)

# Predict clusters
y_kmeans = kmeans.predict(X)

# Visualize the clusters
plt.scatter(X[:, 0], X[:, 1], c=y_kmeans, s=50, cmap='viridis')

# Visualize the centroids
centers = kmeans.cluster_centers_
plt.scatter(centers[:, 0], centers[:, 1], c='red', s=200, al-
pha=0.75, marker='X')
plt.title('k-means Clustering')
plt.xlabel('Feature 1')
plt.ylabel('Feature 2')
plt.show()
```

Explanation of the Code

1. Generating synthetic data: `make_blobs` is used to generate a synthetic dataset with 4 centers (clusters) and a standard deviation of 0.60 for each cluster. This allows us to visualize how k-means groups points around these centers.

2. Applying k-means: A k-means model is initialized with $k = 4$ clusters. The model is fitted to the input data X, and then cluster labels are predicted for each data point.

3. Visualizing results: The data is visualized in a 2D plot where the points are colored according to the cluster they belong to. The centroids of each cluster are marked with a red X, highlighting their location in the feature space.

Advantages and Applications of the k-means Algorithm

The k-means algorithm is simple to implement and scale, making it a popular choice for many applications. Some of the most common applications include:

- **Customer segmentation:** Grouping customers into clusters with similar behaviors allows companies to personalize their marketing campaigns and improve customer satisfaction.

- **Image compression:** k-means can be used for color reduction in an image, grouping similar colors and representing them with a single mean value.

- **Document clustering:** In natural language processing, k-means is used to group documents with similar content, which is useful in recommendation engines and search engines.

- **Behavioral pattern analysis:** k-means helps identify patterns in app usage data or sensor data, which can be useful for anomaly detection.

Additional Considerations

Scalability: k-means is computationally efficient and can handle large datasets, especially when used alongside techniques like k-means++ for initialization.

Data preprocessing: It is important to scale the features before applying k-means, as Euclidean distance is sensitive to feature scales. Normalizing or standardizing the data can significantly improve the algorithm's performance.

Advanced implementations: There are improved versions of k-means, such as mini-batch k-means, which can handle large volumes of data by processing small batches of data in each iteration.

The k-means algorithm, despite its limitations, remains a great tool in the arsenal of clustering techniques. Its simplicity and ability to discover underlying structures in the data make it invaluable in a variety of data science and machine learning applications.

12.3.2. Hierarchical Clustering

Hierarchical clustering is a clustering technique that organizes data into a hierarchy of clusters. Unlike the k-means method, which requires the number of clusters k to be predefined, hierarchical clustering creates a hierarchical structure (or dendrogram) that allows exploration of multiple levels of grouping. This method is particularly useful when the optimal number of clusters is not known in advance or when a more detailed view of the internal structure of the data is desired.

Types of Hierarchical Clustering

There are two main approaches to hierarchical clustering: agglomerative and divisive.

1. Agglomerative hierarchical clustering (AGNES - Agglomerative Nesting):
- This is the most commonly used approach. It starts by treating each observation as an individual cluster.
- Then, at each step, the two most similar clusters are merged into one.
- This process continues until all the data is grouped into a single cluster or until a stopping criterion is reached, such as a specific number of clusters.
- The result is a dendrogram, a decision tree that represents the merging of clusters at each level.

2. Divisive hierarchical clustering (DIANA - Divisive Analysis):
- This approach is the opposite of agglomerative. It starts with all data in a single cluster.
- At each step, the most dissimilar cluster is split into two.
- This process repeats until each data point is in its own cluster.
- Although less common than the agglomerative method, it is useful when the data structure is known and a progressive subdivision is desired.

Distance Metrics and Linkage Criteria

The success of hierarchical clustering largely depends on how the "distance" between clusters is defined. The most common distance metrics are Euclidean distance, Manhattan distance, and Minkowski distance. Once a distance metric is defined, it is necessary to determine how the distance between clusters will be measured. This is done using one of the following linkage criteria:

1. Single linkage:
- The distance between two clusters is defined as the smallest distance between any pair of points, one from each cluster.
- This method tends to create elongated clusters and can be sensitive to noise and outliers.

2. Complete linkage:
- The distance between two clusters is defined as the largest distance between any pair of points, one from each cluster.
- This approach tends to produce compact and similarly sized clusters.

3. Average linkage:
- The distance between two clusters is defined as the average of the distances between all pairs of points from the clusters.
- It is a balance between the single linkage and complete linkage approaches.

4. Ward's method:
- Minimizes the sum of variances within clusters. The merge that minimizes the increase of total variance in the combined clusters is chosen.
- It tends to produce similarly sized clusters and is very useful in most cases.

Visualization with Dendrograms

The dendrogram is a visual tool that represents the hierarchical structure of clustering. Each merge in the dendrogram represents a combination of clusters. The height of the merge reflects the distance or dissimilarity between the merged clusters. The choice of the number of clusters can be made by cutting the dendrogram at a specific height, which groups the data into clusters.

Implementation in Python

Let's now look at an example of how to implement agglomerative hierarchical clustering in Python using `scipy` and `matplotlib` to visualize the dendrogram.

```
import numpy as np
import matplotlib.pyplot as plt
from scipy.cluster.hierarchy import dendrogram, linkage
from sklearn.datasets import make_blobs

# Generate sample data
X, _ = make_blobs(n_samples=100, centers=3, cluster_std=0.6, ran-
dom_state=42)

# Perform agglomerative hierarchical clustering
Z = linkage(X, method='ward')

# Create the dendrogram
plt.figure(figsize=(10, 7))
dendrogram(Z)
plt.title('Hierarchical Clustering Dendrogram')
plt.xlabel('Sample index')
plt.ylabel('Distance (Ward)')
```

```
plt.show()
```

Explanation of the code

1. Generation of synthetic data: A synthetic dataset with three clusters is generated using `make_blobs`. This dataset will serve to demonstrate how hierarchical clustering works.

2. Hierarchical clustering: The linkage function from `scipy` is used to perform agglomerative hierarchical clustering. The linkage method used is Ward's method, which minimizes the total variance within clusters.

3. Dendrogram visualization: The `dendrogram` function is used to create a dendrogram that shows the hierarchical structure of the clusters. The height of the merges indicates the dissimilarity between the merged clusters.

Advantages and Disadvantages of Hierarchical Clustering

Advantages:
- **Does not require a predetermined number of clusters**: Unlike k-means, hierarchical clustering does not need the number of clusters to be specified from the start.
- **Ability to capture hierarchical structures:** It is useful when data has a natural hierarchical structure, such as biological taxonomies.
- **Flexibility:** Allows experimenting with different grouping levels by cutting the dendrogram at different heights.

Disadvantages:
- **Scalability:** Hierarchical clustering has high computational complexity, especially for large datasets. This is because it requires calculating the distance between all pairs of points.
- **Sensitivity to noise and outliers**: Like k-means, hierarchical clustering can be sensitive to noise and outliers, which can significantly affect the structure of the dendrogram.
- **Difficulty in deciding the dendrogram cut:** Although the dendrogram is a useful tool, deciding the optimal cut point to determine the number of clusters can be subjective.

Common applications of hierarchical clustering

Hierarchical clustering is used in a variety of fields due to its ability to reveal hierarchical structures in data. Some of its applications include

Biology: It is widely used in the hierarchical classification of species and in the creation of phylogenetic trees.

Market analysis: It allows the segmentation of customers into hierarchical groups based on behavioral similarities or demographic characteristics.
Natural language processing: It is used to group words, documents, or terms into clusters based on semantic or contextual similarities.
Computer vision: It helps in grouping similar features or patterns in images for tasks such as object detection or image segmentation.

Practical Considerations

Data preprocessing: Before applying hierarchical clustering, it is crucial to standardize or normalize the data, as distance metrics can be sensitive to the scale of the data.

Choice of linkage criterion: The choice of linkage criterion can significantly affect clustering results. It is advisable to test different methods (such as Ward, complete, or average) and evaluate which produces the most useful or interpretable clusters for the problem at hand.

Interpretation of the dendrogram: It is important to keep in mind that the dendrogram offers a hierarchical representation, but it is not always easy to determine the optimal number of clusters. Additionally, a horizontal cut in the dendrogram represents the division into clusters at that specific level of dissimilarity.

Hierarchical clustering is used to discover structures in data, especially when a hierarchical representation is sought or when the appropriate number of clusters is unknown. Despite its scalability limitations, its ability to provide a detailed view of the data makes it an invaluable tool in data analysis.

12.3.3. DBSCAN

DBSCAN (Density-Based Spatial Clustering of Applications with Noise) is a clustering algorithm that identifies clusters based on the density of points in a feature space. Unlike other methods such as k-means or hierarchical clustering, DBSCAN does not require specifying the number of clusters in advance and is especially useful for discovering clusters of arbitrary shape as well as identifying outliers (anomalous values) as noise points. This algorithm is widely used in various applications due to its ability to handle noisy and complex data.

Fundamentals of DBSCAN

The DBSCAN algorithm is based on two main concepts: point density and the notion of point neighborhood.

1. Eps (ε) - Neighborhood radius: Defines the radius around a point within which other neighboring points are searched. This radius determines how close points must be to be considered part of the same cluster.

2. MinPts - Minimum number of points: Specifies the minimum number of points that must be within the ε radius for a point to be considered a "core point." If a point has at least `MinPts` neighbors within its ε neighborhood, it is considered a core point.

Types of points in DBSCAN

In DBSCAN, points are classified into three categories based on the ε and `MinPts` parameters:

- **Core Points:** A point is considered a core point if it has at least `MinPts` neighboring points within its ε radius. These points are fundamental in forming the core of the cluster.

- **Border Points:** These are points that have fewer than `MinPts` neighbors within their ε neighborhood but are within the ε radius of a core point. They form the periphery of the cluster.

- **Noise Points:** These are points that are neither core nor border points, meaning they do not have enough neighboring points within their ε neighborhood and are not within the ε radius of any core point. These points are considered outliers and are not grouped into any cluster.

How the Algorithm works

The clustering process with DBSCAN is carried out as follows:

1. Initialization: A random point is selected from the dataset. If this point has at least `MinPts` neighbors within its ε radius, it is marked as a core point, and the formation of a new cluster begins.

2. Cluster expansion: All neighboring points within the ε radius of a core point are added to the cluster. If any of these points are also core points, the expansion process continues until no more points can be added.

3. Point classification: Points that cannot be part of any cluster (that is, those without enough neighbors within ε) are classified as noise points.

4. Repeat: The process is repeated until all points in the dataset have been processed.

Advantages and Disadvantages of DBSCAN

Advantages:

- **Does not require specifying the number of clusters:** Unlike k-means, DBSCAN automatically determines the number of clusters based on the density of the data.
- **Outlier identification:** DBSCAN naturally classifies outliers as noise points, making it robust against noisy data.
- **Ability to detect clusters of arbitrary shapes:** While k-means tends to form spherical clusters, DBSCAN can identify clusters of any shape.

Disadvantages:

- **Sensitivity to the ε and MinPts parameters**: The choice of parameters can be difficult and may significantly affect the results. An inappropriate ε value can cause the algorithm to identify clusters that are too large or too small.
- **Issues with variable density data:** DBSCAN may struggle with datasets where clusters have different densities, as the optimal ε and `MinPts` parameters may vary across different parts of the dataset.
- **Scalability:** Although it is more efficient than other clustering methods in many cases, DBSCAN can be less efficient on extremely large datasets, especially when using a complex distance metric.

Implementation in Python

Let's look at an example of how to implement DBSCAN in Python using `sklearn`. The code includes visualization of the clustering results.

```
import numpy as np
import matplotlib.pyplot as plt
from sklearn.cluster import DBSCAN
from sklearn.datasets import make_moons
from sklearn.preprocessing import StandardScaler

# Generate example data with moon shape
X, _ = make_moons(n_samples=300, noise=0.1, random_state=42)

# Standardize the data to improve DBSCAN performance
X = StandardScaler().fit_transform(X)

# Apply DBSCAN
db = DBSCAN(eps=0.3, min_samples=5).fit(X)
labels = db.labels_
# Number of clusters in the labels, ignoring noise points (labeled
as -1)
n_clusters_ = len(set(labels)) - (1 if -1 in labels else 0)
n_noise_ = list(labels).count(-1)
```

```
print(f'Estimated number of clusters: {n_clusters_}')
print(f'Estimated number of noise points: {n_noise_}')

# Visualization of the clusters
unique_labels = set(labels)
colors = [plt.cm.Spectral(each) for each in np.linspace(0, 1,
len(unique_labels))]
for k, col in zip(unique_labels, colors):
    if k == -1:
        # Color para los puntos de ruido.
        col = [0, 0, 0, 1]

    class_member_mask = (labels == k)
    xy = X[class_member_mask & (labels != -1)]
    plt.plot(xy[:, 0], xy[:, 1], 'o', markerfacecolor=tuple(col),
markeredgecolor='k', markersize=6)

    xy = X[class_member_mask & (labels == -1)]
    plt.plot(xy[:, 0], xy[:, 1], 'x', markerfacecolor=tuple(col),
markeredgecolor='k', markersize=3)

plt.title('DBSCAN Clustering')
plt.show()
```

Code Explanation

1. Synthetic data generation: The `make_moons` function from `sklearn.datasets` is used to generate a dataset with a moon shape. This type of data is ideal to demonstrate DBSCAN's ability to identify clusters of arbitrary shapes.

2. Data standardization: `StandardScaler` is applied to standardize the data, which improves DBSCAN performance since it is sensitive to data scale.

3. Applying DBSCAN: The algorithm is applied with eps set to 0.3 and `min_samples` set to 5. These values are adjusted for this specific dataset.

4. Visualization of results: The clusters identified by DBSCAN are visualized. Noise points are marked with an "x," while points that belong to clusters are marked with circles of different colors.

Practical Considerations for using DBSCAN

- **Parameter selection:** Choosing appropriate `eps` and `MinPts` is crucial for DBSCAN performance. These parameters can be adjusted using techniques such as the elbow curve or by visually inspecting the data.

- **Scalability:** Although DBSCAN is more efficient than other methods in many scenarios, its computational complexity can increase significantly with data size. For large datasets, it may be necessary to use optimized implementations or distributed versions of the algorithm.

- **Distance metrics:** DBSCAN can be used with different distance metrics, not just Euclidean distance. For complex data, such as spatial or text data, it may be necessary to use distance metrics better suited to the nature of the dataset.

- **Common applications:** DBSCAN is widely used in geospatial analysis, anomaly detection, image processing, and clustering of sensor data, among other fields. Its ability to handle noisy data and discover clusters of arbitrary shapes makes it a valuable tool in situations where other methods may fail.

DBSCAN is a powerful and versatile algorithm suitable for a wide range of applications. Its ability to identify clusters of arbitrary shapes and handle noise effectively sets it apart from other clustering methods. However, its effectiveness largely depends on the correct choice of parameters, which requires a deep understanding of the dataset and experimentation to achieve the best results.

PART V

Implementation and Production Deployment

Part V: Implementation and Production Deployment

13. Deployment of AI Models

The deployment of Artificial Intelligence models is a crucial phase in the lifecycle of any AI project. After developing, training, and evaluating a model, the next step is to bring it into production, where it can be used by real applications and generate value for the organization. This process not only involves moving the model from a development environment to a production one, but also ensuring that the model operates efficiently, securely, and scalably in a production environment.

In the current context, the deployment of AI models faces several challenges, ranging from model versioning management to the need to monitor and update models based on new data. As models are increasingly integrated into critical business systems, the need for robust and practical solutions for deployment becomes more evident.

One of the main aspects to consider in AI model deployment is the AI development lifecycle. This cycle covers various phases, from the conception of the model to its eventual retirement. It is essential to understand best practices in each of these phases to ensure that the model not only works well in a controlled environment but also adapts to changing production conditions. During this process, support tools play a vital role, facilitating the tracking and management of each stage.

Another critical aspect is the selection of tools and frameworks for deployment. With the growing popularity of containers and orchestration, technologies such as Docker and Kubernetes have emerged as standard solutions for packaging, distributing, and scaling AI applications. These tools allow AI models to be deployed consistently and reproducibly across different environments, significantly reducing compatibility issues and increasing flexibility.

TensorFlow Serving is another widely used framework for serving Machine Learning models in production. This tool facilitates the deployment of models trained in TensorFlow, providing a robust interface for real-time predictions and efficient model version management. Similarly, MLflow is a platform that enables lifecycle management of models, including experiment tracking, reproducibility of results, and deployment management.

Once the model is in production, it is essential to establish monitoring and maintenance practices to ensure its continuous performance. AI models can degrade over time due to changes in the data or the environment in which they operate. Constant monitoring allows these degradations to be detected and timely adjustments to be made, such as updating models or retraining using new data. Additionally, model versioning management is crucial to maintain strict control over different iterations of a model and ensure that updates are carried out in a controlled manner without service interruptions.

The deployment of AI models is a complex process that requires careful planning, the selection of appropriate tools, and the implementation of effective monitoring and maintenance strategies. Each of these areas will be explored in detail in the following subpoints, providing the reader with a comprehensive guide to take AI models from the development phase to successful implementation in production environments.

13.1. Lifecycle of AI Development

13.1.1. Phases in AI Model Development

The development of Artificial Intelligence models follows a structured set of phases that guide the process from conceptualization to deployment and maintenance of a model in production. These phases, although they may vary slightly depending on the methodology adopted, generally include key stages such as problem definition, data collection, preprocessing, feature selection, model construction, training, validation, deployment, and monitoring. Each of these phases plays a crucial role in ensuring that the model is effective, efficient, and aligned with the project objectives.

1. The first phase is problem definition. This stage is critical because it lays the foundation upon which the entire project will be built. The problem to be solved must be clearly identified, formulating key questions such as: What is the model's goal? What kind of results are expected? How will success be measured? It is essential to understand the business context or application in which the model will be deployed, as well as to define the specific requirements and constraints of the project. This also includes identifying the stakeholders involved and their expectations.

2. Once the problem is clearly defined, the process moves on to data collection and exploration. This phase involves obtaining the necessary data to train the model. The data can come from various sources such as internal databases, APIs, sensors, or even public datasets. It is essential to ensure that the collected data is relevant, representative, and of high quality. During data exploration, datasets are analyzed to understand their structure and distribution and to detect potential issues such as missing or outlier values.

Statistical techniques and visualization tools can be used to discover patterns and relationships within the data.

3. The data preprocessing phase follows data collection and exploration. At this stage, the data is cleaned to ensure it is in an appropriate format for modeling. This includes the removal of duplicates, handling of missing values, normalization and standardization of data, and the transformation of categorical variables into numerical ones. Preprocessing is crucial to ensure that the model can learn from the data effectively and that the results are accurate and reliable. This stage also includes splitting the dataset into training, validation, and test sets for use in later phases.

4. Feature selection is the next phase. Here, the most relevant variables to be used for training the model are chosen. Feature selection significantly impacts the model's complexity and performance. Several techniques exist for performing this selection, ranging from statistical approaches to algorithm-based methods. Dimensionality reduction can also be applied in this phase to simplify the model without sacrificing its predictive capabilities. This is particularly important in large and complex datasets, where many features may be irrelevant or redundant.

5. With the data preprocessed and features selected, the model construction phase begins. At this stage, the Machine Learning or Deep Learning algorithms that best fit the specific problem are selected. The choice of algorithm depends on the type of problem (regression, classification, clustering, etc.) as well as the nature and volume of the data. Models are built and configured, including defining the architecture in the case of neural networks, and the initial tuning of hyperparameters such as learning rate or number of layers. It is common practice to test several different models to identify the one with the best performance.

6. The training phase follows model construction. During training, the model is adjusted to the training data using an optimization algorithm to minimize a loss function. This phase may involve multiple iterations through the data, adjusting the model's internal weights and parameters to improve its predictive ability. The training process can be resource-intensive, especially in the case of complex models such as deep neural networks. This is where it becomes clear whether the model is learning correctly or facing issues such as overfitting, which can compromise its ability to generalize to new data.

7. Model validation is crucial to assess its performance on a dataset that is independent from the one used for training. Validation allows the identification of issues not evident during training, such as overfitting or sensitivity to certain data features. Techniques such as cross-validation are used to ensure that the model is robust and its performance consistent. The validation phase may also involve hyperparameter tuning and comparison between different models to select the most suitable one.

8. Once the model has been validated, it proceeds to implementation and deployment. This phase involves moving the model into a production environment, where it begins to process data in real-time or batch mode. Implementation may require integrating the model with existing systems, developing APIs for its use, or deploying it to cloud platforms. It is crucial that the model be optimized for the production environment, ensuring it is scalable, fast, and secure. Furthermore, procedures must be established to monitor its performance and apply updates as needed.

9. The final phase is monitoring and maintenance. After the model has been deployed, it is essential to continuously monitor its performance to ensure it continues to meet the established objectives. This includes detecting potential performance degradation due to changes in input data or the operating environment. Monitoring may lead to the need for retraining the model or adjusting its parameters. Additionally, model versioning must be managed to ensure that updates or improvements do not interrupt service or introduce errors.

It is important to note that each project is different, and the number and nature of phases in this example represent the foundational framework upon which each project can be developed. Each of these phases is essential to the success of an Artificial Intelligence project. By following a methodical and systematic approach, it can be ensured that the models developed are not only technically sound but also generate real and sustainable value in practical applications.

13.1.2. Best Practices in each Phase

In each phase of the development of Artificial Intelligence models, it is essential to apply best practices to ensure the process is efficient, the results are accurate, and the model meets the project's objectives. We have already mentioned some; now let's make a list of all of them.

During problem definition, it is crucial to involve all relevant stakeholders from the beginning. This includes not only developers and data scientists but also domain experts, business analysts, and those who will be affected by the model's use. A clear and detailed definition of the problem helps avoid misunderstandings and ensures that the project aligns with strategic goals. Additionally, it is advisable to document all assumptions and expectations, as well as to define success metrics that are specific, measurable, achievable, relevant, and time-bound.

As we know, in the data collection and exploration phase, quality is fundamental. Procedures must be implemented to verify the integrity, consistency, and accuracy of the collected data. A recommended practice is to carry out a thorough exploratory data analysis (EDA) to identify patterns, relationships, and possible anomalies. Visualization techniques should be used to better understand the data distribution and to detect outliers or missing values. It is also advisable to consider diverse data sources to improve the model's representativeness and robustness.

As you have seen throughout the book, for data preprocessing, it is essential to apply cleaning techniques methodically. Removing duplicates, handling missing values consistently, and ensuring the consistency of formats are steps that help avoid errors in later stages. Normalization and standardization of data should be considered when features have different scales. Additionally, it is important to apply categorical variable transformation techniques, such as one-hot encoding, so they are compatible with Machine Learning algorithms.

In feature selection, best practices include carefully evaluating the relevance and redundancy of each feature. Automatic techniques such as correlation analysis, removing low-variance features, and feature selection methods like Recursive Feature Elimination (RFE) can be very helpful. However, it is equally important to consider domain knowledge to make informed decisions about which features to include or exclude. Documenting the reasons behind each feature selection is a recommended practice to facilitate future model reviews or audits.

Model building should begin with thorough research on the most suitable algorithms for the problem at hand. It is advisable to implement several baseline models and compare their results before deciding which one to use in production. Modularity is key; the model should be built in a way that allows for adjustments and improvements without needing to rewrite all the code. It is also advisable to use well-supported and up-to-date frameworks and libraries to ensure long-term scalability and maintenance.

During model training, it is essential to closely monitor the model's behavior in each iteration to detect potential problems such as overfitting or underfitting. A good practice is to split the data into training, validation, and test sets so that the model can be validated continuously during training. Using techniques such as cross-validation can help ensure the model is generalizable. Additionally, it is recommended to use regularization techniques, such as L1 or L2 penalties, to prevent overfitting.

In the validation phase, appropriate performance metrics should be used for the type of problem and applied consistently. It is advisable to evaluate the model across multiple metrics (for example, accuracy, recall, F1-score) to obtain a complete picture of its performance. One should avoid the temptation to tweak the model solely to improve a specific metric, as this can lead to undesirable trade-offs in other areas. It is also a good practice to carry out a sensitivity analysis to understand how the model responds to different inputs.

For implementation and deployment, it is crucial to carefully plan the transition of the model from the development environment to the production environment. This includes creating automated pipelines for continuous deployment, thorough testing in staging environments to identify potential issues before production deployment, and integration with existing systems via APIs or cloud services. It is advisable to use orchestration tools and containers to ensure the model is scalable and can be consistently replicated across different environments.

Finally, in the monitoring and maintenance phase, continuous monitoring mechanisms should be established to detect performance degradations of the model in real-time. This includes implementing automatic alerts and collecting logs to facilitate problem diagnosis. It is essential to plan and document model retraining processes to ensure it stays up to date with new data. Version control is equally important to track changes and revert to previous versions if necessary.

These best practices not only guarantee a more robust and efficient development but also ensure that deployed models are reliable, maintaining their value over time.

13.1.3. Support Tools

Let's make a summary list again with the most important tools. In the development of Artificial Intelligence models, it is essential to have support tools that facilitate each stage of the process, from the initial conceptualization to the deployment and continuous monitoring of the model. These tools not only optimize the workflow but also help maintain quality and consistency at every phase of the AI development lifecycle. Below are the most relevant support tools and their specific applications in each phase.

For project management and collaboration in multidisciplinary teams, platforms such as JIRA and Trello are widely used. JIRA is a robust tool that allows task management, incident tracking, and sprint planning in agile environments, which is crucial to keep control over the project's progress.

Trello, though simpler, is very effective for visual task management and facilitates collaboration through boards that can be customized according to the team's needs. These tools help ensure that all stakeholders are aligned with the project objectives and that tasks are carried out in an orderly manner and within established deadlines.

During data collection and preparation, tools like Apache NiFi and Talend stand out for their ability to automate and manage complex data flows. Apache NiFi provides a flexible platform for ingesting, processing, and distributing data in real-time, allowing data integration from various sources. Talend, on the other hand, offers a complete suite of tools for data integration and transformation, with capabilities to clean, combine, and enrich data before they are used in modeling. These tools are essential to ensure that the data used in building the model are of high quality and in the correct format.

Regarding exploratory data analysis and visualization, Python with its libraries Pandas, Matplotlib, and Seaborn is a standard option in the industry. Pandas facilitates the manipulation of large datasets, allowing data scientists to perform descriptive analyses and transformations efficiently. Matplotlib and Seaborn provide powerful visualization capabilities, enabling the identification of patterns, trends, and anomalies in data effectively. Additionally, tools like Tableau and Power BI offer more sophisticated and user-friendly visual solutions for presenting data, which is especially useful when presenting results to non-technical stakeholders.

For building and training models, TensorFlow, PyTorch, and Scikit-learn are fundamental. TensorFlow is widely used to build Machine Learning and Deep Learning models, offering great flexibility and scalability. PyTorch is preferred by many researchers due to its intuitive design and ease of use, especially in tasks that require rapid and experimental development. Scikit-learn, with its wide range of implemented algorithms, is ideal for quick prototyping and applications where simplicity and efficiency are key. Additionally, Keras, which runs on top of TensorFlow, provides a simpler API for creating neural networks, facilitating experimentation and quick iteration in model development.

During hyperparameter tuning and evaluation, tools like GridSearchCV and RandomizedSearchCV in Scikit-learn are essential. These tools automate the search process for optimal hyperparameters by evaluating multiple possible combinations based on model performance on a validation set. For more advanced and efficient tuning, Optuna and Hyperopt are libraries that implement more sophisticated optimization techniques, such as Bayesian search, which can significantly reduce the computation time needed to find the best hyperparameter configuration.

In model implementation and deployment, Docker and Kubernetes are key tools. We will look at these in the next section. On the one hand, Docker allows packaging applications and their dependencies into containers that can be run consistently across different environments, ensuring that the model behaves the same way in production as it does in development. Kubernetes, meanwhile, offers a platform for container orchestration, enabling automatic scalability, network traffic management, and the implementation of update and failure recovery strategies. These tools are fundamental to ensure that models can be deployed efficiently and remain operational and scalable in production environments.

For monitoring and maintaining models in production, Prometheus and Grafana are widely used. Prometheus is a monitoring and alerting tool that collects performance and availability metrics of models in real-time. Grafana, complementarily, offers advanced visualization capabilities, allowing DevOps teams and data scientists to monitor model performance through customizable dashboards. Additionally, MLflow is a tool that facilitates experiment tracking, model management, and deployment, providing a complete framework for managing the Machine Learning lifecycle.

Regarding documentation and traceability, tools like Jupyter Notebooks and Sphinx are essential. Jupyter Notebooks allows data scientists to combine code, visualizations, and explanatory text in a single document, which is ideal for documenting experiments and presenting results. Sphinx is used to generate technical documentation from source code, facilitating the creation of coherent and well-structured documentation for developed AI models and applications.

For version control and code management, Git and GitHub are indispensable tools, and when you learn to use them, you will see for yourself the great potential they have and the number of lines of code they will save you from writing. Git is a version control system that allows teams to effectively manage changes in source code, facilitating collaboration and the recovery of previous code versions if necessary. GitHub also offers a platform for project collaboration, with additional capabilities for code review, continuous integration, and automated deployment.

These support tools not only make AI model development easier but also ensure that processes are replicable, transparent, and efficient, allowing data teams to focus on innovation and the continuous improvement of model performance.

13.2. Tools and frameworks for deployment

13.2.1. Docker and Kubernetes

Docker and Kubernetes are two fundamental technologies in the implementation and deployment of applications, especially in the context of Artificial Intelligence models. Both tools have transformed the way applications are built, deployed, and scaled, allowing greater flexibility, consistency, and efficiency in development and operations processes.

Docker is a platform that allows packaging applications and their dependencies into containers. A container is a standardized unit of software that packages the application code along with all the libraries, dependencies, and configurations needed to run in any environment. This approach eliminates the problem of "environment compatibility" by ensuring that the application runs consistently regardless of where it is deployed: on a developer's local machine, in a test environment, or in production.

The main benefit of Docker is its ability to encapsulate applications in a way that makes them completely portable. Developers can define all dependencies and configurations in a Dockerfile, which is then used to build a Docker image. This image is a template from which containers are created, which are instances of the running image. Each container is isolated and has its own file system, network, and process space, ensuring that the applications inside them do not interfere with each other or with the host operating system.

In terms of deploying AI models, Docker facilitates reproducibility of the development, testing, and production environments. An AI model trained in a Docker container in the development environment can be deployed in an identical container in production, ensuring that the model's behavior does not vary between environments. This is especially critical when working with specific libraries and versions that are sensitive to changes in the underlying environment.

On the other hand, Kubernetes is a container orchestration platform used to manage containerized applications at scale. While Docker allows you to create and run containers, Kubernetes manages the deployment, scalability, and operation of those containers in a cluster of servers. A Kubernetes cluster is composed of a set of nodes (servers) running the containers, and Kubernetes provides an abstraction layer over these nodes, allowing operators to manage the cluster centrally.

Kubernetes automates many container management tasks, such as workload distribution (load balancing), automatic recovery in case of failures (retrying failed container executions), automatic scaling (adjusting the number of containers based on demand), and configuration and secret management (such as passwords and API keys). These features are essential to maintain robust and scalable AI applications in production.

In the context of an AI workflow, Kubernetes allows deploying models at scale and managing them efficiently. For example, if an AI model needs to be deployed in multiple instances to handle a high demand for real-time predictions, Kubernetes can automate the creation of additional containers and distribute requests evenly among them. Additionally, if a node in the cluster fails, Kubernetes can move the affected containers to other available nodes, minimizing downtime.

One of the great advantages of using Kubernetes in combination with Docker is the ability to manage the entire lifecycle of AI applications, from development to production, in a coherent and automated environment. Kubernetes also facilitates zero-downtime deployments (through rolling updates) and running different versions of a model simultaneously (using patterns like canary releases or blue-green deployments).

Furthermore, Kubernetes supports integration with CI/CD tools (Continuous Integration/Continuous Deployment), which allows fully automating the development and deployment workflow. This is particularly useful in AI projects where models may require frequent updates based on new data or adjustments to algorithms.

Here is an example of a basic Dockerfile that could be used to create an image of an AI model using `TensorFlow`:

```
# Use an official TensorFlow image as the base image
FROM tensorflow/tensorflow:2.4.1

# Set the working directory inside the container
WORKDIR /usr/src/app

# Copy the content of the current directory into the container at
/usr/src/app
COPY . .

# Install any necessary packages specified in requirements.txt
RUN pip install --no-cache-dir -r requirements.txt

# Make port 80 available to the outside world
EXPOSE 80

# Define an environment variable
ENV NAME World
```

```
# Run app.py when the container starts
CMD ["python", "./app.py"]
```

This Dockerfile defines a Docker image based on `TensorFlow` that copies the application code into the container, installs the necessary dependencies, and exposes port 80 for communication with the container.

Here is a basic example of a Kubernetes deployment file (YAML) that could be used to deploy the container in a Kubernetes cluster:

```
apiVersion: apps/v1
kind: Deployment
metadata:
  name: my-tensorflow-app
spec:
  replicas: 3
  selector:
    matchLabels:
      app: my-tensorflow-app
  template:
    metadata:
      labels:
        app: my-tensorflow-app
    spec:
      containers:
      - name: tensorflow-container
        image: my-tensorflow-image:latest
        ports:
        - containerPort: 80
```

This YAML file defines a deployment in Kubernetes with three replicas of a container based on the previously created TensorFlow image. Kubernetes orchestrates these replicas, ensuring that the service is available and scalable as needed.

13.2.2. TensorFlow Serving

If I'm not mistaken, TensorFlow Serving is a system designed specifically, and I mean "specifically," for the production and deployment of Machine Learning models in TensorFlow. It is a robust and flexible solution that allows trained models to be served efficiently, ensuring they are available to make real-time predictions from new inputs. This tool is optimized to handle Machine Learning models in production environments, where low latency and high availability are essential.

The main goal of TensorFlow Serving is to provide an infrastructure that facilitates the deployment of Machine Learning models in production without needing to rewrite or significantly modify the trained model's code. This is achieved through the ability to serve multiple versions of a model simultaneously and manage hot updates (without interrupting the service).

Key features of TensorFlow Serving:

- **Model Management:** TensorFlow Serving allows managing multiple models and model versions. This means that in a production environment, developers can deploy new versions of a model while keeping the previous versions running. This is essential in environments where A/B testing or comparing the performance of different versions of a model is required. The ability to serve multiple versions facilitates iterative development and deployment of models.

- **Dynamic Model Loading:** TensorFlow Serving supports dynamic model loading, meaning a model can be loaded into memory at runtime without needing to restart the server. This is crucial in production environments where service availability must be maintained without interruptions.

- **Configuration and flexibility:** TensorFlow Serving is highly configurable and flexible, allowing users to customize aspects such as request routing, automatic scaling based on load, and traffic routing policies between model versions. This level of customization ensures that TensorFlow Serving can adapt to different production needs.

- **Performance optimization:** TensorFlow Serving is designed to deliver low-latency predictions. It is optimized to handle large volumes of real-time prediction requests, making it an ideal choice for applications that require fast responses, such as recommendation systems, fraud detection, and automated medical diagnostics.

- **Prediction APIs:** TensorFlow Serving exposes both REST and gRPC APIs, making it easy to integrate with various applications and services. gRPC is a popular choice in high-demand environments due to its efficiency and support for communication between services in different programming languages.

- **Support for Batch and Streaming:** In addition to serving real-time predictions, TensorFlow Serving also supports batch processing and data streaming. This makes it versatile for different types of applications, from those requiring immediate responses to those processing large data volumes more slowly.

TensorFlow Serving Architecture

TensorFlow Serving follows a modular architecture, where each module can be configured and extended as needed. The main architecture includes the following components:

- **Model Server:** This is the core component of TensorFlow Serving that loads and serves models. This server is responsible for managing models, making predictions, and handling communication with client applications.

- **Servables:** These are the main units that TensorFlow Serving manages and serves. A servable can be a Machine Learning model, a lookup table, or any other artifact. TensorFlow Serving can load and handle multiple servables simultaneously.

- **Loader:** This component is responsible for loading servables. Whenever a model or servable is updated or changed, the loader loads it into the server without needing to stop the service.

- **Source:** This is the source from which TensorFlow Serving obtains the servables. It can be a file system, a database, or any other model storage. The source also monitors changes in the servables and notifies the server to perform the necessary updates.

- **Manager:** The manager coordinates the loading and access to the servables. It ensures that the correct versions of the servables are available and manages the transition between versions.

- **Core:** This is the core of TensorFlow Serving, which manages the central logic, such as resource allocation and performance optimization.

Implementation Example with TensorFlow Serving

Let's look at a basic example of how TensorFlow Serving could be configured to serve a trained TensorFlow model. Suppose you have a TensorFlow model trained and exported to a directory called model.

1. Export the model: First, the model must be exported in a format compatible with TensorFlow Serving. This process is usually done during or after training the model.

```
import tensorflow as tf
from tensorflow import keras

# Create a simple model
```

```
model = keras.Sequential([
    keras.layers.Dense(128, activation='relu', input_shape=(784,)),
    keras.layers.Dense(10, activation='softmax')
])

# Compile and train the model
model.compile(optimizer='adam',
              loss='sparse_categorical_crossentropy',
              metrics=['accuracy'])

# Export the model to a SavedModel format
tf.saved_model.save(model, 'model/1/')
```

In this example, the model is saved in a format that TensorFlow Serving can load. The model version is indicated in the subdirectory 1.

2. Run TensorFlow Serving: To serve the exported model, TensorFlow Serving must be configured to point to the directory where the model is located.

If you are using Docker, you can run TensorFlow Serving with the following command:

```
docker run -p 8501:8501 \
  --name=tf-serving \
  --mount type=bind,source=$(pwd)/model,target=/models/my_model \
  -e MODEL_NAME=my_model -t tensorflow/serving
```

In this command:

- `-p 8501:8501` exposes port 8501, which is the default port where TensorFlow Serving listens for requests.
- `--mount type=bind,source=\$(pwd)/model,target=/models/my\_model` mounts the directory where the model is located into the Docker container.
- `-e MODEL\_NAME=my\_model` sets the model name for TensorFlow Serving.

3. Make predictions: Once TensorFlow Serving is running, you can make predictions using the REST or gRPC API. Below is an example using the REST API:

```
import requests
import json

# Define the input data
data = {"instances": [[0.0, 0.0, 0.0, ..., 0.0]]}  # Input data
shape must match the model

# Make a POST request to the TensorFlow Serving API
```

```
response = requests.post('http://localhost:8501/v1/mod-
els/my_model:predict', json=data)

# Print the prediction
print(response.json())
```

This script sends a POST request to the TensorFlow Serving server to get predictions from the served model.

13.2.3. MLflow

MLflow is an open-source platform designed to manage the complete lifecycle of Machine Learning models, from initial experimentation to production deployment and continuous monitoring. Created by Databricks, MLflow provides a set of integrated tools that allow data science and Machine Learning teams to efficiently manage all phases of model development and deployment. MLflow has become a popular option due to its flexibility, scalability, and ability to integrate with multiple frameworks and work environments.

The main features of MLflow are grouped into four key components: MLflow Tracking, MLflow Projects, MLflow Models, and MLflow Registry. Below is a detailed description of each of these components.

1. MLflow Tracking

MLflow Tracking is a tool that allows exhaustive tracking of Machine Learning experiments. Through MLflow Tracking, developers can log and compare metrics, parameters, and artifacts generated during model training. This functionality is essential for iterative experimentation, where different model configurations must be evaluated and compared.

Some of the key functions of MLflow Tracking include:

- Logging of training parameters, such as learning rates, number of epochs, and other hyperparameters.
- Logging of performance metrics, such as accuracy, recall, F1-score, among others.
- Storage of artifacts, which can include model files, charts, configuration files, and more.
- Visualization of experiment results through an intuitive web interface, making it easier to compare different runs.

The following code shows a basic example of how MLflow Tracking is used to log parameters and metrics for a Machine Learning model trained with `scikit-learn`:

```
import mlflow
import mlflow.sklearn
from sklearn.ensemble import RandomForestClassifier
from sklearn.datasets import load_iris
from sklearn.model_selection import train_test_split
from sklearn.metrics import accuracy_score

# Load the dataset
iris = load_iris()
X_train,  X_test,  y_train,  y_test  =  train_test_split(iris.data,
iris.target, test_size=0.2, random_state=42)

# Define the model hyperparameters
n_estimators = 100
max_depth = 3

# Start an MLflow experiment
with mlflow.start_run():
    # Train the model
    model      =      RandomForestClassifier(n_estimators=n_estimators,
max_depth=max_depth)
    model.fit(X_train, y_train)

    # Make predictions
    predictions = model.predict(X_test)

    # Calculate accuracy
    accuracy = accuracy_score(y_test, predictions)

    # Log parameters and metrics to MLflow
    mlflow.log_param("n_estimators", n_estimators)
    mlflow.log_param("max_depth", max_depth)
    mlflow.log_metric("accuracy", accuracy)

    # Save the model
    mlflow.sklearn.log_model(model, "model")
```

2. MLflow Projects

MLflow Projects provides a standard format for defining and packaging Machine Learning projects. Each project in MLflow is defined by an MLproject file, which describes the required dependencies, instructions for running the project, and adjustable parameters. This allows projects to be easily reproducible and shareable across different development environments.

The key features of MLflow Projects include:

- **Portability:** Projects defined with MLflow Projects can be run in any environment that supports MLflow, whether locally, on remote servers, or in the cloud.
- **Reproducibility:** By explicitly defining dependencies and execution commands, MLflow Projects ensures that a project can be reproduced exactly the same way in different environments.
- **Flexibility:** MLflow Projects can integrate with any programming language or Machine Learning framework, making it suitable for a wide range of applications.

A simple example of an MLproject file can be seen below:

```
name: MyMLProject

conda_env: conda.yaml

entry_points:
  main:
    parameters:
      learning_rate: {type: float, default: 0.01}
      epochs: {type: int, default: 10}
    command: "python train.py --learning_rate {learning_rate} --
epochs {epochs}"
```

In this example, the file defines a project named `MyMLProject`, which uses a Conda environment defined in `conda.yaml` and runs through the command specified in `entry_points`.

3. MLflow Models

MLflow Models provides a standard way to package Machine Learning models for deployment. A model packaged with MLflow Models includes not only the model file itself but also metadata about how it should be used, making it easier to implement across different platforms.

Models in MLflow can be packaged and deployed in a variety of environments, including:

- **Local systems:** For quick testing and validation.
- **Production systems:** Via TensorFlow Serving, Kubernetes, or AWS SageMaker.
- **REST API:** MLflow Models can deploy a model as a web service using `mlflow.models.serve`.

An example of how to package a model with MLflow Models is as follows:

```
import mlflow
import mlflow.sklearn
from sklearn.ensemble import RandomForestClassifier
from sklearn.datasets import load_iris
from sklearn.model_selection import train_test_split

# Load the dataset
iris = load_iris()
X_train, X_test, y_train, y_test = train_test_split(iris.data,
iris.target, test_size=0.2, random_state=42)

# Train the model
model = RandomForestClassifier(n_estimators=100, max_depth=3)
model.fit(X_train, y_train)

# Save the model in MLflow format
mlflow.sklearn.log_model(model, "model")
```

This code saves the trained model in a format compatible with MLflow Models, which can then be used for deployment.

4. MLflow Registry

MLflow Registry is a registry system to manage model versions, track their evolution, and handle their lifecycle from development to production. This component is especially useful in environments where multiple versions of a model may be at different stages of their lifecycle (development, testing, production).

Key features of MLflow Registry include:
- **Versioning:** Each time a model is updated, it can be registered as a new version in the registry, making it easier to track the model's evolution.
- **Lifecycle management:** Models can move through different stages like `Staging`, `Production`, or `Archived`, allowing precise control over which versions are active in production.
- **Annotations and Descriptions**: Models and their versions can be annotated with descriptions, tags, and comments, making collaboration between teams easier.

MLflow covers all aspects of the Machine Learning model lifecycle, from experimentation and tracking to deployment and version management. Its ability to integrate with a variety of frameworks and platforms makes it ideal for Machine Learning development and production environments, providing data science teams with a flexible and efficient infrastructure to manage their projects effectively.

13.3. Model Monitoring and Maintenance

13.3.1. Model Monitoring Techniques

Monitoring Machine Learning models in production is a crucial task to ensure their continuous performance and to detect any type of drift that may affect the quality of predictions. This practice is fundamental because models can degrade over time due to changes in input data or the environment in which they operate. There are various techniques and tools that allow data science and operations teams to effectively monitor models in production, ensuring they continue to meet accuracy and efficiency requirements.

1. Model Performance Monitoring

The performance of a Machine Learning model in production must be constantly monitored to ensure its predictions remain accurate and useful. The metrics used in this monitoring include, but are not limited to, accuracy, recall, precision, F1-score, and the area under the ROC curve (AUC-ROC) for classification models, or mean squared error (MSE) and mean absolute error (MAE) for regression models. Continuously comparing these metrics with the values obtained during the validation phase can help identify whether the model is experiencing performance degradation.
An example of how this type of monitoring can be performed in code is as follows:

```
import numpy as np
from sklearn.metrics import accuracy_score

# Simulated production predictions
actual_labels = np.array([1, 0, 1, 1, 0, 1, 0, 1])
predicted_labels = np.array([1, 0, 1, 0, 0, 1, 1, 1])

# Calculate accuracy in production
accuracy = accuracy_score(actual_labels, predicted_labels)
print(f"Model accuracy in production: {accuracy:.2f}")
```

This code calculates the model's accuracy in production by comparing the actual labels with the predictions made. This type of calculation should be performed at regular intervals and compared with the results obtained during the model's development and validation.

2. Data Drift Monitoring

Data drift is one of the most common reasons why a model's performance may degrade. There are two main types of data drift: feature drift and concept drift. Feature drift occurs when the distribution of input features changes over time, while concept drift refers to changes in the relationship between the features and the output labels.

To monitor data drift, statistical techniques are used to compare the distribution of the training data with the current production data. A common method for drift detection is the Kolmogorov-Smirnov test, which measures the difference between two distributions. Below is an example of how this could be implemented in code:

```
from scipy.stats import ks_2samp

# Simulated training and production data
train_feature = np.random.normal(0, 1, 1000)
production_feature = np.random.normal(0.5, 1, 1000)

# Kolmogorov-Smirnov test for feature drift detection
ks_statistic, p_value = ks_2samp(train_feature, production_feature)
print(f"KS Statistic: {ks_statistic:.2f}, P-value: {p_value:.2f}")

# If p-value is small, it indicates significant drift
if p_value < 0.05:
print("Significant feature drift detected.")
else:

print("No significant feature drift detected.")
```

In this example, it is detected whether the distribution of a feature in the production data significantly differs from the distribution of that same feature in the training data.

3. Latency and Operational Performance Monitoring

In addition to accuracy and data drift, latency and the model's operational performance are key factors that must be monitored. Latency refers to the time it takes a model to return a prediction after receiving a request. If the response time increases significantly, it may indicate performance issues that need to be addressed, such as code inefficiencies, system overload, or scalability problems.

The following code simulates measuring a model's latency:

```
import time

# Simulate the prediction process
def predict():
time.sleep(0.05)  # Simulates a prediction that takes 50 ms
return "Prediction"

# Measure latency
```

```
start_time = time.time()
prediction = predict()
latency = time.time() - start_time

print(f"Model latency: {latency:.3f} seconds")
```

This type of measurement can be automated to run with each prediction or at regular intervals, storing the latency times and alerting if certain predefined thresholds are exceeded.

4. Monitoring Model Stability

Model stability refers to its ability to maintain consistent performance under different input conditions. Instability may appear as predictions that vary drastically with similar inputs or as high variance in performance metrics over time. To monitor stability, techniques such as cross-validation on live data or observation of predictions on specific data subsets can be applied.

One approach to monitor stability may involve evaluating the model on various production data subsets and analyzing the variation in performance:

```
from sklearn.model_selection import KFold

# Simulated production dataset
X_production = np.random.randn(100, 10)
y_production = np.random.choice([0, 1], size=100)

# K-Fold Cross Validation to monitor stability
kf = KFold(n_splits=5)
model_stability_scores = []

for train_index, test_index in kf.split(X_production):
    X_train, X_test = X_production[train_index], X_produc-
tion[test_index]
    y_train, y_test = y_production[train_index], y_produc-
tion[test_index]

    model.fit(X_train, y_train)
    accuracy = model.score(X_test, y_test)
    model_stability_scores.append(accuracy)

stability_variance = np.var(model_stability_scores)
print(f"Model stability variance: {stability_variance:.4f}")
```

In this code, the variance in the model's accuracy across different partitions of the production data is measured, providing an indication of how stable the model is under varying conditions.

5. Monitoring Interpretability and Explainability

In some cases, it is important to monitor not only the model's performance but also its interpretability and explainability, especially in environments where model-based decisions must be justified. Tools such as SHAP (SHapley Additive exPlanations) or LIME (Local Interpretable Model-agnostic Explanations) can be used to explain model predictions in real time and ensure that these explanations are consistent with expected domain knowledge.

Below is an example of how SHAP could be used to monitor a model's explainability:

```
import shap
explainer = shap.TreeExplainer(model)
shap_values = explainer.shap_values(X_test)

# Visualization of SHAP values to monitor interpretability
shap.summary_plot(shap_values, X_test)
```

This technique helps understand how each feature contributes to the model's final prediction, which is crucial in sensitive applications requiring high interpretability.

It is very important to keep in mind that monitoring Machine Learning models is an essential aspect of ensuring that deployed models continue to perform optimally over time. Using a set of techniques covering performance evaluation, drift detection, latency monitoring, and stability checks, teams can identify and address issues before they significantly impact the business. A combination of automated tools and manual analysis enables robust supervision, ensuring that models remain effective and reliable.

13.3.2. Retraining and Updating Models

Retraining and updating models are critical aspects of the lifecycle of a Machine Learning model in production. As environmental conditions change or new data becomes available, it is necessary to adjust or retrain models to maintain performance. Retraining not only ensures that models remain accurate and useful but also helps prevent issues such as model drift and obsolescence.

1. Model Retraining

Retraining refers to the process of re-training an existing model using new data that better reflects the current environment. This process may be necessary for several reasons:

- **Change in data distribution:** The distribution of input data may change over time, known as data drift. If a model trained on an old data distribution faces a new one, its performance may degrade.
- **Availability of new data:** As more data is collected, it can provide additional information that the original model did not consider, allowing for improved accuracy.
- **Update of the problem definition:** In some cases, the model's objective may change, requiring the model to be adjusted to align with the new problem definition.

The retraining process generally involves several steps:

1. **Collection of new data:** New data is collected and stored, ideally in a format that allows immediate use for retraining.
2. **Evaluation of the need for retraining:** The current model's performance is monitored to determine if retraining is necessary. This is done by comparing current performance metrics with historical metrics.
3. **Data preparation:** The data is preprocessed similarly to the original data used to train the model. This includes cleaning, normalizing, and transforming the data.
4. **Retraining:** The model is retrained using the new data. This may involve retraining the model from scratch or adjusting an existing model using techniques like transfer learning.
5. **Evaluation of the retrained model:** After retraining, the model is evaluated to ensure it has improved compared to the previous model. This evaluation includes comparing key metrics and testing on a validation dataset.
6. **Deployment of the updated model:** If the retrained model proves superior to the existing model, it is deployed in production.

Here is an example of how a basic retraining process could be implemented in Python using a logistic regression model:

```
from sklearn.linear_model import LogisticRegression
from sklearn.model_selection import train_test_split
from sklearn.metrics import accuracy_score

# Let's assume we have new data available
new_data = ...  # New data
new_labels = ...  # Labels corresponding to the new data
```

```
# Split the new data into training and test sets
X_train, X_test, y_train, y_test = train_test_split(new_data,
new_labels, test_size=0.2, random_state=42)

# Retrain the model
model = LogisticRegression()
model.fit(X_train, y_train)

# Evaluate the retrained model
y_pred = model.predict(X_test)
accuracy = accuracy_score(y_test, y_pred)
print(f"Accuracy of retrained model: {accuracy:.2f}")
```

This example shows a simple retraining process where new data is collected, trained on a logistic regression model, and the retrained model's performance is evaluated.

2. Model Updating

Model updating goes beyond simple retraining and involves deeper adjustments to the model, its architecture, or even its methodology. Updates may be needed when:

- **Technological evolution:** New modeling techniques or algorithm improvements can offer better results than existing models.
- **Change in business requirements:** If business goals or key metrics change, the existing model may need an update to align with these new objectives.
- **Incorporation of new features:** If new features are discovered that could improve the model's performance, an update may be required.

The process of updating models is more complex than retraining, as it may involve changes in the model architecture, the use of different algorithms, or the integration of new preprocessing and data transformation techniques.

A basic example of updating a model could involve switching from a simpler algorithm like logistic regression to a more complex model like a random forest:

```
from sklearn.ensemble import RandomForestClassifier

# Updated data and labels
updated_data = ...  # Data with new features
updated_labels = ...  # Labels corresponding to the updated data

# Train a new model with Random Forest
new_model = RandomForestClassifier(n_estimators=100, ran-
dom_state=42)
new_model.fit(updated_data, updated_labels)
```

```
# Evaluate the new model
new_y_pred = new_model.predict(X_test)  # X_test is the test set
new_accuracy = accuracy_score(y_test, new_y_pred)

print(f"Accuracy of updated model: {new_accuracy:.2f}")
```

This example shows how an existing model can be updated using a more advanced algorithm to improve performance.

3. Considerations for Retraining and Updating

Several key considerations exist when retraining and updating models:

- **Automating retraining:** In dynamic environments, it is useful to automate the retraining process to run regularly or in response to certain performance thresholds. This can be achieved using Machine Learning pipelines that automatically detect the need for retraining and execute the process.
- **Continuous monitoring:** Monitoring the model's performance is essential to determine when retraining or an update is necessary. Tools like MLflow can be used to track and compare the performance of different model versions.
- **A/B testing and shadow testing:** Before deploying a retrained or updated model, it is advisable to conduct A/B tests or shadow tests to compare the new model with the existing one in a controlled environment.

A/B testing involves splitting traffic between the old and new models to compare their real-time performance. Shadow testing, on the other hand, involves running the new model in parallel with the existing model, without the new model affecting production decisions, to compare results.

```
# Simple example of A/B testing (assumes a deployment environment)
def ab_test(model_A, model_B, data):
    # Split the data traffic between the models
    results_A = model_A.predict(data[:len(data)//2])
    results_B = model_B.predict(data[len(data)//2:])

    # Compare the results
    accuracy_A = accuracy_score(true_labels[:len(data)//2], re-
sults_A)
    accuracy_B = accuracy_score(true_labels[len(data)//2:], re-
sults_B)

    print(f"Model A accuracy: {accuracy_A:.2f}")
    print(f"Model B accuracy: {accuracy_B:.2f}")

# Assuming we have an existing model (model_A) and a new model (mo-
del_B)
ab_test(model_A, model_B, X_test)
```

4. Impact of Retraining and Updating

Retraining and updating models can have a significant impact on performance and operational efficiency. While retraining allows models to adapt to minor changes and maintain their performance, updating models can lead to substantial improvements in accuracy, efficiency, and the ability to handle more complex data. However, both processes must be carefully managed to avoid risks such as over-optimization or introducing errors into the production system.

In production environments, it is important to balance the need to keep models updated with system stability. This involves establishing clear policies on when and how retraining and updating processes should be carried out, ensuring that all changes are thoroughly validated and tested before being deployed to production.

Retraining and updating models are processes that allow our models to continue delivering value and adapt to new realities and data, and are therefore essential in maintaining Machine Learning models in production.

13.3.3. Model Versioning Management

Model versioning management in Machine Learning projects is a fundamental aspect to ensure reproducibility, traceability, and effective maintenance of models over time. As models are deployed and updated, multiple versions are generated, each with potential differences in data, algorithms, hyperparameter configurations, and results. Managing these versions effectively is crucial to avoid confusion, ensure system integrity, and allow quick recovery in case of issues.

1. Importance of Model Versioning Management

In traditional software development, version control is an established practice to maintain control over source code. Similarly, in Machine Learning, model versioning management ensures that each model can be replicated exactly as it was trained and evaluated, even if multiple versions are deployed at different times or environments.

The key reasons for implementing solid model versioning management are:

- **Traceability:** Allows identifying which version of a model was used at a given time, essential for audits and retrospective analyses.
- **Reproducibility**: Ensures that a model's results can be reproduced at any time using the same model version, data, and configurations.

- **Regression Handling:** Facilitates comparison between different model versions to identify whether an update has improved or worsened performance.
- **Failure Recovery:** Enables quick rollback to a previous model version if the new version introduces errors or its performance is unsatisfactory.

2. Key Elements in Model Versioning Management

Model versioning management involves several key elements that must be managed together to ensure a complete and usable model version:

- **Trained Model:** The file containing the weights and structure of the model after training.
- **Training and Validation Data:** The data used to train and validate the model. It is crucial to store data versions along with the model to ensure reproducibility.
- **Hyperparameter Configurations:** The specific hyperparameter values used to train the model. This includes configurations such as learning rate, number of layers, and other relevant parameters.
- **Training Code:** The code that defines how the model was trained. This may include preprocessing scripts, architecture definitions, and evaluation procedures.
- **Results and Performance Metrics:** The results obtained during training and evaluation of the model, including metrics such as accuracy, recall, F1-score, among others.
- **Metadata:** Additional information about the context in which the model was trained, such as creation date, hardware and software environment, or the conditions under which it was deployed.

3. Tools for Model Versioning Management

There are several tools that facilitate model versioning management.

- **MLflow:** MLflow is an open-source platform that facilitates the management of the Machine Learning model lifecycle. It offers functionalities for experiment tracking, model versioning, and model deployment to production.

```
import mlflow
import mlflow.sklearn

# Save a model with MLflow
with mlflow.start_run():
    mlflow.sklearn.log_model(model, "model")
    mlflow.log_params({"param1": value1, "param2": value2})
    mlflow.log_metric("accuracy", accuracy_value)
```

```
# Retrieve a saved model
model_uri = "runs:/<run_id>/model"
loaded_model = mlflow.sklearn.load_model(model_uri)
```

- **DVC (Data Version Control):** DVC is a tool that allows versioning data and Machine Learning models similarly to how Git manages source code. DVC tracks versions of data, trainings, and results, integrating these changes directly with Git for unified management.

- **Git LFS (Large File Storage):** Git LFS is an extension of Git that allows managing large files, such as trained models, within Git repositories. Although Git LFS is not specialized in Machine Learning, it is a simple solution for projects already using Git for version control.

- **TensorFlow Model Management Tools: TensorFlow** offers native tools for model versioning through TensorFlow Serving. These tools allow tagging and managing multiple versions of a model on a server, facilitating deployment and continuous updating.

4. Model Versioning Strategies

Implementing a clear and well-documented versioning strategy is essential to effectively manage multiple model versions. Below are some common strategies:

- **Semantic Versioning:** Similar to software versioning, semantic versioning assigns version numbers in a MAJOR.MINOR.PATCH format. A change in the MAJOR number indicates significant changes in the model's structure or purpose, while changes in MINOR and PATCH indicate incremental improvements or bug fixes.

Example:

- `1.0.0`: First version of the model
- `1.1.0`: Added a new feature set to the model
- `1.1.1`: Fixed a bug in data preprocessing

- **Git Tags and Branches:** Using tags in Git to mark specific model versions or using dedicated branches for the development of new versions can help maintain clear control over which versions are in development, testing, or production.

- **Experiment Tracking:** In addition to model versioning, it is important to track the experiments conducted during model development. This includes different hyperparameter configurations, datasets, and model architectures. Tools like MLflow and DVC are especially useful for this purpose.

5. Security and Compliance Considerations

Model versioning management must also take into account security and compliance aspects, especially in regulated industries such as healthcare or finance. Some considerations include:

- **Access Control:** Ensuring that only authorized personnel can access or modify critical model versions to prevent unauthorized changes.
- **Auditing:** Maintaining detailed records of all model versions, including who made the changes and when, to comply with audit and traceability regulations.
- **Regulatory Compliance:** Storing model versions in compliance with industry-specific regulations, such as GDPR in Europe or HIPAA in the United States, to ensure the protection of sensitive data.

6. Challenges in Model Versioning Management

Despite the available tools, model versioning management presents challenges that must be carefully addressed:

- **Storage Space:** Machine Learning models, especially those trained with large datasets, can occupy a significant amount of storage space. It is important to have strategies to manage this space, such as archiving old versions.
- **Compatibility Maintenance:** As models are updated, it is crucial to maintain compatibility with the applications that consume these models. This may require maintaining multiple versions of the same model in production.
- **Deployment Complexity:** Managing multiple versions in a production environment can complicate the deployment and update process. Tools like Kubernetes and TensorFlow Serving can help manage this complexity, but require proper configuration.

Implementing a robust versioning strategy, supported by appropriate tools and security practices, is essential for long-term success in managing models in production.

14. Infrastructure and Scalability

14.1. Infrastructure Considerations

14.1.1. Types of Infrastructure (on-premise, cloud)

In the context of developing and deploying Artificial Intelligence and Big Data systems, choosing the type of infrastructure is a critical decision that affects not only the performance and scalability of the systems but also costs, security, and operational flexibility. There are two main approaches to infrastructure: on-premise and cloud. Each of these approaches has its own characteristics, advantages, and disadvantages, and the choice between them will depend on specific project factors, such as processing requirements, security policies, available budget, and the scalability capacity needed.

On-Premise Infrastructure

On-premise infrastructure refers to the hardware and software setup that is physically located within an organization's premises. This includes servers, storage, networks, and other components needed to run AI and Big Data applications. Traditionally, this has been the preferred approach for many organizations due to the total control it provides over resources and data security.

One of the main advantages of on-premise infrastructure is full control over the IT environment. Organizations can customize their infrastructure to meet specific performance, security, and compliance requirements. Additionally, companies that manage their own data centers can avoid some of the recurring costs associated with cloud computing, such as subscription fees and pay-as-you-go charges.

However, the on-premise approach also presents several challenges. The initial investment in hardware and software can be significant, which poses a barrier to entry for some organizations, especially small and medium-sized enterprises. Moreover, on-premise infrastructure may require ongoing maintenance, including hardware and software updates, security patches, and hiring specialized personnel to manage the systems.

Another important challenge is scalability. While it is possible to scale on-premise infrastructure, doing so can be complex and costly, as it involves acquiring additional hardware and reconfiguring the IT environment. In situations where a rapid increase in processing or storage capacity is needed, on-premise infrastructure may not be agile enough to meet these demands.

Cloud Infrastructure

Cloud infrastructure, on the other hand, relies on the provision of IT resources through online services offered by providers such as Amazon Web Services, Microsoft Azure, Google Cloud Platform, among others. Instead of purchasing and maintaining physical hardware, organizations can rent computing resources, storage, and other services on demand, allowing them to scale quickly and adapt to changing business needs.

One of the main advantages of the cloud is its flexibility and scalability. Organizations can easily adjust resources based on demand, which is especially useful for AI and Big Data projects that may have significant workload peaks. Additionally, cloud providers offer a wide range of managed services, from databases to Machine Learning, allowing organizations to focus on developing their applications without worrying about the underlying infrastructure.

The cloud cost model is also different from on-premise infrastructure. Instead of making a significant upfront investment, organizations pay only for the resources they use, which can be more cost-effective for projects with fluctuating needs. However, cloud costs can add up quickly if not managed properly, especially in environments where resource usage is not well optimized.

Another important advantage of the cloud is the ability to access global infrastructure. Major cloud providers have data centers in multiple regions around the world, allowing organizations to deploy their applications closer to their end users to reduce latency and improve the user experience. Additionally, the cloud facilitates global collaboration, enabling distributed teams to work on the same projects with access to the same resources.

However, the cloud also has its disadvantages. One of the main concerns is data security and privacy. Although cloud providers offer a wide range of tools and services to secure data, organizations must rely on a third party to manage these critical aspects. Furthermore, regulatory compliance can be more complex in the cloud, especially in highly regulated industries.

Comparison and Considerations

When comparing on-premise and cloud infrastructure, it is important to consider the specific needs of the organization and the project. On-premise infrastructure may be more suitable for organizations that require full control over their resources and have the financial and human resources to manage a complex IT environment. It is particularly relevant in cases where data security is paramount and where strict regulatory compliance is required.

On the other hand, cloud infrastructure is ideal for organizations that need flexibility, rapid scalability, and a cost model more aligned with variable resource use. It is particularly beneficial for startups, small and medium-sized enterprises, or projects that require quick access to advanced resources without the need for a large upfront investment.

In practice, many organizations opt for a hybrid approach that combines elements of both on-premise and cloud infrastructure, leveraging the strengths of both approaches. This allows organizations to maintain control over their most sensitive data and applications while using the cloud to scale resources or for projects that require agile and flexible infrastructure.

The choice between on-premise and cloud infrastructure is not trivial and should be based on a careful analysis of project needs, organizational capabilities, and security and compliance requirements.

14.1.2. Selecting Suitable Infrastructure

Selecting suitable infrastructure for Artificial Intelligence and Big Data projects is a strategic decision that can significantly impact the success of the project. This decision should be based on a thorough analysis of various factors, including the project's technical requirements, costs, security, scalability, flexibility, and regulatory compliance.

1. Project Technical Requirements

The first step in selecting infrastructure is understanding the project's technical requirements. This includes the type and amount of data to be processed, the AI algorithms and models to be used, and the processing and storage needs. Big Data projects often involve managing large volumes of data, which requires scalable storage systems and efficient processing. Additionally, AI models, especially those based on Deep Learning, may require substantial computational resources, such as GPUs or TPUs, to train models efficiently.

2. Cost Analysis

Cost is a critical factor in infrastructure selection. It is essential to evaluate not only the initial implementation costs but also the long-term operational costs. On-premise infrastructure may require a significant initial investment in hardware and software, in addition to ongoing costs for maintenance, power, and technical staff. On the other hand, cloud infrastructure operates under a pay-as-you-go model, which can be more economical for projects with fluctuating demands. However, cloud costs can rise quickly if not managed properly, making it crucial to monitor and optimize resource usage.

3. Security and Regulatory Compliance

Data security and compliance with legal regulations are fundamental considerations, especially in regulated industries such as healthcare, finance, and the public sector. On-premise infrastructure offers greater control over data security, as data remains within the organization's premises. This can be essential for meeting strict regulations that require sensitive data to be kept on local servers. However, cloud providers also offer advanced security and compliance tools, including data encryption, security audits, and compliance with regulations such as GDPR and CCPA. The choice between on-premise and cloud should take into account the organization's security policies and applicable regulatory requirements.

4. Scalability and Flexibility

The ability to scale IT resources according to project needs is another important factor in selecting infrastructure. AI and Big Data projects may experience demand spikes during certain phases, such as model training or processing large data volumes. Cloud infrastructure is particularly advantageous in this regard, as it allows resources to be scaled quickly and easily. In contrast, scalability in on-premise infrastructure may be slower and more expensive, as it involves acquiring additional hardware. Flexibility is also key, as projects may evolve over time, requiring different resource configurations. The cloud offers unmatched flexibility in resource management, allowing organizations to adapt to changes in project requirements without needing to completely restructure their infrastructure.

5. Integration with existing tools and services

When selecting infrastructure, it is important to consider how it will integrate with the existing tools and services used by the organization. Many organizations already have significant investments in software and management systems that need to be compatible with the new infrastructure. In the case of cloud infrastructure, major providers offer a wide range of services and APIs that facilitate integration with existing systems, such as databases, storage systems, and Machine Learning tools. On-premise infrastructure, on the other hand, may require more customization and development to ensure smooth integration.

6. Fault tolerance and disaster recovery

The ability of the infrastructure to handle failures and recover from disasters is another critical consideration. AI and Big Data systems are often fundamental to an organization's operations, so it is crucial that the chosen infrastructure has robust fault tolerance and disaster recovery capabilities. Cloud providers generally offer advanced options for data redundancy, automatic failover, and replication across multiple geographic regions, ensuring that systems can continue operating even in the event of a catastrophic failure at a single location. In an on-premise infrastructure, implementing these capabilities can be more complex and costly, as it requires setting up secondary data centers and managing data replication.

7. Maintainability and support

The maintenance and support of the infrastructure are key factors that influence its long-term viability. On-premise infrastructure requires the organization to maintain a skilled technical team to manage the hardware and software, which can be challenging if the appropriate resources are not available. In contrast, cloud infrastructure offers provider-managed support, which can significantly reduce the operational burden for the organization. Cloud services also typically include automatic updates, security patches, and 24/7 technical support, which can be a major advantage for organizations that do not want to manage their infrastructure directly.

8. Implementation time

The time required to implement the infrastructure is also an important factor to consider. Cloud infrastructure allows organizations to quickly deploy their applications and services, as there is no need to wait for hardware acquisition and installation. This is especially valuable for projects that require a rapid launch or in situations where time to market is critical. On-premise infrastructure, on the other hand, may require considerable time for hardware acquisition, physical installation, and system configuration, which can delay the start of the project.

9. Environmental considerations

Environmental considerations are becoming increasingly important in infrastructure selection. Cloud infrastructure can be more energy-efficient due to the optimization and scalability offered by data centers managed by large providers. These providers are often committed to sustainability, using renewable energy and applying measures to reduce their carbon footprint. On-premise infrastructure, by contrast, may be less efficient in terms of energy consumption, especially if systems are not optimized for resource use or if facilities are not designed with sustainability criteria.

Let's make an assessment to establish an understanding of selecting the right infrastructure. This is a complex process that must consider multiple technical, financial, and strategic factors. The decision between on-premise and cloud infrastructure will depend on the specific needs of the project, the organization's capabilities, and operational constraints. In many cases, a hybrid approach that combines the best of both worlds can be the optimal solution, allowing organizations to leverage the advantages of the cloud while maintaining control and security of their most sensitive data in an on-premise infrastructure. If you are going to be responsible in your company or in projects, I recommend that you get up to date.

14.1.3. Costs and Performance

Cost and performance analysis is another fundamental aspect in the selection and management of infrastructure for Artificial Intelligence and Big Data projects. These two factors are intrinsically related, as the pursuit of optimal performance can incur significant costs, while cost reduction may negatively affect performance.

1. Infrastructure costs

Infrastructure costs are divided into several main categories, each with direct implications for the project's budget and feasibility.

Initial capital expenditures (CAPEX): These include the acquisition of hardware and software, as well as the construction or leasing of facilities for data centers in the case of on-premise infrastructures. In cloud projects, although there is no initial investment in hardware, there may be costs associated with the initial implementation and configuration of cloud services, such as architecture design and integration with existing systems.

Operating costs (OPEX): These are the recurring costs associated with the daily operation of the infrastructure. For on-premise infrastructures, they include hardware maintenance, power consumption, cooling, technical staff, and software licenses. In the cloud, operating costs are reflected in the pay-as-you-go model, where organizations pay for computing capacity, storage, and other services based on their actual usage. Although the pay-as-you-go model can offer flexibility, costs can rise quickly if not managed properly.

Scalability costs: The ability to scale infrastructure based on project needs also has cost implications. In the cloud, scalability is more flexible, but scaling up or down has associated costs. For example, additional storage, increased computing capacity, or the use of specialized services like GPUs or TPUs have a direct cost. In on-premise infrastructures, scalability involves acquiring additional hardware, which entails a significant capital investment and longer implementation times.

Opportunity costs: These are indirect costs associated with decision-making regarding infrastructure. For example, choosing a less expensive but lower-performing solution can lead to longer processing times, which could delay obtaining critical insights and ultimately impact business competitiveness.

2. Performance evaluation

Infrastructure performance should be evaluated based on several key criteria that directly impact the efficiency and effectiveness of Artificial Intelligence and Big Data projects.

Processing capacity: This is a crucial factor, especially in projects that require processing large volumes of data or training deep learning models. Infrastructure performance must be able to support workloads without causing bottlenecks. This includes processor speed, available RAM, and parallel processing capacity using GPUs or TPUs.

Latency and response time: In applications where speed is critical, such as real-time recommendation systems or automated decision-making, latency and response time are essential performance metrics. Cloud infrastructure can offer advantages in terms of latency, as providers usually have geographically distributed data centers that allow for lower latency for users in different locations.

Availability and resilience: Performance should also be evaluated in terms of the infrastructure's ability to remain operational at all times. High availability and fault resilience are crucial for critical applications. This involves having disaster recovery mechanisms, data redundancy, and failover systems that allow operations to continue without significant interruptions.

Resource efficiency: Resource efficiency is a performance measure that examines how the available capacity is used. An efficient system maximizes the use of CPU, memory, and storage, avoiding waste of resources. This is especially important in cloud infrastructures, where pay-as-you-go requires resources to be used optimally to minimize costs.

Scalability: Performance should also be measured in terms of the infrastructure's ability to scale without significant performance degradation. The infrastructure should be able to handle workload increases efficiently, whether through horizontal scaling (adding more servers or instances) or vertical scaling (increasing the capacity of existing servers).

3. Cost and performance comparison between on-premise and cloud infrastructure

Comparing on-premise and cloud infrastructure is essential to determine the option that best fits the project's needs.

On-premise: On-premise infrastructure can offer full control over costs and performance, allowing organizations to optimize each system component according to their specific needs. However, this comes with the downside of high initial costs and a greater maintenance burden. Performance can be optimized for specific workloads, but scalability and flexibility are more limited and expensive.

Cloud: Cloud infrastructure, on the other hand, offers greater flexibility and scalability. Initial costs are low, but operating costs can rise significantly over time if not managed properly. Cloud performance can be very high due to the availability of resources like GPUs and TPUs on demand, but it is important to monitor usage to avoid billing surprises. The cloud also offers advantages in terms of high availability and disaster recovery, with reduced downtime.

4. Cost and performance optimization

To maximize return on investment (ROI) in infrastructure, it is essential to implement optimization strategies that balance costs and performance.

Continuous monitoring and adjustment: Implementing monitoring tools to track resource usage and performance in real-time is crucial. This allows dynamic adjustment of resources according to project needs, reducing costs and improving performance.

Autoscaling and elastic workloads: In the cloud, leveraging autoscaling can help automatically adjust capacity based on demand, thus optimizing resource use and controlling costs.

Architecture optimization: Designing the infrastructure architecture efficiently can reduce operating costs. For example, using cold storage for infrequently accessed data or splitting workloads across different types of cloud instances based on their specific performance needs.

Negotiating with providers: For large-scale projects, negotiating with cloud service providers can result in discounts and customized rates, which can significantly reduce long-term costs.

Cost and performance evaluation is an ongoing process that requires periodic review as project needs change and available technologies evolve. It is important to maintain a balance between these two factors to ensure the infrastructure supports project objectives without incurring unnecessary costs or compromising performance, basically so it doesn't absorb the budget.

14.2. Scalability and Performance Optimization

14.2.1. Horizontal and Vertical Scalability Techniques

There are two main approaches to scaling an infrastructure: horizontal scalability and vertical scalability. Each approach has its own methods, advantages, and limitations, and the choice between them depends on the specific needs of the project, the nature of the workloads, and the available resources.

1. Horizontal scalability

Horizontal scalability, also known as scaling out, involves adding more machines or nodes to a system. Instead of increasing the capacity of a single machine, workloads are distributed across multiple machines to handle a larger volume of data or simultaneous users. This approach is commonly used in distributed systems and cloud-based applications.

Horizontal scalability techniques

1. Load balancing: Load balancing is fundamental in horizontal scalability. It distributes network traffic or service requests among several servers to ensure that none are overloaded. Load balancers can be specialized hardware or software, and they work by distributing incoming requests evenly or according to specific criteria, such as the fewest current connections or server performance.

2. Sharding: Sharding is a technique mainly used in databases and storage systems where data is split into smaller segments (shards) and stored on different servers or nodes. Each shard contains a portion of the complete dataset, and operations are performed only on the relevant shard, which reduces the load on each node and improves overall system performance.

3. Clustering: In a clustered system, multiple servers work together as a single cohesive system. Each node in the cluster can handle part of the workload, and if one node fails, other nodes can take over its load, providing high availability and redundancy. Clustering is common in application servers, databases, and distributed file systems.

4. Containerization and orchestration: The use of containers, such as Docker, facilitates horizontal scalability by allowing applications and services to be deployed uniformly across multiple nodes. Container orchestration with tools like Kubernetes enables automatic management of scalability, ensuring that the appropriate number of instances is available based on demand.

5. Replication: Replication involves creating duplicate copies of data or services across multiple nodes. This technique is used to improve availability and fault tolerance. For example, in distributed databases, data is replicated across several nodes to ensure information is always available, even if one node fails.

Advantages of horizontal scalability

Flexibility: Additional capacity can be added simply by adding more nodes to the system. This is especially advantageous in cloud environments, where resources can be added quickly without significant capital investment.

High availability and redundancy: Horizontal scalability facilitates the creation of highly available and redundant systems since the load is distributed across multiple nodes, and the failure of one node does not significantly affect the entire system.

Gradual costs: Instead of making a large investment in high-performance hardware, organizations can scale gradually, adding nodes as demand grows, allowing for better cost management.

Limitations of horizontal scalability

Management complexity: Horizontal scalability introduces complexities in system management, especially in coordinating between nodes, data consistency, and failure recovery.

Latency and synchronization: Distributing workloads across multiple nodes can introduce additional latencies and challenges in data synchronization, especially in globally distributed systems.

2. Vertical scalability

Vertical scalability, also known as scaling up, involves increasing the capacity of a single machine by adding more resources, such as faster CPUs, more RAM, or additional storage. Instead of distributing the load across multiple nodes, the performance of a single node is improved to handle larger workloads.

Vertical scalability techniques

1. Hardware upgrade: The most direct technique for vertical scalability is upgrading the hardware of the existing server. This can include adding more memory, upgrading the processor, or installing faster storage, such as SSDs instead of traditional hard drives. This approach allows a machine to handle more load without changing the system architecture.

2. Use of hyperthreading and overclocking: In some cases, a server's performance can be improved with techniques like hyperthreading, which allows each CPU core to handle multiple processing threads, or overclocking, which increases the CPU speed beyond its standard specifications. These techniques can provide short-term performance boosts, although with risks related to stability and power consumption.

3. Increasing storage capacity: Expanding the storage capacity of a server, either by adding additional disks or using more advanced storage technologies, is another form of vertical scalability. This is especially useful in systems that require large volumes of locally stored data, such as high-performance databases.

4. Software optimization: In addition to hardware improvements, software optimization, such as database tuning, code optimization, and algorithm enhancement, can increase the efficiency of the existing infrastructure, allowing a machine to handle more load without the need for hardware upgrades.

Advantages of vertical scalability

Ease of management: Vertical scalability is easier to manage compared to horizontal scalability because it does not introduce the complexity of managing multiple nodes. Administration focuses on a single system.

Lower latency: By not having to distribute the load across multiple nodes, vertical scalability can offer lower latency in operations, which is beneficial for applications that require fast responses.

Clear initial costs: Although it may require significant investment in hardware, the costs are clearly defined and do not depend on the complexity of a distributed architecture.

Limitations of vertical scalability

Physical limits: There is a limit to the resources that can be added to a single machine. Once that limit is reached, the only option to improve performance is to move to a larger infrastructure or switch to horizontal scalability.

Single point of failure: Unlike horizontal scalability, where the load is distributed, vertical scalability places the entire load on a single node, meaning that if that node fails, the entire system may become inoperative.

High costs: High-performance hardware upgrades can be expensive and often are not cost-effective compared to large-scale horizontal scalability.

Comparison and choice between horizontal and vertical scalability

The choice between horizontal and vertical scalability depends on several factors, such as the nature of the application, the available budget, performance requirements, and the need for high availability.

Use cases for horizontal scalability:
- Web applications with a large number of simultaneous users.
- Distributed systems requiring high availability and fault tolerance.
- Big Data processing where data is distributed across multiple nodes.

Use cases for vertical scalability:
- Critical applications that require low latency and high processing speed.
- Environments where management simplicity is a priority.
- Legacy systems that cannot be easily distributed.

In many cases, organizations and companies may choose a combination of both approaches, using vertical scalability to maximize the performance of individual nodes and horizontal scalability to distribute the load and increase redundancy. The optimal strategy will depend on the specific objectives of the project, the nature of the workload, and the limitations of the operating environment.

14.2.2. Model Performance Optimization

Model performance optimization is a crucial aspect in the development and deployment of Artificial Intelligence solutions. Improving model performance not only enables more accurate and efficient predictions but also reduces inference time and computational cost, which are key factors in real-time applications and large-scale systems. Optimizing performance involves working on various areas, ranging from hyperparameter selection and tuning to optimization of the underlying code and infrastructure.

Hyperparameter Optimization

Hyperparameters are model settings that are not learned during training but are set before the learning process begins. Hyperparameter optimization can significantly enhance model performance. There are several techniques to optimize these parameters:

Grid Search: This technique involves an exhaustive search through a predefined hyperparameter space. Although simple and guaranteed to find the best set of parameters within the grid, it can be computationally expensive, especially if the search space is large.

Random Search: Instead of testing all possible combinations, random search selects random combinations of hyperparameters. While it may not guarantee finding the best solution, it is more efficient in terms of time and computational resources.

Bayesian Optimization: This technique is based on building a probabilistic model of the hyperparameter space and selecting hyperparameter values that maximize an expected objective criterion. It is more efficient than grid and random search, especially in complex search spaces.

Specific Hyperparameter Optimization Methods: For certain models, such as deep neural networks, specialized techniques like learning rate scheduling, batch normalization, and advanced weight initialization are used to improve model performance.

Model Optimization

Beyond hyperparameters, the design and structure of the model also influence its performance.

Feature Selection: Choosing a subset of relevant features can improve model efficiency and reduce the risk of overfitting. Feature selection and dimensionality reduction techniques, such as Principal Component Analysis and Linear Discriminant Analysis, are useful for this purpose.

Regularization: Regularization is a technique that introduces a penalty for model complexity, helping to prevent overfitting. Common forms of regularization include L1 (Lasso) and L2 (Ridge) regularization, as well as regularization in neural networks using techniques like Dropout.

Training Algorithm Optimization: Some models, like deep neural networks, can benefit significantly from optimizing the training algorithm. Techniques such as adaptive learning rate reduction and optimization using advanced algorithms like Adam, RMSprop, or AdaGrad can accelerate convergence and improve performance.

Model Size Reduction: In resource-constrained environments or when aiming to reduce inference latency, minimizing model size is crucial. This can be achieved through compression techniques such as neural network pruning, weight quantization, and using lightweight models like MobileNet or SqueezeNet.

Code Optimization

A model's performance depends not only on its structure and parameters but also on the efficiency of the code that implements it. Code optimization can include:

Parallelization: Leveraging parallelization in training and inference can significantly improve performance. This involves dividing tasks among multiple CPU cores or GPUs to speed up processing. Tools like TensorFlow and PyTorch make it easy to implement parallelization.

Vectorized Code Optimization: Instead of using iterative loops, vectorization allows operations on blocks of data simultaneously, which significantly reduces computation time.

Use of Optimized Libraries: Using optimized libraries for mathematical and processing operations, such as cuDNN for neural networks on GPUs, can greatly enhance performance. These libraries are designed to fully leverage the underlying hardware architecture.

Caching of Intermediate Results: Storing intermediate results of costly computations can avoid the need to recompute them, reducing computational load and improving efficiency.

Infrastructure Optimization

The infrastructure where a model runs also plays a key role in its performance. Some considerations include:

Hardware Selection: Choosing the right hardware is essential for model performance. For example, for models requiring intensive floating-point operations, such as deep neural networks, GPUs or TPUs can offer significant improvements compared to traditional CPUs.

Use of Cloud Infrastructure: Cloud platforms allow dynamic adjustment of resources according to demand. This not only improves performance but also optimizes cost by paying only for the resources used.

Load Distribution: In large-scale applications, distributing the load across multiple machines can enhance performance and resilience. This includes using computing clusters and load balancing services.

Auto-Scaling: The ability to automatically scale resources based on workload helps maintain optimal performance at all times. Cloud platforms offer auto-scaling services that adjust resources in real time.

Continuous Monitoring and Maintenance

Performance optimization is not a one-time process; it requires continuous monitoring and maintenance. A model's performance can degrade over time due to data changes, software updates, or infrastructure changes. It is crucial to establish a monitoring system to proactively detect and address these issues.

Performance Monitoring: Implementing monitoring systems that log key model metrics, such as accuracy, inference latency, and resource usage, allows identification of performance issues before they impact end users.

Periodic Retraining: Over time, data may change, which can lead to model performance degradation. Performing periodic retraining with updated data ensures the model maintains its accuracy and relevance.

Continuous Adjustments and Improvements: Based on data collected through monitoring, continuous adjustments to the model configuration, hyperparameters, or infrastructure can sustain improved performance.

Debugging and Testing Practices

Performance optimization also involves effective debugging and testing practices. Ensuring that the code is error-free and that the model functions as expected is essential to avoid performance issues.

Unit and Integration Testing: Implementing a robust set of unit and integration tests ensures that each model component functions correctly and that updates do not introduce new issues.

Bottleneck Debugging: Identifying and eliminating bottlenecks in the code or model architecture can free up resources and improve performance. Code profiling and performance analysis tools are useful in this process.

Model performance optimization is a multifaceted process that involves enhancing various aspects, from hyperparameters and model architecture to code efficiency and infrastructure choices. These efforts not only ensure that models are accurate and fast but also make them scalable and cost-effective to operate.

14.2.3. Caching and Parallelization

Caching and parallelization are two fundamental strategies to improve performance and efficiency in systems that handle large volumes of data or require complex computations. These techniques are especially relevant in the context of Big Data, Artificial Intelligence, and real-time applications, where optimizing computational resources is crucial to maintain scalability and minimize processing times.

Caching

Caching is a technique used to temporarily store the results of computations or data that are costly to generate or retrieve repeatedly. By saving these results in fast-access memory, such as RAM or distributed cache storage, access times in future requests are significantly reduced. Effective use of caching can have a positive impact both on processing speed and in reducing the load on backend systems or databases.
Types of Caching:

In-memory caching: This is the most common type of cache, where data is stored in RAM for fast access. Tools like Redis and Memcached are popular examples of in-memory caching systems. These are especially useful in web applications to store frequently queried data, such as user settings or database query results.

Disk caching: Although slower than in-memory caching, disk caching is used when data volumes are too large to store in RAM. Data is written to fast storage disks, such as SSDs, so it is available when needed again. This is useful in data analysis applications where intermediate data is generated and needs to be reused in later processing stages.

Distributed caching: In distributed environments, such as computing clusters or cloud services, distributed caching allows cached data to be shared between different nodes. This improves efficiency and reduces redundancy in accessing common data. Tools like Apache Ignite or Hazelcast are examples of distributed caching solutions.

Cache expiration and update strategies:

TTL (Time to Live): Setting a lifespan for cached data ensures that information is not kept indefinitely and that outdated data is removed or updated. This technique is crucial in scenarios where data changes frequently.

Cache invalidation: This is the process of invalidating or removing cached data when it has changed at the original source. Invalidation strategies include event-based invalidation (when a change in the data triggers cache removal) and manual or scheduled invalidation.

Cache warming: Preloading the cache with data that is likely to be used in the future can reduce wait times for initial requests. This strategy is useful in applications that anticipate load spikes or where pre-computations are costly.

Parallelization

Parallelization is the process of dividing a task into smaller sub-tasks that can be executed simultaneously on multiple CPU cores, threads, or even on different machines in a cluster. This is essential in high-demand applications and large data volumes, as it allows maximum utilization of available resources and reduces processing times.

Types of parallelization:

Data-level parallelization: In this strategy, data is divided into blocks or partitions that are processed independently in parallel. This approach is common in Big Data and Machine Learning algorithms that can operate on data subsets, such as MapReduce in Hadoop or operations on RDDs (Resilient Distributed Datasets) in Apache Spark.

Task-level parallelization: Here, different tasks or functions are executed in parallel. This technique is useful when a process can be divided into different independent stages or functions, allowing simultaneous execution. Data processing pipelines and analysis workflows often benefit from this strategy.

Thread-level parallelization: In multicore systems, thread-level parallelization allows a single task to run across multiple threads, each handling a part of the work. This is common in software applications where a computation can be broken into smaller parts to run in parallel on different CPU cores.

Implementation of parallelization:

MapReduce: This is a distributed programming model that allows breaking down a large data processing task into small tasks that can be executed in parallel. The Map and Reduce phases enable efficient processing and combining of results. This technique is widely used on platforms like Hadoop.

DAGs (Directed Acyclic Graphs): In systems like Apache Spark, tasks are organized in directed acyclic graphs, where nodes represent tasks and edges indicate dependencies. Parallel execution of tasks in a DAG optimizes workflow by allowing independent tasks to run simultaneously.

MPI (Message Passing Interface): This is a standard library used for parallel computing in computer clusters. MPI allows multiple processes on different nodes to communicate and coordinate their efforts in distributed tasks. It is especially useful in scientific and engineering applications that require high computational performance.

Considerations in parallelization:

Synchronization and consistency: When parallelizing tasks, it is essential to ensure that synchronized tasks share resources correctly to avoid race conditions and ensure data consistency. Mechanisms like locks and semaphores are common to manage synchronization.

Load balancing: In distributed environments, it is important to ensure that tasks are distributed evenly across available resources. Dynamic load balancing adjusts task allocation in real time, based on performance and resource availability.

Minimizing communication: In distributed parallelization, communication between nodes can become a bottleneck. Minimizing the need for communication and optimizing data transfers between nodes can significantly improve overall system performance.

Caching and parallelization in real applications

In practice, caching and parallelization are often used together to maximize performance. For example, in real-time recommendation systems, such as those used by streaming or e-commerce platforms, caching stores previously generated recommendations, while parallelization processes new requests in parallel.

In Artificial Intelligence, parallelization is key in training Deep Learning models, where intensive computations are distributed across multiple GPUs. At the same time, caching is used to store intermediate data and avoid costly recomputations during training.

Proper implementation of caching and parallelization can make a significant difference in performance and the ability to handle large data volumes in critical applications.

14.3. Use of Containers and Orchestration (Docker, Kubernetes)

14.3.1. Basic Concepts of Containers

Containers are a lightweight virtualization technology that allows packaging and running applications consistently across different environments. Unlike traditional virtual machines, which emulate complete hardware, containers share the same underlying operating system but run in isolated environments. This enables greater efficiency and portability, making containers a popular choice for developing, deploying, and scaling applications in the cloud computing and microservices era.

Key container concepts:

1. Container images: Container images are immutable templates that include everything needed to run an application, such as the source code, libraries, dependencies, and necessary configurations. An image is generally built from a definition file known as a Dockerfile (in the case of Docker, the most common container system) that specifies how the image should be constructed. Once created, the image can be shared and run in any environment that supports containers, ensuring the application behaves the same across different systems.

2. Containers: A container is a running instance of an image. Each container has its own file system, processes, network, and user space, providing it with an isolated and secure environment. Unlike virtual machines, which require a full operating system for each instance, containers share the host operating system's kernel, significantly reducing resource consumption. This sharing allows multiple containers to run efficiently on the same machine.

3. Isolation: Isolation is one of the fundamental features of containers. Each container operates in its own environment, separated from the rest, meaning processes in one container cannot directly interfere with processes in another container. This isolation is provided by technologies such as namespaces and cgroups in Linux. Namespaces separate system resources, such as process IDs, networks, and mount points, while cgroups control the amount of system resources, such as CPU, memory, and network bandwidth, that a container can use.

4. Portability: One of the greatest advantages of containers is their portability. Because they encapsulate everything needed to run an application, container images can be moved between different environments without affecting the application. This facilitates development, testing, and production across different platforms, such as local environments, on-premise servers, and public or private clouds. The container ensures that the application runs the same way, regardless of where it is deployed.

5. Data persistence: Containers are designed to be ephemeral, meaning that data generated inside a container is lost when it is deleted. To handle persistent data, it is common to use data volumes or mount host directories in the container. Volumes are the recommended way to persist data in Docker because they are outside the container's lifecycle and can be shared between multiple containers. This is essential for applications that require permanent storage, such as databases.

6. Networking and communication between containers: Each container has its own virtual network stack, allowing it to communicate with other containers, the host, or the outside world. Containers can be connected to specific virtual networks to facilitate communication between them. Docker, for example, offers several network options, such as bridge, host, and overlay mode, which are used depending on the application's connectivity and isolation requirements. The bridge mode is the default and allows containers on the same host to communicate with each other, while the overlay mode is used in cluster environments to connect containers on different hosts.

7. Container management: Container management includes orchestration, monitoring, and scaling of containers in production environments. Orchestration tools like Kubernetes, Docker Swarm, and OpenShift are used to automate the deployment, management, scaling, and networking of containers. These platforms allow defining policies for managing multiple containers in server clusters, ensuring that applications remain available and scalable according to demand.

8. Security: Security in containers is critical since they share the underlying operating system kernel. However, containers offer several built-in security mechanisms, such as process isolation, network segmentation, and role-based access control capabilities. Additionally, it is important to apply security practices such as vulnerability scanning in images, running containers as non-privileged users, and restricting unnecessary capabilities in containers.

9. Container use cases: Containers are ideal for a wide range of use cases, including developing and testing applications, deploying microservices, running legacy applications in modern environments, and orchestrating large volumes of cloud services. In DevOps environments, containers are essential for building efficient CI/CD pipelines, where the same container can move from development to production without changes.

Understanding the basic concepts of containers is essential to leverage their advantages in implementing and operating modern applications. I would even say they are important for virtually any project.

14.3.2. Orchestration with Kubernetes

Kubernetes is an open-source container orchestration platform that automates the deployment, management, scaling, and operation of containerized applications. Originally developed by Google and now maintained by the Cloud Native Computing Foundation (CNCF), Kubernetes has become the de facto standard for container orchestration in the industry. Its ability to manage container clusters distributed across multiple nodes makes it an essential tool for managing modern applications that require high availability, scalability, and portability.

Key Kubernetes concepts:

- **Kubernetes Cluster:** A Kubernetes cluster consists of a set of nodes running containers under the supervision of a centralized control plane. The control plane is responsible for maintaining the desired state of the cluster, while the nodes run the workloads. A typical cluster includes a master node (or multiple for high availability) that manages the control plane and multiple worker nodes where the containers run.

- **Nodes:** Nodes are the physical or virtual machines that are part of the cluster and that run the containers. Each node contains an agent called kubelet, which is responsible for communicating with the control plane to receive instructions and report the status of the node. Additionally, each node runs a container runtime (such as Docker or containerd) that executes and manages the containers.

- **Pods:** The pod is the smallest deployment unit in Kubernetes and represents one or more containers running in a shared environment. Containers within a pod share the same storage, network, and lifecycle, allowing them to communicate efficiently with each other. Pods are ephemeral and can be created and destroyed by Kubernetes as needed by the application.

- **Services:** A service in Kubernetes is an abstraction that defines a logical set of pods and a policy to access them. Services provide a stable and reliable way to access pods, regardless of their location in the cluster. This is essential for service discovery and load balancing in distributed applications.

- **Controllers:** Controllers are Kubernetes components that manage the desired state of resources. There are different types of controllers, such as Deployment, which ensures that a specific number of pod replicas are running at all times, or StatefulSet, which manages pods with identity and persistent storage.

- **Namespaces:** Namespaces are a way to divide a Kubernetes cluster into isolated virtual environments. This allows logical separation of resources within the same cluster, making it easier to manage applications that require isolation, such as development, testing, and production environments.

Orchestration and management in Kubernetes:

1. Automatic scalability: Kubernetes allows applications to scale automatically based on demand. Using the Horizontal Pod Autoscaler, Kubernetes can increase or decrease the number of pod replicas based on metrics such as CPU utilization or network load. It is also possible to scale the cluster itself using external tools to add or remove nodes according to the workload.

2. Configuration and secrets management: Kubernetes provides mechanisms to manage application configurations and secrets (sensitive information such as credentials or keys). ConfigMaps and Secrets are resources that allow configuration to be separated from application code, facilitating management and security in dynamic environments.

3. Updates and deployments: Kubernetes supports different deployment strategies to update applications without downtime. Strategies such as Rolling Update allow gradual updates of pods, while Canary deployment strategies allow testing new versions of the application on a subset of users before a full rollout. Kubernetes also provides automatic rollback in case of failure.

4. Load balancing and networking: Kubernetes has built-in load balancing capabilities, allowing traffic distribution between the pods that make up a service. Kubernetes also manages internal networking between pods through a flat network model, where all pods can communicate with each other unless network policies are applied to restrict this communication.

5. Monitoring and logging: Monitoring and logging are critical aspects of managing applications in Kubernetes. Kubernetes facilitates integration with monitoring tools such as Prometheus and logging tools such as Fluentd to collect and analyze metrics and logs at both application and system levels. This allows proactive problem identification and resolution.

Kubernetes in practice

Kubernetes is widely used in the deployment of microservices applications, where resilience, scalability, and portability are essential. Kubernetes integrates with CI/CD tools, facilitating a continuous development workflow, and supports deploying applications in public clouds, private clouds, or hybrid environments. Using Kubernetes allows companies to manage complex infrastructures efficiently and consistently, ensuring that applications are always available and ready to scale as needed.

Here is a basic example of how to define a deployment and a service in Kubernetes using YAML files:

```
apiVersion: apps/v1
kind: Deployment
metadata:
  name: nginx-deployment
spec:
  replicas: 3
  selector:
    matchLabels:
      app: nginx
  template:
    metadata:
      labels:
        app: nginx
    spec:
      containers:
      - name: nginx
        image: nginx:1.14.2
        ports:
        - containerPort: 80

---
apiVersion: v1
kind: Service
metadata:
```

```
  name: nginx-service
spec:
  selector:
    app: nginx
  ports:
  - protocol: TCP
    port: 80
    targetPort: 80
  type: LoadBalancer
```

This code defines a deployment that deploys three replicas of an Nginx container, and a service that balances the load between these replicas. Kubernetes ensures that the three replicas are running at all times and that the service distributes incoming traffic evenly among them.

This basic example only scratches the surface of Kubernetes' capabilities, which include advanced tools for configuration management, security, scaling, and monitoring, making this platform an essential standard in modern application development and deployment.

14.3.3. Benefits of using Containers

The use of containers in application development and deployment has revolutionized the way organizations manage their technology infrastructures. Containers offer a series of benefits ranging from consistency in the runtime environment to improved resource efficiency and ease of application management.

1. Portability:

Containers encapsulate all the dependencies needed to run an application, including libraries, configurations, and code, ensuring that the application runs consistently in any environment. This means that a container that works in the development environment will work the same in production, regardless of differences in the operating system or underlying infrastructure. This portability simplifies the development and deployment process, significantly reducing compatibility issues between environments.

2. Consistency and reproducibility:

Containers provide an isolated and predictable runtime environment. Every time a container runs, it starts in the same state, ensuring that the application behaves identically on each run. This is crucial to ensure that testing, development, and production are consistent, making it easier to identify and fix errors and ensuring that application updates do not introduce unexpected behaviors.

3. Application isolation:

Each container operates in its own isolated space, meaning multiple containers can run on a single host without interfering with each other. This isolation improves security and stability, as a problem in one container does not affect the others. It also allows different versions of the same application or different applications with conflicting dependency requirements to run on the same system without issues.

4. Scalability:

Containers are extremely lightweight compared to traditional virtual machines, allowing a large number of containers to run on a single server. This resource efficiency facilitates horizontal scaling, where multiple instances of an application can be deployed in different containers to handle increases in demand. Orchestration platforms like Kubernetes automate this process, dynamically adjusting the number of containers based on traffic needs.

5. Resource efficiency:

Unlike virtual machines, which require a complete operating system for each instance, containers share the host's operating system kernel, making them much lighter in terms of resource consumption. This efficiency means containers can start and stop quickly, allowing for more dynamic and efficient use of infrastructure, reducing costs, and improving application responsiveness.

6. Deployment and development speed:

Containers can be built, deployed, and updated quickly. This fast lifecycle is especially useful in agile development environments, where frequent updates and deployments are common. With containers, developers can work in environments that accurately replicate the production environment, accelerating the development, testing, and implementation of new features.

7. Ease of management and automation:

The integration of orchestration tools like Kubernetes enables automatic management of containers at scale. These tools can handle the distribution of containers across cluster nodes, perform automatic scaling, manage continuous updates, and provide high availability by redistributing containers in the event of a node failure. The ability to define infrastructure as code also allows automation of repetitive tasks and simplifies maintenance.

8. Enhanced security:

Containers offer several inherent security mechanisms, such as process isolation and access control to system resources, minimizing the attack surface in case of a vulnerability. Additionally, security updates can be applied quickly by rebuilding and redeploying container images. Tools like Docker also allow image verification to ensure that only trusted sources are used.

9. Reduced operational costs:

Resource efficiency and the ability to maximize workload density on fewer physical servers or cloud instances translate into significant operational cost savings. By making the most of existing infrastructure, organizations can reduce spending on hardware, energy, and system administration, resulting in greater profitability and a faster return on investment.

10. Flexibility and adaptability:

Containers are highly adaptable and can easily integrate with various tools and technologies. For example, they can be used in microservices architectures, where each component of the application runs in its own container and can be managed, scaled, and updated independently. This flexibility allows organizations to adopt new technologies and deployment strategies without the need to completely restructure their infrastructure.

11. Support for DevOps and CI/CD:

Containers are fundamental in implementing DevOps practices and continuous integration and continuous deployment (CI/CD) pipelines. They enable automation of the software development, testing, and deployment lifecycle, ensuring that code changes are integrated and deployed quickly in production. This reduces time to market for new features and improves software quality through continuous testing in consistent environments.

Containers have completely influenced the way applications are developed, deployed, and managed, offering benefits that range from portability and efficiency to security and scalability. These benefits make containers one of the most important tools for any organization or company seeking to optimize its technology infrastructure and improve the agility of its software development.

PART VI

Ethics, Privacy, and the Future

Part VI: Ethics, Privacy, and the Future

15. Ethics and Responsibility in AI

Ethics and responsibility in Artificial Intelligence are central topics in the development and implementation of AI-based technologies.

With this chapter, my goal is to explore the fundamental ethical principles that should guide the development and implementation of AI systems, as well as examine the possible social and economic consequences of their use. Artificial Intelligence technology is not just a technical tool but also an agent with the potential to significantly influence society. Therefore, it is crucial that its development and application be carried out in a way that maximizes benefits while minimizing risks.

15.1. Ethical Principles in AI Development

15.1.1. Transparency and Explainability

Transparency and explainability in Artificial Intelligence systems are fundamental concepts to ensure trust and the acceptability of these technologies across various fields, from medicine to justice. As AI algorithms become more complex and are used in critical decisions that affect people and organizations, the need to understand how and why certain decisions are made becomes increasingly imperative.

Transparency in Artificial Intelligence refers to the clarity with which the internal operations of an AI system can be observed and understood. A transparent system allows developers, users, and other stakeholders to inspect how the model processes information, makes decisions, and generates results. This is not only vital for detecting and correcting errors but also to ensure that the system operates according to established ethical and regulatory standards.

One of the greatest challenges in the transparency of AI systems is the inherent complexity of many models, especially those based on deep neural networks and other advanced algorithms. These models, often referred to as "black boxes," are difficult to interpret due to the large number of parameters and the nonlinear nature of their operations. Although they produce highly accurate results, understanding how they arrived at those results can be extremely complicated. This lack of transparency can lead to a lack of trust in the system, especially in contexts where decisions have a significant impact on people's lives.

On the other hand, explainability refers to the ability of an AI system to provide understandable explanations about its decisions and results. Explainability goes a step beyond transparency, as it not only involves the system being transparent in its operation but also being able to effectively communicate in understandable terms how it arrived at a specific decision. Explainability is crucial in applications where end users do not have deep technical knowledge but need to trust the system's decisions, such as doctors using AI for diagnoses or judges reviewing recommendations generated by algorithms.

The lack of explainability in AI systems can lead to several problems. For example, in the legal field, if an AI system suggests a sentence for a court case but cannot clearly explain how it reached that conclusion, judges and lawyers might question the validity of the recommendation, or at least they should. In healthcare contexts, a diagnosis system based on AI that cannot explain its reasoning might be considered unreliable, putting patients' lives at risk if its results are blindly trusted.

To address these challenges, several techniques have been developed to improve the explainability of AI models. One such technique is breaking down the model into simpler components that are easier to understand. For example, in machine learning models, developers can use visualization techniques that show how different input features affect the model's output. Another technique is the creation of explanatory models that simplify the decisions of the original model. These models are less accurate but their simplicity makes them easier to interpret.

In addition, approaches like LIME and SHAP have been proposed to enhance explainability. LIME, for example, generates simplified linear models around a specific prediction to explain how each feature influences that prediction. SHAP, on the other hand, uses game theory to assign values to different features, helping to understand their importance in the final prediction. Both methods are model-agnostic, meaning they can be applied to a wide range of AI algorithms.

The implementation of transparent and explainable AI systems is also linked to ethical and legal aspects. In some industries, regulation already requires minimum levels of explainability for certain types of automated decisions. For example, the European Union's General Data Protection Regulation includes provisions that could be interpreted as a right to an explanation when automated decisions significantly affect individuals. This means companies must be prepared to provide clear and understandable explanations about the decisions made by their AI systems.

However, there is a delicate balance that must be maintained between explainability and model performance. In many cases, making a model more explainable can reduce its accuracy, which raises a dilemma about how much explainability should be prioritized over accuracy. This is an ongoing debate in the Artificial Intelligence community, and the solution often depends on the context in which the AI system is being used.

Organizational culture also plays a key role in promoting transparency and explainability. Organizations should foster an environment where understanding and explaining automated decisions are a priority. This not only involves adopting tools and methods that facilitate explainability but also the continuous education and training of development teams to consider explainability as an essential component in the design of AI systems.

This topic will continue to evolve as Artificial Intelligence becomes more deeply integrated into society, and the pressure for greater transparency and explainability comes from both regulators and public opinion. The ability to provide clear and understandable explanations will be crucial for the success and acceptance of Artificial Intelligence in the future, without a doubt.

15.1.2. Fairness and Equity

Fairness and equity in the development and deployment of Artificial Intelligence systems are fundamental issues that directly affect the legitimacy and acceptance of these technologies in society. As AI systems become increasingly integrated into decision-making in areas such as hiring, criminal justice, resource allocation, and public service provision, it becomes imperative to ensure that these systems do not perpetuate or exacerbate existing inequalities.

Fairness in the context of Artificial Intelligence refers to the impartiality with which a system treats different groups or individuals. This means that algorithms must be designed and trained in such a way that they do not unfairly favor one group over another. The lack of fairness in an AI system can manifest in various ways, from direct discrimination to biased outcomes that negatively affect certain demographic groups, such as women, ethnic minorities, or people with disabilities.

One of the main challenges in promoting fairness in AI is the presence of biases in the data used to train these models. Biases can be inadvertently introduced if the data reflect historical patterns of discrimination or inequality. For example, if a hiring algorithm is trained with data from a company that has historically hired mostly men for leadership positions, it is likely that the system will perpetuate this bias, recommending men more than women for those roles in the future.

To address the problem of fairness, it is crucial to implement measures that identify and mitigate biases in the data and models. This can include collecting more diverse data that better represent all parts of society, using data preprocessing techniques to remove biases, and rigorously validating models to ensure that results do not unfairly favor any group.

Equity, on the other hand, refers to equality in treatment and opportunity for all individuals, regardless of their demographic characteristics such as gender, race, age, religion, or socioeconomic status. In the context of Artificial Intelligence, an equitable system ensures that automated decisions do not introduce unfair disparities between different groups of people. However, equity can be a more complex concept to implement than fairness, as it involves not only the absence of bias but also the consideration of diversity in society and the need to design systems that respect and promote that diversity.

A common approach to improving equity in AI systems is the use of fairness-aware Machine Learning techniques. These techniques aim to adjust algorithms to produce more equitable outcomes. For example, in a credit scoring system, these techniques could modify the model to ensure that loan approval rates do not disproportionately favor one racial group over another, ensuring that all applicants are evaluated fairly.

However, it is important to recognize that equity does not always mean treating everyone exactly the same but sometimes requires differentiated treatment to compensate for historical or structural disadvantages that certain groups have faced. This approach, known as proportional equity or compensatory equity, is particularly relevant in contexts where historical disparities have affected access to opportunities or resources.

Another crucial aspect of equity is transparency in how these policies are implemented and monitored in AI systems. It is necessary for AI developers and the organizations implementing them to be transparent about the criteria and metrics used to evaluate equity, and to communicate these clearly to users and the public. This not only helps build trust in the systems but also allows for greater accountability.

Moreover, equity in Artificial Intelligence is not limited to the model development stage but must also be considered throughout the entire system life cycle. This includes continuous monitoring of model performance to detect any drift toward unfair or inequitable results, as well as regularly updating models to reflect changes in society or underlying data.

An additional challenge is that equity in Artificial Intelligence is a topic intrinsically linked with broader ethical and philosophical questions, such as the very definition of what is "fair" and "equitable." Different cultures and societies may have different perceptions of what constitutes fair or equitable treatment, which further complicates the task of developing AI systems that are universally accepted as fair.

To move toward more fair and equitable AI systems, it is essential that organizations adopt a culture of ethics and responsibility in technology development. This includes not only implementing policies and practices that promote fairness and equity but also creating diverse teams and including voices from underrepresented communities in the AI development process. It is also vital for regulators, academics, and rights advocates to participate in creating regulatory frameworks that ensure Artificial Intelligence is used in a way that benefits all of society without perpetuating or exacerbating existing inequalities.

15.1.3. Responsibility and Accountability

Responsibility and accountability in the development and use of Artificial Intelligence systems are fundamental aspects that ensure not only public trust in these technologies but also their ethical and safe use. The question of who is responsible when things go wrong is becoming increasingly relevant.

Responsibility in the context of Artificial Intelligence involves identifying who should be held accountable for the actions and decisions of an AI system. This issue is complex due to the autonomous nature of many AI systems that often make decisions without direct human intervention. However, behind every AI system, there are people, companies, and organizations that designed, developed, implemented, and operated it, and these entities must take responsibility for the outcomes produced by the system.

One of the first considerations in the discussion of responsibility is the development phase of the AI system. The developers and engineering teams who create the AI models are responsible for ensuring that these models are designed and trained ethically, safely, and fairly. This includes selecting appropriate training data, implementing safeguards to prevent bias, and thoroughly validating the model to ensure it performs as expected. However, responsibility does not end once the model is in production; the organizations that deploy and use these models must also ensure continuous monitoring to detect any failures or unwanted behavior.

An additional complication is the opacity of some AI systems, especially those based on deep learning techniques, which can make it difficult to identify failures or understand how certain decisions were made. This "black box" can make it hard to determine who is responsible when an AI system fails, posing unique challenges for accountability.

Accountability in AI is also closely linked to the concept of "traceability," which is the ability to track and document how an automated decision was made. This is essential not only for understanding the behavior of an AI system but also for properly attributing responsibility. Organizations must ensure their AI systems are traceable, which involves documenting key decisions during the development and implementation of the system, as well as keeping detailed records of how the system operates in real time.

A critical aspect of responsibility is the question of who is legally liable when an AI system causes harm or makes an incorrect decision. Laws and regulations regarding Artificial Intelligence are under development in many parts of the world, and there is still considerable legal uncertainty about how to address these issues. In many cases, liability may fall on the organizations that implement the AI system, although developers or even data providers may also be responsible, depending on the circumstances. Responsibility can also be shared, involving a networked approach where multiple actors assume different degrees of accountability.

Another important factor is the creation of internal policies within organizations that use AI. Companies should establish clear mechanisms for accountability, including the designation of specific individuals responsible for overseeing the ethics and safety of AI use. This could include creating AI ethics committees, adopting responsibility principles in product design, and continuously training employees on the risks and responsibilities associated with AI.

In addition, accountability in AI does not only refer to actions taken after an incident occurs but also involves being proactive in managing the risks associated with AI systems. This can include thorough testing before deployment, rigorous validation of the system under different conditions, and implementing contingency plans to address any failures or malfunctions.

Regarding regulation, governments and international organizations are beginning to address these issues more directly. For example, in the European Union, the General Data Protection Regulation already establishes that organizations must be able to explain and justify decisions made by algorithms, especially in contexts that significantly affect individuals. This type of regulation is a step toward formalizing responsibility in Artificial

Intelligence, although there is still a long way to go to establish a coherent global framework.

An additional challenge is the speed at which AI technology is advancing, which often outpaces the ability of legal and regulatory frameworks to keep up. This means that organizations must be responsible not only for complying with current regulations but also for anticipating potential future issues and acting ethically and proactively, even in the absence of specific legal requirements.

It is very important for organizations to be transparent about their management of responsibility and accountability in AI. This not only involves complying with legal regulations but also being open with the public and stakeholders about how AI systems are being used, what risks are associated with them, and how those risks are being mitigated. Transparency in these processes is essential for building and maintaining public trust in Artificial Intelligence technologies.

15.2. Biases in Algorithms and How to Mitigate Them

15.2.1. Types of Biases in AI

Biases in Artificial Intelligence are a critical challenge that can significantly affect the fairness, accuracy, and effectiveness of AI systems. These biases arise from various sources and can manifest in different ways, influencing the automated decisions made by algorithms. Understanding the different types of biases is essential to mitigate their effects and develop fairer and more responsible AI systems.

One of the most common types of biases in AI is selection bias. This type of bias occurs when the dataset used to train the model is not representative of the target population. For example, if a facial recognition model is trained with data that mainly includes images of people from a specific ethnicity, the model may perform poorly when it encounters images of people from other ethnicities. This happens because the model has learned to make assumptions based on a limited dataset and does not generalize well to other contexts.

Another important type is confirmation bias, which occurs when the model designers, intentionally or not, select features and parameters that reinforce their pre-existing expectations or beliefs. This bias can lead to models that perpetuate stereotypes or prejudices, as the model reflects the implicit biases of the development team. For example, a job recommendation system that prioritizes candidates with educational backgrounds similar to current employees of a company could perpetuate a lack of diversity in hiring.

Clustering bias is another relevant type of bias in AI, especially in classification and segmentation algorithms. This bias occurs when the model tends to group data into pre-existing or dominant categories, ignoring diversity within the categories. A classic example of this bias is when an AI model groups people from different cultural backgrounds into the same category due to common superficial characteristics, which can result in inappropriate recommendations or decisions that do not consider cultural differences.

Omission bias manifests when certain relevant data or variables are not included in the training set, either by oversight or due to lack of availability. This can lead to models that fail to consider crucial factors, resulting in suboptimal or unfair decisions. For example, a credit algorithm that does not take into account the economic circumstances of a specific region may assign unfair credit scores to residents of that region.

Interpretation bias occurs when the model's results are interpreted incorrectly or biasedly by users or the systems interacting with the model. This can happen due to a lack of understanding of the model's limitations or a tendency to blindly trust automated decisions without critical analysis. In situations where AI models are used in legal or medical processes, this type of bias can have serious consequences.

Algorithmic bias is related to decisions made during the algorithm design phase, where certain assumptions or simplifications can introduce biases into the final model. This bias is especially problematic in algorithms that learn from historical data that already contains human biases. For example, a crime prediction model based on historical police data could perpetuate the same biases that already existed in the judicial system, such as racial discrimination.

Presentation bias occurs when the way data or model results are presented to users affects the decisions made based on those results. For example, if a recommendation model displays products or services in a way that favors certain options over others, users may be influenced in a biased manner in their purchasing decisions.

Another less discussed but equally important type of bias is survivorship bias, which occurs when only the data or cases that have "survived" a certain process are considered, ignoring those that have not. This bias can lead to incorrect conclusions about the effectiveness of a system or process. For example, when analyzing the success of startups, if only the successful ones are considered, the lessons that could be learned from those that failed are ignored.

Temporality bias is a type of bias that arises when models are trained with data reflecting a specific temporal reality and do not adapt well to future changes or evolving trends. This type of bias is common in financial models that use historical data to predict future market movements without considering that macroeconomic conditions can change significantly over time.

Identification bias occurs in systems that associate personal data with individuals, which can lead to privacy violations or decisions that negatively affect certain individuals. This type of bias is particularly concerning in AI applications that handle large volumes of personal data, such as in healthcare or surveillance.

It is important to highlight that these types of biases are not mutually exclusive; a single AI system can be affected by multiple biases at the same time, which further complicates the identification and mitigation of these issues. The existence of biases in AI systems underscores the need for a conscious and proactive approach in the design, development, implementation, and monitoring of these systems to ensure they are as fair and equitable as possible.

15.2.2. Methods for Identifying and Correcting Biases

To identify and correct biases in Artificial Intelligence systems, a series of methods and practices must be employed, ranging from data preparation and analysis to continuous evaluation of the models in production.

The first fundamental step to identify biases is to conduct a thorough exploratory data analysis before training any model. This analysis involves examining the distribution of variables in the dataset, looking for imbalances that may indicate the presence of biases. For example, if a categorical variable such as "gender" or "ethnicity" is disproportionately represented in the dataset, it is likely that the resulting model will reflect these imbalances in its predictions. To perform this analysis, statistical tools and visualizations such as histograms, box plots, and contingency tables can be used, which help identify potential sources of bias in the data.

Once a potential bias has been identified, one of the most common methods to correct it is through data stratification or resampling. This method consists of adjusting the training dataset so that underrepresented categories have adequate weight in the model's learning process. There are different techniques to achieve this, such as oversampling minority classes, undersampling majority classes, or creating synthetic samples using techniques like SMOTE (Synthetic Minority Over-sampling Technique). These techniques allow the representations within the dataset to be balanced, thereby reducing the risk of the model perpetuating existing bias.

In addition to resampling, another crucial technique is preprocessing the data to remove or transform variables that may induce biases. This can include anonymizing sensitive data or removing variables that are correlated with protected attributes such as race or gender. In some cases, instead of removing variables, one may opt for encoding and transformation techniques that reduce the likelihood of these variables introducing biases into the model.

Fairness analysis of the model is another important step. This analysis is conducted after training the model and consists of evaluating whether the model produces fair results for different population groups. Fairness metrics, such as outcome parity, opportunity parity, or error rate differences between groups, are key tools in this analysis. These metrics help detect whether the model favors or disadvantages certain groups, which may indicate the presence of biases. For example, if a credit model tends to approve more loan applications from one ethnic group compared to another, this suggests the need to adjust the model to correct this imbalance.

The post-hoc adjustment technique is a strategy used after the model has been trained. This method involves applying corrections to the model's predictions to ensure they are fair and equitable. A common approach is reweighting predictions to ensure that underrepresented groups receive equitable treatment. Another post-hoc technique is threshold adjustment, where the model's decision thresholds are modified for different groups, with the goal of achieving equity in error and acceptance rates.

To ensure that bias corrections are effective and sustainable in the long term, it is crucial to establish mechanisms for continuous model monitoring. This involves implementing monitoring processes that evaluate the model's performance in production, ensuring that biases are not reintroduced or that new biases do not emerge as data or environmental conditions change. Continuous monitoring allows for detecting deviations in fairness metrics and making dynamic adjustments to the model, thus maintaining an acceptable level of fairness over time.

In the context of bias correction, model transparency and explainability are essential. More transparent and explainable models allow developers and auditors to identify how and why certain results are produced, which facilitates the detection of biases. Interpretability tools, such as LIME and SHAP, are useful for breaking down a model's decisions and understanding how different features contribute to predictions, helping to identify potential sources of bias.

It is important to mention the role of external auditing and peer review in identifying and correcting biases. External audits conducted by independent third parties can offer an objective and neutral perspective on the model's operation, identifying biases that the internal team may have overlooked. Peer review, on the other hand, allows experts in the field to evaluate and challenge the assumptions and methodologies used in the model's development, which can lead to significant improvements in fairness and system performance.

Identifying and correcting biases in Artificial Intelligence models requires a combination of statistical analysis, preprocessing techniques, continuous monitoring, and interpretability tools.

Only through a rigorous and multifaceted approach can it be ensured that AI systems operate fairly and equitably, minimizing the risk of perpetuating or amplifying existing inequalities in society.

15.2.3. Examples and Case Studies

Examples and case studies are essential for understanding how biases in Artificial Intelligence systems can manifest in real-world situations and the consequences they can have.

One of the most well-known cases is the COMPAS (Correctional Offender Management Profiling for Alternative Sanctions) risk assessment algorithm, used in the United States judicial system to predict the likelihood of offenders reoffending. A 2016 investigation by ProPublica revealed that the algorithm exhibited significant racial bias: African Americans were nearly twice as likely as whites to be incorrectly classified as high risk for recidivism. This bias arose despite race not being an explicitly used variable in the model, highlighting how characteristics correlated with race, such as criminal history and socioeconomic background, can introduce implicit bias into model outcomes. This case underscored the need for fairness analyses in models used in sensitive contexts such as criminal justice and for employing post-hoc correction techniques to adjust predictions according to affected groups.

Another notable example is gender bias in facial recognition models. A 2018 study by researcher Joy Buolamwini revealed that several commercial facial recognition systems, including those from companies like IBM, Microsoft, and Face++, showed significantly higher error rates when identifying women, especially dark-skinned women, compared to light-skinned men. This bias was attributed to a lack of diversity in the training data used to develop these models, which predominantly consisted of images of white men. In response to these findings, the companies involved committed to improving their datasets and implementing better practices in data collection, ensuring a more diverse and equitable representation of the population.

In the field of Artificial Intelligence in recruitment and selection, Amazon developed an automated resume screening system that was discovered to show bias against women. The system, which had been trained on a dataset of resumes received by the company over a ten-year period, learned to favor male candidates for technical roles because the majority of historical resumes belonged to men. The model penalized terms like "women's" in candidate descriptions and favored language commonly used in male resumes. Upon identifying this issue, Amazon decided to discontinue the use of this system, acknowledging the inherent challenges of eliminating biases in models trained with historical data that reflect gender inequalities.

A case in the healthcare sector involved bias identified in a risk prediction algorithm used by hospitals in the United States to determine patient access to preventive care programs. Researchers discovered that the algorithm underestimated the risk of Black patients compared to white patients, resulting in Black patients receiving less access to healthcare programs. This bias arose because the algorithm used the cost of prior medical treatment as a key variable for predicting risk, and since Black patients have historically had less access to high-quality healthcare, their costs were generally lower, leading the algorithm to incorrectly classify their risk. To address this issue, the algorithm was modified to include variables more representative of the patient's health instead of relying on treatment costs.

In the realm of digital advertising, a 2015 investigation showed that Google Ads algorithms displayed high-paying job ads more frequently to men than to women. This gender bias in advertising can have significant effects, perpetuating and amplifying gender inequalities in the job market. The cause of the bias was not fully determined, but it is suspected to be related to decisions made by the automated bidding system, which optimizes ad impressions based on the likelihood of clicks, where historical user behavior, influenced by gender factors, affected the algorithm's decisions. This case highlighted the importance of auditing and adjusting advertising algorithms to prevent the perpetuation of biases in personalized content delivery.

In the finance field, biases have been observed in credit evaluation models, where certain ethnic and socioeconomic groups tend to receive lower credit scores. This is concerning because it directly affects people's ability to access loans and other financial services. A specific case occurred in 2019 when the Apple Card, managed by Goldman Sachs, was accused of discriminating against women by granting them significantly lower credit limits than men, even when applications came from individuals with similar financial profiles. Investigations revealed that the discrepancies could be related to the algorithm used to determine credit limits, although Goldman Sachs denied that gender data was used in the process. This incident led to increased scrutiny of credit evaluation algorithms and demands for financial institutions to provide clear explanations of how decisions are made.

Biases in AI can arise in a variety of contexts, from criminal justice to advertising and healthcare, and the consequences of these biases can be broad and harmful. Identifying and correcting biases, as we have seen since the beginning of the book, is crucial to ensuring that AI systems are fair and equitable, and these case studies serve as important lessons for developers and regulators in creating more inclusive and responsible technologies.

15.3. Social and Economic Implications

15.3.1. Impact on Employment

The impact of Artificial Intelligence on employment is a highly relevant topic, as the adoption of advanced technologies in various sectors is significantly transforming the nature of work. The discussion around this impact involves multiple dimensions, from task automation to the creation of new job roles, including the redefinition of required skills and changes in the labor market structure.

One of the main concerns related to AI is the automation of tasks and the potential loss of jobs. AI has the capacity to automate repetitive and rule-based tasks that were previously performed by humans. This includes jobs in sectors such as manufacturing, logistics, customer service, and accounting. For example, chatbot systems and virtual assistants have reduced the need for human agents in customer service centers by efficiently handling basic queries. Similarly, automated accounting analysis systems can process invoices and carry out simple audits without human intervention. Automation in factories through industrial robots has displaced many workers on production lines. This type of automation can lead to a reduction in demand for certain types of jobs, especially in roles that do not require high qualifications.

However, not all effects of AI on employment are negative. The adoption of AI technologies also has the potential to create new jobs and industrial sectors. With the development of AI, additional needs arise in areas such as the design, implementation, and maintenance of AI systems, driving demand for professionals in fields such as machine learning, data science, cybersecurity, and software engineering. In addition, the need to interpret results provided by AI systems creates opportunities for data analysts and experts in various industries who can apply these results effectively. For example, the proliferation of AI in the healthcare sector has created a growing demand for bioinformaticians and AI specialists working on the development of diagnostic systems based on machine learning.

Another important dimension is the redefinition of skills and competencies. AI is causing a shift in the skills valued in the labor market. Routine and data-based tasks are being taken over by automated systems, increasing the value of human skills that cannot be replicated by AI, such as critical thinking, creativity, empathy, and the ability to manage complex situations. For example, although AI can automate many aspects of medical diagnosis, clinical judgment and empathy in patient interactions remain exclusive domains of human healthcare professionals. This trend is leading to greater investment in retraining programs and continuing education to equip the workforce with the necessary competencies to adapt to a constantly evolving work environment. Companies and governments are collaborating on initiatives to train workers in new technologies, ensuring that they can transition to more advanced or emerging roles.

It is also important to consider the effect of AI on economic inequality. There is concern that AI-driven automation could exacerbate inequality, as the economic benefits of automation may be concentrated in the hands of a few, while displaced workers may face difficulties in finding new quality jobs. Jobs that are most vulnerable to automation are often those held by people with lower levels of education and skills, which could lead to a polarization of the labor market. Highly skilled jobs requiring advanced technical abilities may see an increase in demand and salaries, while lower-skilled jobs could become scarcer and less well paid.

An aspect that should not be overlooked is the psychological and social impact of AI on employment. Uncertainty about job security and the need to acquire new skills can cause stress and anxiety among workers. This impact can be especially pronounced in sectors and regions where automation is advancing rapidly. Companies have the responsibility to manage these changes ethically, providing support and resources to facilitate workers' transition to new job opportunities. Well-being programs, counseling, and continuous training can help mitigate the negative impact of these changes.

The implementation of AI in the workplace also raises questions about governance and employment regulation. Governments and labor organizations are debating how to regulate the use of AI to protect workers and ensure that the benefits of automation are distributed fairly. Employment policies will need to adapt to address challenges such as protecting the rights of displaced workers, promoting equal opportunities in the digital economy, and ensuring that AI technologies are developed and used in ways that respect the dignity and well-being of workers.

While AI has the potential to automate tasks and displace workers, it also offers opportunities for the creation of new jobs, improved productivity, and the redefinition of the skills required in the labor market. The key to addressing these challenges lies in proactive management of the transition to a technology-driven work environment, ensuring that the benefits of AI are shared fairly and equitably throughout society.

15.3.2. Privacy and Surveillance

The issue of privacy and surveillance in the context of Artificial Intelligence is one of the most controversial and relevant topics in the digital era. As AI technologies become increasingly integrated into various areas of daily life, the amount of personal data collected and processed by these technologies has grown significantly. This has raised concerns about how that data is handled, who has access to it, and how it is used to influence individuals' behavior and decisions.

Data privacy is one of the main concerns in this field. With the growing capacity of AI systems to collect, analyze, and use large volumes of personal data, it has become crucial to ensure that individuals' privacy is protected. The data collected by these systems can include highly sensitive information such as medical history, personal preferences, geographic location, online behavior, and private communications. The concern is that this data may be used for purposes that individuals do not anticipate or consent to, which could lead to violations of their privacy.

A clear example is the use of personal data for targeted advertising. Online platforms use AI algorithms to analyze user behavior and predict their interests, allowing them to display personalized ads. While this can improve the relevance of advertising, it also raises serious questions about the level of intrusion into people's private lives. Additionally, there is the risk that the collected data could be sold to third parties without the users' knowledge or explicit consent, which further exacerbates the situation.

Mass surveillance is another critical issue linked to the use of AI. Governments and corporations have the capability to use AI systems to monitor large populations continuously. Technologies such as facial recognition, social media monitoring, and data collection from smart devices allow tracking and analyzing individuals' activities in real-time. This level of surveillance can be used for a wide range of purposes, from crime prevention to the suppression of political dissent. In authoritarian regimes, these technologies can be employed to control the population, identify and repress opponents, and maintain strict control over information.

The lack of transparency in how data is collected, processed, and used is also a source of concern. In many cases, users are not fully aware of the amount of data being collected about them, how that data is being used, or who has access to it. This lack of transparency can undermine trust in AI technologies and in the institutions that use them. The opacity in algorithms and decision-making models can make it difficult to identify biases and errors, which in turn can lead to unfair or discriminatory decisions.

Additionally, the capacity for data anonymization is a critical aspect of privacy protection. While techniques can be implemented to anonymize personal data before its use in AI analysis, the effectiveness of these techniques can be limited. Re-identification, that is, the ability to identify an individual from supposedly anonymous data, is a growing concern, especially as AI algorithms become more sophisticated and capable of cross-referencing different data sources to reconstruct identities.

AI-based surveillance also poses challenges in terms of discrimination and human rights. Facial recognition technologies, for example, have been criticized for their propensity for errors and biases, especially in recognizing people of color, women, and other minority groups. These biases can lead to unfair law enforcement and violations of civil rights, such as the wrongful detention of innocent individuals or discrimination in access to public and private services.

Another important challenge is the management and regulation of privacy and surveillance in a global environment. Data protection laws and regulations vary widely between countries and regions. For example, while the European Union has implemented the General Data Protection Regulation to ensure data privacy, other countries have much less strict regulations. This disparity creates challenges for the effective protection of privacy at a global level, especially in a world where data easily crosses borders.

In the corporate sphere, companies have the responsibility to ensure that their data collection and usage practices are transparent, ethical, and compliant with current regulations. This includes informing users about how their data is collected and used, implementing robust security measures to protect data against unauthorized access, and respecting users' rights to control their own data, including the right to be forgotten.

Surveillance and privacy in the age of AI also require an ethical reflection on the limits of technology. It is crucial that both technology developers and policymakers consider the long-term impacts of mass surveillance and the extensive use of personal data. This involves not only appropriate regulation but also a commitment to ethical principles that prioritize human dignity and respect for fundamental rights.

The relationship between privacy, surveillance, and Artificial Intelligence is complex and requires a balanced approach that promotes technological innovation without sacrificing individual rights. Protecting privacy and managing surveillance in the age of AI are challenges that must be addressed comprehensively, through legislation, technology, and an ethical commitment by all actors involved.

15.3.3. Regulation and Public Policies

Regulation and public policies in the field of Artificial Intelligence are vital topics that are gaining relevance as AI technologies are integrated into more aspects of daily life and have therefore become a crucial debate in our society. The need to establish an adequate regulatory framework arises from the risks and challenges associated with AI, including privacy, surveillance, algorithmic bias, impact on employment, and the ethical implications of automated decisions.

One of the first challenges in AI regulation is the clear definition of what constitutes Artificial Intelligence. AI is a broad and diverse field that ranges from simple automation algorithms to complex deep learning systems that can make real-time decisions. This breadth makes it difficult to create specific and adequate regulations that address all possible applications of AI. To tackle this problem, lawmakers must work together with technical experts to develop precise definitions and categorizations that can guide regulation without stifling innovation.

Another critical aspect is the protection of data privacy. As discussed earlier, AI heavily depends on access to large volumes of data to train models and make predictions. However, the collection, storage, and use of these data pose significant risks to individuals' privacy. Legislation in this field must ensure that data are handled responsibly and ethically, with adequate measures to protect personal information. In this regard, regulations such as the General Data Protection Regulation in the European Union have set strict standards for data protection, serving as a model for other jurisdictions. However, much remains to be done to ensure that privacy protection keeps pace in a world where AI technologies are evolving rapidly.

Accountability and responsibility are also key elements in AI regulation. As AI systems take on functions previously performed by humans, the question arises of who is responsible when these systems fail or cause harm. Regulation must clearly establish the legal responsibilities of developers, providers, and users of AI technologies. This includes defining the obligations of those who implement AI systems regarding supervision, transparency in automated decision-making processes, and the ability to explain and justify AI decisions. Additionally, the creation of legal mechanisms that allow people affected by automated decisions to seek remedies must be considered.

Managing algorithmic bias is another area where public policies are fundamental. AI algorithms, being trained with historical data, can perpetuate and amplify existing biases, which can lead to unfair and discriminatory decisions. Regulation must require organizations to implement procedures to detect, mitigate, and correct biases in their AI models. This could include regular audits of algorithms, diversification of the datasets used for training, and promoting transparency in the criteria used by AI models. Furthermore, policies should foster research and development of techniques to ensure that AI is fair and equitable.

The impact on employment from automation and AI is another area where public policies must intervene. As AI and automation replace jobs that were previously performed by humans, significant disruption in the labor market is likely. Public policies must anticipate and mitigate these effects by creating training and retraining programs for affected workers, promoting new employment opportunities in emerging sectors, and establishing a social safety net to support workers in transition. Additionally, a focus on education is necessary to prepare future generations for a labor market increasingly dominated by technology.

Moreover, surveillance and public security are areas that require careful regulation. AI technologies, especially when combined with mass data collection and surveillance, can be powerful tools for maintaining order and public safety, but they can also be used for darker purposes, such as mass surveillance and political repression. Regulation must establish clear limits on the use of AI for surveillance, ensuring that human rights and civil liberties are respected. This includes the need for transparency in how these technologies are used, who has access to the collected data, and what measures are implemented to prevent abuses.

At the international level, cooperation between countries is essential for effective AI regulation. Since AI is a global technology, isolated national policies may be insufficient to address issues that transcend borders, such as the use of AI in cybersecurity, competition in the global market, and privacy protection on the internet. International organizations such as the UN, the

OECD, and the European Union are beginning to develop cooperation frameworks for AI regulation, but this is a rapidly evolving field that will require continuous and effective coordination.

AI regulation must balance the protection of rights and the promotion of innovation. Public policies must be designed in a way that does not stifle technological development, which is crucial for economic and social progress. This means that regulations must be flexible and adaptive, allowing adjustments as technology evolves and new AI applications emerge. Moreover, it is crucial to involve all stakeholders, including governments, companies, researchers, and civil society, in the policy-making process to ensure that regulations reflect a wide range of perspectives and needs.

Regulation and public policies around Artificial Intelligence are essential to ensure that this important technology is developed and used in a way that benefits society as a whole. Privacy protection, accountability, fairness, and the balance between security and innovation are central issues that must be addressed urgently and precisely in the AI era.

16. Data Privacy and Security

The issue of data privacy and security is one of the most critical aspects in the development and deployment of Artificial Intelligence and Big Data technologies. As these technologies become increasingly integrated into different sectors, from healthcare to finance, the proper handling of data has become a central concern for both developers and users. The ability to collect, store, process, and analyze large volumes of data entails significant risks, especially concerning individual privacy and information security.

One of the main challenges posed by the use of large volumes of data is ensuring that individuals' privacy remains intact. Artificial Intelligence and Big Data heavily rely on the mass collection of data, which often includes sensitive personal information such as medical, financial, and behavioral data. This raises concerns about how these data are used, who has access to them, and how they are protected against misuse or unauthorized access. Privacy is not just a technical issue but also an ethical and legal matter, implying the need for strict and clear regulations that protect individuals' rights.

To address these concerns, regulations and policies have been developed in different parts of the world that set guidelines on how personal data should be handled. These regulations include laws such as the General Data Protection Regulation in the European Union and the California Consumer

Privacy Act in the United States. These laws not only impose restrictions on the collection and use of personal data but also grant individuals certain rights over their data, such as the right to know what data are collected, how they are used, and with whom they are shared, as well as the right to request the deletion of their data.

Despite the existence of these regulations, the effective implementation of data privacy and security policies requires the use of advanced data protection techniques. These techniques include anonymization, which aims to remove or modify personal information in the data so that it cannot be easily associated with a specific individual, and encryption, which protects data during transmission and storage, ensuring that only authorized parties can access them. These techniques are essential to minimize the risks of data breaches and to comply with legal and ethical requirements.

Moreover, cybersecurity is a key component in data protection in the context of Artificial Intelligence and Big Data. Systems that handle large volumes of data are attractive targets for cyberattacks, which can have serious consequences, such as the theft of personal data, information manipulation, or disruption of critical services. Cybersecurity involves not only protection against external attacks but also the implementation of internal controls that limit access to data and ensure that only authorized persons can perform certain actions.

Technological advancement has also brought new threats and vulnerabilities in the field of cybersecurity, requiring a comprehensive security strategy that combines preventive measures, such as continuous monitoring and system updates, with quick and effective responses in the event of incidents. Security tools must be capable of detecting and mitigating threats in real time, and organizations must be prepared to manage crises and recover quickly from any security breach.

Data security is not just a technical issue but also a strategic matter that affects public trust and the reputation of organizations. Consumers and end users are increasingly aware of the risks associated with handling their data and expect companies and institutions to adopt rigorous measures to protect their privacy. The lack of adequate measures can not only result in legal penalties but also in loss of trust and long-term damage to the organization's image.

It is important to recognize that data privacy and security in the field of Artificial Intelligence and Big Data are constantly evolving topics. As technologies advance and new applications are developed, new challenges and threats arise, requiring constant monitoring and continuous adaptation of security policies and practices. Organizations must be prepared to proactively update their data privacy and security approaches, ensuring that they keep up with best practices and the latest regulations.

Protecting personal information, complying with regulations, implementing advanced security techniques, and preparing for cyber threats are essential tasks to ensure that the use of these technologies is safe, ethical, and respectful of individuals' rights. The responsibility for maintaining data privacy and security lies not only with developers and organizations but also with governments and regulators, who must establish an adequate legal and ethical framework to guide the development and application of these technologies.

16.1. Regulations and Compliance (GDPR, CCPA)

16.1.1. GDPR Principles and Requirements

The General Data Protection Regulation is one of the most rigorous and comprehensive regulations regarding personal data protection worldwide. Adopted by the European Union and applicable since May 25, 2018, the GDPR establishes a legal framework that protects the rights of European citizens concerning the processing and safeguarding of their personal data. The regulation not only applies to organizations within the EU but also has extraterritorial reach, affecting any entity that processes data of EU citizens, regardless of its location.

One of the central aspects of the GDPR is its fundamental principles, which guide how personal data should be handled. These principles are:

1. Lawfulness, fairness, and transparency: This principle states that personal data must be processed lawfully, fairly, and transparently in relation to the individual to whom it belongs. Lawfulness refers to the need to have a valid legal basis for processing data, such as the individual's explicit consent, compliance with a legal obligation, or the protection of vital interests. Fairness and transparency require organizations to be clear about how and why data is being collected and used, providing individuals with easy-to-understand information about these practices.

2. Purpose limitation: According to this principle, personal data must only be collected for specific, explicit, and legitimate purposes and must not be further processed in a way that is incompatible with those purposes. This means organizations must clearly define the purpose of data collection from the outset and cannot use the data for other purposes without obtaining new consent from the individual or fulfilling a new legal basis.

3. Data minimization: This principle dictates that the personal data collected must be adequate, relevant, and limited to what is necessary in relation to the purposes for which it is processed. In other words, organizations must ensure they do not collect more data than they truly need to achieve the established purposes, thus avoiding unnecessary data storage.

4. Accuracy: Personal data must be accurate and, where necessary, kept up to date. This principle requires organizations to take reasonable steps to ensure that inaccurate data is corrected or deleted promptly. Accuracy is crucial to avoid incorrect decisions based on erroneous data.

5. Storage limitation: Personal data must be kept in a form that allows the identification of data subjects only for as long as necessary for the purposes for which it is processed. Once the data is no longer needed for these purposes, it must be deleted or anonymized. This principle helps reduce the risk of data being misused or accessed without authorization.

6. Integrity and confidentiality: Personal data must be processed in a manner that ensures appropriate security, including protection against unauthorized or unlawful processing and against accidental loss, destruction, or damage, using appropriate technical and organizational measures. This means organizations must implement security measures such as encryption, access control, and system auditing to protect data.

7. Accountability: This principle requires organizations to be responsible for complying with all the above principles and to be able to demonstrate compliance. This includes taking steps such as conducting data protection impact assessments, appointing a data protection officer when necessary, and properly documenting all data protection-related decisions.

In addition to these principles, the GDPR sets out several specific requirements that organizations must meet:

Consent: When the processing of personal data is based on consent, it must be explicit, informed, and freely given. Organizations must be able to demonstrate that valid consent has been obtained and that individuals have been adequately informed about how their data will be used. Furthermore, individuals have the right to withdraw their consent at any time.

Data subject rights: The GDPR grants individuals several rights over their personal data, including the right to access their data, the right to rectification, the right to erasure (also known as the "right to be forgotten"), the right to restrict processing, the right to data portability, and the right to object to processing. Organizations must have procedures in place to respond to data subject requests promptly and effectively.

Data Protection Impact Assessment (DPIA): In situations where data processing may involve a high risk to individuals' rights and freedoms, organizations must carry out a data protection impact assessment. This assessment must identify potential risks and the measures to be taken to mitigate them.

Data breach notification: The GDPR stipulates that, in the event of a personal data breach, organizations must notify the relevant supervisory authority without undue delay and, in most cases, within 72 hours of becoming aware of the breach. If the breach poses a high risk to individuals' rights and freedoms, it is also necessary to inform the affected individuals directly.

International data transfers: The GDPR imposes strict restrictions on the transfer of personal data outside the European Economic Area (EEA) to ensure that data continues to be adequately protected. Such transfers may only be made to countries that provide an adequate level of data protection or through approved transfer mechanisms, such as standard contractual clauses or binding corporate rules.

Compliance with the GDPR is not only a legal obligation but is also fundamental to protecting individuals' privacy and maintaining public trust in organizations that handle personal data. Penalties for non-compliance can be severe, with fines of up to 4% of the organization's annual global turnover or 20 million euros, whichever is greater. Therefore, it is essential for organizations to take a proactive approach to ensure all aspects of the GDPR are implemented and maintained continuously.

16.1.2. CCPA Requirements

The California Consumer Privacy Act (CCPA) is one of the most significant regulations in the United States governing how businesses must handle and protect the personal information of California residents. Enacted in 2018 and effective since January 1, 2020, the CCPA represents a milestone in privacy legislation in the United States, offering consumers greater control over their personal data and setting strict requirements for businesses that collect and process it.

Scope of application

The CCPA applies to any business that operates in California and meets at least one of the following criteria:

1. Has annual gross revenues exceeding 25 million dollars.
2. Buys, receives, or sells the personal information of 50,000 or more consumers, households, or devices.

3. Derives at least 50% of its annual revenue from selling consumers' personal information.

These provisions ensure that both large corporations and data-driven tech companies are required to comply with the CCPA.

Key CCPA requirements

1. Right to know: The CCPA grants consumers the right to know what personal information is being collected about them, the sources of that information, the purposes for which it is being used, the categories of third parties with whom it is shared, and the specific information that has been collected about them in the past 12 months. Businesses must provide this information in an accessible and understandable manner, usually through detailed and updated privacy policies.

2. Right to delete: Consumers have the right to request that a business delete any personal information it has collected about them, with certain exceptions. Businesses may refuse to delete data if it is necessary to complete a transaction, comply with a legal obligation, detect security incidents, protect against malicious activities, conduct scientific, historical, or statistical research, and other exceptions stipulated by the law.

3. Right to opt out of data sales: One of the CCPA's most notable features is the consumer's right to opt out of the sale of their personal data. Businesses must provide a clear link on their website titled "Do Not Sell My Personal Information" to allow consumers to easily exercise this right. This right also extends to minors under 16, for whom explicit parental or guardian consent is required before their data can be sold.

4. Right to non-discrimination: The CCPA prohibits businesses from discriminating against consumers who exercise their rights under the law. This means businesses cannot deny goods or services, charge different prices, or provide a different level of service to consumers who choose to exercise their rights. However, the law allows businesses to offer financial incentives in exchange for the collection, sale, or retention of personal information, as long as such incentives are lawful and clearly disclosed.

5. Notice of data collection: Businesses must inform consumers, at the time of data collection, about the categories of personal information that will be collected and the purposes for which it will be used. This transparency obligation requires businesses to keep consumers informed about how and why their data is being used, allowing for greater clarity and trust in interactions between consumers and businesses.

6. Data security: Although the CCPA does not prescribe specific technical requirements, it establishes that businesses must implement and maintain reasonable security procedures to protect personal information. The law allows consumers to bring private lawsuits if a security breach occurs due to a lack of adequate security measures. Penalties may include statutory damages of up to \$750 per incident per affected consumer, encouraging businesses to strengthen their cybersecurity practices.

Compliance and penalties

Compliance with the CCPA is overseen by the California Attorney General, who has the authority to impose fines for non-compliance. Fines can reach \$2,500 for each unintentional violation and up to \$7,500 for each intentional violation. Additionally, as mentioned earlier, the CCPA grants consumers the right to sue in the event of a security breach resulting from a lack of reasonable security measures.

To comply with the CCPA, businesses must review and potentially redesign their privacy policies, data management systems, and security practices to ensure they meet the requirements for transparency, access, deletion, and data protection. They must also establish clear procedures to respond to consumer requests within the timeframes set by the law, which is generally 45 days, with the possibility of a 45-day extension under certain circumstances.

Additional considerations

In addition to the requirements described, the CCPA is subject to amendments and updates that may change its provisions. For example, the California Privacy Rights Act (CPRA), approved in November 2020, modifies and expands several aspects of the CCPA, including the creation of a specific agency for privacy protection and the strengthening of consumer rights regarding sensitive personal information.

Businesses operating in multiple jurisdictions must also consider how the CCPA interacts with other privacy laws, such as the GDPR in Europe, to ensure consistent and global compliance. This is especially relevant for international companies that must navigate the complexities of multiple regulatory frameworks simultaneously.

The CCPA is a complex legal framework that requires businesses to adopt a rigorous and proactive approach to managing personal data. Compliance is essential not only to avoid penalties but also to maintain consumer trust in an increasingly privacy-conscious digital environment.

16.1.3. Compliance and Best Practices

Compliance with data protection regulations, such as the General Data Protection Regulation and the California Consumer Privacy Act, is essential for companies that handle personal information. Proper implementation of these regulations not only avoids legal penalties but also protects the company's reputation and strengthens customer trust. To ensure effective compliance, it is crucial that companies adopt a series of best practices that address the different aspects of personal data management, from collection to deletion.

1. Data Protection Impact Assessment (DPIA)

A Data Protection Impact Assessment (DPIA) is a key tool for identifying and mitigating risks associated with the processing of personal data. This assessment is particularly relevant when a new technology or process is introduced that could affect individuals' privacy. DPIAs allow organizations to anticipate privacy issues and take preventive measures before they occur. Although not always mandatory under the GDPR, conducting a DPIA is considered a best practice when processing data that could result in a high risk to individuals' rights and freedoms.

2. Clear and Transparent Privacy Policies

Privacy policies must be clear, accessible, and understandable for all users. They should explicitly detail what types of data are collected, how they are used, with whom they are shared, and the rights users have regarding their data. It is essential that these policies are available at all data collection points, including online forms, mobile apps, and any other digital channel. Transparency is a fundamental principle of the GDPR and the CCPA, and companies should strive to communicate their privacy practices in a way that leaves no doubt for the consumer.

3. Mechanisms for Obtaining Consent

Under the GDPR, consent must be explicit, informed, and freely given. This means that organizations must implement mechanisms that allow users to actively consent to the processing of their personal data. It is important that consent is not implicit or bundled with other terms and conditions. Companies must provide clear options for users to accept or reject the collection of their data and must allow users to withdraw their consent at any time. These mechanisms must be clearly documented so that the company can demonstrate compliance in the event of an audit or investigation.

4. Implementation of Appropriate Security Measures

Data security is a crucial component of regulatory compliance. Companies must adopt appropriate technical and organizational measures to protect personal data against unauthorized access, loss, alteration, or disclosure. This may include encrypting data in transit and at rest, implementing role-based access control (RBAC) policies, and regularly auditing systems and processes. In addition, it is essential to conduct periodic security tests to identify and correct vulnerabilities before they can be exploited. Ongoing staff training in cybersecurity is also vital to ensure employees understand and follow security best practices.

5. Maintenance of Processing Activity Records

The GDPR requires organizations to maintain detailed records of data processing activities. These records must include information about the categories of data processed, the purposes of the processing, data transfers to third countries, and the security measures implemented. Keeping these records is not only a legal obligation but also facilitates data management and helps organizations identify potential risks or non-compliance. These records must be updated regularly and be available for review in the event of an audit by data protection authorities.

6. Management of Data Subject Rights Requests

Both the GDPR and the CCPA grant individuals specific rights regarding their personal data, such as the right of access, rectification, deletion, and objection to processing. Companies must establish effective procedures to manage and respond to these requests within the timeframes established by law. It is essential that these procedures are known to all relevant employees and that the necessary tools are in place to comply with requests efficiently and completely. Documenting and tracking these requests are fundamental to demonstrate compliance in case of disputes or investigations.

7. Regular Assessments and Audits

To ensure continuous compliance with data protection regulations, it is advisable for organizations to carry out regular assessments and audits. These reviews allow companies to identify areas for improvement and adjust their practices as necessary. Audits also provide an opportunity to review data processing records, verify that policies and procedures are up to date, and ensure that all security mechanisms are working properly. Additionally, audits can help organizations prepare for possible inspections by data protection authorities.

8. Staff Training and Awareness

Regulatory compliance is a shared responsibility across the organization. It is crucial that all employees, from senior management to operations staff, understand the basic principles of data protection and their role in compliance. Regular training and awareness campaigns can help prevent security incidents and foster an organizational culture focused on privacy and data protection. Training should be tailored to the specific responsibilities of each employee group and include updates on regulatory changes and new privacy threats.

9. Incident Response and Breach Notification

The GDPR establishes that companies must notify data protection authorities of any security breach affecting personal data within 72 hours of detection. The CCPA also has breach notification requirements, although with different deadlines and conditions. Organizations must have a well-defined incident response plan that includes procedures for detecting, containing, mitigating, and notifying security breaches. It is essential that this plan is tested and known by all relevant staff to ensure a rapid and effective response in case of an incident.

10. Commitment to Continuous Improvement

The regulatory and technological environment around data protection is constantly evolving. Today's best practices may not be sufficient tomorrow, so organizations must commit to the continuous improvement of their compliance policies and procedures. This involves staying informed about regulatory developments, updating security technologies, and regularly reviewing internal policies to ensure they remain effective. Additionally, organizations must be prepared to adapt their practices as new regulations and expectations in the field of data protection emerge.

Compliance with the GDPR, the CCPA, and other privacy regulations is a complex process that requires a combination of robust policies, technical and organizational measures, and an organizational commitment to privacy. Adopting these best practices not only helps ensure regulatory compliance but also contributes to strengthening customer trust and protecting the organization's reputation in an increasingly privacy- and security-conscious world.

16.2. Anonymization and Data Protection Techniques

16.2.1. Anonymization Techniques (k-anonymity, l-diversity)

Anonymization is a fundamental technique in handling personal data to protect individuals' privacy. This practice focuses on modifying data in such a way that the people to whom it belongs cannot be identified directly or indirectly. As the processing of personal data is an increasing concern in the digital age, anonymization has become a crucial tool to comply with regulations such as the GDPR and the CCPA, as well as to protect privacy in Big Data and Machine Learning projects.

k-Anonymity

The concept of k-anonymity is one of the most widely used techniques for data anonymization. The basic idea behind k-anonymity is to ensure that each record in a dataset is indistinguishable from at least k-1 other records in terms of certain attributes that can be used to identify a person, known as quasi-identifiers.
In a dataset that complies with k-anonymity, each combination of quasi-identifier values appears at least k times. This means that, for any attempt at reidentification based on these attributes, the attacker cannot distinguish an individual from at least k-1 others, significantly reducing the possibility of identification.

To achieve k-anonymity, techniques such as generalization and suppression of data are commonly used. Generalization involves replacing specific attribute values with more general values (for example, replacing exact birth dates with age ranges). Suppression, on the other hand, consists of deleting certain values that could make a record unique.

A practical example of k-anonymity would be a patient dataset where birth dates are replaced with five-year age ranges and postal codes are reduced to only the first two digits. If each combination of these attributes is repeated in at least k records, the dataset is considered k-anonymous.

l-Diversity

While k-anonymity is effective, it has significant limitations, especially in scenarios where the values of a sensitive attribute are homogeneous within a group of k-anonymous records. This can lead to vulnerabilities in cases where the sensitive information in a k-anonymous group is the same or shows little variability. To address this limitation, the concept of l-diversity was introduced.

L-diversity extends k-anonymity by requiring that, for each group of records indistinguishable in terms of quasi-identifiers, there are at least l "well-represented" values of the sensitive attribute. In other words, each k-anonymous group must contain at least l distinct and frequent values for the sensitive attributes, making it even harder to identify an individual or infer sensitive information.

There are different variants of l-diversity to ensure that sensitive values are properly distributed within the groups:

1. **Distinct l-diversity:** Requires at least l distinct values of the sensitive attribute in each k-anonymous group.
2. **Entropy l-diversity:** Uses entropy to measure diversity within a group, ensuring that sensitive values are evenly distributed.
3. **Recursive (or classic) l-diversity:** Ensures that the most common values do not dominate the k-anonymous group.

The application of l-diversity is particularly useful in datasets where simple anonymization through k-anonymity could lead to the disclosure of sensitive information. For example, if all records within a k-anonymous group have the same medical diagnosis, an attacker could infer that condition for any individual within that group, even if they cannot directly identify the patient.

Limitations and Challenges

Although k-anonymity and l-diversity are powerful techniques, they are not foolproof. One of the main challenges is that applying these techniques can result in a significant loss of information, which may reduce the utility of the dataset for analysis or Machine Learning. Moreover, these techniques do not protect against more sophisticated attacks, such as correlation attacks, where an attacker uses additional external information to reidentify anonymous data.

Another challenge is that in very large and complex datasets, ensuring k-anonymity and l-diversity can require significant computational processing, which can be an obstacle for real-time implementation. Additionally, choosing the values of k and l is critical; a k or l value that is too low may not provide adequate anonymization, while a value that is too high could remove so much information that the dataset loses its value.

Practical Implementation

In practice, implementing k-anonymity and l-diversity often involves using specific algorithms designed to modify data while minimizing information loss. Here is an example of Python code that illustrates how to perform anonymization of a dataset using the k-anonymity technique:

```
import pandas as pd
from sklearn.preprocessing import KBinsDiscretizer

# Example data
data = {
    'age': [34, 45, 56, 67, 78, 89],
    'zipcode': [12345, 12345, 12345, 67890, 67890, 67890],
    'disease': ['diabetes', 'cancer', 'diabetes', 'flu', 'flu',
'cancer']
}

df = pd.DataFrame(data)

# Generalize age into ranges (generalization)
k_bins = KBinsDiscretizer(n_bins=3, encode='ordinal', strategy='uni-
form')
df['age_group'] = k_bins.fit_transform(df[['age']])

# Partial suppression of postal code (generalization)
df['zipcode'] = df['zipcode'].astype(str).str[:3] + 'XX'

print(df)
```

This code creates generalized age groups and suppresses part of the postal code to help ensure k-anonymity. However, this is a simplified example, and in practice, the implementation would require additional adjustments and careful evaluation to ensure that the appropriate level of anonymization is met without compromising data utility.

In summary, both k-anonymity and l-diversity are valuable tools in the arsenal of data protection techniques. However, they must be implemented carefully and in combination with other security techniques to ensure robust privacy protection without sacrificing the quality and utility of the anonymized data.

16.2.2. Data Encryption

Data encryption is a fundamental security technique that protects information by converting it into a format that is unreadable to anyone who does not have the necessary key to decrypt it. In the context of data privacy and security, encryption plays a crucial role in ensuring that sensitive data, whether in transit or at rest, is protected against unauthorized access, even if it is intercepted or stolen.

Types of Encryption

There are several types of encryption commonly used to protect data, each with its own methods and specific use cases. The two main approaches are symmetric encryption and asymmetric encryption.

- **Symmetric encryption:** In this type of encryption, the same key is used both to encrypt and decrypt the data. This approach is fast and efficient, making it ideal for encrypting large volumes of data. However, the security of this method depends on keeping the key secret. Some of the most widely used symmetric encryption algorithms are AES (Advanced Encryption Standard), DES (Data Encryption Standard), and 3DES (Triple DES).

- **Asymmetric encryption:** Unlike symmetric encryption, asymmetric encryption uses a pair of keys: a public key to encrypt the data and a private key to decrypt it. This approach is more secure for key distribution, as the public key can be freely shared while the private key is kept secret. However, it is slower and therefore generally used to encrypt small blocks of data or to establish secure channels through which symmetric keys can be shared. Common examples of asymmetric encryption algorithms include RSA (Rivest-Shamir-Adleman) and ECC (Elliptic Curve Cryptography).

Encryption in Transit and at Rest

Data encryption can be applied both when data is in transit (that is, when it is being sent across a network) and when it is at rest (stored on devices or storage systems). Securing both states is crucial for complete information protection.

- **Encryption in transit:** This type of encryption protects data while it is moving across networks, such as the internet. Without encryption in transit, data can be vulnerable to attacks like interception and eavesdropping. To protect data in transit, protocols like TLS (Transport Layer Security) or SSL (Secure Sockets Layer) are used, which secure communication between devices by creating an encrypted channel.

- **Encryption at rest:** Encryption at rest ensures that stored data, whether on hard drives, databases, or in the cloud, is protected against unauthorized access. Even if storage devices are stolen or compromised, access to the data requires the encryption key. Tools like BitLocker (for hard drives) and integrated database encryptions, such as Transparent Data Encryption (TDE) in SQL Server, are examples of encryption at rest.

Common Methods and Algorithms

- **AES (Advanced Encryption Standard):** AES is the most widely used symmetric encryption standard and is known for its security and efficiency. AES supports key sizes of 128, 192, and 256 bits, with AES-256 being the strongest. AES is widely used in both software and hardware applications, from disk encryption to network security.

- **RSA (Rivest-Shamir-Adleman):** RSA is a widely used asymmetric encryption algorithm in data security. It is based on the difficulty of factoring large integers, which provides strong security. RSA is commonly used to secure the transmission of sensitive data and for identity authentication.

- **ECC (Elliptic Curve Cryptography):** ECC is a form of asymmetric encryption that offers a security level comparable to RSA but with much smaller keys, making it more efficient in terms of resource usage. ECC is especially useful in devices with limited resources, such as mobile phones and IoT devices.

Implementing Encryption in Python

To illustrate how data encryption can be implemented, here is an example of Python code using the cryptography library, which applies AES to encrypt and decrypt a message (we will look at a different example with the same library later):

```
from cryptography.hazmat.primitives.ciphers import Cipher, algo-
rithms, modes
from cryptography.hazmat.backends import default_backend
import os

# Generate a 256-bit key (32 bytes)
key = os.urandom(32)

# Generate a 128-bit initialization vector (IV) (16 bytes)
iv = os.urandom(16)

# Create the AES cipher in CBC mode
cipher = Cipher(algorithms.AES(key), modes.CBC(iv), backend=de-
fault_backend())
encryptor = cipher.encryptor()

# Message to encrypt (must be a multiple of the 128-bit block size)
plaintext = b'This is a secret message'

# Ensure the message is a multiple of the block size using padding
from cryptography.hazmat.primitives import padding
padder = padding.PKCS7(algorithms.AES.block_size).padder()
padded_data = padder.update(plaintext) + padder.finalize()
```

```
# Encrypt the message
ciphertext = encryptor.update(padded_data) + encryptor.finalize()

print(f'Ciphertext: {ciphertext}')

# To decrypt the message
decryptor = cipher.decryptor()
decrypted_padded_data = decryptor.update(ciphertext) + decryptor.fi-
nalize()
# Remove the padding
unpadder = padding.PKCS7(algorithms.AES.block_size).unpadder()
decrypted_data = unpadder.update(decrypted_padded_data) + unpad-
der.finalize()

print(f'Decrypted message: {decrypted_data}')
```

This code generates a key and an initialization vector (IV), then uses AES in CBC mode to encrypt and decrypt a message. Padding ensures the message is the right size for encryption. Although this is a simple example, in practice, key management and encryption/decryption handling must be done carefully to avoid vulnerabilities, so don't get carried away thinking you're Mr. Robot.

Challenges of Encryption

Despite its effectiveness, encryption presents several challenges. One of the main ones is secure key management. If an encryption key is compromised, all data encrypted with that key is also compromised. Therefore, organizations must implement strict key management policies, including the use of hardware security modules (HSM), secure storage, and regular key rotation.

Another challenge is performance. Encryption, especially for large volumes of data or in real time, can be resource-intensive. Organizations must balance the need for security with performance requirements, opting for solutions that offer a good compromise between the two.

Encryption is not a universal solution for data security. While it protects data confidentiality, it does not guarantee integrity or availability. Therefore, it must be part of a broader security strategy that includes access controls, continuous monitoring, and incident response measures.

As you know, data encryption is an essential tool for protecting sensitive information in digital environments, from messages to photos, emails, and in general all our data. By implementing encryption, organizations can ensure that data remains confidential, even if it is compromised. However, the success of encryption depends on proper key management, the selection of appropriate algorithms, and integration with other security measures.

16.2.3. Data Protection Tools

Data protection tools are essential to ensure the privacy and security of information in an increasingly digital and connected environment. These tools cover a wide range of technologies designed to protect data against unauthorized access, loss, alteration, and other risks. Let's now explore some of the most important tools that can be employed at different levels and contexts within an organization to safeguard sensitive data.

Encryption Tools

Encryption is one of the most effective techniques to protect data, both in transit and at rest. The most common techniques and algorithms, such as AES and RSA, have already been discussed, but it is equally important to consider the tools that facilitate the secure and efficient implementation of these techniques.

- **VeraCrypt:** VeraCrypt is an open-source tool that allows the creation of encrypted volumes. It is widely used to encrypt entire hard drives, partitions, or specific files. Its ease of use makes it accessible to both individual users and small organizations.

- **BitLocker:** BitLocker is a full-disk encryption tool integrated into Windows operating systems. It allows the encryption of entire disk drives, thus protecting data stored on devices such as laptops that may be stolen or lost. BitLocker uses AES encryption and can be managed through group policies in corporate environments.

- **OpenSSL:** OpenSSL is a robust library that provides an implementation of the SSL and TLS protocols for encrypting data in transit. It also supports a variety of symmetric and asymmetric encryption algorithms and is widely used to secure network communications, including HTTPS connections.

Data Anonymization Tools

Anonymizing data is crucial to protect individuals' privacy when working with datasets that may contain personally identifiable information (PII). Various tools and techniques exist to achieve this, some of which are detailed below.

- **ARX Data Anonymization Tool:** ARX is an advanced data anonymization tool that supports a variety of techniques, including k-anonymity, l-diversity, and t-closeness. ARX allows users to apply these techniques to datasets and evaluate the impact of anonymization on data utility. It is useful for compliance with regulations such as the GDPR, which require the protection of personal data.

- **SdcMicro:** SdcMicro is a tool in R for statistical disclosure control of microdata, used to apply anonymization techniques such as data perturbation and value suppression. It is ideal for organizations handling statistical data that need to ensure privacy without compromising information quality.

Data Loss Prevention (DLP) Tools

Data loss prevention solutions are fundamental to ensure that sensitive information does not leave the organization without authorization. These tools monitor, detect, and block unauthorized access to sensitive data, both inside and outside the corporate network.

- **Symantec Data Loss Prevention:** Symantec DLP is a comprehensive solution that offers a wide range of features, including monitoring of data in use, in transit, and at rest. It uses predefined or customizable policies to identify and protect sensitive information, ensuring compliance with regulations.

- **McAfee Total Protection for Data Loss Prevention:** This tool offers advanced monitoring and control capabilities, enabling organizations to protect data on endpoints, networks, and in the cloud. It is ideal for large organizations requiring a comprehensive approach to data protection.

- **Digital Guardian:** Digital Guardian is another DLP solution focused on protecting confidential data. It offers real-time monitoring and protection for both structured and unstructured data, providing visibility and control over how data is used inside and outside the organization.

Key Management Tools

Proper management of cryptographic keys is crucial for the success of any encryption strategy. Without adequate management, keys can be vulnerable to theft or loss, compromising the security of encrypted data.

- **AWS Key Management Service (KMS):** AWS KMS allows centralized management of cryptographic keys used to encrypt data stored in AWS services. It offers a high level of security and complies with strict regulations. Additionally, KMS facilitates key rotation and auditing.

- **HashiCorp Vault:** Vault is an open-source tool that enables organizations to securely manage secrets, including certificates, passwords, and encryption keys. It offers advanced features such as automatic key rotation and detailed access auditing.

- **Microsoft Azure Key Vault:** Similar to AWS KMS, Azure Key Vault is a service that allows the secure management of cryptographic keys in the Microsoft Azure cloud. It provides capabilities such as key generation, storage, and management, with direct integration with other Azure services to protect data and applications.

Auditing and Compliance Tools

To ensure that organizations comply with data protection laws and regulations, it is essential to have tools that facilitate auditing and continuous compliance.

- **Splunk:** Splunk is a data analysis platform that allows organizations to monitor and analyze activities in their infrastructure in real time. In the context of data protection, Splunk can be used to audit access to and usage of sensitive data, detecting and responding to security incidents.

- **Varonis Data Security Platform:** Varonis provides a comprehensive data security solution, offering auditing, monitoring, and risk analysis capabilities. It is particularly useful for compliance with data protection regulations, as it allows organizations to identify and mitigate both internal and external threats.

- **Netwrix Auditor:** Netwrix Auditor is a tool designed to facilitate the auditing of changes and access within the IT infrastructure. It enables organizations to track how sensitive data is used and ensure compliance with regulations such as GDPR and CCPA.

Cloud Protection Tools

As many organizations have migrated their operations and data storage to the cloud, it is vital to use tools that protect data in these environments. These tools offer encryption, access control, and monitoring specifically for cloud services.

- **Microsoft Azure Security Center:** Azure Security Center provides a unified view of security across all Azure workloads. It offers security recommendations, threat detection, and automatic incident response, ensuring that data stored in Azure is protected.

- **Google Cloud Security Command Center:** This Google Cloud tool provides centralized visibility over the security of cloud resources. It enables vulnerability detection, risk mitigation, and ensures that data stored in Google Cloud complies with security regulations.

- **AWS CloudTrail:** AWS CloudTrail is a service that allows organizations to monitor and record activity within their AWS accounts. This includes auditing access to and use of data, facilitating compliance with security policies and regulations.

Implementing Protection Tools in Python

Although the tools mentioned above are complete products, it is possible to implement certain basic data protection functionalities using code. The following is a different and simple example of how the cryptography library in Python could be used to implement another data encryption:

```
from cryptography.hazmat.primitives.kdf.pbkdf2 import PBKDF2HMAC
from cryptography.hazmat.primitives import hashes
from cryptography.hazmat.primitives.ciphers import Cipher, algo-
rithms, modes
from cryptography.hazmat.backends import default_backend
import os
import base64

# Function to generate a key derived from a password
def generate_key(password, salt):
    kdf = PBKDF2HMAC(
        algorithm=hashes.SHA256(),
        length=32,  # 32 bytes = 256 bits
        salt=salt,
        iterations=100000,
        backend=default_backend()
    )
    return kdf.derive(password)  # We do not use Base64 here

# Function to encrypt a message
def encrypt_message(key, message):
    iv = os.urandom(16)
    cipher = Cipher(algorithms.AES(key), modes.CFB(iv), ba-
ckend=default_backend())
    encryptor = cipher.encryptor()
    ciphertext = iv + encryptor.update(message) + encryptor.fina-
lize()
    return base64.urlsafe_b64encode(ciphertext)

# Usage example
password = b'my_secret_password'
salt = os.urandom(16)
key = generate_key(password, salt)

message = b'Sensitive data that needs protection'
ciphertext = encrypt_message(key, message)
```

```
print(f'Ciphertext: {ciphertext}')
```

This code generates a key based on a password using PBKDF2, a key derivation algorithm, and then encrypts a message using AES in CFB mode. This implementation is a simplified example of how organizations can integrate encryption techniques into their applications to protect sensitive data.

Final Considerations

The choice of data protection tools should align with the specific needs of the organization, taking into account factors such as the type of data handled, applicable regulations, and the technological environment in which they operate. Additionally, it is essential for organizations to maintain a holistic approach to data protection, combining these tools with robust security policies, employee education and training, and continuous monitoring of emerging threats. In this way, sensitive information can be safeguarded against a wide range of risks in today's complex digital landscape.

16.3. Cybersecurity in Big Data Projects

16.3.1. Threats and Vulnerabilities

Threats and vulnerabilities in Big Data projects are critical issues that can compromise the integrity, confidentiality, and availability of data, which can have devastating consequences for an organization, especially for small or medium-sized enterprises. With the increase in the volume, variety, and velocity of processed data, the attack surfaces expand, introducing new challenges to the security of Big Data systems.

Common threats in Big Data projects

- **Cyberattacks and security breaches:** Cyberattacks represent one of the most significant threats to any Big Data infrastructure. These attacks can take various forms, from denial-of-service (DDoS) attacks that attempt to overload systems to SQL injections and phishing attacks designed to gain unauthorized access to data. The resulting security breaches can expose large volumes of sensitive information, leading to legal and reputational consequences for organizations.

- **Ransomware:** Ransomware is a type of malware that encrypts an organization's data, blocking access until a ransom is paid. This type of attack can paralyze an organization's operations, especially when it affects critical Big Data systems that support essential business functions. Given the volume of data involved, restoring these systems can be costly and time-consuming.

- **Data exfiltration:** Data exfiltration is the process by which an attacker transfers valuable information from an organization to an external location without authorization. This can occur due to network vulnerabilities being exploited or through insider attacks where employees with legitimate access to data extract it for malicious purposes.

- **Insider attacks:** Insider attacks, carried out by current or former employees with privileged access, are a considerable threat in Big Data environments. These individuals can abuse their permissions to access, manipulate, or steal confidential data. Since these users usually have authorized access, detecting these attacks can be more complicated and damaging.

- **Supply chain compromise:** Big Data systems often rely on a complex network of providers and third-party services, from cloud storage to analytics software. A compromise in one of these components can lead to a chain attack, where unauthorized access to an external service compromises the security of the entire system. This threat has increased with the growing dependence on cloud services and the integration of multiple platforms.

- **Data tampering:** Data tampering is a threat where data is maliciously altered, compromising its integrity and the decision-making processes based on that data. This can have devastating effects in sectors such as banking, where data integrity is crucial for risk assessment and financial decision-making.

- **Malware infections:** Big Data systems, especially those that rely on multiple nodes and distributed servers, are vulnerable to malware infections. These can spread quickly across the network, affecting system availability and performance, and jeopardizing data confidentiality.

Vulnerabilities in Big Data projects

- **Poor security configuration:** Incorrect configuration of systems and services is one of the most common vulnerabilities in Big Data infrastructures. This includes weak security settings such as unnecessary open ports, weak password policies, or lack of encryption in data transmission and storage. These bad practices can be easily exploited by attackers to gain access to the systems.

- **Vulnerabilities in software and applications:** The software used in Big Data projects, including storage, processing, and analytics platforms, may contain vulnerabilities that can be exploited. Examples include vulnerabilities in NoSQL database systems, in frameworks like Hadoop or Spark, or in analytics applications that have not been updated or patched.

- **Issues with access and permissions management:** Inadequate management of access and permissions is a significant vulnerability. If users have more privileges than necessary or if permissions are not properly revoked when a user no longer needs access, the risk of a successful attack increases. This situation is particularly critical in Big Data environments, where multiple users may need access to large volumes of data.

- **Lack of encryption:** Not properly encrypting data, both at rest and in transit, is a critical vulnerability. If data is not encrypted, it can be intercepted and read by attackers during transmission or if they gain access to storage media. This is particularly serious in Big Data systems, where the data volumes may include highly sensitive information.

- **Vulnerabilities in network infrastructure:** The network infrastructure that supports Big Data systems can have vulnerabilities such as misconfigured routers, lack of network segmentation, or the absence of proper firewalls. These vulnerabilities can be exploited to intercept data or introduce malicious traffic into the system.

- **Lack of monitoring and detection:** The absence of effective monitoring and detection systems is a vulnerability that can allow attackers to operate undetected for long periods. Without monitoring tools such as IDS/IPS (Intrusion Detection and Prevention Systems), SIEM (Security Information and Event Management), or behavioral analysis tools, it is difficult to detect anomalous activity or ongoing attacks.

- **Dependence on third parties and cloud services:** Relying on third-party services, such as cloud storage providers, introduces vulnerabilities that are beyond the direct control of the organization. If these providers do not apply adequate security measures, the organization that relies on them is also exposed. Shared security in the cloud requires a clear understanding of responsibilities and associated risks.

Factors increasing vulnerabilities

1. System scalability and complexity: Big Data systems are, by nature, highly scalable and complex. As more nodes, services, and users are added to the system, the attack surface expands, making it more difficult to effectively secure each component. The complexity can also make it harder to identify and mitigate vulnerabilities.

2. Inadequate updating and patching: Keeping systems updated with the latest security patches is crucial to protect against known vulnerabilities. However, in Big Data environments, where multiple systems and applications are interconnected, applying updates can be complex and error-prone, potentially leaving security gaps open.

3. Lack of security culture: A lack of awareness and training in cybersecurity among employees can make them the weakest link in the security chain. Without a proper security culture, users may fall for phishing scams, use weak passwords, or fail to follow established security policies.

4. Use of emerging technologies: The rapid pace of technological innovation in the Big Data and AI field means that organizations often adopt new technologies that have not yet been fully tested or lack robust security controls. This can introduce new vulnerabilities that attackers can exploit.

Examples of threats and vulnerabilities in action

Equifax attack (2017): One of the most notorious attacks in recent history was the hacking of Equifax, one of the largest credit agencies in the world. Attackers exploited a vulnerability in the Apache Struts software to gain access to Equifax's network. As a result, personal data of approximately 147 million people was exposed. This incident underscores the importance of timely and proper patching of software vulnerabilities.

Data exposure in MongoDB (2019): In 2019, multiple MongoDB database instances were found open and unprotected, exposing millions of personal data records. This situation was caused by poor security configurations that left the databases publicly accessible without authentication. Attackers took advantage of these vulnerabilities to extract and, in some cases, delete data, demanding ransoms for its restoration.

Vulnerability in Hadoop YARN (2018): In 2018, a critical vulnerability was discovered in Hadoop YARN (Yet Another Resource Negotiator) that allowed attackers to execute code remotely on Hadoop servers. If unpatched, this vulnerability could be exploited to fully compromise a Hadoop cluster, highlighting the importance of proactively monitoring and applying security patches in Big Data infrastructures.

The proactive identification and mitigation of these vulnerabilities not only protect the organization's assets but also ensure user trust and regulatory compliance in an increasingly regulated environment.

16.3.2. Mitigation Strategies

To mitigate threats and vulnerabilities in Big Data projects, it is crucial to implement a robust set of strategies that address both preventive protection and reactive response to incidents. Since Big Data environments are complex and handle large volumes of information, these strategies must be comprehensive, covering everything from infrastructure to organizational policies.

Proactive mitigation strategies

- **Continuous risk assessment:** Performing regular risk assessments is essential to identify and prioritize the most relevant threats to the Big Data infrastructure. This assessment should include vulnerability analysis, threat modeling, and the implementation of penetration testing (pentesting) to identify weaknesses before they can be exploited.

- **Layered security implementation (defense in depth):** A defense-in-depth strategy involves implementing multiple layers of security to protect Big Data systems. This includes network segmentation, firewalls, intrusion detection and prevention systems (IDS/IPS), encryption of data at rest and in transit, and strict access and permissions management. Each layer acts as an additional barrier to stop or slow down attackers.

- **Robust data encryption:** Implementing strong encryption for data at rest and in transit is essential to protect the confidentiality of information. Encryption keys must be securely managed, using practices such as regular key rotation and storing them in hardware security modules (HSM) to prevent unauthorized access.

- **Identity and access management (IAM):** Implementing strict controls over who has access to which data is key to minimizing the risk of unauthorized access. This includes using multi-factor authentication (MFA), least privilege policies, and constant monitoring of access to quickly detect and respond to suspicious activity.

- **Regular system updates and patching:** Since many vulnerabilities are exploited through outdated software, it is crucial to keep all components of the Big Data infrastructure—including operating systems, databases, frameworks, and applications—updated with the latest security patches. Updates should be applied regularly and in a controlled environment to minimize operational impact.

- **Network segmentation and isolation:** Segmenting the network by creating isolated subnets helps contain any security incident, limiting the lateral movement of attackers within the infrastructure. This isolation can include separating production, development, and sensitive data networks, as well as using demilitarized zones (DMZ) to control network traffic to and from critical systems.

- **Continuous monitoring and security analysis:** Implementing a continuous monitoring system to supervise network traffic, data access, and user activity is essential to detect anomalous behavior and potential threats in real time. Security Information and Event Management (SIEM) tools are useful for collecting, correlating, and analyzing security events, providing early alerts about possible incidents.

- **Use of Artificial Intelligence and Machine Learning:** AI and Machine Learning technologies can be used to enhance threat detection by identifying unusual patterns that may indicate an attack. These technologies can efficiently analyze large volumes of data, helping to discover threats that might go unnoticed with traditional methods.

Reactive mitigation strategies

- **Incident response plans (IRP):** Having a well-defined incident response plan is essential for effectively managing any security breach. The plan should include clear protocols for identifying, containing, eradicating, and recovering from incidents, as well as internal and external communication during and after the incident.

- **Data backup and recovery:** Maintaining regular and secure backups is a critical strategy to ensure quick recovery after an incident, such as a ransomware attack. Backups should be encrypted and stored in secure locations, with regular restoration tests to ensure that data can be recovered when needed.

- **Digital forensic analysis:** In the event of a security incident, performing a digital forensic analysis helps understand how the attack occurred, which systems were compromised, and what data was affected. This information is vital for improving defenses and preventing similar future attacks.

- **Communication and transparency:** In the event of a security breach, it is important to have a communication plan that addresses how to inform stakeholders, including employees, customers, and regulators. Transparency in communication can help mitigate reputational damage and comply with legal and regulatory obligations.

- **Continuous improvement and lessons learned:** After managing a security incident, it is crucial to review what happened, identify areas for improvement, and update security policies, procedures, and controls accordingly. Continuous improvement should be an integral part of the security strategy, ensuring that the organization learns and strengthens with each incident.

Tools and technologies for mitigation

Intrusion detection and prevention systems (IDS/IPS): These tools are essential for identifying and blocking attacks in real time. IDS/IPS analyze network traffic for known attack patterns and take measures to prevent these attacks from succeeding.

Encryption tools: Solutions such as OpenSSL, BitLocker, and those offered by cloud services (AWS KMS, Google Cloud KMS) facilitate the implementation of strong encryption for data at rest and in transit, ensuring that sensitive information remains protected even if intercepted.

SIEM platforms: Tools like Splunk, IBM QRadar, and ArcSight collect, analyze, and correlate security events from multiple sources, providing a centralized view of the organization's security posture and real-time alerts about possible incidents.

Identity and access management (IAM) systems: Solutions like Azure Active Directory, Okta, and AWS IAM allow granular access management, ensuring that only the right people have access to the data and systems they need for their work—and nothing more.

Next-generation firewalls (NGFW): These devices not only filter traffic based on predefined rules but also offer deep packet inspection (DPI) and can block traffic based on specific applications and users, providing an additional layer of defense against advanced threats.

Considerations

The effective implementation of mitigation strategies in Big Data projects requires a combination of advanced technologies, good management practices, and an organizational culture that prioritizes security. Threats are dynamic and constantly evolving, demanding a proactive and adaptive attitude from organizations. Collaboration between security, development, and operations teams, along with ongoing training for all members of the organization, is crucial to create a Big Data environment that is not only efficient but also secure.

16.3.3. Security Tools

In the context of Big Data, where large volumes of information are handled and complex infrastructures are used, the implementation of security tools is essential to protect data, ensure privacy, and comply with legal regulations. These tools help identify, mitigate, and respond to threats and vulnerabilities. Below are the main categories of security tools, as well as specific examples that are particularly relevant for Big Data environments.

1. Security Information and Event Management (SIEM) Systems

SIEM tools collect and analyze in real time the security events generated by all systems within an organization, providing a centralized view of the security posture and enabling early threat detection.

Examples of SIEM tools:

- **Splunk:** One of the most popular SIEM platforms, used for monitoring, analyzing, and visualizing machine data in real time. Splunk allows the collection of large volumes of data from various sources and facilitates anomaly detection, alert generation, and report creation.

- **IBM QRadar:** This SIEM system is known for its ability to correlate security events in real time and its ease of integration with other security tools. QRadar offers advanced forensic analysis features, allowing efficient investigation of security incidents.

- **ArcSight:** From Micro Focus, ArcSight is another widely used SIEM solution, known for its ability to handle large volumes of data and its flexibility to integrate with various data sources, making it suitable for Big Data environments.

2. Endpoint Protection Platforms (EPP) and Endpoint Detection and Response (EDR) tools

EPP and EDR solutions focus on protecting individual devices within the network (endpoints) against threats such as malware, ransomware, and other targeted attacks.

Examples of EPP/EDR tools:

- **CrowdStrike Falcon:** This EDR is known for its ability to prevent and respond to advanced threats on endpoints. It uses Artificial Intelligence to detect suspicious behaviors and take automatic measures to neutralize threats.

- **Symantec Endpoint Protection:** Provides comprehensive threat protection for endpoint devices, combining malware protection, firewall, and device controls in a single solution. It is highly scalable and suitable for enterprise environments with large volumes of data.

- **Carbon Black:** Offered by VMware, Carbon Black provides an EDR platform that allows continuous and real-time monitoring of endpoints, quickly identifying and responding to emerging threats.

3. Identity and Access Management (IAM) tools

IAM tools are essential for controlling who has access to which resources within an organization. They ensure that only authorized individuals can access sensitive data and enable the enforcement of strict access policies.

Examples of IAM tools:

- **Okta:** A cloud-based IAM solution that facilitates identity and access management for applications and devices. It offers features such as multifactor authentication, single sign-on (SSO), and detailed permission management.

- **Azure Active Directory (AAD):** From Microsoft, AAD is an IAM solution that provides authentication and authorization for Azure cloud applications and services. It is particularly useful in enterprise environments that use hybrid or fully cloud-based infrastructures.

- **AWS Identity and Access Management (IAM):** This tool is used to manage access to Amazon Web Services resources and services. AWS IAM allows detailed access policy definitions for users and roles and integrates with other AWS security tools for comprehensive management.

4. Next-Generation Firewalls (NGFW)

NGFWs provide advanced protection by going beyond the basic functions of traditional firewalls. They offer deep packet inspection, application control, and protections against advanced threats such as zero-day attacks.

Examples of NGFW:

- **Palo Alto Networks:** Palo Alto Networks firewalls are known for their ability to integrate deep packet inspection, threat prevention, and application control in a single platform. They are recognized for their effectiveness in stopping sophisticated attacks.

- **Cisco ASA with FirePOWER:** This NGFW combines firewall functionality with advanced threat protection. It offers comprehensive defense against attacks on corporate networks and is highly scalable.

- **Fortinet FortiGate:** A robust NGFW solution that provides protection against a wide range of threats, including malware and network attacks. FortiGate easily integrates with other security solutions and offers centralized management.

5. Intrusion Detection and Prevention Systems (IDS/IPS)

IDS/IPS tools are essential for identifying and blocking intrusion attempts in real time. They monitor network traffic for suspicious behaviors and take measures to prevent these from becoming security incidents.

Examples of IDS/IPS tools:

- **Snort:** One of the most popular open-source IDS, used to detect attacks by inspecting network traffic in real time. Snort is highly configurable and supports the creation of custom rules for detecting specific threats.

- **Suricata:** Similar to Snort, Suricata is an IDS/IPS tool that offers deep packet inspection and network monitoring to detect malicious activities. It stands out for its ability to process traffic at high speeds, making it ideal for Big Data environments.

- **Cisco Firepower:** Combines IDS/IPS functionality with that of a next-generation firewall, providing advanced protection against both known and unknown threats. It is a comprehensive solution adaptable to networks of any size.

6. Audit and compliance tools

These tools help organizations ensure they comply with security regulations and standards, as well as perform internal and external audits.

Examples of audit and compliance tools:

- **AuditBoard:** A platform that facilitates compliance management and the execution of internal audits. It provides tools for automating audit processes and documenting regulatory compliance.

- **Qualys Compliance Suite:** Offers a range of services for security and compliance management, including configuration audits, compliance assessments, and continuous monitoring.

- **Netwrix Auditor:** An auditing solution that monitors changes in configuration, file access, and other critical events in IT systems. It is useful for ensuring compliance with security policies and regulations such as GDPR or CCPA.

7. Incident response tools

Incident response tools enable organizations to effectively manage security incidents, from detection to resolution.

Examples of incident response tools:

- **TheHive:** An open-source platform designed for security incident management. It offers functionalities for creating, tracking, and resolving incidents and integrates with forensic analysis tools like Cortex.

- **Cortex XSOAR (formerly Demisto):** From Palo Alto Networks, this tool facilitates the automation of incident response, coordinating actions across different security systems and providing a unified framework for incident management.

- **Splunk Phantom:** A security automation platform that allows security teams to respond quickly to incidents by automating repetitive tasks and orchestrating responses across multiple tools.

Selecting and implementing appropriate security tools in a Big Data environment is a complex challenge that requires a holistic approach. Companies and organizations must consider both external threats and internal vulnerabilities, ensuring that every component of the infrastructure is comprehensively protected. It is important to integrate these security tools within a coherent security strategy that includes continuous training, regular vulnerability testing, and ongoing review of security policies.

17. The Future of AI and Big Data

The future of Artificial Intelligence and Big Data is shaping up to be one of the most exciting and transformative in the history of technology and science. As these two disciplines continue to evolve, it is important to understand not only the emerging trends and disruptive technologies that are shaping this landscape but also the broader implications they will have on society, the economy, and various industries.

We are currently witnessing an unprecedented pace of innovation in the field of AI and Big Data. This is driven by a combination of advances in hardware, algorithms, and the availability of massive data. These innovations are paving the way for new applications that were unthinkable just a decade ago.

The future of AI and Big Data is undoubtedly bright and full of possibilities, but it is also fraught with challenges that must be collectively addressed by the global community. It is a rapidly evolving field where the decisions we make today will have lasting repercussions on the society of tomorrow.

17.1. Emerging trends and disruptive technologies

17.1.1. Generative AI (GANs, Transformers)

Generative Artificial Intelligence is an emerging branch of AI that has captured the attention of the scientific community and industry due to its ability to generate new and realistic content, such as images, text, music, and more. Within this field, two of the most prominent technologies are Generative Adversarial Networks (GANs) and Transformer models. These technologies have shown significant potential to transform various industries and open new creative and technical possibilities.

Generative Adversarial Networks were introduced in 2014 by Ian Goodfellow and his team, and have become a key tool in synthetic content generation. A GAN consists of two neural networks, known as the generator and the discriminator, which compete against each other in a zero-sum game. The generator creates fake data (such as images or text) that it tries to pass off as real data, while the discriminator evaluates this data and tries to distinguish between real and generated data. As this iterative process continues, the generator improves its ability to produce increasingly realistic data, while the discriminator becomes more skilled at detecting fakes. This approach has led to impressive applications, such as the generation of human faces that do not exist in reality, the creation of original works of art, and the enhancement of low-resolution images. So at this point you've probably stopped wondering how generative AIs achieve such realistic faces.

Well, however, despite their advances, GANs present several challenges. One of the main problems is the stability of training. Since GANs depend on a delicate balance between the generator and the discriminator, it is common for one of the models to outperform the other, which can lead to ineffective training or convergence to suboptimal solutions. In addition, GANs can be prone to what is known as "mode collapse," where the generator learns to produce only a limited set of outputs, rather than generating a diverse variety of examples.

On the other hand, Transformer models, introduced by Vaswani et al. in 2017, have revolutionized the way natural language processing tasks are approached and, more recently, content generation. Transformers use an attention mechanism that allows them to focus on different parts of a data sequence, such as words in a sentence, to capture long-term relationships more effectively than previous architectures, such as recurrent neural networks. This approach has enabled significant advances in tasks such as machine translation, text generation, and document summarization. To put it plainly, transformers marked a huge before-and-after moment.

A key development based on Transformers is the GPT model (Generative Pre-trained Transformer), which has demonstrated a remarkable ability to generate coherent and contextually relevant text. GPT-3, for example, is a model with 175 billion parameters that can write essays, answer questions, and perform complex tasks in a way that is almost indistinguishable from a human. And I say "almost indistinguishable" because obviously it's not. It's as easy to recognize AI-generated text as it is to spot an AI-generated image. These types of models have not only shown a high level of competence in specific tasks, but have also raised important questions about creativity and the role of AI in content production.

However, like GANs, Transformers also face challenges. One of the main problems is the need for large amounts of data and computational resources to train large models, making them inaccessible to many researchers and small organizations. Additionally, the complexity of these models poses challenges in terms of interpretability, making it difficult to understand how and why the model generates certain outputs, which is critical in applications where transparency and accountability are required.

Despite these challenges, generative AI, driven by technologies such as GANs and Transformers, is at the forefront of many innovations. In the entertainment industry, these technologies are being used to create new characters, scripts, and visual effects. In the design field, they are being used to generate prototypes and sketches that designers can then refine. Even in medicine, GANs are being explored to enhance the quality of medical images and to generate synthetic data that can aid research without compromising patient privacy.

The proliferation of generative AI has also raised ethical and security concerns. Since these technologies can generate highly realistic content, there is a risk that they will be used to create false information or impersonate people, posing significant challenges to information authenticity and digital security. Therefore, it is crucial to develop ethical frameworks and regulations that guide the development and use of generative AI, ensuring it is used responsibly and with minimal risk.

GANs and Transformers represent two of the most innovative technologies in the field of generative AI. Although both face technical and ethical challenges, their ability to create new and realistic content has the potential to transform a wide range of industries and applications. The future of generative AI is promising, and as these technologies continue to evolve, we are likely to see an even greater impact on creativity, entertainment, medicine, and beyond.

17.1.2. Quantum Computing and its Impact on AI

Quantum computing is one of the most exciting and complex frontiers of contemporary science and technology. Unlike classical computing, which is based on bits that represent binary states (0 and 1), quantum computing uses qubits, which can exist in a superposition of states, allowing the representation of multiple values simultaneously. This approach opens the door to exponentially faster processing capabilities for certain types of problems, which has the potential to revolutionize many fields, including Artificial Intelligence.

Superposition is one of the fundamental principles of quantum computing. While a classical bit can be in a state of 0 or 1, a qubit can be in a combination of both, thanks to superposition. This capability allows qubits to perform calculations in parallel, exponentially increasing processing power compared to classical systems. In addition to superposition, another key principle is quantum entanglement, which allows two qubits to be correlated in such a way that the state of one instantly determines the state of the other, regardless of the distance between them. This phenomenon can be harnessed to create incredibly fast and secure communication and data processing systems.

In the context of AI, quantum computing could address some of the most significant challenges in terms of processing and optimization. Machine learning algorithms, which often require exploring a very large solution space, could benefit enormously from the speed and efficiency of quantum algorithms. For example, search and optimization methods, which are fundamental in many AI problems, could be drastically accelerated by using quantum algorithms like Grover's algorithm, which offers a quadratic advantage in unstructured search. This capability could make solving complex problems that are currently intractable with classical computers feasible.

One area where quantum computing could have a transformative impact is in the training of deep neural networks. Training these models is a resource-intensive process involving the optimization of millions or even billions of parameters. This process could benefit from quantum algorithms, such as variational quantum optimization (VQA) algorithms, which can find global minima in high-dimensional loss functions more efficiently than classical methods. This could significantly reduce the time and cost associated with training complex models, making advanced AI more accessible and applicable to a wider range of problems.

Another promising field is quantum simulation, which can be used to model complex systems much more efficiently than traditional methods. In AI, this could allow more accurate simulations of neural networks or other intelligent systems, enabling advances in areas such as behavior simulation, outcome prediction, and the creation of more robust and precise models. Quantum simulations could also be used to model complex natural processes, such as quantum chemistry, potentially leading to discoveries in areas like drug design or advanced materials, with direct implications for AI in biomedicine and nanotechnology.

However, despite its potential, quantum computing still faces several challenges before it can be effectively integrated into AI systems. One of the main challenges is creating stable and scalable quantum hardware. Current qubits are extremely sensitive to environmental interference, resulting in calculation errors that must be corrected using sophisticated quantum error correction techniques. In addition, creating a sufficient number of entangled qubits to perform useful calculations remains a significant challenge. The practical implementation of quantum computing will also require the development of new programming techniques and quantum algorithms, which demands a shift in how software engineers and data scientists approach problems.

Another important consideration is security and privacy. Quantum computing has the potential to break many of today's cryptographic systems, posing significant risks to data security. At the same time, it also offers the possibility of developing new forms of quantum cryptography, which could protect data in ways that are impossible with current technology. For AI, this means that while quantum computing could enable advances in the privacy and security of data systems, it could also require a complete reassessment of the data protection techniques in use today.

As the technology advances, the convergence of quantum computing and AI promises to create a new era of computational capabilities, enabling the resolution of problems that are currently beyond the reach of even the most advanced computers. Potential applications range from optimization and modeling to the creation of new forms of Artificial Intelligence that could learn and adapt at levels that today seem like science fiction. However, it is important to recognize that these advances will also bring ethical and technical challenges that must be carefully managed to ensure that the benefits of quantum computing in AI are realized safely and fairly.

17.2. The impact of AI and Big Data on various industries

17.2.1. Industry 4.0

Industry 4.0 is a term that describes the transformation of manufacturing industries through the integration of advanced technologies such as Artificial Intelligence, the Internet of Things, robotics, cloud computing, and automation, with the goal of creating smart factories. This new industrial era is characterized by the interconnection and digitalization of all production processes, allowing for greater flexibility, efficiency, and customization in the production of goods. The term itself is not new, but if you woke up y-esterday after a long winter nap, well, it might sound new to you.

One of the most notable aspects of Industry 4.0 is the interconnection of devices and systems. Through IoT, sensors, machines, and management systems are networked, enabling real-time communication between them. This interconnection allows for the collection and analysis of large volumes of data throughout the value chain, from the supply of raw materials to the delivery of the final product. The data collected can be used to optimize production processes, predict machine maintenance, and reduce resource waste.

AI plays a fundamental role in Industry 4.0, as it enables advanced data analysis and automated decision-making. AI algorithms are used to detect patterns in production data, predict equipment failures, optimize production routes, and adjust manufacturing parameters in real time to improve product quality and reduce costs. In addition, AI enables the implementation of predictive maintenance systems, where machines are constantly monitored and repairs are carried out before failures occur, reducing downtime and increasing productivity.

Advanced automation is another key component of Industry 4.0. Smart factories are equipped with robots and automated systems that can perform complex tasks with high precision and speed. These systems are capable of working autonomously or in collaboration with human workers, known as collaborative robotics or "cobots." Automation not only improves production efficiency but also enables mass customization, where products can be tailored to specific customer needs without compromising production speed or cost.

Another important aspect of Industry 4.0 is production customization. Thanks to advanced technologies, factories can produce small batches of customized products at a cost similar to that of mass production. This is possible through techniques such as additive manufacturing (3D printing), which allows for the rapid production of customized parts without the need for special tools or molds. Mass customization is a response to the growing consumer demand for unique products tailored to their individual needs.

Cloud computing is also an essential component of Industry 4.0. Cloud platforms enable the storage and processing of large volumes of data generated by smart factories. This data can be accessed and analyzed in real time from anywhere in the world, facilitating informed decision-making and collaboration across different parts of the supply chain. In addition, cloud computing allows for the implementation of production management systems based on SaaS (Software as a Service), which can be scaled according to the company's needs without requiring costly physical infrastructure.

In supply chain management, Industry 4.0 introduces complete product traceability throughout its life cycle. Through technologies such as blockchain and IoT sensors, companies can track raw materials from their origin to their transformation into finished products and delivery to consumers. This not only improves transparency and efficiency in the supply chain but also allows companies to respond quickly to changes in demand, quality issues, or supply disruptions.

Cybersecurity is a major challenge in Industry 4.0, due to the high interconnection of systems and the growing reliance on digital technology. As more devices and systems connect to the network, the risk of cyberattacks that could compromise production or data integrity increases. To mitigate these risks, companies must implement advanced security measures, such as data encryption, multi-factor authentication, and continuous network monitoring to detect and respond to threats in real time.

Sustainability is a central theme in Industry 4.0. The ability to monitor and optimize resource use in real time enables companies to reduce their environmental impact and increase energy efficiency. Smart factories can implement more sustainable production processes, such as material recycling, waste reduction, and the use of renewable energy sources. Sustainability is not only beneficial for the environment but can also be a key competitive factor, as consumers and regulations increasingly demand responsible business practices.

In short, the term Industry 4.0 represents a profound transformation in the way products are manufactured and supply chains are managed. Through the integration of advanced technologies such as AI, IoT, robotics, and cloud computing, smart factories are redefining efficiency, customization, sustainability, and security in industrial production. However, it also presents significant challenges, especially in terms of cybersecurity and the need for a highly skilled workforce to manage and operate these new technologies.

17.2.2. Health and Biotechnology

The convergence of Artificial Intelligence and biotechnology has revolutionized the healthcare field, offering new possibilities for the diagnosis, treatment, and prevention of diseases, as well as for biotechnological research. And I say "has" because in this case, the revolution is already happening like never before in this field. This intersection of technologies is transforming the way we understand and treat diseases while driving significant advances in areas such as personalized medicine, genetic engineering, and drug development.

One of the most impactful applications of AI in the healthcare sector is AI-assisted medical diagnosis. AI algorithms, especially those based on deep learning, are being trained to analyze medical images, such as X-rays, CT scans, and MRIs, with a precision that rivals or even surpasses that of human radiologists. For example, in the early detection of breast cancer, convolutional neural networks have demonstrated remarkable ability to identify tumors in mammograms, enabling faster and more accurate diagnoses, which is crucial for effective treatment.

In addition to image analysis, AI is being used to predict disease progression and treatment response. By analyzing large volumes of clinical data, including medical histories, lab test results, and genomic data, AI models can identify patterns that predict how a disease will evolve in a specific patient. This is especially useful in chronic diseases like diabetes or Alzheimer's, where AI can help doctors personalize treatment plans based on each patient's individual characteristics.

In the field of personalized medicine, AI and biotechnology are working together to develop treatments tailored to the specific needs of each patient. This approach is based on the idea that every person has a unique genetic makeup, meaning diseases can manifest and progress differently in each individual. AI is used to analyze genomic data and other biomarkers, allowing doctors to identify the therapies that will be most effective for each patient. This approach is proving particularly promising in cancer treatment, where targeted therapies based on the genetic profile of the tumor are improving success rates and reducing side effects.

Another significant advancement is the use of AI in genetic engineering. Gene-editing tools like CRISPR-Cas9 have opened new possibilities for DNA modification, and AI is playing a crucial role in optimizing these processes. AI is used to design guide RNA sequences that direct CRISPR to the correct locations in the genome, increasing precision and reducing the risk of off-target effects. Additionally, AI is helping scientists explore vast libraries of genetic data to identify new therapeutic targets and develop innovative treatments for genetic diseases.

In drug development, the combination of AI and biotechnology is significantly accelerating the process, which has traditionally been costly and time-consuming. AI algorithms can analyze large databases of chemical compounds to identify those with the potential to become new drugs. This approach, known as AI-assisted drug discovery, allows researchers to identify promising candidates in a fraction of the time it would take using conventional methods. Furthermore, AI is being used to optimize the phases of clinical testing and development, predicting how different patient populations will respond to new treatments and helping to design more efficient clinical trials.

The impact of AI and biotechnology on public health management is also significant. AI models are being used to predict the spread of infectious diseases, enabling governments and health organizations to take proactive measures to contain outbreaks before they become epidemics. During the COVID-19 pandemic, AI played a key role in tracking the spread of the virus, identifying mutations, and accelerating vaccine development.

Despite these advances, the integration of AI and biotechnology in healthcare raises ethical and regulatory challenges. Genetic manipulation, for example, raises questions about the long-term implications for humanity and the environment. Additionally, the collection and analysis of large amounts of personal health data require strict safeguards to protect patient privacy. Regulators and the scientific community are working together to establish ethical and regulatory frameworks that guide the development and use of these technologies in ways that maximize their benefits while minimizing risks.

17.2.3. Finance and Insurance

The impact of AI and Big Data on the finance and insurance sectors has been transformative, reshaping processes, improving decision-making, and optimizing operational efficiency. The integration of these technologies is enabling financial institutions and insurers to innovate in critical areas such as risk management, fraud detection, service personalization, and predictive analytics. Below, we will look at some of the most significant applications of AI and Big Data in these sectors.

In the financial field, one of the most important applications is risk management. Financial institutions have adopted advanced AI models to assess and mitigate risks associated with investments, loans, and other financial operations. Machine Learning algorithms analyze large volumes of historical and real-time data to identify patterns and foresee potential risks. For example, in the case of credit risk, AI can assess the likelihood of a customer defaulting on a loan based on multiple variables such as credit history, income, spending behavior, and even macroeconomic variables. These models not only increase the precision of decision-making but also enable continuous and dynamic risk assessment, adjusting to changes in the market and customer behavior.

Fraud detection is another area where AI has proven to be crucial. Traditional fraud detection systems relied on predefined rules that were often insufficient to identify new fraud patterns. In contrast, AI models, particularly those based on Machine Learning and predictive analytics, can detect anomalous behavior in real-time, quickly adapting to new fraud tactics. These systems analyze millions of financial transactions instantly, identifying suspicious patterns that could indicate fraudulent activities, such as unusual credit card usage or atypical bank transfers. Moreover, AI algorithms can continuously improve as they process more data, increasing their ability to detect fraud more accurately and quickly.

In the insurance sector, the personalization of policies and risk assessment have greatly benefited from the use of AI and Big Data. Insurers can now design personalized products for their customers based on detailed analyses of behavior data, claims history, lifestyle, and other relevant factors. For example, in auto insurance, companies can offer policies based on the driving behavior of the insured, collected through telematics devices installed in vehicles. This personalization allows insurers to adjust premiums more accurately, rewarding safe drivers and mitigating risks for the company. Similarly, in health insurance, data collected from wearable health devices can be used to create insurance plans more tailored to individual needs, promoting a more proactive approach to health management.

Algorithmic trading, another key application of AI in finance, uses advanced algorithms to execute buy and sell orders of financial assets at speeds and volumes impossible for human traders. These algorithms are designed to analyze large amounts of market data in fractions of a second, identifying arbitrage opportunities, price patterns, and trading signals that can be exploited for profit. AI not only enables the execution of these strategies at high speed but also the continuous optimization of algorithms based on Machine Learning, which improves the accuracy and profitability of operations. Additionally, the use of AI in trading reduces the impact of human bias in decision-making, as operations are based on data and predefined rules rather than emotions or intuitions.

The optimization of operational processes is another area where AI and Big Data have demonstrated their value in finance and insurance. Institutions are using AI-powered chatbots and virtual assistants to improve customer experience by providing immediate and accurate responses to common inquiries, processing claims, and managing basic transactions. These tools not only improve operational efficiency by reducing the workload of human employees but also increase customer satisfaction by offering faster and more accessible service.

Furthermore, AI in financial forecasting is transforming business planning and strategy. Predictive models analyze large volumes of historical and real-time data to forecast economic trends, market fluctuations, and changes in consumer behavior. These models enable financial institutions and insurers to anticipate market movements, adjust their strategies accordingly, and make more informed decisions that minimize risks and maximize opportunities.

In the context of regulation and compliance, AI also plays a fundamental role. Financial institutions are required to comply with complex regulations that vary by jurisdiction. AI can automate much of the compliance process by analyzing transactions and documentation to ensure they meet current regulations. This not only reduces the risk of non-compliance and associated penalties but also frees up human resources to focus on higher-value tasks.

However, the adoption of AI and Big Data in finance and insurance is not without challenges. Ensuring transparency in AI models, particularly in critical decisions such as loan approvals or premium setting, is essential to maintain customer trust and comply with regulations. Additionally, data security and privacy remain major concerns, given the sensitive nature of the financial and personal information handled by these institutions.

To fully capitalize on these advances, institutions must address the ethical, security, and regulatory challenges associated, ensuring that the use of these technologies aligns with the highest standards of transparency, accountability, and data protection.

PART VII

Practical Cases and real Projects

Part VII: Practical cases and real projects

18. Case Studies

From the beginning of the book, I have been talking to you and giving different examples of the use of AI in different sectors and in many contexts. You are almost finishing the book now, and I want to take the opportunity to delve into real cases so that, with everything you have learned, you gain more knowledge in this aspect and also reinforce the idea of the importance of data during development and of AI at the business and social levels.

Currently, AI is at a stage where it not only improves existing processes but also enables new possibilities that were previously unthinkable. From medical diagnosis assisted by algorithms to the optimization of production lines in smart factories, AI demonstrates its ability to increase efficiency, reduce costs, and enhance data-driven decision-making. Its impact extends to virtually all sectors, redefining the way we interact with technology and the world around us.

The current applications of AI can be classified into a wide variety of areas. In the health field, to recap, AI is used to improve diagnostic accuracy, personalize treatments, and accelerate the research of new drugs. In industry, intelligent systems optimize manufacturing processes, predictive maintenance, and quality control. In the transportation sector, AI is used to improve the safety and efficiency of autonomous vehicles and to manage traffic in smart cities.

Additionally, AI has found a significant space in customer service, where chatbots and virtual assistants have revolutionized the way companies interact with their consumers. In the food sector, AI contributes to crop optimization through the analysis of climate and soil data, as well as improving distribution logistics. In the scientific field, Artificial Intelligence is a fundamental tool in physics and chemistry, helping to model complex phenomena and discover new materials. Likewise, its application in environmental and biodiversity preservation allows for the monitoring of ecosystems and the early detection of environmental threats.

Throughout the following sections, we will explore in detail how Artificial Intelligence is transforming each of these sectors, presenting specific cases that illustrate its impact and the opportunities it offers for the future. In all my books, I always try to give different examples and place the reader in various contexts, so I will try to do the same here. We will also reflect on the role of data in the evolution of AI and on the challenges it faces in its development and implementation. As if you haven't had enough already, right?

Although we have already mentioned many examples, I have prepared a section in which I will tell you how Artificial Intelligence and Big Data are being used in very important sectors. The idea is that, through specific examples, you can see not only how these technologies are revolutionizing these areas but also the challenges and considerations that arise when applying them. Every example helps to understand the potential of AI and the importance of Big Data for it, and I am sure that the end of the book will be no different in that respect.

In health, for example, I will show you how AI is helping doctors make more precise and faster diagnoses, something we have already discussed several times throughout the book, but because it is really changing patients' lives. Then we move on to marketing, where Big Data allows companies to better understand their customers and create more personalized and effective campaigns. We will also see how, in the world of finance, AI is transforming the way risks are managed and investment decisions are made. And finally, I will end the chapter by giving you many examples in other areas that will surprise you. Well, that depends on the experience you already have.

What I want you to take away from this section is a clear vision of how AI and Big Data can be applied in the real world and how, although they bring many benefits, there are also challenges that we cannot ignore. My goal is that in the end, after this part of the book, you feel inspired and with a deeper understanding of how these technologies can make a difference in your field of work.

18.1. AI in Health: Diagnosis and Treatment

Artificial Intelligence has proven to be a revolutionary tool in the field of medicine, not only in widely known areas such as imaging diagnostics or drug development but also in less obvious but equally impactful applications.

Early detection of neurodegenerative diseases through speech
One of the most innovative fields in the application of AI in medicine is speech analysis for the early detection of neurodegenerative diseases such as Parkinson's and Alzheimer's. Machine Learning algorithms can analyze voice patterns and microvariations in intonation, speech speed, and pauses to identify early biomarkers of these diseases. This approach not only allows

earlier detection than traditional methods but also facilitates non-invasive monitoring of disease progression over time.

Optimization of organ transplants
The allocation of organs for transplants is a complex process that depends on multiple factors such as genetic compatibility, the recipient's health status, and the organ's ischemia time. AI models can analyze donor and recipient databases in real time, optimizing organ allocation and reducing waiting times. Additionally, algorithms are being developed that can predict the likelihood of transplant success based on variables such as the patient's medical history and the quality of the donated organ, thus improving postoperative survival rates.

Disease detection through artificial smell analysis
Another surprising application of AI in medicine is the use of electronic sensors, known as electronic noses, combined with deep learning algorithms to detect diseases through the analysis of chemical compounds present in patients' breath. This method has proven effective in detecting diseases such as lung cancer, diabetes, and even bacterial infections, allowing quick and non-invasive diagnoses.

AI in mental health monitoring
Mental illnesses such as depression and anxiety can be difficult to diagnose due to the subjectivity of the symptoms. AI is revolutionizing this field through the analysis of behavioral data obtained from mobile devices, social networks, and sleep patterns. Algorithms can detect early signs of mental deterioration by analyzing app activity, changes in the way text messages are written, or variations in physical activity, providing early alerts and personalized recommendations for intervention.

Use of AI for tissue regeneration
One of the most promising areas in regenerative medicine is AI-assisted 3D bioprinting. Machine Learning algorithms can optimize the combination of biomaterials and stem cells to print functional tissues, which could revolutionize the treatment of severe injuries and degenerative diseases. This technology has already shown its potential in printing skin for patients with severe burns and in creating vascular structures to improve wound healing.

Prediction of infectious disease outbreaks
The analysis of Big Data together with Artificial Intelligence allows for the prediction of infectious disease outbreaks by analyzing internet search patterns, weather data, and real-time medical reports. This type of prediction has been key in the fight against pandemics, allowing health systems to prepare in advance and respond more effectively to the spread of diseases.

18.1.1. Applications in Imaging Diagnostics

The use of Artificial Intelligence in imaging diagnostics has revolutionized medical practice, allowing for greater accuracy and speed in disease detection. This advance is based on the application of deep learning algorithms, especially convolutional neural networks, which are particularly effective in analyzing medical images such as X-rays, CT scans, MRIs, and mammograms.

One of the first and most prominent examples of AI in imaging diagnostics is its application in the early detection of breast cancer. Algorithms trained with thousands of mammogram images have proven capable of identifying anomalies with accuracy comparable to, and in some cases surpassing, that of human radiologists. This not only improves the early detection rate but also reduces the workload of health professionals, allowing them to focus on more complex cases.

Another area where AI has shown significant impact is in the diagnosis of lung diseases such as pneumonia and tuberculosis through the analysis of chest X-rays. Algorithms can detect subtle patterns that might go unnoticed by the human eye, enabling more precise and earlier identification of these diseases. Additionally, during the COVID-19 pandemic, AI was used to analyze chest CT scans, helping doctors assess the severity of the infection and make informed treatment decisions.

In the field of neurology, AI has been used to analyze brain MRI scans, facilitating the diagnosis of neurological disorders such as multiple sclerosis, Alzheimer's, and strokes. Algorithms can accurately measure the volumes of different brain regions, detect lesions, and monitor changes in the brain over time, which is crucial for tracking degenerative diseases.

In addition to these specific examples, AI is also being used to improve diagnostic accuracy in other areas, such as the detection of skin lesions in dermatology, where algorithms can differentiate between different types of lesions and assist in the early identification of melanomas. In ophthalmology, AI is used to analyze retinal images, enabling early detection of eye diseases such as diabetic retinopathy and macular degeneration.

The training of these AI models is carried out using large datasets that include images labeled by human experts. As the algorithms learn to identify specific patterns and features in the images, their accuracy improves over time. However, it is important to highlight that, although AI has proven to be a valuable tool in imaging diagnostics, its application should be considered as a complement to the clinical judgment of health professionals and not as a replacement.

The implementation of AI in imaging diagnostics also raises important ethical and privacy considerations, especially regarding the handling of patient data. AI systems must comply with data protection regulations and ensure the privacy and security of medical information. Additionally, it is essential to ensure that the algorithms are transparent and explainable so that health professionals can trust the decisions made by AI and understand how these conclusions have been reached.

Its success depends on the quality of the data used to train the models, effective integration with clinical work, and adherence to strict ethical principles.

18.1.2. Predictive Models for Treatments

Predictive models for treatments in the medical field represent one of the most revolutionary applications of Artificial Intelligence and machine learning. These models allow predicting a patient's response to different treatment options, facilitating clinical decision-making and personalizing medical care according to the individual characteristics of each patient.

One of the main areas where predictive models have proven valuable is oncology. Cancer treatment often involves a combination of surgery, radiotherapy, chemotherapy, and targeted therapies. However, patients' responses to these treatments can vary significantly depending on factors such as the type of cancer, the patient's genetics, and the stage of the disease. Predictive models help oncologists anticipate which treatments will be most effective for a particular patient, minimizing side effects and improving clinical outcomes.

These models are built using historical patient data, which includes information on diagnoses, previous treatments, treatment outcomes, and demographic and genetic characteristics. Using supervised learning techniques, algorithms analyze this data to identify patterns and relationships that are not evident to humans. For example, a predictive model could identify that certain genetic profiles are associated with a better response to a specific type of chemotherapy, while other profiles may indicate a higher likelihood of adverse effects.

Another key area of application is predicting the effectiveness of treatments in chronic diseases such as diabetes and cardiovascular diseases. In these cases, predictive models can assess the likelihood of a patient experiencing serious complications, such as a heart attack or stroke, based on their medical history, lifestyle habits, and other risk factors. This allows doctors to proactively adjust treatment plans, for example, by intensifying medication or recommending lifestyle changes to prevent adverse events.

In addition to predicting treatment response, these models are also useful in planning long-term treatment strategies. In the case of neurodegenerative diseases such as Alzheimer's, predictive models can help determine which interventions may slow the progression of the disease based on the clinical evolution of previous patients. This is particularly important in diseases where current treatments can only manage symptoms rather than offer a cure.

In the field of personalized medicine, predictive models play a crucial role in optimizing drug treatments. Pharmacogenomics, which studies how a person's genes affect their response to medications, greatly benefits from these models. For example, patients with certain genetic variants may metabolize drugs more slowly, which could lead to drug accumulation and a higher risk of side effects. Predictive models can suggest dose adjustments or switching to a different drug based on the patient's genetics, resulting in safer and more effective treatment.

However, implementing predictive models in clinical practice is not without challenges. One of the main challenges is the need for high-quality, well-labeled data. The accuracy of the models largely depends on the quantity and quality of the available data. Moreover, it is crucial that the data used are representative of the population to which the models will be applied to avoid biases and ensure that the results are generalizable.

Another challenge is integrating these models into the clinical workflow. Doctors must be trained to interpret the predictions generated by the models and use them as a decision-support tool rather than relying solely on them. Collaboration between AI developers and healthcare professionals is essential to design user interfaces that present the information clearly and accessibly and to ensure that recommendations are understandable and useful in the clinical context.

Additionally, predictive models must comply with strict ethical and privacy standards. Since these models are often trained with sensitive patient data, it is essential to implement robust data protection measures to ensure patient privacy is not compromised. Likewise, it is important that the models are transparent and explainable so that doctors and patients understand how the predictions are generated and can trust their reliability.

As technology advances, predictive models are expected to become increasingly accurate and personalized. With the integration of genomic data, biomarkers, and other advanced data sources, these models have the potential to transform medicine, enabling more precise, effective, and personalized treatments. However, the success of these models will depend on continuous collaboration between technology and medicine, as well as a commitment to ethical principles and patient privacy protection.

18.1.3. Ethics in the Use of AI in Healthcare

The use of Artificial Intelligence in healthcare has led to significant advances in diagnosis, treatment, and disease prevention. However, it also raises a series of ethical challenges that must be carefully considered to ensure that its application benefits patients without compromising the fundamental principles of medicine and human rights.

One of the main ethical challenges in the use of AI in healthcare is the issue of transparency and explainability. Many AI tools, especially those based on deep learning algorithms, operate as "black boxes," where the decisions or recommendations generated cannot be easily explained or understood by humans. In such a sensitive environment as medicine, where decisions can mean life or death, the lack of explainability can generate distrust among both healthcare professionals and patients. Transparency in how these systems are trained, validated, and used is essential to ensure that AI-based decisions are reliable and can be audited if necessary.

Another critical ethical aspect is the inherent bias in the data used to train AI algorithms. If training data are not representative of the general population, models may perpetuate or even amplify existing inequalities in the healthcare system. For example, if a model is trained mainly with data from patients of a certain ethnic or socioeconomic group, it may not generalize properly to other groups, resulting in disparities in diagnosis and treatment. Addressing these biases requires a conscious and proactive approach to data collection and use, ensuring that models are developed with diverse and representative data.

Privacy and data protection are also fundamental ethical concerns in the use of AI in healthcare. AI systems require large amounts of personal data to function effectively, including highly sensitive information such as medical histories, genomic data, and other intimate details of patients' lives. Improper handling or vulnerability of these data can lead to privacy breaches, which could have devastating consequences for the individuals affected. Moreover, the possibility that these data may be used for commercial purposes or without proper consent raises serious ethical concerns. Therefore, it is crucial that organizations implementing AI in healthcare adopt rigorous data protection practices and comply with legal regulations such as the General Data Protection Regulation in Europe.

Accountability and responsibility in the use of AI in healthcare is another highly relevant ethical issue. When an AI system makes a mistake or fails in its performance, the question arises as to who is responsible: the software developers, the data providers, the healthcare professionals who used the AI to make decisions, or the institutions that implemented the technology. The lack of clarity in this area can lead to situations where victims of errors cannot obtain justice or adequate compensation. It is essential to establish clear frameworks of responsibility that define who is accountable for AI system failures in healthcare.

Moreover, the use of AI in medicine also touches on ethical aspects related to patient autonomy and informed consent. As AI systems become more integrated into medical decision-making, there is a risk that patients and doctors may blindly trust the AI's recommendations without fully questioning or understanding the processes behind those recommendations. This could undermine patient autonomy, as treatment decisions might be more influenced by algorithms than by human judgment. Therefore, it is vital that patients are informed of the involvement of AI in their care and that they give their informed consent before decisions based on these technologies are made.

The use of AI in healthcare also raises questions about access and equity. Implementing advanced AI technologies can exacerbate existing inequalities in access to medical care, especially in regions or communities with fewer resources. If AI technologies are only available to those who can afford them or who live in areas with advanced infrastructure, there is a risk that health disparities between different populations will widen. It is essential that public health policies promote equitable access to technological innovations and that consideration is given to how AI tools can benefit all patients, regardless of their location or economic status.

18.2. Big Data in Marketing: Segmentation and Personalization

18.2.1. Customer Behavior Analysis

Customer behavior analysis is a fundamental tool in modern marketing, especially in the context of Big Data and Artificial Intelligence. This type of analysis allows companies to better understand the needs, preferences, and purchasing patterns of their customers, which in turn helps them make more informed decisions and personalize their offers more effectively.

The process of customer behavior analysis involves collecting and examining large volumes of data from various sources, such as purchase transactions, online interactions, satisfaction surveys, social media, and more.

These data are analyzed to identify patterns, trends, and recurring behaviors that can provide deep insight into the customer profile. The key is to use advanced data analysis tools and Machine Learning models to detect hidden patterns that would not be evident with traditional analysis methods.

One of the most common applications of customer behavior analysis is customer segmentation. This process involves dividing customers into smaller, more homogeneous groups based on specific characteristics, such as demographics, purchasing behavior, interests, and values. Segmentation allows companies to target their marketing efforts more precisely, personalizing messages and offers for each specific group. For example, an online store could identify a segment of customers who tend to buy luxury products and design specific campaigns for this group, thus maximizing the effectiveness of its marketing efforts.

Another critical aspect of customer behavior analysis is the prediction of future behavior. Using predictive models, companies can anticipate which products or services a customer is likely to buy, when they are most likely to do so, and even how much they are willing to spend. These models are based on historical data and behavior patterns and can be used to optimize inventory management, improve production planning, and design more effective promotions. For example, a retailer could use predictive models to identify customers who are about to leave their service and direct personalized offers to retain them.

Customer behavior analysis is also used to improve the customer experience. By better understanding customer preferences and expectations, companies can personalize the shopping experience, offer more accurate product recommendations, and reduce friction in the buying process. An example of this is the use of recommendation engines on e-commerce platforms, which suggest products based on previous purchases and the customer's browsing behavior. This type of personalization not only improves customer satisfaction but also increases the likelihood of additional sales.

In addition, customer behavior analysis is crucial for fraud detection and risk management. By monitoring transactions and customer behavior in real-time, Machine Learning algorithms can identify anomalous patterns that might indicate fraudulent activities. For example, if a customer who normally makes small purchases suddenly makes a very large purchase in a foreign country, this could be a sign of fraud. Companies can set up automatic alerts to investigate these cases and take preventive measures.

In terms of implementation, customer behavior analysis requires a robust Big Data infrastructure that can handle and process large volumes of data in real time. It is also essential to have a team of data analysts and data scientists who can design, implement, and refine analytical models. Data visualization tools are also important, as they allow marketing and sales teams to interpret the analysis results more intuitively and make informed decisions based on the insights obtained.

The challenge of this type of analysis lies in integrating data from multiple sources, which are often in different formats and may vary in quality. Data cleaning and normalization are crucial steps to ensure that analytical models produce accurate and useful results.

Customer behavior analysis not only benefits companies but can also enhance the customer experience by making interactions with the company more relevant and satisfying. However, it is important for companies to use these data ethically, respecting customer privacy and ensuring that the use of AI and Big Data aligns with the values and expectations of their customers.

Artificial Intelligence has revolutionized customer service, transforming the way companies interact with their users, and likewise the way users interact with them. Although chatbots and virtual assistants are the most well-known applications, there are other atypical and equally relevant ways in which AI is impacting this field.

Emotion detection in service calls
Some companies have implemented AI to analyze the tone of voice and emotions of customers during phone calls. The algorithms can detect whether a customer is frustrated, impatient, or satisfied, allowing agents to adjust their response tone or for the system to transfer the call to a more experienced crisis management agent.

AI systems for sign language interpretation
Companies focused on inclusion have developed tools that use neural networks to translate sign language in real-time into text or voice, facilitating communication between deaf people and customer service agents.

AI-based personalization engines
In e-commerce, some companies have implemented AI systems that personalize navigation and recommendations according to user behavior. Without the customer having to communicate with a representative, the AI anticipates their needs and adapts the shopping experience, generating frictionless interactions.

Microexpression analysis in video calls
In the financial and luxury services sectors, some entities use AI to analyze facial microexpressions during video call interactions. This helps detect

levels of interest, concern, or doubt in customers, allowing agents to adjust their sales or advisory strategy in real-time.

Optimization of email responses with contextual AI
Advanced AI systems can analyze incoming emails and generate highly personalized automatic responses. These models not only use the content of the received email but also the history of previous interactions to ensure that the responses are coherent and relevant.

Customer service robots in physical stores
Some retail chains have incorporated AI-powered robots that can guide customers within the store, answer questions about products in real-time, and even handle processes such as returns or assistance with online purchases.

Prediction of customer needs through predictive AI
AI systems can analyze large volumes of data on customers' previous interactions and predict when they might need assistance. For example, in the telecommunications sector, AI can foresee imminent technical problems in a service and alert the user before the issue occurs, offering proactive solutions.

AI for claims management with document recognition
In sectors such as insurance and banking, AI is used to analyze documents submitted by customers in claims or support requests. The algorithms can identify errors, validate information, and speed up the approval process, significantly reducing waiting times.

18.2.2. Personalization of Offers and Campaigns

The personalization of offers and campaigns is one of the most powerful applications of data analysis and Artificial Intelligence in the field of marketing. This strategy involves tailoring products, services, promotions, and messages to the individual needs and preferences of customers. Unlike traditional marketing, which uses a generalized approach to reach as many people as possible, personalization seeks to create a deeper and more relevant connection with each customer, which can significantly increase the effectiveness of campaigns and customer satisfaction.

Personalization begins with the collection and analysis of customer data. These data can come from multiple sources, such as purchase history, online activity, social media interactions, and survey responses. Through the analysis of these data, companies can identify behavior patterns, preferences, and specific needs of each customer. For example, an online store could identify that a customer has shown recurring interest in technology products and therefore could personalize its offer for this customer by suggesting related products or sending specific promotions about technology.

One of the most common techniques used in personalization is advanced segmentation. While basic segmentation divides customers into large groups based on general characteristics such as age or location, advanced segmentation uses Machine Learning algorithms to create much more specific and dynamic segments. These segments can be based on recent behaviors, propensity to perform certain actions, or even psychological and emotional factors. This allows companies to design campaigns that resonate more precisely with the individual motivations of each customer group.

In addition, personalization also extends to the content and the channel through which it is delivered. For example, a company could personalize not only the offer itself but also the medium through which it is communicated, such as emails, text messages, push notifications, or social media ads. This ensures that the message reaches the customer at the time and place where they are most likely to respond positively. For instance, a customer who regularly checks their email in the morning could receive personalized offers at that time of day, while another who spends more time on social media might see the same offers as personalized ads in their feed.

Another crucial aspect of personalization is real-time adaptation. Thanks to Big Data technologies and predictive analytics, it is possible to adjust offers and campaigns based on the customer's real-time interaction. For example, if a customer adds products to their shopping cart but does not complete the purchase, a personalization system can immediately offer them a discount or a special promotion to encourage them to finalize the purchase. This type of real-time personalization is especially effective in e-commerce and mobile apps, where purchasing decisions are often quick and influenced by immediate factors.

In addition, Artificial Intelligence enables the creation of highly effective recommendation engines, which are one of the most visible forms of personalization. These engines use historical customer data and Machine Learning algorithms to suggest products or services that the customer is likely to find interesting. A classic example of this is Amazon's recommendation engine, which suggests products based on previous purchases, viewed items, and general purchasing trends among users with similar profiles. This type of personalization not only improves the customer experience but also increases cross-selling and upselling, enhancing the customer's lifetime value for the company.

It is important to note that although personalization can offer great benefits, it also presents significant challenges, especially in terms of privacy and data management. Companies must be transparent about how customer data are collected and used, and must ensure compliance with all relevant regulations, such as the GDPR in Europe or the CCPA in California.

In terms of implementation, the personalization of offers and campaigns requires a solid data infrastructure that can handle large volumes of information and process it efficiently. Companies must invest in Big Data technologies, advanced analysis tools, and automated marketing platforms that allow personalization at scale. In addition, they need to have a team of data analysts, data scientists, and marketing professionals who can interpret the data and design effective personalization strategies.

18.2.3. Marketing Tools and Platforms

In the world of modern marketing, marketing tools and platforms play a fundamental role in helping companies execute, manage, and analyze their campaigns efficiently. With the advancement of technology and the widespread adoption of Artificial Intelligence and Big Data, these tools have evolved to offer more sophisticated capabilities, such as mass personalization, campaign automation, and predictive analysis. Below, some of the most important marketing tools and platforms are explored and how they contribute to the effectiveness of marketing strategies.

One of the most commonly used types of tools in marketing is the marketing automation platform. These platforms allow companies to automate repetitive tasks, such as sending emails, posting on social media, and audience segmentation. Examples of these platforms include HubSpot, Marketo, and Pardot. These tools not only save time but also enable more precise personalization and real-time results analysis. For example, HubSpot offers features to create automated workflows that personalize the customer experience based on their previous behavior, such as interactions with emails or website visits.

Customer Relationship Management (CRM) platforms are also crucial in the marketing toolset. A CRM like Salesforce, Microsoft Dynamics, or Zoho CRM allows companies to centralize all customer information in a single database accessible to all teams. This ensures that each customer interaction is consistent and based on accurate data. Additionally, many CRMs offer integrations with marketing automation tools, allowing campaigns to be more personalized and tailored to the specific needs of each customer. For example, Salesforce can integrate with Pardot to automate lead capture and track customer interactions throughout the entire sales funnel.

Regarding campaign management, ad management platforms such as Google Ads, Facebook Ads Manager, and LinkedIn Campaign Manager are essential. These tools enable companies to create, manage, and optimize online advertising campaigns efficiently. They use advanced algorithms to segment audiences, optimize budgets, and measure return on investment (ROI) in real time. Additionally, they offer remarketing capabilities, allowing companies to reconnect with users who have previously interacted with their website or ads. These platforms are fundamental for any digital marketing strategy, as they allow reaching a broad and precisely segmented audience.

Data analytics tools such as Google Analytics, Adobe Analytics, and Tableau are equally crucial. These platforms allow companies to monitor user behavior on their websites and apps, understand which content is most effective, and optimize their campaigns based on data. Google Analytics, for example, provides a detailed view of web traffic, allowing marketers to see where their visitors come from, which pages are most visited, and how long they stay on each. On the other hand, Tableau facilitates the visualization of complex data, enabling companies to make decisions based on detailed analyses and present results clearly to stakeholders.

Additionally, content management systems (CMS) like WordPress, Drupal, and Joomla allow companies to create and manage their online content efficiently. A CMS facilitates publishing new content, updating information, and managing multiple digital channels from a single place. These tools are important for maintaining a consistent and attractive online presence, which is fundamental for any digital marketing strategy.

In the area of personalization, tools like Dynamic Yield, Optimizely, and Adobe Target allow companies to personalize the user experience in real time. These platforms analyze user behavior and adapt the content, offers, and messages shown based on their preferences and previous actions. For example, Dynamic Yield can modify a webpage's content in real time to display recommended products based on what the user has previously browsed. This personalization capability not only enhances the user experience but also increases conversion rates and customer satisfaction.

In the context of social media management, tools like Hootsuite, Buffer, and Sprout Social are indispensable. These platforms allow companies to manage all their social media accounts from a single place, schedule posts, interact with their audience, and monitor brand mentions in real time. Additionally, they offer detailed analytics on social media campaign performance, enabling strategies to be adjusted as needed to maximize reach and engagement. Hootsuite, for example, allows marketers to schedule posts on multiple social platforms and analyze which content is generating the most engagement.

Regarding search engine optimization (SEO), tools like SEMrush, Ahrefs, and Moz are vital. These platforms offer detailed keyword analysis, ranking tracking, website audits, and competitor analysis. This enables companies to improve their visibility in search results, which is crucial for attracting high-quality organic traffic. For example, SEMrush allows users to track their keyword performance, discover new SEO opportunities, and monitor their competitors' SEO strategy.

In the area of email marketing, platforms like Mailchimp, SendGrid, and Campaign Monitor are fundamental. These tools allow the creation of attractive email campaigns, audience segmentation, and performance analysis. Mailchimp, for example, offers advanced features such as list segmentation, automation of email campaigns based on user behavior, and integration with other marketing tools to deliver a consistent and personalized customer experience.

These tools not only facilitate the execution of complex campaigns but also provide the data and analysis necessary to make informed decisions tailored to customer needs and behaviors in real time. By using these platforms in an integrated manner, companies can significantly improve the efficiency of their marketing operations, offer more personalized experiences to their customers, and ultimately achieve better results in their campaigns.

18.3. AI in finance: Risk analysis and Algorithmic Trading

18.3.1. Predictive Credit Risk Models

The development of predictive credit risk models is a crucial area within the financial sector, as it allows institutions to assess the probability of a borrower defaulting before granting a loan. These models are based on Machine Learning techniques and advanced statistics, and their proper implementation can significantly reduce losses associated with bad debts, improve risk management, and optimize capital allocation.

Predictive credit risk models typically use historical data of the borrower, as well as other economic and market factors, to predict their future behavior. The information analyzed generally includes demographic data, credit history, payment behavior, income, debt levels, and other relevant factors. One of the most commonly used methodologies is logistic regression, which estimates the probability of a binary event, such as payment default (that is, whether the borrower will meet their credit obligations or not).

For example, a logistic regression model might take as input variables such as the applicant's age, total debt amount, history of late payments, and type of employment. The trained model would use this data to predict the probability that the applicant will default on a new loan. The model's output, which is a probability, can be used to classify applicants into different risk categories, from low to high risk.

In addition to logistic regression, other Machine Learning methods such as decision trees, random forests, and support vector machines are also commonly used in credit risk prediction. Decision trees are particularly useful for their interpretability, as they allow visualization of how decisions are made at each step based on the applicant's characteristics. Random forests, an extension of decision trees, combine multiple trees to reduce overfitting and improve model accuracy.

A more advanced technique in this field is the use of neural networks, which can capture nonlinear relationships and complex patterns in the data. Although neural networks are usually less interpretable than simpler models, their ability to handle large amounts of data and detect subtle patterns can offer superior performance in some applications.

The accuracy of a credit risk model is generally measured using metrics such as the AUC-ROC (Area Under the Receiver Operating Characteristic Curve) and accuracy. The AUC-ROC is particularly useful because it measures the model's ability to discriminate between borrowers who will meet their payments and those who will not, regardless of a specific threshold.

A critical aspect of implementing predictive credit risk models is continuous validation and recalibration. Financial data and borrower behavior can change over time due to macroeconomic factors, changes in legislation or credit policies, and new market trends. Therefore, models must be reviewed and recalibrated periodically to maintain their effectiveness. This involves retraining the model with more recent data and adjusting parameters as needed.

Fairness is another crucial issue in developing these models. It is important that credit risk models do not introduce biases that could harm certain groups of people. For example, if a model relies on variables that are correlated with protected characteristics such as race, gender, or religion, it could generate unfair decisions. To mitigate these risks, it is essential to apply fairness techniques in Machine Learning, which aim to ensure that models make fair and equitable decisions for all applicants.

In terms of technical implementation, predictive credit risk models are generally integrated into automated decision systems that can process credit applications in real time. These systems extract the relevant information from the applicant, apply the predictive model, and return a decision along with the calculated risk probability. This process allows financial institutions to make more informed credit decisions and reduce the risk of default.

Let's look at a simplified example in Python that illustrates how a logistic regression model could be trained to predict credit risk:

```
import pandas as pd
from sklearn.model_selection import train_test_split
from sklearn.linear_model import LogisticRegression
from sklearn.metrics import roc_auc_score, accuracy_score

# Load data from a CSV file
# Make sure that the file 'credit_data.csv' is in the same directory
or provide the full path
data = pd.read_csv('credit_data.csv')

# Display the first rows of the DataFrame to verify correct data
loading
print(data.head())

# Select features and target variable
X = data[['age', 'total_debt', 'income', 'payment_history']]  # Fea-
tures
y = data['default']  # Target variable, 1 if there is a default, 0
otherwise

# Split data into training and testing sets
X_train, X_test, y_train, y_test = train_test_split(X, y,
test_size=0.3, random_state=42)

# Create and train the logistic regression model
model = LogisticRegression()
model.fit(X_train, y_train)

# Make predictions
y_pred = model.predict(X_test)
y_pred_prob = model.predict_proba(X_test)[:, 1]

# Evaluate the model
auc = roc_auc_score(y_test, y_pred_prob)
accuracy = accuracy_score(y_test, y_pred)

print(f"AUC-ROC: {auc}")
print(f"Accuracy: {accuracy}")
```

In this code, a logistic regression model is used to predict the probability of default based on various borrower characteristics. Key metrics such as AUC-ROC and accuracy are evaluated to measure the model's performance.

The development and implementation of predictive credit risk models is a complex process that requires a combination of knowledge in finance, Machine Learning, and risk management. However, when done correctly, it offers significant value to financial institutions by improving decision-making and reducing credit risk.

18.3.2. Trading Algorithms

Trading algorithms have revolutionized the way financial markets operate, allowing traders to make automated, data-driven decisions in fractions of a second. These algorithms are essential in algorithmic trading, also known as automated trading, where buy and sell orders are executed automatically by a computer program based on a set of predefined rules. Trading algorithms can be designed for different strategies, from high-frequency trading execution to trading based on fundamental or technical analysis.

One of the best-known types of trading algorithms is high-frequency trading (HFT). These algorithms execute a large number of trades in milliseconds, taking advantage of small inefficiencies in the market. The strategy is based on speed, where profits are derived from accumulating small margins across many trades. HFT algorithms typically use real-time market data and operate in multiple markets simultaneously to identify and exploit arbitrage opportunities, which involve buying and selling an asset simultaneously in different markets to take advantage of price differences.

Another approach is momentum-based trading, where algorithms are designed to identify trends in asset prices and trade in the same direction as the trend. These algorithms analyze technical indicators, such as moving averages, oscillators, or the relative strength index (RSI), to determine the right time to enter or exit a position. For example, a momentum algorithm might be programmed to buy an asset when its price crosses above its 50-day moving average and sell it when it crosses below.

Statistical arbitrage trading is another common approach. This type of algorithm seeks to identify deviations in the price relationship between two or more assets that have historically shown a stable correlation. For example, if two stocks usually move in tandem but one temporarily deviates from its historical correlation, the algorithm could execute buy orders in the undervalued stock and sell orders in the overvalued one, expecting the prices to return to their historical relationship.

In addition to these approaches, trading algorithms based on fundamental analysis focus on evaluating economic and financial data to make investment decisions. These algorithms can analyze financial reports, valuation ratios, macroeconomic data, news, and other fundamental indicators to determine the intrinsic value of an asset. Based on this evaluation, the algorithm can execute buy or sell orders, taking advantage of long-term investment opportunities.

Risk management is an integral part of trading algorithms. The algorithms are designed to calculate the risk of each trade and adjust positions accordingly. This includes the use of stop-losses, which are predetermined sell orders to limit losses if the market moves against the trader's position, and take-profits, which are sell orders to secure gains when the market moves in favor.

Regarding technical implementation, trading algorithms are developed using programming languages such as Python, C++, or R, among others. Libraries like NumPy, Pandas, and Scikit-learn facilitate data analysis and the implementation of machine learning models for trading. Let's look at a simplified Python example of a basic moving average trading algorithm, a commonly used strategy to identify trends:

```
import pandas as pd
import numpy as np

# Load price data (assume 'data' is a DataFrame with 'Date' and
'Close' columns)
data = pd.read_csv('market_data.csv', parse_dates=['Date'], in-
dex_col='Date')

# Calculate moving averages
data['SMA_50'] = data['Close'].rolling(window=50).mean()
data['SMA_200'] = data['Close'].rolling(window=200).mean()

# Generate buy/sell signals
data['Signal'] = 0
data['Signal'][50:] = np.where(data['SMA_50'][50:] >
data['SMA_200'][50:], 1, 0)
data['Position'] = data['Signal'].diff()

# Print trading signals
print(data[['Close', 'SMA_50', 'SMA_200', 'Signal', 'Posi-
tion']].tail())
```

In this code, the algorithm calculates two moving averages (50 and 200 days) and generates buy signals when the short-term moving average (50 days) crosses above the long-term moving average (200 days), and sell signals when the opposite occurs. This type of strategy is simple but effective for capturing market trends.

The use of trading algorithms offers multiple benefits, such as eliminating emotions in decision-making, the ability to operate 24 hours a day, and the possibility of executing complex strategies that would be impossible for a human. However, it also presents risks, especially in volatile markets or during unexpected events that can cause sharp price movements. It is crucial that algorithms are well designed and rigorously tested before being deployed in a production environment.

Regulation is an essential aspect to consider in the development and implementation of trading algorithms. Different jurisdictions have specific regulations for algorithmic trading, aimed at preventing unfair practices and ensuring the stability of financial markets. Developers of these algorithms must ensure compliance with all applicable regulations to avoid penalties and preserve market integrity.

18.3.3. Regulation and Compliance in Finance

Regulation and compliance in the financial sector are fundamental to ensuring the integrity, transparency, and stability of financial markets. In an environment where electronic transactions, trading algorithms, and advanced technologies such as Artificial Intelligence play a crucial role, regulatory oversight has intensified to mitigate systemic risks and protect investors and the economy in general.

One of the main motivations for regulation in finance is to prevent systemic risk, which refers to the possibility that a disruption in a financial institution or an asset class spreads to the entire financial system, causing severe economic crises. Events such as the 2008 financial crisis demonstrated how the lack of adequate regulation and non-compliance could have devastating global effects. Since then, regulatory bodies have strengthened regulations and introduced new laws and guidelines to prevent such crises from recurring.

An essential regulatory framework in the financial context is Basel III, established by the Basel Committee on Banking Supervision. This framework, following Basel I and Basel II, aims to strengthen the regulation, supervision, and risk management of the banking sector. Basel III introduces stricter requirements regarding capital adequacy, leverage, and liquidity, forcing banks to maintain higher capital reserves to absorb potential losses and reduce the risk of insolvency.

Another critical component of financial regulation is the Dodd-Frank Wall Street Reform and Consumer Protection Act in the United States, enacted in 2010 in response to the 2008 financial crisis. This law implements a series of reforms aimed at improving financial stability, protecting consumers, ending "too big to fail," and creating greater transparency in financial markets. Dodd-Frank establishes stricter capital and leverage requirements for financial institutions and regulates derivatives markets, which were at the center of the 2008 crisis.

In the European Union, the General Data Protection Regulation (GDPR) and the Markets in Financial Instruments Directive (MiFID II) are key regulations affecting financial institutions. MiFID II, in particular, seeks to enhance investor protection and increase transparency in financial markets, setting new rules for the operation of investment firms, information disclosure, and order execution.

MiFID II also introduces specific regulations for algorithmic and high-frequency trading, imposing requirements for firms using these methods to have adequate risk controls, as well as supervision and audit systems. This includes ensuring that algorithms do not cause market destabilization, prevent market manipulation, and ensure that operations are conducted in the best interest of clients.

The Sarbanes-Oxley Act, also in the United States, is another example of legislation designed to improve transparency and accountability in finance. Enacted in 2002 after the Enron and WorldCom accounting scandals, this law establishes strict requirements for financial disclosure and corporate responsibility, including the obligation for senior executives to personally certify the accuracy of their companies' financial statements.

In terms of compliance, financial institutions must implement robust risk management and compliance frameworks to ensure they operate within the law. This includes creating dedicated compliance teams that monitor operations, identify potential risks, and ensure all internal and external policies and procedures are followed. Technology plays an important role in compliance, as Big Data analytics tools and automated fraud detection systems allow companies to monitor large volumes of transactions in real-time and detect suspicious activities.

Compliance also involves regular audits by regulatory bodies, as well as internal audits to review the effectiveness of control systems and ensure all areas of the organization comply with relevant regulations. Penalties for non-compliance can be severe, including substantial fines, criminal sanctions, and reputational damage to the company.

Moreover, regulatory compliance is not only about avoiding legal penalties but also about maintaining the trust of investors, clients, and other stakeholders. In a market where trust is fundamental, companies perceived as lacking transparency or failing to comply with regulations can suffer significant business losses.

Regarding the technology used for compliance, RegTech (regulatory technology) tools have gained prominence. These solutions help financial companies automate compliance processes, manage large volumes of regulatory data, and quickly adapt to changes in regulations. RegTech covers a wide range of applications, from risk management and client identification to continuous monitoring and regulatory reporting.

It is important to mention the role of international regulatory agencies, such as the International Organization of Securities Commissions (IOSCO) and the Financial Stability Board (FSB), which coordinate regulation and supervision at the global level. These organizations work to establish international standards and promote cooperation between different jurisdictions to address global risks, improve transparency, and ensure the stability of the international financial system.

Regulation and compliance in finance are dynamic and constantly evolving to address new challenges and emerging technologies. Financial institutions must continuously adapt and improve their compliance practices to keep up with the ever-changing regulatory environment and avoid the risks associated with non-compliance.

18.4. AI in Industry

Artificial Intelligence has revolutionized the industrial sector with applications that go beyond typical cases such as predictive maintenance and production line automation. There are lesser-known but equally crucial implementations that are transforming various areas of industry.

Fabric Optimization in the Textile Industry
In garment and textile manufacturing, AI is used to minimize fabric waste through cutting optimization algorithms. Machine Learning models analyze patterns and garment shapes, calculating the best way to distribute cuts on the fabric to reduce leftover material. Sustainable fashion companies have implemented this technology to improve efficiency and reduce their environmental impact.

AI for Defect Detection in Marble and Natural Stone
The construction and decoration industry uses Artificial Intelligence to inspect blocks of marble and granite for cracks or internal imperfections that are not visible to the naked eye. Using neural networks trained with

reference images, companies can classify and select the best pieces before processing, reducing waste and improving the quality of the final product.

Fermentation Monitoring in Beverage Production
Breweries, wineries, and other producers of fermented goods have begun implementing smart sensors and AI algorithms to monitor the fermentation process in real time. This allows adjustments to variables such as temperature, pH, and sugar concentration, optimizing the quality of the final product and reducing losses from defective batches.

Failure Prediction in Cutting Tools in Manufacturing
In the metalworking industry, cutting tools like drills and milling cutters have a limited lifespan, and unexpected failures can halt production. AI systems analyze vibrations, temperature, and wear patterns to predict when a tool will fail, allowing it to be replaced before a critical problem occurs.

Waste Sorting in Industrial Processes
Companies that produce large volumes of waste have adopted AI to improve waste management. Smart sensors and computer vision classify recyclable and non-recyclable materials in real time, increasing recycling efficiency and reducing operational costs.

Generation of Optimized Designs for Lightweight Structures
In sectors such as aerospace and automotive, Artificial Intelligence is used to design structures optimized for weight and strength. Generative optimization algorithms can create designs that use less material without compromising safety, reducing costs and improving product performance.

AI in Perfume and Aroma Manufacturing
The creation of fragrances and aromas is an art now supported by AI. Through deep learning models, companies can predict ingredient combinations that will result in pleasant and unique scents. These algorithms can even anticipate how the fragrance will change over time, improving product formulation.

Simulation of Extreme Conditions in the Aerospace Industry
Space agencies and aerospace companies use AI to simulate extreme conditions that materials and equipment will face in space. Advanced models can predict how different materials will respond to cosmic radiation or abrupt temperature changes, allowing for the development of more resistant and durable components.

18.5. AI in Transportation

Artificial Intelligence is transforming the transportation industry in surprising ways. While autonomous vehicles and traffic optimization are well-known examples, there are less obvious but equally revolutionary applications that demonstrate AI's impact on mobility.

AI in Predictive Maintenance of Infrastructure

One of the most significant advances in transportation is the implementation of AI in predictive maintenance of infrastructure. Machine learning models analyze large volumes of data from sensors installed on roads, bridges, and tunnels to detect wear patterns and predict structural failures before they occur. This approach not only improves safety but also reduces repair costs and minimizes mobility disruptions.

A notable case is the use of drones equipped with computer vision to inspect railways and roads. These devices can identify microscopic cracks or corrosion in critical structures, allowing preventive maintenance before serious incidents occur.

AI for Noise Reduction at Airports

Airports have begun applying AI to reduce noise pollution generated by air traffic. Advanced algorithms analyze takeoff and landing patterns in real time to adjust flight paths and minimize noise impact in urban areas.
Additionally, some airlines have integrated AI into engine management to dynamically modify thrust levels and reduce noise emissions without compromising safety or flight efficiency.

AI in Maritime Fleet Management

Maritime transport is a sector where Artificial Intelligence is bringing unexpected innovations. Machine learning models predict the best routes for ships based on weather data, maritime traffic, and historical navigation patterns, reducing travel times and fuel consumption.

A notable example is the implementation of AI in optimizing loading and unloading at ports. Sensors and computer vision algorithms allow containers to be arranged on ships in an optimal way, improving stability and reducing waiting times.

AI in Predicting Traffic Jams in Undersea Tunnels

Undersea tunnels, due to their enclosed nature and high vehicle density, are prone to severe congestion. AI is being used to predict and mitigate these traffic jams by combining real-time data from traffic sensors, weather conditions, and vehicle flow models.

An example is the Channel Tunnel, where AI systems predict traffic build-ups up to an hour in advance, allowing proactive measures such as adjusting recommended speeds and opening additional lanes at access points.

AI in Personalized Public Transport
Some cities are experimenting with dynamic public transport services powered by AI. Instead of fixed routes, buses and minibuses can adjust their routes based on real-time demand.

For example, in Helsinki, Finland, on-demand transport systems have been implemented that use machine learning algorithms to group passengers with similar journeys, optimizing service efficiency and reducing the number of vehicles in circulation.

18.6. AI in Food

Artificial Intelligence has revolutionized numerous sectors, and food is no exception. However, beyond typical cases such as supply chain optimization and automation in the food industry, there are lesser-known but equally relevant applications that are transforming the sector in innovative ways.

Creation of New Flavors
One of the less conventional uses of AI in food is the creation of new flavors and ingredient combinations. Specialized companies have developed AI models that analyze the chemical composition of thousands of ingredients to identify unexpected but harmonious combinations. These systems use neural networks to predict pleasant flavors and create entirely new recipes, helping chefs and food companies innovate with unique products.

Detection of Food Fraud
Another lesser-known example is the use of AI in detecting food fraud. Food adulteration is a global problem, and AI is helping to combat it by analyzing spectroscopic and chemical data to detect counterfeit or incorrectly labeled ingredients. Thanks to deep learning, these systems can identify small variations in product composition and alert regulators before products reach the market.

Analysis of Ripeness of Fruits and Vegetables
In precision agriculture, an unusual but highly efficient case is the use of AI to analyze the ripeness of fruits and vegetables in real time. Advanced sensors coupled with AI systems can accurately assess product quality, allowing them to be harvested at the optimal time. This technology has been implemented in crops such as avocados and bananas, where ripeness can

change quickly and affect transport and marketing. Some companies generally use this technology for harvesting.

Use of AI to Create Meat Alternatives

Another innovative case is the application of AI in creating meat alternatives. Machine learning models analyze the texture, flavor, and nutritional composition of various plant sources to develop products that closely mimic meat. Food tech companies are using these tools to develop burgers and other plant-based meat products that are more sustainable and have a convincing flavor profile.

AI in Reducing Food Waste

A lesser-explored but highly impactful aspect is the use of AI in reducing food waste. Restaurants and supermarkets use AI systems to predict demand more accurately, optimize inventories, and minimize waste. Some advanced programs can even suggest recipes and ways to reuse ingredients that are about to expire, helping reduce the amount of food discarded.

AI in Personalized Nutrition

AI is also playing a crucial role in personalized nutrition. AI-powered platforms can analyze health data, eating habits, and individuals' nutritional needs to recommend personalized diets. Some applications even use computer vision to identify foods on a plate and calculate their nutritional value in real time, facilitating healthier and more balanced eating.

As you can see, AI in food goes far beyond process automation and has a profound impact on culinary innovation, food safety, sustainability, and health.

18.7. AI in Physics

Artificial Intelligence has also revolutionized many areas of physics, from theoretical research to experimentation in cutting-edge laboratories. While the most well-known examples include accelerating quantum simulations or analyzing particle collision data at CERN, there are lesser-known but equally impactful applications.

AI in the Study of Exotic Materials

One of these examples is the use of AI for the study of exotic materials. Researchers have used neural networks to predict the properties of topological quantum materials, which could revolutionize quantum computing. Thanks to deep learning, patterns can be identified in experimental data that could lead to the discovery of materials with superconducting characteristics at room temperature.

AI for Astronomical Image Reconstruction
Another atypical application of AI in physics is the reconstruction of astronomical images. A paradigmatic case was the use of deep learning algorithms to complete observations from very long baseline interferometry (VLBI) telescopes (Event Horizon Telescope (EHT) Project). These systems enabled the historic image of the black hole in M87. AI reconstructed the missing information between the different observations, improving the resolution and quality of the data obtained.

AI to Stabilize Nuclear Reactors
In the field of plasma physics, AI has also proven to be a valuable tool. Control systems based on reinforcement learning are helping to stabilize nuclear fusion reactors. A particular example is the control of the magnetic configuration in tokamaks like ITER. Neural networks can predict plasma instabilities in real time and adjust the magnetic fields to prevent disturbances that could compromise reactor stability.

Reconstruction of Physical Theories
Another interesting case is the use of AI in reconstructing physical theories from experimental data. Some projects have used machine learning algorithms to deduce fundamental equations of physics without prior knowledge of the studied systems. For example, AI models have been able to derive the laws of motion from observations of moving particles, without explicitly programming Newton's equations.

AI in the Study of Dark Matter
In cosmology, AI is helping to solve one of the greatest mysteries of the universe: dark matter. Machine learning algorithms have been trained to analyze the distribution of galaxies and estimate the presence and distribution of this invisible matter, allowing the creation of three-dimensional maps of its gravitational influence with unprecedented precision.

AI is proving not only to accelerate calculations and improve precision in physical experiments but also to enable the discovery of new phenomena and to reformulate theories in previously unthinkable directions. As AI continues to evolve, its impact on physics will only keep expanding, opening new frontiers in our understanding of the universe, beyond what humans can now even imagine.

18.8. AI in Chemistry

Another field that Artificial Intelligence is also completely revolutionizing is chemistry in its various areas, from the design of new materials to the optimization of industrial processes. While many classic examples include drug discovery or reaction modeling, there are lesser-known but equally important applications that demonstrate the impact of AI in this field.

Discovery of Synthetic Minerals
One of the most surprising uses of AI in chemistry is the identification of new compositions for synthetic minerals. Deep learning algorithms can analyze combinations of elements and predict stable crystal structures that do not exist in nature. This has applications in advanced electronics, enabling the creation of new semiconductors or superconducting materials.

Modeling of Fragrances and Flavors
Neural networks have been used to predict the interaction of aromatic compounds and create synthetic fragrances that mimic natural scents without relying on animal-derived materials or scarce natural resources. Companies in the food and perfume sectors are adopting these models to design new flavors and aromas without traditional testing, reducing costs and experimentation time.

AI for the Generation of Efficient Catalysts
Catalysts are fundamental in the chemical industry as they accelerate reactions without being consumed in the process. AI is helping to design more efficient catalysts by predicting which combinations of metals and molecular structures optimize the desired reactions. This is being applied in the production of synthetic fuels and the reduction of industrial pollutants.

Quantum Chemistry and Molecular Simulation
AI algorithms are helping to solve quantum mechanics equations more quickly, allowing for precise simulation of complex molecules. This is key to understanding the reactivity of new compounds before conducting costly laboratory experiments.

Automated Chemical Recycling
The development of AI systems to identify and separate molecules in industrial waste is enabling highly efficient chemical recycling processes. These models can analyze the composition of waste in real time and suggest optimal chemical processes to recover valuable materials without generating additional pollution.

Manufacturing of Sustainable Dyes and Pigments
The textile and paint industries face the challenge of reducing the environmental impact of their processes. AI is used to find alternative compounds to traditional toxic dyes, formulating pigments that maintain quality and durability while reducing water consumption and polluting agents in their manufacture.

Prediction of Corrosion in Infrastructure
Another little-explored field is the application of AI in predicting corrosion in construction materials and industrial infrastructures. Machine learning models analyze data on the chemical composition of metals, climatic conditions, and exposure to chemical agents to foresee structural failures before they occur, allowing proactive maintenance strategies.

The application of AI in lesser-explored areas, such as material optimization, synthetic fragrance creation, corrosion prediction, and chemical recycling, demonstrates its potential to transform the industry and improve sustainability.

18.9. AI in Environmental and Wildlife Preservation

Artificial Intelligence is playing a crucial role in environmental preservation and wildlife protection. Through advanced algorithms, neural networks, and machine learning techniques, it is becoming possible to identify environmental patterns, predict climate changes, and mitigate human impact on fragile ecosystems. While many of the best-known applications include detecting deforestation through satellite images or monitoring wildlife with drones, there are less conventional but equally relevant examples that demonstrate the potential of AI in this field.

Monitoring Coral Bleaching Through Sound
Coral bleaching is a critical problem caused by rising water temperatures, which leads to the expulsion of symbiotic algae essential for coral survival. Researchers have developed AI algorithms capable of analyzing reef sounds to detect changes in biodiversity and determine the health of the marine ecosystem. Instead of relying only on satellite images, this auditory approach allows continuous and less invasive monitoring, providing real-time data on the health of coral reefs.

Control of Invasive Species with Autonomous Robots
Invasive species pose a serious threat to native ecosystems, displacing native species and altering the natural balance. AI has been integrated into underwater and terrestrial robots that can identify and eradicate invasive species without affecting the surrounding biodiversity. For example, in Australia, deep learning robots have been developed that identify and eliminate crown-of-thorns starfish, which are responsible for the destruction of coral reefs. These systems enable more efficient management of invasive populations without harming the ecosystem.

Analysis of Light Pollution and Its Impact on Wildlife

Excessive artificial lighting alters the behavioral patterns of many species, affecting bird migration, sea turtle reproduction, and pollinator insect activity. AI algorithms can analyze nighttime images captured by satellites to map the areas most affected by light pollution and suggest strategies to mitigate its impact. This type of information has enabled the implementation of adaptive lighting in cities and coastal areas, reducing the negative effects on nocturnal wildlife.

Optimization of Crops with AI-Assisted Pollination

The decline in bee populations has raised global concern due to their key role in crop pollination. Autonomous drones equipped with AI algorithms have been developed to identify flowers and perform artificial pollination. While these devices cannot completely replace natural pollinators, they represent an alternative solution in environments where pollination has drastically decreased. Additionally, AI is also being used to analyze data on bee colony health and predict disease outbreaks, helping beekeepers make informed decisions.

Neural Networks for Early Detection of Forest Fires

Forest fires are one of the main threats to biodiversity and contribute significantly to greenhouse gas emissions. AI models have been developed that analyze data from thermal sensors and surveillance cameras to detect fires in their early stages. Unlike traditional monitoring methods, which rely on human observation or satellites with limited review times, these systems can alert to possible fire outbreaks with unprecedented speed, facilitating immediate response and reducing fire spread.

As you can see, the use of Artificial Intelligence in environmental and wildlife preservation is revolutionizing the way we tackle ecological challenges. Beyond conventional applications, the use of AI for monitoring underwater sounds, eradicating invasive species, reducing light pollution, artificial pollination, and early fire detection demonstrates its versatility and importance. Thanks to the combination of AI with conservation strategies, it can play an even more significant role in protecting the planet.

★★★★★

I truly hope you enjoyed the book. If so, if you liked it, or maybe it helped you understand Artificial Intelligence better, or perhaps even sparked your curiosity to learn more about AI, then I kindly ask you to write a review.

Did you know that, according to statistics, 67% of customers write a review after a positive experience, while 40% do so after a negative one? However, based on my own research, this is completely wrong and actually the opposite is true. Satisfied customers rarely write reviews, while dissatisfied ones tend to write them almost immediately. At the same time, 93% of consumers read online reviews before making a purchase decision. One study shows that 55% of the reviews on the internet are fake, but according to many investigative reports, the percentage of fake reviews is actually much higher. Still, 94% of consumers avoid a product or company due to negative feedback.

Your review is very valuable and can help me tremendously to keep writing.

★★★★★

Acknowledgments

Dear reader,

I want to take this moment to sincerely thank you for making it this far and investing your time in reading this book. I applaud you and tip my hat to you. Your dedication and commitment to learning reflect your desire to stay at the forefront of a field as dynamic and ever-evolving as Artificial Intelligence and Big Data. I hope the knowledge shared has been useful to you and inspires you to keep exploring the endless possibilities these technologies offer.

Artificial Intelligence is not just a technology of the present, but one that will continue to shape the future in ways we can barely imagine. It is crucial that you keep learning, stay updated, and develop skills that will allow you not only to adapt but also to lead in this era of digital transformation. Every step you take in your learning journey will not only increase your knowledge but also bring you closer to new opportunities to make an impact on your environment, your work, and society.

If you are interested in delving deeper into Artificial Intelligence project management, I invite you to check out my books "AI-Manager" and "AI the *Homo digitalis*." In them, I guide you through best practices, strategies, and tools necessary to become a leader in AI. I am convinced that these will be valuable complements to the knowledge you have gained here and will provide you with a broader perspective on AI, both professionally and personally.

Once again, thank you for joining me on this journey. I encourage you to keep learning, exploring, and expanding your horizons in the fascinating world of Artificial Intelligence. The future is in your hands!

With immeasurable gratitude and best wishes,

Juan García
CEO, AI Expert, AI Manager, IBM Advanced ML Specialist
SMART &PRO AI
DEEP ATHENA

About the Author

Juan García is a passionate technology expert and tireless researcher of the transformative potential of Artificial Intelligence. Born in Almería, Spain, and with a professional career that has taken him through several European countries, he has dedicated more than 25 years to learning, teaching, and sharing knowledge in the industrial sector—especially in areas such as automation and optimization, and since 2019, particularly in Artificial Intelligence, Machine Learning, and Big Data.

His approach does not merely follow technological trends but stems from deep reflection on how human intelligence can be extended through machines. He sees AI as an extension of our innate curiosity to understand the world and solve complex problems, guided by a vision that combines technical, ethical, and social implications.

As a AI Manager, trainer, consultant, and founder of SMART &PRO AI, based in Germany, he has applied his expertise in consulting, automation, and process optimization across 11 different industrial sectors since January 2022. His reputation as a strategic partner is built on combining specialized knowledge with a highly practical approach, adapting AI, Machine Learning, and Big Data solutions to the specific challenges of each company.

He is certified by IBM as an Advanced Machine Learning Specialist and has designed and delivered training programs, workshops, lectures, and customized solutions for professionals and executives in Germany, Switzerland, Spain, Austria, Belgium, Macedonia, and the Netherlands. Thanks to his ability to explain complex concepts in an accessible way, he has helped industrial companies adopt these technologies with tangible results in efficiency and competitiveness.

In 2025, he founded DEEP ATHENA, his own publishing house specialized in AI, Machine Learning, and Big Data, with the aim of promoting didactic, philosophical, and practical content, and establishing a benchmark brand in science and technology. DEEP ATHENA stays away from the hype and sensationalism that often surrounds these topics, offering high-quality content developed by the people who build the machines—not by the machines themselves.

Juan is the author of several books on Artificial Intelligence, including "AI-Manager," "AI the Book," and "AI the *Homo digitalis*." His works combine technical expertise with a critical perspective on the social and cultural impacts of AI and have been well received and translated into several languages.

"AI & Big Data" is the first book published under the DEEP ATHENA label. In it, he not only explores the technical foundations of intelligent systems and large-scale data analysis but also invites readers to reflect on the role we want to assign to these technologies in our lives and within the industrial business context.

Beyond his professional work, Juan stands out as a passionate communicator and educator, convinced that education has the power to transform lives. He doesn't just write about Artificial Intelligence—he lives immersed in it, with the goal of making technology a tool in the service of humanity. He emphasizes that what truly matters is not what AI can do for us, but what we choose to do with it.

Recommended Books

- **AI-Manager:** For professionals who want to dive into AI professionally, no matter the path you choose.

- **AI the *Homo digitalis:*** A book that presents Juan García's unique vision of Artificial Intelligence as an evolutionary catalyst for humanity toward a new stage: the *Homo digitalis*. It is aimed at readers who wish to understand AI not only from a technical or scientific perspective, but as a cultural, philosophical, and transformative phenomenon that redefines what it means to be human in the digital age.

www.ingramcontent.com/pod-product-compliance
Lightning Source LLC
Chambersburg PA
CBHW071414230926
51846CB00001B/84
9783912099072